PJ2

FLEET HISTORY

OF

OPERATORS of the BAILIWICK of GUERNSEY
(including ALDERNEY)

PUBLISHED BY

THE PSV CIRCLE

JUNE 2019

FOREWORD

The draft for this publication was prepared by Bob Howes. Other valued contributions have come from Peter Bates, Stewart Brett, John Carman, David Corke, Ian Everson, Richard Gadsby, Tony Holdsworth, John Jones, Peter Tulloch and Fred Ward. Reference was also made to the following excellent publications which have helped immensely towards the accuracy of this Fleet History:

Channel Island Transport Fleet Histories:
    Volume 1 – Bailiwick of Guernsey – Guernsey & Alderney bus operators by WJ Carman (1991)
    A history of Guernsey's Buses, Coaches & Trams by WJ Carman (2009)
    Railways in Guernsey by Frank E Wilson.

This publication contains all material available in June 2019.

Photographs have kindly been supplied by Dave Arnold, The Bus Archive, John Carman, Chris Elkin, Peter Henson, Roy Marshall Collection, Geoffrey Morant, Mike Penn, Mike Streete and Peter Tulloch.

Notes:
This is one of a range of publications produced by The PSV Circle primarily as a service to its members. The information contained herein has been taken from the range of sources indicated above; either from observation or other research, as well as the content of PSV Circle monthly news sheets and also includes information provided from other reputable sources. Considerable time and effort have been taken to ensure that the content of this publication is as complete and accurate as possible but no responsibility can be accepted for any errors or omissions.

Contents:

Any general comments on this publication may be sent to the Publications Manager, The PSV Circle, 4th Floor, Crown House, Linton Road, Barking, IG11 8HG or via email to publications.manager@psvcircle.org.uk.

Details of how to join The PSV Circle and a list of all our publications can be obtained from The PSV Circle website - www.psvcircle.org.uk.

ISBN: 978-1-910767-38-2
Published by the PSV Circle.
© The PSV Circle June 2019

INTRODUCTION

The Channel Islands consist of of number of islands in the English Channel off the French coast of Normandy. They consist of two Crown dependencies: The Bailiwick of Jersey and the Bailiwick of Guernsey, the latter consisting of three jurisdictions: Guernsey, Alderney and Sark. Jersey, Guernsey and Alderney contain most of the population and are the only ones permitting motorised transport. They are not (technically) part of the United Kingdom or the European Union, although the UK is responsible for defence and international relations. The total population of the islands is around 165,000 of which 100,000 live on Jersey, 63,000 on Guernsey and 2,000 on Alderney. Jersey covers an area of (approximately) 45 square miles, Guernsey 25 square miles and Alderney 3 square miles.

The other inhabited islands in the Bailiwick include Sark (just over 2 square miles) with around 500 inhabitants and Herm (0.75 square miles) with a population of around 60. Neither permits motorised transport apart from agricultural machinery. Sark does permit horse-drawn (and more recently tractor-drawn) trailers (known as buses) to be operated to convey visitors from the harbour and also on island tours whilst there is record of one former Guernsey vehicle ending up on Herm just after World War 2, where it was probably deployed in the postwar reconstruction of the island

GUERNSEY
Guernsey comprises of ten parishes which are listed below under the next section. Each is presided over by a senior and a junior Connetable (Constable) together with their Douzaine (Parish Council), which is headed by a Dean. The major town is St Peter Port where the main harbour for passenger and freight traffic is located. A second harbour at St Sampson is used for some bulk cargo ships. The airport is located at Forest. Historically agriculture was the main industry on Guernsey, but in recent times, this has been overtaken by international banking and insurance.

HORSE BUSES
Although horse buses first appeared in the latter years of the eighteenth century when James Macey established a livery stables business, it was not until March 1823 when the first timetabled public transport appeared. This was when Thomas Martin advertised a stagecoach service running tours around the island on three days per week. It was not until 1837 when John Roberts' *'Defiance'* service ran between St Peter Port and St Sampson. This route was later provided by trams and motor buses and with the exception of the Second World War years, has been operated continuously for more than 180 years.

During the 1840s, a few services were tried from St Peter Port to King's Mills and St Peter-in-the-Wood, but for the most part, horse-drawn buses to other areas did not flourish. They were mainly operated by livery stables or cab operators, mostly as a secondary source of income. The St Peter Port and St Sampson services did flourish however and was subject to severe competition which led at times to standards declining. By 1877, there was said to be 44 licensed vehicles on the road between the two ports.

From the late 19th century, all horse-drawn commercial vehicles were issued with an identifying number from their Parish Constable which was painted on vehicles together with a parish code letter (although the number was allocated to the owner rather than the vehicle). These were originally listed in French, with the English version (used in this publication) alongside:

A	Saint Pierre Port	St Peter Port
B	Saint Samson	St Sampson
C	Le Valle	Vale
D	Catel	Castel
E	Saint Sauveur	St Saviour
F	Saint Pierre du Bois	St Peter-in-the-Wood
G	Torteval	Torteval
H	Foret	Forest
I	Saint Martin	St Martin
K	Sanit Andre	St Andrew

TRAMWAYS
Early railway proposals for a route between St Peter Port and L'Ancresse were put forward in 1845 by the Island of Guernsey Railway (later Guernsey Railway and Pier Co) and although the company was well capitalised, nothing came of it. Further ideas followed including connecting quarries in the north of the island to St Peter Port which was eventually rejected by the States.

In 1874 the first tramway proposal - 'Projet de Loi' (Law Project) was approved although construction was never started. A revised proposal was granted in 1877 and a Hughes steam tram was subsequently demonstrated on a temporary track. The Guernsey Steam Tramway Co Ltd was incorporated in London in May 1878 and construction between St Peter Port and the harbour at St Sampson was started soon afterwards, opening in June 1879.

The trams consisted of a steam tram drawing first-class closed and second-class open trailers. Unfortunately, the tramway soon ran into financial and maintenance difficulties caused in part by its structure, partly due to the cheap horse-bus competition along its route and partly by unreliable rolling stock.

It was felt locally that Guernsey was ready for a well-organised island-wide horse-bus service and the Guernsey Omnibus Co was formed in early 1888 and quickly grew to be the largest horse-bus operator on the island. They operated garden-seat double-deck buses of the latest London design to a regular timetable and had purpose-built stables. Services were soon extended to Cobo, L'Ancresse and L'Islet and on 5 January 1889, the tramway succumbed to the pressure and had ceased running. Other livery stable owners, taking the lead from Guernsey Omnibus, established regular bus services to St Martin, St Saviour and St Peter.

Meanwhile, some of the shareholders of the Guernsey Steam Tramway set about forming a new locally registered company. The Guernsey Railway Co Ltd emerged and relaunched the tramway after a break of eleven months. Guernsey Railway had more ambitious plans and trials were held in October 1891 to electrify the line and in February 1892, regular services started. As a result, Guernsey had one of the earliest tramway systems to utilise overhead current collection. The tramway now flourished and in 1895, amalgamated with Guernsey Omnibus Co. A tramway to Cobo was considered, but this was dismissed as impractical and the horse-bus services were progressively sold off to the livery stables.

MOTOR BUSES & CLOSURE OF THE TRAMWAY

After the turn of the century, the Guernsey Railway Co considered turning to trolleybuses, but a satisfactory system could not be found. By the end of the first decade, motor buses were beginning to develop and three former London buses were placed on the road in 1909, replacing the horse-drawn services to L'Ancresse and L'Islet as well as providing a tram-replacement service on Sundays; trams being not permitted on the Sabbath.

After World War I, Guernsey Motors Ltd was formed in 1919 (with some of the Railway Co directors on the board) and both they and Guernsey Railway Co constructed a legally binding agreement that neither would encroach on the other's territory. Guernsey Railway Co's territory was the north of the island and Guernsey Motors covered all other parts as well as operating lorries, repairs services, agencies for cars and parts. Within a few years, every road on the island which could be operated on, had a bus service – if not by Guernsey Motors or Guernsey Railway Co, then by one of the smaller companies now springing up.

Because of Guernsey's narrow roads, many buses of unusual makes were deployed. In the early years following World War I, many former army lorry chassis were purchased and fitted with bus bodies. These had solid tyres and some were left-hand drive, both aspects being later prohibited. Other than models such as Bean, Dennis Falcon, Arrow Minor, Leyland Cub and Vulcan, most vehicles available in the 1920s and 1930s were too wide for the island's maximum permitted width of 6ft 6in. This led to many former lorry chassis being adapted extensively over the years.

Local coachbuilders who built bus bodies flourished during the years between the two World Wars and included the following:

FT Bennett, St Peter Port	1924-28
T Davies, St Peter Port	c1900-20
S Frampton, St Peter Port	1881-1920
T Le Huray, St Peter Port	from c1900
F Mallett, St Sampson	from c1920
WJ Rugg, St Sampson	1925-46

By 1934, the tramway was ageing and a decision was taken to close it and replace its services with motor bus operated ones. The tramway had been unable to extend its lines due to geographical constraints and restrictions by the island's roads and terrain and had for the last 15 years, suffered serious competition from motor buses, including those it owned itself. Over these years, the Guernsey Railway Co had diversified its activities including operation of a refuse incinerator (providing electricity for the trams and its workshops), engineering and plumbing work, ship repairs and a foundry.

WARTIME
Following the outbreak of World War II in September 1939, the German forces invaded and occupied the Channel Islands from June 1940. Bus services immediately ceased, but later a skeleton service was re-established and some attempts were made to resurrect horse-drawn buses in some country districts, but without lasting success. Vehicles were nominally impressed by the States of Guernsey (under German control) although in many cases continued to be driven by the former owners, or staff attached to the newly formed Civil Transport Service. The States also controlled a Military Transport Service. Later many more vehicles were impressed for use at various military establishments around the island and to provide much needed scrap metal for the War effort, whilst others were sent to France for similar purposes.

Much of the island's transport was only possible through the use of gazogene, a gas produced by a wood burning device to fuel a modified petrol engine. By 1944, even this form of propulsion was running low on materials.

POST-WAR REBUILDING
The liberation of the islands came in 1945 and work began on renewing the infrastructure. There was obviously an urgent need to replace the buses that had been lost during the War years. Prior to this time, the narrow roads on the island had led to the maximum vehicle width of 6ft 6in being imposed. Roads that had been subjected to German military vehicles for five years had been widened and this led to the law being changed in 1945 to permit vehicles of 7ft width. Even this meant that the choice was somewhat restricted, vehicle makes and types now appeared that had never been seen before.

The island's transport services were still dominated by Guernsey Motors and Guernsey Railway Co, but in 1946, a long-established former horse-bus and early motor bus operator Thomas Sarre applied for several licences in the name of Sarre Transport Ltd. With the backing of a major garage proprietor who could supply buses and Sarre having acquired WJ Rugg's old established 'Wayfarer' business, he set about challenging the 'big two'.

CHANGES IN OWNERSHIP
Red & White United Transport Ltd of Chepstow in South Wales had been pursuing the major operators on Guernsey since 1946 and succeeded first in taking over Guernsey Railway Co in July 1949 and then Guernsey Motors in August 1950. An early impact was to acquire and absorb the operations of Sarre Transport (with each subsidiary taking half of the business), thus eliminating the major competitor on the island. United Transport, possibly anticipating nationalisation, sold out their UK based subsidiaries to the British Transport Commission, but retained their Guernsey interests before turning their attention further afield in Africa.

Under United Transport's influence, vehicles of Albion manufacture became the standard and later, when suitable Albions were no longer available, a Bedford lorry chassis was suitably modified.

In 1973, the Guernsey Motors fleet was incorporated into Guernsey Railway Co allowing Motors to concentrate on their tourism and other activities.

The next development was in 1978 when United Transport sold the Guernsey Railway Co to a South Wales businessman – William Smith. A fleet of new buses was purchased, the first to the new legal width of 7ft 4in which had been introduced in 1969. William Smith expressed a preference for repainting the fleet into the former Guernsey Motors red livery, but in the event ill health and his subsequent death saw the business being sold on to another Mr Smith – a Scottish businessman called Alex Smith who was connected with the oil industry and in particular, the Kinross Plant & Construction Co Ltd on Tayside. This introduced another new vehicle policy, with a fleet of former Western National Bristol SUs being acquired to replace all of the remaining Albions still in the fleet. These were mostly sold off for preservation at auction in early 1980. The Bristols were 7ft 6in wide and took advantage of a new law for buses used on licensed routes permitted to be of this width. For a time, coaches used the Delta Tours fleet name (which had been the name of a small minibus operator acquired in 1977).

GUERNSEYBUS
The new regime did not last long for the Guernsey Railway Co became insolvent and ceased trading in November 1980. A temporary free minibus service was provided by the States of Guernsey and crewed by the former Railway Co drivers. A public hearing in early 1981 decided in favour of selling the island's bus company to Trafalgar Leisure International, an English company. The name Guernseybus Ltd was adopted and operations commenced in February 1981 with the new company having acquired the premises and fleet of the former Railway Co. Most of the redundant staff were also re-employed by the new company.

FRANCHISING

Over the years (and unlike on Jersey), the island has never supported any large independent coach operator, but in 1976, a new company called Educational Holidays Guernsey Ltd was formed. Their vehicles were restricted to 7ft 4in wide (not being a bus operator), which led to a number of 8ft 2½in wide vehicles being imported from the UK, subsequently cut down and rebuilt to 7ft 4in wide.

In 1993, Educational Holidays' private hire licences were converted to omnibus. This allowed them to operate bus services for the first time, in competition with Guernseybus. The States of Guernsey's desire to improve public services led to them organising the island's bus routes into three packages, to which they invited tenders. The Holidays company secured one package and Guernseybus the other two. As a result, Educational Holidays acquired a number of midi-buses in a variety of types, which they branded 'Roadrunner'.

Declines in passenger numbers led to both company's finances becoming poor in the final years of the 20th century and following the ill-heath of Guernseybus's Managing Director and a failure to find a buyer, the company became insolvent in November 2000. Following this, the States of Guernsey acquired their fleet and in turn, leased it to Educational Holidays, now renamed Island Coachways Ltd. In 2003, the States replaced the old Guernseybus stock with a fleet of 33 new Dennis Dart buses. This state of affairs was maintained until 2012 when the States adopted a franchising model as had been introduced on Jersey previously. There were differences however as the States of Guernsey retained the ownership of the vehicles, leasing them to the operator. CT Plus (who were to successfully bid for the Jersey tender in the following year) were awarded the contract. The Dennis Darts were transferred from Island Coachways and continued to give sterling service, only being replaced in 2017/8 with a new intake of Wright StreetVibe vehicles.

CURRENT SCENE

Since the 1980s, several small minibus operators have sprung up, some of which evolved into operating larger vehicles. Blue Bird Taxis were started in 1987 and Delta Taxis in 1994, the latter taking over Blue Bird in 2004. Delta themselves collapsed and were taken over by a new company, Island Taxis in 2010. The other significant operator still current today is Intransit which was started in 1996.

At the present time, there are seven PSV operators on Guernsey:

One island-wide bus operator	CT Plus Guernsey Ltd
One major coach operator	Island Coachways Ltd
Five smaller operators of coaches and minibuses	Barnabe Ltd
	Executive Car Services Ltd
	Intransit Ltd
	Island Taxis Ltd
	Lambourne Taxis Ltd

REGISTRATION NUMBERS

The first series of registration numbers on Guernsey commenced in 1903 and were controlled by the Constables of St Peter Port. Originally, they were only required to be displayed on the rear of the vehicle, either painted on or on a plate. The first numbers were prefixed 'A'; only four PSVs have ever been recorded displaying this series.

In 1915, the States of Guernsey took over the issuing of registration numbers with initially the same as the original series with the 'A' painted out. From 1919, number plates were issued in vitreous enamel starting with black numbers on a white background for cars, lorries, buses etc and black on red for motorcycles. The following year, the colours were reversed, with the change in appearance indicating that the motor tax had been paid. This pattern was alternated in each succeeding year. From 1928, front number plates were required although these had to be supplied by the owner, the States maintaining supplyl over the rear enamel ones.

From 1931, growing numbers of vehicles led to the system that has been in force ever since. The number plate was no longer an indication that tax had been paid and could be regarded as permanently allocated to the vehicle although strictly, Guernsey registrations are not allocated for life, just the period that the vehicle is licensed for use on the road. Numbers are reused and owners can keep 'cherished' numbers and apply them to successive vehicles. This was particularly popular with Guernseybus in the 1980s and 1990s when they re-used older former Guernsey Motors and Guernsey Railway Co marques several times. Island Coachways today continue to re-use their older registrations (these instances are distinguished by the (unofficial) suffixes [1], [2], [3] etc in this publication.

POLICE PLATES

Police plates were introduced in 1946 to certify that the vehicle had been examined and approved for public use. The Island Police Committee which had been in existence since 1925, was the body that administered this system. Prior to 1946, their approval was directly stenciled on to the vehicle. Numbers were allocated to vehicles run on licensed services. After Guernsey Railway Co closed, Police plates were discontinued and replaced with Public Service Omnibus numbers.

From 1966, vehicles used solely on private hires were allocated Private Hire numbers (which indicated that they were not approved for use on licensed bus services. These are prefixed 'ph' in this publication although these letters are not carried in reality. The third category is 'taxi' plates for vehicles of eight seats or fewer. These are shown with an (unofficial) 't' suffix in this publication.

TRAMS

GUERNSEY STEAM TRAMWAY CO LTD
GUERNSEY RAILWAY CO LTD

The tramway was operated successively by two distinct companies. First, The Guernsey Steam Tramway Co Ltd was incorporated in London in May 1878 with a share capital of £25,000 having hosted a demonstration of a Hughes Steam Tram on a temporary track in late 1877-early 1878. Construction between St Peter Port and the harbour at St Sampson starting in the following June. A certain amount of disquiet existed between the shareholders of the new company, particularly as the cost of construction left very little in hand to buy rolling stock. In any event, the line opened on 6 June 1879. The prospects were good; the horse-bus route in 1877 had 44 operators competing along it, carrying some 2,000 passengers in that year.

The rolling stock comprised initially of three steam trams – two by Merryweather and one built by Stephen Lewin. These were augmented by a further four second-hand locomotives arriving in 1882-1883, but all suffered from unreliability over the years which saw passenger numbers drop which impacted on the finances.

The trams consisted of a steam engine drawing first-class closed and second-class open trailers. Unfortunately, the tramway soon ran into financial and maintenance difficulties caused in part by its structure, partly due to the cheap horse-bus competition along its route and partly by unreliable rolling stock. This saw a re-emergence of the horse-cab operators who took the opportunity to regain some of the ground they lost when the system opened. The emergence of an island-wide horse bus operator – The Guernsey Omnibus Co in 1888 was the final straw and although the possibility of a merger was explored, the tramway system closed on 5 January 1889.

Some of the shareholders of the Guernsey Steam Tramway set about forming a new locally registered company – the Guernsey Railway Co Ltd which was incorporated on 18 September 1888. With an issued share capital of £14,732 it set about acquiring the assets of the Guernsey Steam Railway Co, which it eventually did after an eleven-month break on 2 December 1889. The new company had ambitious plans to electrify the line, but first it had to consolidate the steam operation although the only new rolling stock to be purchased initially was a double-deck Falcon trailer.

In January 1891, permission was granted to electrify the line and Siemens was awarded the contract. Three double-deck Falcon cars fitted with Siemens motors were acquired later in the year which were used to trial the system, with services commencing on 20 February 1892. Reliability was patchy in the early days and on occasions, the steam locomotives had to substitute to keep the service running. Siemens were called on to rectify the problems and it was agreed that they would pay the Guernsey Railway Co £600 plus £20 per week to lease the line and run the services. Thus, the Railway Company only had the track to maintain and during this period and took the opportunity to construct new offices at Hougue a la Pierre. The Siemens lease ran for eighteen months when the railway resumed later in 1893. By now the reliability problems had been resolved but competition from the Guernsey Omnibus Co was keeping passenger numbers down. A proposition to merge the two companies came to fruition on 24 April 1895 and the horse-bus services were progressively sold off although they did not finally disappear until 1911. The system was now profitable and further new and second-hand cars were purchased at intervals up to 1905.

In 1904, an incinerator was constructed which dealt with the refuse from the town and surrounding villages. This plant was connected to the tranway generating equipment and after 1913 supplied power commercially to the town. This allowed the company to make economies and carry out maintenance without interrupting the tram service.

Trams had always been prohibited from running on Sundays, but bus services were never restricted by this. With the advent of motor buses in 1909, the law was amended and from April 1912, Sunday tram services were permitted.

By 1934, the tramway was over 40 years old and the newest car almost 30 years old. Constraints and restrictions by the island's roads and terrain had restricted any possibility of extending it and since the early 1920s, serious competition from motor buses had impacted on its viability. A decision was taken to close the system and replace its services with motor bus operated ones and it ceased on 9 June 1934.

STEAM TRAMS

1879

New steam locomotives:

1	Merryweather & Sons	0-2-0	6/1879	9/1898
2	Merryweather & Sons	0-2-0	6/1879	-/1896
3	Stephen Lewin	0-2-0	12/1879	-/1882

Notes:

1: Named 'Shooting Star'; rebuilt 10/1885.
2: Named 'Sampson'.
3: Was trialled by Portsmouth Tramways before delivery and is believed to be the only tram engine built by Stephen Lewin.

Disposals:

1: Robinson, Guernsey (dealer) for scrap 9/1898.
2: No known disposal.
3: Scrapped (locally) 1882.

New trailers:

1 [1]	SCWC	2-axle / 8 bay	20	6/1879	-/1903
2 [1]	SCWC	2-axle / 8 bay	20	6/1879	-/1903
3 {1]	SCWC	2-axle / 4 bay	20	6/1879	-/1897
4 [1]	SCWC	2-axle / 4 bay	20	6/1879	by-/1890
5	SCWC	2-axle	14	6/1879	by-/1893
6	SCWC	2-axle	14	6/1879	by-/1893

Notes:

Fleet number 7 was a coke truck, new 6/1879 and withdrawn by1891.

1 [1], 2 [1]: Were first class closed saloons only until 1890, when the distinction between first and second class was discontinued.
3-4: Were open sided 'umbrella' cars.
5-6: Were open cars; rebuilt as closed smoking cars by AG Humby, Le Truchot 12/1879.

Disposals:

Disposals are known only for the following trailers.

1 [1]: Rocquaine Bay Tea Rooms, St Peter-in-the-Wood.
3 [2]: Converted to an electric tram car 1901 (qv).
4 [2]: Converted to an electric tram car 1891 (qv).

1881-1890

New trailers:

8	?	3-axle	60	5/1881	-/1896
9	SCWC	2+2-axle / 7+7 bays	46	7/1884	-/1891
4 [2]	Falcon	2+2-axle / 7 bay	32/44	6/1890	-/1891
12	Falcon	2-axle / 5 bay	32	8/1895	6/1934
13	Falcon	2-axle / 5 bay	32	8/1895	6/1934
3 [2]	Milnes	2-axle / 4 bay	22/32	3/1897	-/1901
14	Milnes	2-axle / 5 bay	40	5/1897	6/1934
15	Milnes	2-axle / 5 bay	40	5/1897	6/1934

Notes:

8: Was a double-deck car acquired after being exhibited at a Paris exhibition. It had knife board seating.
9: Was built as a two-compartment car with one compartment for first class and one for second class passengers (up to 1890).
12-13: Were rebuilt after fire damage 1897.

Disposals:

Disposals are known only for the following trailers.

9: Converted to an electric tram car 1891 (as a 48-seater) (qv).
14-15: The body from one of these was in a garden in Jerbourg Road, St Martin whilst the other was at Grosse Hougue, St Sampson.

Acquired steam locomotives:

4	Henry Hughes & Co	0-2-0	-/1877-8	11/1890
5	Henry Hughes & Co	0-2-0	-/1877-8	10/1889
6	Henry Hughes & Co	0-2-0	-/1877-8	10/1889
7	Henry Hughes & Co	0-2-0	-/1877-8	10/1889
8	R & W Hawthorne Leslie	0-2-0	-/1879	9/1898

Previous histories:

4: Its origins are unknown; it was acquired 11/1882.
5-7: Believed to be three of a batch of 12 locomotives supplied to Compagnie des Tramways Sud, Paris (O-F) on a contract commencing 8/1879; the company had ceased by2/1880 and Henry Hughes & Co went into liquidation in 1881. Falcon Engineering & Car Works, Loughborough was formed in 1882 and these were among assets that they wished to dispose of. They were acquired in 5/1883, 7/1883 and 8/1883 respectively.
8: Possibly new to Sunderland Corporation Tramways; it passed to R & W Hawthorne Leslie & Co Ltd, Newcastle upon Tyne at an unknown date; acquired 5/1890.

Notes:

8: Named '*Haro*'.

Disposals:

4: T Ward, Sheffield (dealer) for scrap 11/1890.
5: T Ward, Sheffield (dealer) for scrap 10/1889.
6: T Ward, Sheffield (dealer) for scrap 10/1889.
7: T Ward, Sheffield (dealer) for scrap 10/1889.
8: Robinson, Guernsey (dealer) for scrap 9/1898.

ELECTRIC TRAMS

1891-1905

New cars:18

7	Falcon	Horn block 2 axle	Siemens 27 hp	22/34	7/1891	6/1934
10	Falcon	Horn block 2 axle	Siemens 27 hp	22/34	8/1891	6/1934
11	Falcon	Horn block 2 axle	Siemens 27 hp	22/34	8/1891	6/1934
5	Falcon	Pivotal trucks 2+2 axle	Siemens 2 x 14 hp	32/44	5/1893	3/1931
6	Falcon	Pivotal trucks 2+2 axle	Siemens 2 x 14 hp	32/44	5/1893	6/1934
8	Milnes	Peckham 8ft 2-axle	2 x GE800	36/44	7/1896	6/1934
2 [2]	Brush	Peckham 6E 2-axle	1 x GE800	22/30	5/1903	6/1934
1 [2]	Brush	Brill 21E	1 x GE800	22/30	3/1905	6/1934

Notes:

1 [2], 2 [2]: Were of 3-bay double-deck design; rebuilt to 6-bay design 1912.

5: Was of 7-bay double-deck design; its original equal-wheel pivotal trucks were replaced with Brill 22E maximum traction trucks and GE800 motors 1914.

6: Was of 7-bay double-deck design; its original equal-wheel pivotal trucks were replaced with Brill 22E maximum traction trucks and GE800 motors 1913.

7: Was of 8-bay double-deck design; its original truck with axel horn blocks was replaced with a Peckham 7B truck 1895 and later a Peckham 6E truck; it was also fitted with a GE800 motor and a K2 controller.

8: Was of 6-bay double-deck design; its extra-long cantilever extension truck was replaced with Peckham pivotal trucks 1896.

10-11: Were of 8-bay double-deck design; their original trucks with axel horn blocks were replaced with Peckham 6E trucks 1895; they were also fitted with a GE800 motors and K2 controllers.

Disposals:

Disposals (dates unknown) are known only for the following vehicles.

7 (or 11): E Best, St Andrew.

8: S Duquemin, Vazon as a race-track grandstand.

10: At Pitronnerie Road, St Peter Port.

Rebuilt cars:

9	SCWC	Plate frame 2+2 axle	Siemens 14 hp	48	7/1884	-/1914
4 [2]	Falcon	Plate frame 2+2 axle	Siemens 14 hp	32/44	6/1890	-/1905
3 [2]	Milnes	Peckham 9A 2-axle	2 x GE800	22/32	3/1897	6/1934

Previous histories:

3 [2]: Was originally a steam tram trailer converted to an electric tram car 1901 (qv).

4 [2]: Was originally a steam tram trailer converted to an electric tram car 1891 (qv).

9: Was originally a (46-seat) steam tram trailer converted to an electric tram car 1891 (qv).

Notes:

3 [2]: Was of 4-bay double-deck design.

4 [2]: Was a double-deck of 7-bay design; converted to a single-deck car 6/01

9: Was built as a two-compartment car (7+7 bays).

Disposals:

Disposals (dates unknown) are known only for the following vehicles.

3 [2]: Body to a summer house / shed 1934; two members of Guernsey Old Car Club for preservation 1975/76; C Brouard, La Villiaze, Forest at an unknown date; States Ancient Monuments Committee, Guernsey for preservation by8/93; Guernsey Museum & Art Gallery & Heritage Service for preservation by10/04.

9: One saloon to WJ Caparne, St Martin as an artist's studio; the other saloon to Delancey, St Sampson as a summer house.

Acquired cars:

16	Falcon	2-axle / 6 bay	18/26	-/1893	6/1934
17	Falcon?	2-axle / 7 bay	18/26	-/1893?	-/1933
18	Falcon	2-axle / 6 bay	18/26	-/1893	6/1934
19	Falcon?	2-axle / ? bay	18/26	-/1893?	-/1928

Previous histories:

16-19: Were new or second hand to Cardiff Tramways Co Ltd as double-deck horse trams in 1893; Cardiff Corporation Tramways Department 12/1901; acquired in 4/1903.

Notes:

17 and 19 may have been of Electric Railway & Tramway Carriage Works or Milnes Voss manufacture.

17 was rebuilt as a single-deck smoking car in 4/22.

Disposals:

Disposals are known only for the following vehicle.

17: Body found at Cobo Motor Works, Castel 1/86; J Carman, St Sampson for preservation 1986.

GUERNSEY MOTORS LTD

On 1 July 1919, a group of local businessmen formed Guernsey Motors Ltd with ambitious aims:

- Establishing and maintaining a frequent service of motor buses between St Peter Port and other parts of the island.
- The equipping of up-to-date motor engineering workshops to undertake the repair of motor cars, motorcycles, motor boats and general engineering of every description.
- The provision of motor lorries for cartage of coal, growers' produce and any other form of merchandise which may be conveniently and profitably handled.
- The establishment of a depot for carrying on the business of vendors of motor cars, motorcycles, marine engines, tyres and all spare parts.

Accommodation was obtained and a garage and works leased from the States of Guernsey on Castle Walk. One of the first acts performed was to draw up an agreement with the Guernsey Railway Co Ltd which held that:

- Guernsey Motors would not operate to St Sampson, L'Ancresse or L'Islet
- Guernsey Railway Co would not operate in the rest of the island

This agreement stayed in force until 1941 when it was formally terminated during the Occupation. That the companies operated in the main amicably was due to the fact that the founders of Guernsey Motors were also shareholders and directors of the Railway Company.

To start operations, 20 Ford TT chassis were obtained, 12 of which were bodied by Slope Bros of Camberley, Surrey, others were fitted with former horse-drawn coaches. The first of these entered service on 18 December 1919. A short-lived parcels service ('Express Parcels') was also started, but this was unprofitable and the van was quickly converted to a bus.

Good coverage of the island was achieved within a year and more spacious premises were obtained, these being former stables at Brock Road. A contract was obtained from the Royal Hotel and an specially yellow-liveried vehicle was placed in service. An early rival was JH Miller who had been the previous tenant at the Brock Road Stables and had been ousted when Guernsey Motors took over the lease. His business was acquired in October 1921. This brought with it nine vehicles (one being a chassis only) and nine approved routes. With new Ford chassis being difficult to obtain, former Army lorry chassis were obtained from the Slough Trading Company including some Packards which became a favoured make. These robust vehicles were fitted with new Baico bodies or recycled horse-drawn units and some lasted until after World War II.

Up to 1926, further small operators were acquired, including the business of Thomas Sarre (August 1922) and Le Cheminant {Saints Bus Service} and Le Valliant & Robert {Britannia} in August 1925. Part of the WN Priaulx / Ozanne Bros {Primrose} business was also obtained in May 1924. These were interspersed with further ex-War Department vehicles.

In October 1927, the Perchard's Livery Stables were acquired and the Perchards name was later used for a hearse and taxi arm of the company. The stables would become a major source of income during the Occupation. Two further acquisitions during late 1928 were the businesses of AE Langmead {The Robin} and WT Robilliard {Reindeer}.

From the start of the 1930s, an attempt at standardization was made with the purchase of Vulcans. During the decade, 14 new and 9 secondhand examples were acquired which replaced many of the early vehicles. Others underwent a refurbishment programme which included the fitting of in-house built bodies including two with toastrack style bodies.

The largest acquisition to date came in November 1931 when the established business of Ulric Ash was acquired. Other than nine buses, Ash's taxi business was also acquired. The yellow livery of these vehicles was adopted as standard for the remainder of the prewar period.

A setback occurred at Easter 1936 when a fire at Brock Road destroyed three vehicles and damaged a number of others. Replacements were obtained, but these were amongst the last Vulcans to be manufactured and so attention was turned towards Dennis products. The last prewar acquisition was LN Lenfestey's Lorina business which came with four vehicles of Reo manufacture in February 1939. The other notable purchase of the year was a Bedford WTB coach which was acquired to operate a service to the newly opened States Airport. It was painted in a green livery and was bodied by WL Thurgood – the original owner of Guernsey and Jersey Airways.

At the outbreak of War in September 1939 and the German Occupation in the following June, normal services were suspended, but the stables ensured that the company remained profitable. A total of 55 vehicles were impressed by the German Military of which only 12 were eventually recovered, and those in very poor condition. Ulric Ash (who had been associated with the company since 1928 and whose own business had been acquired in 1931) was appointed General Manager in 1946. He immediately set upon renewing and replacing the fleet. Some utility specification Bedford OBs arrived in and ex-War Department Commer chassis were obtained in 1947/48, but these were followed by batches of 33-seat Austin K4s which were now available. 27 of these were obtained over the next three years, a number being fitted with locally constructed and second-hand bodies.

Red & White United Transport Ltd of Chepstow had acquired Guernsey Railway Co Ltd on 1 July 1949 and in parallel opened negotiations with Guernsey Motors Ltd. The acquisition was concluded in August 1950 with the results that both companies came under common management. The taxi business had already earlier been divested to Ash Ltd, Ulric Ash's company in April 1950.

Red & White's vehicle policy of buying Albions through their associate Watts Factors of Lydney, Gloucestershire was implemented fairly quickly with the Railway Company, but probably due to the recent large intake of Austins, it was not until 1953 that this make arrived in the Motors fleet. It remained the standard vehicle in both companies up to 1965 when production ceased; 37 of this type had been acquired over this period. The other notable addition was the joint acquisition of Sarre Transport Ltd, a major competitor since the War with the assets being equally between both Railway and Motors companies.

With Albion vehicles no longer available after 1965, it had become difficult to source a standard vehicle that seated around 35 but was only 7ft wide. Eventually a chassis based on the Bedford J4 was chosen and this became the standard in both fleets. 15 of these entered service with Guernsey Motors up to the final purchases in 1972.

In October 1973, it was decided to rationalize the two company's activities. Guernsey Motors fleet was incorporated into Guernsey Railway Co allowing Guernsey Motors to concentrate on their tourism and other activities. 54 vehicles (39 Albion and 15 Bedford) were transferred.

1919

New vehicles:

2		Ford TT	?	Baico	B14F	12/19	-/--
3		Ford TT	?	Slope Bros	B14F	12/19	-/--

Notes:

These vehicles had their chassis modified by Baico.
Fleet number 1 was a Ford TT lorry – to service 11/19.

2: Rebodied Baico COB18F at an unknown date.

Disposals:

No disposals are known for these vehicles.

1920

New vehicles:

4		Ford TT	?	?	B—F	1/20	-/--
7		Ford TT	?	Slope Bros	B14F	3/20	-/--
8		Ford TT	?	Slope Bros	B14F	3/20	-/--
9		Ford TT	?	Slope Bros	B14F	3/20	-/--
10		Ford TT	?	?	Ch20	3/20	-/--
11		Ford TT	?	?	OB--R	3/20	-/--
12		Ford TT	?	?	Ch14	4/20	-/--
13	2659	Ford TT	?	?	OB--R	6/20	by-/35
14		Ford TT	?	Slope Bros	B14F	6/20	-/--
15		Ford TT	?	Slope Bros	B14F	6/20	-/--
17		Ford TT	?	Baico	Ch--	6/20	-/--
18		Ford TT	?	Slope Bros	B14F	6/20	-/--
19		Ford TT	?	Slope Bros	B14F	6/20	-/--
20	478	Ford TT	?	Slope Bros	B23F	6/20	-/--
22		Ford TT	?	Baico	COB18F	-/20	-/--

Notes:

These vehicles had their chassis extended by Baico.

Slope Bros (of Camberley) supplied six B14F bodies for fitting to Ford chassis by3/20. Subsequently, a further six were ordered. In addition, six Baico COB18F bodies were delivered for fitting to Ford chassis, three of which were fitted with modified Baico extension attachments. Some of these bodies replaced earlier lorry and those from former horse-drawn vehicles.

Fleet numbers 5 and 6 were Ford TT lorries (5 with its chassis modified by Baico), new 2/20.

4: Was fitted with one of two van bodies purchased in London 10/19; originally intended for the 'Express Parcels' fleet.

10: Was fitted with an ex horse-drawn body; rebodied Baico COB18F at an unknown date.

12: Was purchased for the Royal Hotel contract and painted in a special livery.

22: Was of unknown origin, fitted with a Baico body with its chassis modified by Baico 1920.

2659 (13): Was fitted with an ex horse-drawn body) the registration 2659 was not its first); it was rebodied Baico COB18F and re-registered 2659 by1929.

Disposals:

No disposals are known for these vehicles (three of these were withdrawn by1924; a further four by1928 and the rest by1935.

Vehicle acquired from an unknown source 6/20:

16		Cadillac	?	Guernsey Motors	Ch--	-/--	by-/24

Notes:

16: Acquired as a car 3/20; fitted with a charabanc body by Guernsey Motors Ltd 6/20.

Vehicle acquired from War Department (GOV) 7/20:

21	413	Packard E	?	Guernsey Motors	Ch27	-/--	10/42

Previous history:

413 (21): Chassis was new as a War Department (army) (GOV) lorry, acquired from Slough Trading Depot and fitted with a Guernsey Motors charabanc body 7/20.

Notes:

413 (21): Rebodied B24F at an unknown date.

Disposal:

413 (21): Impressed by German Military Authorities (Military Truck Compound) (GOV) 10/42; scrapped locally at an unknown date (or sent to France for scrapping).

1921

Vehicles acquired from JH Miller, St Peter Port (CI) 11/21:

27		Maxwell 25 cwt	?	T Davies	?	-/--	by-/39
28		Maxwell 25 cwt	?	T Davies	?	-/--	by-/39
29		De Dion Bouton	?	T Davies	?	-/--	by-/35
30		Maxwell 25 cwt	?	T Davies	?	-/--	by-/36
31	1151	Maxwell 25 cwt	?	T Davies	OB18R	-/--	by-/39
32	313	Maxwell 25 cwt	?	T Davies	OB18R	-/--	10/42
33	658	Maxwell 25 cwt	?	(chassis only)		-/--	10/42
34	659 [1]	Guy	?	Guy	B--F	-/--	3/23

Previous histories:

27-28, 30 First recorded with JH Miller (CI) - one as B18R in 2/20 and two as Ch20 in 6/20 and the third by1921 (order unknown).

29: First recorded with JH Miller (CI) 1921.

313 (32): New to JH Miller (CI) 7/21.

658 (33): First recorded with JH Miller (CI) 10/21, but not bodied.

659 [1] (34): First recorded with JH Miller (CI) 10/21.

1151 (31): First recorded with JH Miller (CI) 4/20.

Notes:

Two of the Maxwells were rebodied Baico OB19F 1926.

313 (32): Rebuilt as a small-wheeled 'Toast Rack Tourabout' and bodied by Guernsey Motors T14 1933.
658 (33): Fitted with a B—R body at an unknown date; overturned and its roof demolished 1/27; subsequently rebodied B18F.
1151 (31): Probably reseated / rebuilt as B16F c1930.

Disposals:

27-30: No known disposals.
313 (32): Impressed by German Military Authorities (Military Truck Compound) (GOV) 10/42; scrapped locally at an unknown date (or sent to France for scrapping).
658 (33): Impressed by German Military Authorities (Military Truck Compound) (GOV) 10/42; scrapped locally at an unknown date (or sent to France for scrapping).
659 [1] (34): Chassis returned to Guy Motors 3/23; body to Packard 3641 (2) 7/29.
1151 (31): Impressed by German Military Authorities (Military Truck Compound) (GOV) 10/42; scrapped locally at an unknown date (or sent to France for scrapping).

Vehicles acquired from War Department (GOV) 1921:

25		Packard E	?	Baico	OB25F	-/--	-/40
26		Packard E	?	Baico	OB25F	-/--	-/40
23	567 [1]	Packard E	?	Guernsey Motors	OB23C	-/--	9/48
24	612	Packard E	?	?	Ch23	-/--	9/48

Previous histories:

25-26: Chassis were new as War Department (army) (GOV) lorries, acquired from Slough Trading Depot and fitted with new Baico bodies.
567 [1] (23): Chassis was new as War Department (army) (GOV) lorry, acquired from Slough Trading Depot and fitted with a Guernsey Motors body.
612 (24): Chassis was new as a War Department (army) (GOV) lorry, acquired from Slough Trading Depot and fitted with a former horse-drawn excursion car body (one of two) purchased from JH Miller, St Peter Port (CI) 2/20.

Notes:

567 [1] (23) and 612 (as 372 [1]) (24): Probably received two Police plates from 71, 83, 95 in 1946.

567 [1] (23): Chassis rebuilt and rebodied Guernsey Motors B29F 1932; impressed by States of Guernsey Civil Transport Service, St Peter Port (GOV) 2/41; returned to Guernsey Motors Ltd 23 5/45.
612 (24): Chassis rebuilt and rebodied Guernsey Motors B29F 12/34; impressed by States of Guernsey Military Transport Service, St Peter Port (GOV) 7/40; German Military Authorities (Military Truck Compound) (GOV) by10/42; AP Delaney, Castel (GOV) re-registered 372 [1] 10/42; returned to Guernsey Motors Ltd 24 by8/44.

Disposals:

25-26: Chassis scrapped 1940; bodies probably impressed by German Military Authorities (Military Truck Compound) (GOV) 12/42; scrapped locally at an unknown date (or sent to France for scrapping).
372 [1] (ex 612) (24): Scrapped 9/48.
567 [1] (23): Scrapped 9/48.

1922

Vehicles acquired from War Department (GOV) 5-6/22:

10		Packard E	?	Baico	COB23F	-/--	4/36
40	400	Packard E	?	Baico	COB23F	-/--	10/42
5	465	Packard E	?	Baico	COB23F	-/--	9/48
38	737	Packard E	?	Baico	COB23F	-/--	7/40
39	742	Packard E	?	Baico	COB23F	-/--	10/42
36	745	Packard E	?	Baico	COB23F	-/--	10/42
37	784	Packard E	?	Baico	COB23F	-/--	7/40

Police plate (from 1946):

465 (as 295 [1]) (5): Probably one of 71, 83, 95.

Previous histories:

The chassis of these vehicles were new as a War Department (army) (GOV) lorries, acquired from Slough Trading Depot and fitted with Baico bodies. The Packard E was still being imported from USA up to 1924 by W G Gaunt & Co, Piccadilly, London which may have been an alternative souce of supply.

Notes:

10: To service 5/22.

400 (40): To service 6/22.

465 (5): To service 5/22; chassis rebuilt and rebodied Guernsey Motors B29F 3/34; impressed by States of Guernsey Military Transport Service, St Peter Port (GOV) 7/40; German Military Authorities (Military Truck Compound) (GOV) 4/41; AP Delaney, Castel (GOV) re-registered 295 [1] 10/42; returned to Guernsey Motors Ltd 5 by8/44.

737 (38): To service 6/22; chassis rebuilt and rebodied Guernsey Motors B29F between 1933 and 1936.

742 (39): To service 6/22.

745 (36): To service 6/22.

784 (37): To service 6/22; chassis rebuilt and rebodied Guernsey Motors B29F between 1933 and 1936.

Disposals:

10: Destroyed by fire at Brock Road, St Peter Port 4/36.

295 [1] (ex 465) (5): Scrapped 9/48.

400 (40): Impressed by German Military Authorities (Military Truck Compound) (GOV) 10/42; scrapped locally at an unknown date (or sent to France for scrapping).

737 (38): Impressed by States of Guernsey Military Transport Service, St Peter Port (GOV) 7/40; German Military Authorities (Military Truck Compound) (GOV) 12/42; scrapped locally at an unknown date (or sent to France for scrapping).

742 (39): Impressed by German Military Authorities (Military Truck Compound) (GOV) 10/42; scrapped locally at an unknown date (or sent to France for scrapping).

745 (36): Impressed by German Military Authorities (Military Truck Compound) (GOV) 10/42; scrapped locally at an unknown date (or sent to France for scrapping).

784 (37): Impressed by States of Guernsey Military Transport Service, St Peter Port (GOV) 7/40; German Military Authorities (Military Truck Compound) (GOV) 12/42; scrapped locally at an unknown date (or sent to France for scrapping).

Vehicles acquired from TW Sarre, St Peter-in-the-Wood (CI) 8/22:

41	2224	International 25 hp	5520	T Le Huray	Ch19	-/21	3/39
42		International 25 hp	?	?	OB22C	by8/22	c-/29

Previous histories:

42: New to TW Sarre (CI) (as OB19F); HJ Ozanne, Guernsey (dealer) by8/22.

2224 (41): Ordered by TW Sarre, St Peter-in-the Wood (CI) but not operated (or possibly even delivered); HJ Ozanne, Guernsey (dealer) by8/22.

Disposals:

42: No known disposal.

2224 (41): Scrapped 3/39.

Vehicle acquired from K Millard, Guernsey (dealer) 9/22:

43	744	Maxwell 30 cwt	?	?	Ch22	-/22	11/42

Previous history:

744 (43): New to K Millard (dealer) (may have been operated briefly on private hire work with them).

Notes:

744 (43): Rebuilt as a small-wheeled 'Toast Rack Tourabout' and bodied by Guernsey Motors T14 6/34.

Disposal:

744 (43): Impressed by German Military Authorities (Military Truck Compound) (GOV) 11/42; scrapped locally at an unknown date (or sent to France for scrapping).

1923

New vehicle:

34	659 [2]	Guy 25 hp	?	Baico	OB25F	7/23	10/42

Notes:

659 [2] (34): Its chassis was obtained from Guy Motors in exchange for that of 659 [1] of 1921.

Disposal:

659 [2] (34): Impressed by German Military Authorities (Military Truck Compound) (GOV) 10/42; scrapped locally at an unknown date (or sent to France for scrapping).

1924

Vehicle acquired from WN Priaulx / Ozanne Bros {Primrose}, Forest (CI) 5/24:

44		Napier	?	Ridley	Ch16	-/--	c-/35
45	348	Maxwell	?	?	Ch14	-/--	11/42

Previous histories:

44: First recorded with WN Priaulx / Ozanne Bros {Primrose} (CI); UU Ash, St Peter Port (dealer) c5/24.

348 (45): First recorded with WN Priaulx / Ozanne Bros {Primrose} (CI), possibly in 10/22 (as Ch20); UU Ash, St Peter Port (dealer) c5/24.

Disposals:

44: No known disposal.

348 (45): Impressed by German Military Authorities (Military Truck Compound) (GOV) 11/42; scrapped locally at an unknown date (or sent to France for scrapping).

Vehicles acquired from War Department (GOV) 1924:

1	937	Packard E	?	Baico	COB25F	-/--	1/41

Previous histories:

937 (1): Chassis was new as a War Department (army) (GOV) lorry, acquired from Slough Trading Depot and fitted with a Baico body.

Notes:

937 (1): Chassis rebuilt and rebodied Guernsey Motors B29F following a fire 1/33 when its Baico body was destroyed.

Disposals:

937 (1): Impressed by States of Guernsey Military Transport Service, St Peter Port (GOV) 2/41; German Military Authorities (Military Truck Compound) (GOV) 12/42; scrapped locally at an unknown date (or sent to France for scrapping).

1925

Vehicles acquired from F Le Cheminant {Saints Bus Service}, St Martin (CI) 8/25:

46	2251	International 20 hp	?	?	Ch24	-/--	9/37
47		Oldsmobile	?	?	Ch10	-/--	c-/35
48 [2]		Ford TT	?	Le Cheminant	OB14R	-/--	c-/35

Previous histories:

These vehicles were first recorded with F Le Cheminant {Saints Bus Service} (CI) by9/22. A spare body was also acquired.

Disposals:

47: No known disposal.

48 [2]: No known disposal.

2251 (46): Scrapped 3/39; remains impressed by German Military Authorities (Military Truck Compound) (GOV) for scrap metal 12/42.

Vehicles acquired from J Le Valliant & JE Robert {Britannia}, St Peter Port (CI) 8/25:

49	434	Reo Speed Wagon	?	?	OB25F	-/--	c-/35
50		Oldsmobile 1 ton	?	?	Ch15	-/--	c-/40

Previous histories:

These vehicles were first recorded with J Le Valliant & JE Robert {Britannia} (CI). A spare body was also acquired.

Disposals:

434 (49): Impressed by German Military Authorities (Military Truck Compound) (GOV) 11/42; scrapped locally at an unknown date (or sent to France for scrapping).

50: No known disposal.

Vehicles acquired from War Department (GOV) 1925:

22	1027	Packard E	?	Baico	COB25F	-/--	10/42

Previous histories:

1027 (22): Chassis was new as a War Department (army) (GOV) lorry, acquired from Slough Trading Depot and fitted with a Baico body.

Disposals:

1027 (22): Impressed by German Military Authorities (Military Truck Compound) (GOV) 11/42; scrapped locally at an unknown date (or sent to France for scrapping).

1926

Vehicle acquired from War Department (GOV) 1926:

4	1088	Packard E	?	Baico	COB25F	-/--	7/40
52	1957	Packard E	?	Baico	COB25F	-/--	10/42

Previous history:

1088 (4): Chassis was new as a War Department (army) (GOV) lorry, acquired from Slough Trading Depot and fitted with a Baico body.

1957 (52): Chassis was new as a War Department (army) (GOV) lorry, acquired from Slough Trading Depot and fitted with a Baico body.

Disposals:

1088 (4): Impressed by States of Guernsey Military Transport Service, St Peter Port (GOV) 7/40; German Military Authorities (LPA Paris) (GOV) 9/42; German Military Authorities (Military Truck Compound) (GOV) 12/42; scrapped locally at an unknown date (or sent to France for scrapping).

1957 (52): Impressed by German Military Authorities (Military Truck Compound) (GOV) 10/42; scrapped locally at an unknown date (or sent to France for scrapping).

Vehicle acquired from Bird Bros, St Sampson (CI) 1926:

53		W & G du Cros	?	F Mallett	B14-	-/--	c-/35

Previous history:

53: Probably new to Bird Bros (CI) named 'Island Belle' (as B18R) – was used as a lorry for coal deliveries but had a detachable bus body for passenger use.

Disposal:

53: No known disposal.

1928

Vehicles acquired from AE Langmead {The Robin}, St Peter Port (CI) 9/28:

35		Wallace 25 hp	B510	?	Ch29	by7/21	c-/28
20		Renault PB	?	Underhill	OB18F	-/--	c-/36

Previous histories:

20: Its origins are unknown; AE Langmead {The Robin} (CI) 1926?.

35: Probably new to Sansum's Central Garage, Paignton (DN) registered TA 1738 (as C20-); last licensed 3/25; AE Langmead {The Robin} (CI) 1925?.

Notes:

35: Named 'Edgar'.

Disposals:
>20: No known disposal.
>35 (ex TA 1738): No known disposal.

Vehicle acquired from WT Robilliard {Reindeer}, St Peter Port (CI) 11/28:

| 7 | 1601 | GMC | ? | FT Bennett | OB23F | -/-- | 10/42 |

Previous history:
>1601 (7): First recorded with WT Robilliard {Reindeer} (CI) (as OB22F).

Disposal:
>1601 (7): Impressed by German Military Authorities (Military Truck Compound) (GOV) 10/42; scrapped locally at an unknown date (or sent to France for scrapping).

Vehicle acquired from War Department (GOV) 1928:

| 3 | 2536 | Packard E | ? | Baico | COB25F | -/-- | 10/42 |

Previous history:
>2536 (3): Chassis was new as a War Department (army) (GOV) lorry, acquired from Slough Trading Depot and fitted with a Baico body.

Disposal:
>2536 (3): Impressed by German Military Authorities (Military Truck Compound) (GOV) 10/42; scrapped locally at an unknown date (or sent to France for scrapping).

1929

Vehicle acquired from AJ Marquand, St Peter Port (GCI) 1/29:

| 8 | 753 | Packard E | ? | Guernsey Motors | Ch23 | -/-- | 10/42 |

Previous history:
>753 (8): Was new as a lorry; chassis only acquired from AJ Marquand (GCI) and fitted with a Guernsey Motors body.

Disposal:
>753 (8): Impressed by German Military Authorities (Military Truck Compound) (GOV) 10/42; scrapped locally at an unknown date (or sent to France for scrapping).

Vehicle acquired from E Best, St Andrew (GCI) 3/29:

| 42 | 448 | Packard E | ? | ? | B29F | -/-- | 7/40 |

Previous history:
>448 (42): Was new as a lorry; chassis only acquired from E Best (GCI) and fitted with a bus body of unknown make.

Disposal:
>448 (42): Impressed by States of Guernsey Military Transport Service, St Peter Port (GOV) 7/40; German Military Authorities (Military Truck Compound) (GOV) 12/42; scrapped locally at an unknown date (or sent to France for scrapping).

Vehicle acquired from War Department (GOV) 7/29:

| 2 | 3641 | Packard E | ? | Guy | B24F | -/-- | 7/40 |

Previous history:
>3641 (2): Chassis was new as a War Department (army) (GOV) lorry, acquired from Slough Trading Depot and fitted with the Guy body from 659 (34) of 1921.

Notes:
>3641 (2): Used as a van on the Royal Mail contract until 1933 when it was rebodied Guernsey Motors B29F.

Disposal:

3641 (2): Impressed by States of Guernsey Military Transport Service, St Peter Port (GOV) 7/40; German Military Authorities (Military Truck Compound) (GOV) 12/42; scrapped locally at an unknown date (or sent to France for scrapping).

1930

New vehicles:

17	2783	Vulcan Duke	3XS68	Metcalfe	B19F	1/30	2/41
55	2791	Vulcan Duke	3XS63	Metcalfe	B19F	2/30	2/55
56	2792	Vulcan Duke	3XS62	Metcalfe	B19F	2/30	4/41
57	2793	Vulcan Duke	3XS64	Metcalfe	B19F	3/30	-/49

Police plate (from 1946):

2791 (55) (as 3450 (29)): 66

Notes:

2791 (55): Damaged by fire at Brock Road, St Peter Port 4/36; rebuilt to a Vulcan Duchess specification; rebodied Vulcan B29F, numbered 29 and re-registered 3450 9/36; impressed by States of Guernsey Military Transport Service, St Peter Port 2/41; returned to Guernsey Motors Ltd 29 at an unknown date; fitted with an Austin engine at an unknown date (post-WW2).

2793 (57): Impressed by States of Guernsey Military Transport Service, St Peter Port (GOV) 2/41; German Military Authorities (Military Truck Compound) (GOV) 12/42; AP Delaney, Castel (GOV) at an unknown date re-registered 266; returned by8/44.

Disposals:

266 (ex 2793) (57): No known disposal.

2783 (17): Impressed by States of Guernsey Military Transport Service, St Peter Port (GOV) 2/41; German Military Authorities (Military Truck Compound) (GOV) 12/42; scrapped locally at an unknown date (or sent to France for scrapping).

3450 (ex 2791) (29, ex 55): Scrapped 2/55.

2792 (56): Impressed by States of Guernsey Military Transport Service, St Peter Port (GOV) 4/41; German Military Authorities (Fortress Engineer Staff) (GOV) 7/42; scrapped locally at an unknown date (or sent to France for scrapping).

1931

New vehicles:

9	2976	Vulcan Duchess	?	Vulcan	B26F	4/31	4/36
19	2982	Vulcan Duchess	D51	Vulcan	B26F	5/31	9/49
47	2985	Vulcan Duchess	D52	Vulcan	B26F	4/31	7/40
15	2987	Vulcan Duchess	D53	Vulcan	B26F	4/31	7/40

Notes:

2982 (19): Impressed by States of Guernsey Military Transport Service, St Peter Port (GOV) 7/40; German Military Authorities (Fortress Engineer Staff) (GOV) 7/42; returned at an unknown date; it received a Police plate, probably one of 62, 63, 78, 79, 85 in 1946.

Disposals:

2976 (9): Destroyed by fire at Brock Road, St Peter Port 4/36.

2982 (19): Scrapped 1/55.

2985 (47): Impressed by States of Guernsey Military Transport Service, St Peter Port (GOV) 7/40; German Military Authorities (Military Truck Compound) (GOV) 11/42; scrapped locally at an unknown date (or sent to France for scrapping).

2987 (15): Impressed by States of Guernsey Military Transport Service, St Peter Port (GOV) 7/40; German Military Authorities (Military Truck Compound) (GOV) 12/42; scrapped locally at an unknown date (or sent to France for scrapping).

Vehicles acquired from UU Ash, St Peter Port (CI) 11/31:

62		Acason 3 ton	?	Baico	Ch26	by8/22	by-/33
64		Maxwell 30 cwt	?	?	Ch18	by4/22	by-/41
65		Willys-Overland 25 cwt	?	?	Ch18	-/--	by-/37
63	48	Maxwell 30 cwt	?	?	Ch18	6/23	10/42
60	885	Vulcan 30 cwt	?	?	Ch19	-/24	10/42

61	987	Vulcan 3 ton	?	?	Ch28	-/24	10/42
59	2220	Vulcan Duke	3XS06	Spicer	Ch19	11/27	10/42
58	2840	Vulcan Duke	3XS65	?	Ch23	4/31	9/50
18	2965	Vulcan Duke	3XS70	?	Ch23	-/31	9/49

Police plates (from 1946):
2840 (58): Probably one of 72, 76, 81, 84, 89.
2965 (18): Probably one of 62, 63, 78, 79, 85.

Previous histories:
62: First recorded with UU Ash (CI) (as Ch28).
64: First recorded with UU Ash (CI) (as Ch22).
65: First recorded with UU Ash (CI).
48 (63): New to WT Robilliard {Reindeer}, St Peter Port (CI) (as Ch20); UU Ash (CI) at an unknown date (as Ch22).
885 (60): New to WN Priaulx / Ozanne Bros {Primrose}, Forest (CI) named 'Queen of the Isles' (as Ch20); UU Ash (CI) 5/24.
987 (61): New to WN Priaulx / Ozanne Bros {Primrose}, Forest (CI) named 'Princess Ena'; UU Ash (CI) 5/24.
2220 (59): Probably new as a demonstrator with Vulcan Motors Ltd, Southport registered WM 1405 (as Ch20); it was also recorded as registered GD 9128 12/27); UU Ash (CI) named 'Rambler' 3/28.
2840 (58): New to UU Ash (CI).
2965 (18): New to UU Ash (CI).

Disposals:
62: No known disposal.
64: No known disposal.
65: No known disposal.
48 (63): Impressed by German Military Authorities (Military Truck Compound) (GOV) 10/42; scrapped locally at an unknown date (or sent to France for scrapping).
885 (60): Impressed by German Military Authorities (Military Truck Compound) (GOV) 10/42; scrapped locally at an unknown date (or sent to France for scrapping).
987 (61): Impressed by German Military Authorities (Military Truck Compound) (GOV) 10/42; scrapped locally at an unknown date (or sent to France for scrapping).
2220 (59): Impressed by German Military Authorities (Military Truck Compound) (GOV) 10/42; scrapped locally at an unknown date (or sent to France for scrapping).
2840 (58): Scrapped 1/55.
2965 (18): Ash Ltd, St Peter Port (dealer) for scrap 11/49.

1934

Vehicle acquired from E Stead {La Rapide}, St Sampson (CI) 3/34:

62	1073	Dodge LB	?	FT Bennett	OB24F	8/25	10/42
	1295	Dodge A	A577835	FT Bennett	OB21F	4/26	9/34

Previous histories:
1073 (62): New to E Stead {La Rapide} (CI) 2 (as OB23F); withdrawn 1931.
1295: New to E Stead {La Rapide} (CI) 3; withdrawn 1932.

Disposals:
1073 (62): Impressed by German Military Authorities (Military Truck Compound) (GOV) 10/42; scrapped locally at an unknown date (or sent to France for scrapping).
1295: Guernsey Railway Co Ltd (CI) 15 9/34; withdrawn 12/36; scrapped 12/39.

1935

New vehicles:

12	558	Vulcan Duchess	D125	Vulcan	B29F	8/35	7/40
14	1016	Vulcan Duchess	D12-	Vulcan	B29F	8/35	10/42

Disposals:
    558 (12): Impressed by Impressed by States of Guernsey Military Transport Service, St Peter Port (GOV) 7/40; German Military Authorities (Air Force Local Command) (GOV) 8/42; scrapped locally at an unknown date (or sent to France for scrapping).

    1016 (14): Impressed by German Military Authorities (Military Truck Compound) (GOV) 10/42; scrapped locally at an unknown date (or sent to France for scrapping).

Acquired vehicle from Shaw, Warrington (CH) 3/35:

11	4222	Vulcan Duchess	D41	?		B24R	3/30	7/40

Previous history:
    4222 (11): Probably new to Shaw registered ED 5838 (as C26-); Trade Motive, Slough (dealer) at an unknown date.

Notes:
    4222 (ex ED 5838) (11): Fitted with a Meadows 6 cylinder engine.

Disposal:
    4222 (ex ED 5838) (11): Impressed by States of Guernsey Military Transport Service, St Peter Port (GOV) 7/40; German Military Authorities (Military Truck Compound) (GOV) 12/42; scrapped locally at an unknown date (or sent to France for scrapping).

Vehicle acquired from C Major {Red Bus Service}, Worksop (NG) 10/35:

16	4444	Vulcan Duchess	D55	Guernsey Motors	B29F	12/30	9/53

Police plates (from 1946):
    4444 (16): 88

Previous history:
    4444 (16): New to C Major {Red Bus Service} (NG) registered VO 4935 and fitted with a Vulcan B26F body; Albion Motors Ltd (dealer) 12/34; chassis to T Allsop, Sheffield (dealer) 12/34 (its Vulcan body was fitted to Major's Albion PK26 CW 7706 2/35); fitted with a Guernsey Motors B29F body.

Notes:
    4444 (16): Impressed by Impressed by States of Guernsey Military Transport Service, St Peter Port (GOV) 7/40; German Military Authorities (Fortress Engineer Staff) (GOV) 12/42; returned to Guernsey Motors Ltd at an unknown date.

Disposal:
    4444 (16): Burgess & Sons, St Peter Port 9/53; W Head & Son Ltd, St Peter Port (minus engine) 1/55.

Acquired vehicle from an unknown source 1935:

49	507	Reo 25 hp	?	?		OB25F	-/--	11/42

Previous history:
    507 (49): May have been new to H Shaw, Bournemouth (HA) 1926, but this is not verified.

Disposal:
    507 (49): Impressed by German Military Authorities (Military Truck Compound) (GOV) 10/42; scrapped locally at an unknown date (or sent to France for scrapping).

1936

New vehicles:

9	624	Vulcan Duchess	D150	Vulcan	B29F	6/36	9/51
55	630	Vulcan Duchess	D151	Vulcan	B29F	7/36	7/40
10	1846	Vulcan Duchess	D152	Vulcan	B29F	6/36	9/51

Police plates (from 1946):
    624 (9) and 1846 (10): Probably two of 72, 76, 81, 84, 89.

Notes:
    These vehicles were purchased to replace vehicles destroyed in the Brock Road fire in 4/36.

624 (9): Impressed by States of Guernsey Military Transport Service, St Peter Port (GOV) 7/40; AP Delaney, Castel (GOV) 10/42; returned to Guernsey Motors Ltd 9 by8/44.

1846 (10): Impressed by States of Guernsey Military Transport Service, St Peter Port (GOV) 7/40; German Military Authorities (Air Force Construction Staff) (GOV) 8/42; returned to Guernsey Motors Ltd 10 at an unknown date.

Disposals:

624 (9): Scrapped 9/51.

630 (55): Impressed by States of Guernsey Military Transport Service, St Peter Port (GOV) 7/40; German Military Authorities (Fortress Engineer Staff) (GOV) 7/42; scrapped locally at an unknown date (or sent to France for scrapping).

1846 (10): FC Mercer, Hotel Beaulieu, St Martin (XCI) 10/51; EG Priaulx, Guernsey 2/52; R Opie, St Peter Port 4/54.

Vehicle acquired from Northern Ireland Road Transport Board, Belfast (AM) 4/36:

13	4684	Vulcan Duchess	D48	Vulcan		B27F	10/30	by-/55

Police plates (from 1946):

4684 (13, as 1): Probably one of 72, 76, 81, 84, 89.

Previous history:

4684 (13): New to T Nugent, Keady (AH) registered IB 4689 (as a 26-seater); Great Northern Railway (Ireland), Dundalk (EI) 178 1931; Northern Ireland Road Transport Board (AM) H97 8/35; Horne Products, Slough (dealer) 10/35.

Notes:

4684 (ex IB 4689) (13): Impressed by States of Guernsey Military Transport Service, St Peter Port (GOV) 7/40; AP Delaney, Castel (GOV) 10/42; returned to Guernsey Motors Ltd 1 by8/44.

Disposal:

4684 (ex IB 4689) (1, ex 13): Scrapped by1955.

Vehicle acquired from an unknown source 1936:

30	2972 [1]	Vulcan Duke	(3XS) 44	Vulcan		B26F	5/29?	3/41

Previous history:

2972 [1] (30): Was a secondhand Vulcan Duke chassis rebuilt to Vulcan Duchess specification and rebodied Vulcan B26F; if the chassis number quoted is correct, then it was new to W Webster {UNU - U Need Us}, Llangefni (AY) registered EY 3586 5/29 (with an unidentified B20F body); LMS Crosville, Chester (CH) 91 1/30; Crosville Motor Services Ltd, Chester (CH) 91 5/30; withdrawn 1932; Blakes Motors Ltd, Salford (dealer) c10/32; WJ Green, Whaplode (HD) at an unknown date; last licensed 12/36.

Disposal:

2972 [1] (30): Impressed by States of Guernsey Military Transport Service, St Peter Port (GOV) 3/41; German Military Authorities (Air Force Local Command) (GOV) 9/42; transferred to Military Truck Compound (GOV) 11/42; scrapped locally at an unknown date (or sent to France for scrapping).

1937

New vehicle:

20	1814	Vulcan Duchess	D177	Vulcan		B29F	7/37	9/51

Police plate (from 1946):

1814 (20): Probably one of 72, 76, 81, 84, 89.

Notes:

1814 (20): Impressed by States of Guernsey Civil Transport Service, St Peter Port (GOV) 2/41; converted to Gazogene propulsion 9/42; returned to Guernsey Motors Ltd 20 5/45.

Disposal:

1814 (20): Burgess & Sons, St Peter Port 6/53; unidentified owner, Jersey 11/59.

Vehicle acquired from an unknown sources 7/37:

65	176	Overland		?	Guernsey Motors	B14F	-/--	11/42

Previous history:

176 (65): Its origins are unknown other than its chassis was previously a lorry, fitted with a Guernsey Motors B14F body.

Notes:

176 (65): Built and exclusively used on the Richmond Hotel contract.

Disposal:

176 (65): Impressed by German Military Authorities (Military Truck Compound) (GOV) 11/42; scrapped locally at an unknown date (or sent to France for scrapping).

1938

New vehicle:

28	1127	Dennis Arrow Minor	255045	Dennis	B29F	10/38	9/54

Police plate (from 1946):

1127 (28): 87

Notes:

1127 (28): Impressed by States of Guernsey Military Transport Service, St Peter Port (GOV) 2/41; States of Guernsey Civil Transport Service, St Peter Port (GOV) and converted to Gazogene propulsion 2/43; returned to Guernsey Motors Ltd 28 5/45; fitted with a Bedford engine post-WW2.

Disposal:

1127 (28): Delancey Hotel, St Sampson as living accommodation 1/55.

1939

New vehicles:

50	27	Dennis Falcon	280011	Dennis		B31F	10/39	10/54
41	722	Bedford WTB	18200	Thurgood	724	C20F	6/39	9/53

Police plate (from 1946):

27 (50): 65   722 (41): 73

Notes:

27 (50): Impressed by States of Guernsey Military Transport Service, St Peter Port (GOV) 2/41; States of Guernsey Civil Transport Service, St Peter Port (GOV) 7/41; converted to Gazogene propulsion 9/42; returned to Guernsey Motors Ltd 50 5/45.

722 (41): Painted in Channel Island Airways livery for the newly opened Airport service; impressed by States of Guernsey Military Transport Service, St Peter Port (GOV) 4/42; German Military Authorities (Garrison Commander) (GOV) 12/42; returned to Guernsey Motors Ltd 41 at an unknown date; painted in BEA livery 1947.

Disposal:

27 (50): Delancey Hotel, St Sampson as living accommodation 1/55.

722 (41): WP Simon, Alderney (CI) re-registered AY 101 [2] 4/54; withdrawn by 2/60.

Vehicles acquired from NA Lenfestey {Lorina}, Pleinmont (CI) 2/39:

	1419	Reo Speed Wagon F	110536	Heaver	OB20D	3/26	3/26
48	2714	Reo Sprinter	FAA11138	Heaver	B25F	10/29	9/49
44	2719	Reo Sprinter	FAX1430	Heaver	B25F	10/29	9/48
46	3901 [1]	Reo (Speed Wagon?)	TDX20285	Heaver	B29F	6/34	9/49

Police plates (from 1946):

2714 (48), 2719 (44, as 11) and 3901 [1] (46): Probably three of 62, 63, 78, 79, 85.

Previous histories:

1419: New to NA Lenfestey {Lorina} (CI) 2 (as C24D); rebuilt to OB20D at an unknown date.

2714 (48): New to HN & HK Falla {Blue Bird}, Vale (CI) 7 (as B22F); reseated to B25F at an unknown date;
NA Lenfestey {Lorina} (CI) 5 5/37.

2719 (44): New to NA Lenfestey {Lorina} (CI) 3.

3901 [1] (46): New to NA Lenfestey {Lorina} (CI) 4.

Notes:

2714 (48): Fitted with a Silver Crown engine; impressed by States of Guernsey Military Transport Service,
St Peter Port (GOV) 11/41; German Military Authorities (Fortress Engineer Staff) (GOV) 7/42;
returned to Guernsey Motors Ltd 48 at an unknown date.

2719 (44): Impressed by States of Guernsey Military Transport Service, St Peter Port (GOV) 11/41; AP
Delaney, Castel (GOV) 10/42; returned to Guernsey Motors Ltd 44 by8/44; renumbered 11
1945.

3901 [1] (46): Fitted with a Silver Crown engine; impressed by AP Delaney, Castel (GOV) 10/42; returned to
Guernsey Motors Ltd 46 by8/44; fitted with an Austin engine 1947.

Disposals:

1419: Impressed by German Military Authorities (Military Truck Compound) (GOV) 10/42; scrapped locally
at an unknown date (or sent to France for scrapping).

2714 (48): No known disposal.

2719 (11, ex 44): Watson's Garage Ltd {The Greys}, St Martin (CI) 11/48; broken up for spares 1949.

3901 [1] (46): Living accommodation, La Ramee, St Peter Port (later as a shed) 1/50.

1946

New vehicles:

15	261	Bedford OB	35168	Mulliner		B32F	10/46	9/57
2	1292	Bedford OB	12059	Guernsey Motors		B32F	3/46	9/62
7	1833	Bedford OB	17258	Strachan		B32F	6/46	1/60
8	1864	Bedford OB	22228	Strachan		B32F	7/46	1/60
12	2411	Bedford OB	35115	Mulliner		B32F	10/46	9/55
14	2441	Bedford OB	34898	Mulliner		B32F	10/46	9/56
22	4021	Commer Commando	17A0457	Heaver		B31F	11/46	1/57
25	4022 [1]	Commer Commando	17A0458	Heaver		B31F	11/46	9/54

Police plates:

261 (15): 74	1864 (8): 67	4021 (22): 68
1292 (2): 69	2411 (12): 61	4022 [1] (25): 70
1833 (7): 64	2441 (14): 77	

Notes:

261 (15): Was built to utility specification.

1292 (2): Fitted with a rebuilt Guernsey Motors body previously mounted on a pre-war Packard chassis;
rebodied F Mallett B32F 8/53; fitted with a Perkins P6 oil engine 11/54.

1833 (7): Reseated to B33F at an unknown date; fitted with a Perkins P6 oil engine 1951.

1864 (8): Reseated to B33F at an unknown date; fitted with a Perkins P6 oil engine 1951.

2411 (12): Was built to utility specification.

2441 (14): Was built to utility specification.

4021 (22): Reseated to B33F at an unknown date; fitted with a Perkins P6 oil engine 1952.

4022 [1] (25): Reseated to B33F at an unknown date.

Disposals:

261 (15): Unidentified owner (minus engine) 3/58.

1292 (2): St Anthony's Hotel, Vale as living accommodation 3/63.

1833 (7): M Duquemin, Vale as living accommodation 11/60.

1864 (8): Farm shed, St Peter 11/60.

2411 (12): Dismantled 12/55.

2441 (14): Unidentified owner (minus engine) 2/57.

4021 (22): R Niles, Vale 1/57.

4022 [1] (25): Dismantled 12/55.

Vehicle acquired from War Department (GOV) 3/46:

3	1379	Commer Q4	15A1745S	Guernsey Motors		B29F	-/41	9/53

Police plate:
> 1379 (3): 75

Previous history:
> 1379 (3): Chassis acquired as a War Department lorry (GOV) fitted with a Guernsey Motors body transferred from a prewar vehicle.

Disposal:
> 1379 (3): Dismantled 12/55.

Vehicle acquired from War Department (GOV) 8/46:

4	2959	Commer Q4	15A1761S	Guernsey Motors		B33F	-/41	9/53

Police plate:
> 2959 (4): 80

Previous history:
> 2959 (4): Chassis acquired as a War Department lorry (GOV); operated for the States of Guernsey Civil Transport Service, St Peter Port (GOV) until 12/45; fitted with a Guernsey Motors body transferred from a prewar vehicle.

Disposal:
> 2959 (4): Dismantled 12/55.

1947

New vehicles:

30	1506	Austin K4/CXB	98577	Guernsey Motors		B33F	5/47	9/55
31	3462	Austin K4/CXB	98580	Guernsey Motors		B33F	4/47	1/58
26	4023	Commer Commando	17A0539	Heaver		B33F	4/47	9/57
27	4024	Commer Commando	17A0540	Heaver		B33F	4/47	9/59
17	4400	Guy Vixen	LVP30920	Duple	42662	B35F	7/47	9/48

Police plates:

1506 (30): 92	4023 (26): 90	4400 (17): 94
3462 (31): 93	4024 (27): 91	

Notes:
> 1506 (30): Was fitted with a rebuilt Guernsey Motors body previously mounted on an unidentified prewar chassis.
> 3462 (31): Was fitted with a rebuilt Guernsey Motors body previously mounted on an unidentified prewar chassis.
> 4024 (27): Fitted with a Perkins P6 oil engine 10/53.

Disposals:
> 1506 (30): No known disposal.
> 3462 (31): Unidentified owner (minus engine) 9/58.
> 4023 (26): Plaisance, St Peter as living accommodation 12/57.
> 4024 (27): Fort Saumarez Hotel, St Peter-in-the-Wood as living accommodation 3/60.
> 4400 (17): Guernsey Railway Co Ltd (CI) 12 9/48; fitted with a Perkins P6 oil engine 11/52; withdrawn 9/67; unidentified owner (minus engine) 10/67.

1948

New vehicles:

21	3	Austin K8/MB	189	Austin / T Le Huray		B13R	4/48	9/53
5	295 [2]	Austin K4/CXB	122523	Thurgood	490	B32F	9/48	9/63
24	372 [2]	Austin K4/CXB	122521	Thurgood	489	B32F	10/48	9/69
23	567 [2]	Austin K4/CXB	122524	Thurgood	496	B32F	9/48	9/64
33	932	Austin K4/CXB	109760	F Mallett		B24F	4/48	9/59
32	4151	Austin K4/CXB	98575	F Mallett		B33F	1/48	9/61
34	4392	Austin K4/CXB	122522	Thurgood	491	B32F	10/48	9/65
35	4492	Austin K4/CXB	109770	F Mallett		B24F	5/48	1/58
37	4495	Austin K4/CXB	106995	Strachan		B32F	248	12/59
38	4496	Austin K4/CXB	106997	Strachan	50807	B32F	1/48	9/66
39	4498	Austin K4/CXB	107000	Strachan	50809	B32F	2/48	9/62
40	4499	Austin K4/CXB	109704	Strachan		B32F	1/48	9/60
42	4507	Austin K4/CXB	109782	Barnard	BX3	B33F	6/48	9/67
43	4508	Austin K4/CXB	109783	Barnard	DX3	B33F	7/48	9/69
44	4510 [1]	Austin K4/CXB	109792	Barnard	CX3	B33F	5/48	9/69
45	4512	Austin K4/CXB	109793	Barnard	AX3	B33F	6/48	9/69

Police plates:

3 (21): 158	4392 (34): 183	4507 (42): 164
295 [2] (5): 177	4492 (35): 161	4508 (43): 171
372 [2] (24): 181	4495 (37): 154	4510 [1] (44): 162
567 [2] (23): 178	4496 (38): 83	4512 (45): 169
932 (33): 159	4498 (39): 155	
4151 (32): 86	4499 (40): 71	

Notes:

3 (21): Was a conversion of a 'Threeway' van; reseated to B12R shortly after entering service.

295 [2] (5): Reseated to B33F at an unknown date; fitted with a Perkins P6 oil engine 3/57.

372 [2] (24): Fitted with a Perkins P6 oil engine 3/54.

567 [2] (23): Fitted with a Perkins P6 oil engine 4/54.

932 (33): Was built for the Airport service with a luggage compartment at the rear; painted in BEA livery until 1950; reseated to B33F 1950.

4392 (34): Fitted with a Perkins P6 oil engine 6/54.

4492 (35): Was built for the Airport service with a luggage compartment at the rear; painted in BEA livery until 1950; reseated to B33F 1950.

4495 (37): Fitted with a Perkins P6 oil engine at an unknown date.

4496 (38): Fitted with a Perkins P6 oil engine at an unknown date.

4498 (39): Fitted with a Perkins P6 oil engine at an unknown date.

4499 (40): Fitted with a Perkins P6 oil engine at an unknown date.

4507 (42): Fitted with a Perkins P6 oil engine 3/60.

4508 (43): Fitted with a Perkins P6 oil engine 10/62.

4510 [1] (44): Fitted with a Perkins P6 oil engine 3/57.

4512 (45): Fitted with a Perkins P6 oil engine 1/61.

Disposals:

3 (21): Timothy & Sandwith, St Peter Port (GCI) as a van 9/53; W Tostevin, St Peter at an unknown date.

295 [2] (5): E Le Breton, St Peter Port 12/63.

372 [2] (24): Unidentified owner as a shed (or similar) 7/70.

567 [2] (23): Unidentified owner as a shed (or similar) 10/65.

932 (33): Living accommodation at Le Becquet, St Martin 9/62.

4151 (32): No known disposal.

4392 (34): Unidentified owner as a shed (or similar) 9/66.

4492 (35): Martel's Stores, Delancey, St Sampson (GCI) as a mobile shop (with a shortened wheelbase and body altered to suit by F Mallett) 4/59; Guernsey Amusement Centre, Pont Vaillant, Vale 9/64; Parry, Jersey (showman) at an unknown date.

4495 (37): Chassis to W Head & Son, St Peter Port as a boat trailer 8/61; body presumed scrapped.

4496 (38): E Noyon, St Sampson as a shed 10/66 to 1991 at least.

4498 (39): H Sebire, Guernsey as a shed 9/62.

4499 (40): Dismantled 9/60.

4507 (42): Unidentified owner as a shed (or similar) 5/69.

4508 (43): No known disposal.

4510 [1] (44): Guernsey Airport, Forest (XCI) for internal transport 6/70; withdrawn 11/73 (registration re-allocated elsewhere); Guernsey Old Car Club for preservation1/80; re-registered 2725 4/80; fitted with a petrol engine 5/82; Educational Holidays Guernsey Ltd {Island Coachways}, St Peter Port (CI) re-registered 4510 [1] and named 'Katie' 5/84; to service 6/84; Wacton Trading / Coach Sales, Bromyard (dealer) 9/92; Maple. Jacksons Hill (IS) re-registered VVS 913 4/93; moved to Porthcressa (IS) by10/95; withdrawn 3/97; Twynham, Hugh Town (IS) 7/98; to service 3/99; reseated B28F by5/02; Lucas, Hugh Town (IS) 10/06; S Hendra, Truro for preservation 12/14 (collected 4/15); P Whear, Redruth for preservation 11/17; Prof JF Kennedy, Tenbury Wells for preservation 7/18.

4512 (45): Unidentified owner 7/70.

One of 4507 (42), 4508 (43), 4512 (45) was at a vinery, Port Soif, Vale in the early 1970s.

1949

New vehicles:

47	374	Austin K4/CXB	142786	Thurgood	601	B24F	12/49	1/66
46	3901 [2]	Austin K4/CXB	143846	Thurgood	600	B32F	3/50	9/67
36	4493	Austin K4/CXB	109772	F Mallett		B33F	2/49	4/60
48	4548	Austin K4/CXB	143840	Thurgood	603	B32F	12/49	9/69
49	4683	Austin K4/CXB	143844	Thurgood	602	B24F	12/49	9/67
6	5502	Austin K4/CXB	109765	F Mallett		B33F	7/49	9/61
51	6286	Austin K4/CXB	130634	Thurgood	529	B32F	1/49	9/69
52	6287	Austin K4/CXB	130631	Thurgood	531	B32F	1/49	9/69
53	6288	Austin K4/CXB	130603	Thurgood	528	B32F	5/49	4/60
54	6289	Austin K4/CXB	130617	Thurgood	527	B32F	5/49	4/60
55	6290	Austin K4/CXB	130641	Thurgood	530	B32F	5/49	4/60

Police plates:

374 (47): 79	4683 (49): 63	6288 (53): 85
3901 [2] (46): 226	5502 (6): 184	6289 (54): 188
4493 (36): 82	6286 (51): 62	6290 (55): 189
4548 (48): 227	6287 (52): 78	

Notes:

374 (47): Entered service 1/50 on the Airport service with a luggage compartment at the rear; painted in BEA livery until 1959; reseated to B33F c1959; fitted with a Perkins P6 oil engine 4/60.

3901 [2] (46): Entered service 3/50; fitted with a Perkins P6 oil engine 1/55; reseated to B33F at an unknown date.

4548 (48): Entered service 3/50; fitted with a Perkins P6 oil engine 3/55; reseated to B33F at an unknown date.

4683 (49): Entered service 1/50 on the Airport service with a luggage compartment at the rear; painted in BEA livery until 1959; reseated to B33F c1959; fitted with a Perkins P6 oil engine 12/59.

6286 (51): Fitted with a Perkins P6 oil engine 11/53; reseated to B33F at an unknown date.

6287 (52): Fitted with a Perkins P6 oil engine and reseated to B33F at unknown dates.

6288 (53): Fitted with a Perkins P6 oil engine 2/55.

6289 (54): Fitted with a Perkins P6 oil engine 2/55; reseated to B33F at an unknown date.

6290 (55): Fitted with a Perkins P6 oil engine 12/53.

Disposals:

374 (47): Scrapped 8/66.

3901 [2] (46): Scrapped 11/68.

4493 (36): The Cycle Track, St Sampson as a control centre 1/62.

4548 (48): Guernsey Airport, Forest (XCI) as a training vehicle 9/69.

4683 (49): Scrapped 10/67.

5502 (6): Living accommodation at Le Becquet, St Martin 9/62.

6286 (51): No known disposal.

6287 (52): Guernsey Airport, Forest (XCI) as a training vehicle 9/69.

6288 (53): No known disposal.

6289 (54): Living accommodation at Frie au Four, St Saviour at an unknown date; Educational Holidays Guernsey Ltd {Island Coachways}, St Peter Port (CI) (not operated) and broken up for spares 1987.

6290 (55): No known disposal.

1951

New vehicles:

17	1916	Austin KP/CXD	175589	Thurgood	678	B33F	5/51	9/70
18	2247	Austin KP/CXD	175590	Thurgood	679	B33F	5/51	9/70
19	2486	Austin KP/CXD	175591	Thurgood	680	B33F	5/51	9/70

Police plates:

1916 (17): 230	2247 (18): 231	2486 (19): 123

Notes:

These vehicles were fitted with Perkins P6 oil engines from new.

Disposals:

1916 (17): Living accommodation at Vale 1970; demolished 1987.
2247 (18): No known disposal.
2486 (19): Body derelict at Les Monmains, Vale 1970 to 1994 at least; chassis possibly used as a boat trailer.

Vehicles acquired from Sarre Transport Ltd, St Peter Port (CI) 11/51:

9	1557	Bedford OB	24340	Mulliner		B32F	5/46	12/55
1	1558	Bedford OB	23960	Mulliner		B32F	5/46	-/56
61	2711	Dodge	PLW29	WJ Rugg		B25F	-/--	----
20	2818	Bedford OB	43166	Mulliner		B32F	3/47	9/56
56	2851	Bedford OB	43367	Mulliner		B32F	3/47	9/57
10	4101	Bedford OB	30485	Mulliner		B32F	9/46	12/55
60	4414	Bedford OB	105646	Mulliner	T383	B28F	5/49	9/61
57	5184	Bedford OB	76076	Mulliner	SP207	B28F	6/48	9/62
58	5185	Bedford OB	75989	Mulliner	SP206	B31F	6/48	9/62
59	5186	Bedford OB	77409	Mulliner	SP208	B28F	6/48	3/61

Police plates:

1557 (9): 124	2851 (56): 59	5185 (58): 166
1558 (1): 120	4101 (10): 123	5186 (59): 170
2711 (61): 118	4414 (60): 191	
2818 (20): 128	5184 (57): 167	

Previous histories:

1557 (9): New to Sarre Transport Ltd, St Peter-in-the-Wood (CI) 2; moved to St Peter Port (CI) at an unknown date.

1558 (1): New to Sarre Transport Ltd, St Peter-in-the-Wood (CI) 1; moved to St Peter Port (CI) at an unknown date.

2711 (61): Chassis purchased second hand in Jersey and fitted with a WJ Rugg body; WJ Rugg {Wayfarer}, St Sampson (CI) 7 1938; Sarre Transport Ltd, St Peter-in-the-Wood (CI) 7 4/46; moved to St Peter Port (CI) at an unknown date; renumbered 22 at an unknown date.

2818 (20): New to Sarre Transport Ltd, St Peter-in-the-Wood (CI) 12; moved to St Peter Port (CI) at an unknown date.

2851 (56): New to Sarre Transport Ltd, St Peter-in-the-Wood (CI) 13; moved to St Peter Port (CI) at an unknown date

4101 (10): New to Sarre Transport Ltd, St Peter-in-the-Wood (CI) 3; moved to St Peter Port (CI) at an unknown date

4414 (60): New to Sarre Transport Ltd, St Peter-in-the-Wood (CI) 20; moved to St Peter Port (CI) at an unknown date

5184 (57): New to Sarre Transport Ltd, St Peter-in-the-Wood (CI) 17; moved to St Peter Port (CI) at an unknown date

5185 (58): New to Sarre Transport Ltd, St Peter-in-the-Wood (CI) 18; moved to St Peter Port (CI) at an unknown date

5186 (59): New to Sarre Transport Ltd, St Peter-in-the-Wood (CI) 19; moved to St Peter Port (CI) at an unknown date

Notes:

2711 (61): Not operated by Guernsey Motors Ltd.

Disposals:

1557 (9): Dismantled 12/55.

1558 (1): Vazon, Castel as a shed 2/57.

2711 (61): Vandertang's Nurseries, Vale as an office 9/55; broken up when the site was sold at an unknown date.

2818 (20): Unidentified owner 2/57.

2851 (56): Normandy Laundry, St Peter Port as a store 3/59.

4101 (10): Dismantled 12/55.

4414 (60): FJK Reynolds {Cliffways Hotel}, St Martin (CI) 11/61; withdrawn 9/69; LF Le Noury, St Sampson 3/72; scrapped by5/73.

5184 (57): St Anthony's Hotel, Vale as living accommodation 3/63.

5185 (58): JT Carre, Guernsey 10/63.

5186 (59): Unidentified owner 3/61.

1954

New vehicles:

62	6148	Albion FT39AN	73737F	Heaver	1713	B35F	5/54	*
63	6173	Albion FT39AN	73740F	Heaver	1714	B35F	5/54	*
64	6188	Albion FT39AN	73742B	Heaver	1715	B35F	5/54	*

Police plates:

6148 (62): 72　　　　　　6173 (63): 73　　　　　　6188 (64): 89

Notes:

These were the last buses with timber-framed bodies to be purchased by Guernsey Motors Ltd.

6188 (64): Rebuilt with flat sides and sliding windows 1967.

Vehicles marked with an asterisk above, were transferred to Guernsey Railway Co Ltd (CI) 10/73 (qv):

6148 (62), 6173 (63), 6188 (64).

1955

New vehicles:

70	1982	Albion FT39AN	73791K	Heaver		B35F	12/55	*
66	6768 [1]	Albion FT39AN	73779D	Heaver	2465	B35F	4/55	*
65	6771	Albion FT39AN	73771K	Heaver		B35F	3/55	*
67	6773	Albion FT39AN	73779C	Heaver		B35F	4/55	*

Police plates:

1982 (70): 158　　　　　　　　6771 (65): 65

6768 [1] (66): 76　　　　　　　6773 (67): 87

Notes:

These were the first buses with aluminium-framed bodies to be purchased.

Vehicles marked with an asterisk above, were transferred to Guernsey Railway Co Ltd (CI) 10/73 (qv):

1982 (70), 6768 [1] (66), 6771 (65), 6773 (67).

1956

New vehicles:

68	1463 [1]	Albion FT39AN	73787C	Heaver	2753	B35F	1/56	*
69	1529 [1]	Albion FT39AN	73791J	Heaver		B35F	1/56	*
71	2027	Albion FT39AN	73791L	Heaver		B35F	1/56	*
72	4022 [2]	Albion FT39AN	73821E	Heaver		B35F	11/56	*
73	4029	Albion FT39AN	73821F	Heaver		B35F	12/56	*
74	4038	Albion FT39AN	73821H	Heaver		B35F	12/56	*
75	4076	Albion FT39AN	73821J	Heaver		B35F	12/56	*

Police plates:

1463 [1] (68): 70　　　　　1529 [1] (69): 80　　　　　2027 (71): 61

4022 [2] (72): 124　　　　4038 (74): 118

4029 (73): 92　　　　　　　4076 (75): 75

Vehicles marked with an asterisk above, were transferred to Guernsey Railway Co Ltd (CI) 10/73 (qv):
1463 [1] (68), 1529 [1] (69), 2027 (71), 4022 [2] (72), 4029 (73), 4038 (74), 4076 (75).

1958

New vehicles:

76	8226 [1]	Albion FT39KAN	73837K	Reading	2364	B35F	4/58	*
77	8227 [1]	Albion FT39KAN	73840H	Reading	2366	B35F	4/58	*
78	8228 [1]	Albion FT39KAN	73840J	Reading	2369	B35F	6/58	*
79	8229 [1]	Albion FT39KAN	73842E	Reading	2367	B35F	4/58	*

Police plates:
8226 [1] (76): 68   8228 [1] (78): 100
8227 [1] (77): 74   8229 [1] (79): 90

Vehicles marked with an asterisk above, were transferred to Guernsey Railway Co Ltd (CI) 10/73 (qv):
8226 [1]-8229 [1] (76-79).

1960

New vehicles:

80	9436 [1]	Albion NS3N	82051C	Reading	6155	B35F	4/60	*
81	9437	Albion NS3N	82051F	Reading	6156	B35F	4/60	*
82	9438 [1]	Albion NS3N	82052C	Reading	6157	B35F	4/60	*
83	9439 [1]	Albion NS3N	82053B	Reading	6158	B35F	4/60	*

Police plates:
9436 [1] (80): 165   9438 [1] (82): 120
9437 (81): 106   9439 [1] (83): 122

Vehicles marked with an asterisk above, were transferred to Guernsey Railway Co Ltd (CI) 10/73 (qv):
9436 [1] (80); 9437 (81); 9438 [1] (82); 9439 [1] (83).

1961

New vehicles:

84	10484 [1]	Albion NS3AN	82064C	Reading	9664	B35F	7/61	*
85	10485 [1]	Albion NS3AN	82064B	Reading	9665	B35F	7/61	*
86	10486	Albion NS3AN	82064E	Reading	9666	B35F	11/61	*
87	10487	Albion NS3AN	82064H	Reading	9667	B35F	10/61	*

Police plates:
10484 [1] (84): 81   10486 (86): 91
10485 [1] (85): 175   10487 (87): 82

Vehicles marked with an asterisk above, were transferred to Guernsey Railway Co Ltd (CI) 10/73 (qv):
10484 [1]-10485 [1] (84-85); 10486-10487 (86-87).

1962

New vehicles:

88	11674	Albion NS3AN	82065H	Reading	2175	B35F	4/62	*
89	11675 [1]	Albion NS3AN	82065J	Reading	2176	B35F	4/62	*
90	11676	Albion NS3AN	82065A	Reading	2177	B35F	5/62	*

Police plates:
11674 (88): 88   11675 [1] (89): 108   11676 (90): 157

Vehicles marked with an asterisk above, were transferred to Guernsey Railway Co Ltd (CI) 10/73 (qv):
11674 (88), 11675 [1] (89), 11676 (90).

1963

New vehicles:

91	12723 [1]	Albion NS3AN	82066K	Reading	4445	B35F	4/63	*
92	12724	Albion NS3AN	82067A	Reading	4446	B35F	4/63	*
93	12725	Albion NS3AN	82066L	Reading	4447	B35F	4/63	*
94	12726	Albion NS3AN	82066F	Reading	4448	B35F	4/63	*

Police plates:

12723 [1] (91): 69	12725 (93): 109
12724 (92): 167	12726 (94): 155

Vehicles marked with an asterisk above, were transferred to Guernsey Railway Co Ltd (CI) 10/73 (qv):
12723 [1] (1); 12724-12726 (92-94).

Vehicles acquired from HK Falla {Blue Bird}, Vale (CI) 1/63:

27	2960	Commer Commando	17A0442	Heaver		B31F	9/46	10/63
28	2961	Commer Commando	17A0444	Heaver		B31F	10/46	4/64
29	3990	Commer Commando	17A0626	Heaver		B35F	9/47	10/67
25	4869	Albion PK115	25011G	Heaver	9376	FB35F	10/36	10/64
26	5499	Reo (Speed Wagon?)	909	Heaver	2008	FB35F	4/39	10/67
30	5967	Albion SpFT3L	70695H	Strachan	50944	B31F	9/48	10/65

Police plates:

2960 (27): 139	3990 (29): 152	5499 (26): 140
2961 (28): 137	4869 (25): 142	5965 (30): 180

Previous histories:
- 2960 (27): New to HN & HK Falla {Blue Bird} (CI) 2; fitted with a Perkins P6 oil engine 4/56.
- 2961 (28): New to HN & HK Falla {Blue Bird} (CI) 3; fitted with a Perkins P6 oil engine 8/52.
- 3990 (29): New to HN & HK Falla {Blue Bird} (CI) 6; fitted with a Perkins P6 oil engine 4/52.
- 4869 (25): New to HN & HK Falla {Blue Bird} (CI) 5 (with a Heaver FB35F body); rebodied Heaver (9376) FB35F 1/50; fitted with a Perkins P6 oil engine 3/53.
- 5499 (26): New to HN & HK Falla {Blue Bird} (CI) 7 (with a Heaver FB35F body and fitted with a Gold Crown engine); fitted with a Perkins P6 oil engine 3/52; rebodied Heaver (2008) FB35F 1954.
- 5967 (30): New to HN & HK Falla {Blue Bird} (CI) 1; fitted with a Perkins P6 oil engine 4/55.

Disposals:
- 2960 (27): Scrapped 8/65.
- 2961 (28): Unidentified owner 1/67.
- 3990 (29): Dumped at Priaulx's Quarry, St Sampson 2/68.
- 4869 (25): Dumped at Priaulx's Quarry, St Sampson 1966.
- 5499 (26): Scrapped 3/68.
- 5967 (30): No known disposal.

1964

New vehicles:

95	14627	Albion NS3AN	82069C	Reading	7740	B35F	5/64	*
96	14628	Albion NS3AN	82069D	Reading	7741	B35F	4/64	*

Police plates:

14627 (95): 179	14628 (96): 177

Vehicles marked with an asterisk above, were transferred to Guernsey Railway Co Ltd (CI) 10/73 (qv):
14627-14628 (95-96).

1965

New vehicles:

97	16213	Albion NS3AN	82071A	Reading	0500B	B35F	5/65	*
98	16214	Albion NS3AN	82071B	Reading	0501B	B35F	5/65	*

Police plates:

16213 (97): 166	16214 (98): 184

Vehicles marked with an asterisk above, were transferred to Guernsey Railway Co Ltd (CI) 10/73 (qv):
16213-16214 (97-98).

1966

New vehicles:

99	14223 [1]	Bedford J4EZ1	6818558	Reading	2403C	B35F	6/66	*
100	14531 [1]	Bedford J4EZ1	6823213	Reading	2404C	B35F	6/66	*
101	14838 [1]	Bedford J4EZ1	6816013	Reading	2405C	B35F	7/66	*

Police plates:

14223 [1] (99): 173   14531 [1] (100): 180   14838 [1] (101): 183

Vehicles marked with an asterisk above, were transferred to Guernsey Railway Co Ltd (CI) 10/73 (qv):
14223 [1] (99), 14531 [1] (100), 14838 [1] (101).

Vehicle acquired from WS Le Poidevin, Castel (XCI) 1/66:

5895	Morris CVF.13/5	73322	Wadham	C19F	8/48	----

Previous history:
5895: Its origins are unknown; Commercial Company of the Channel Islands, St Peter Port (CI) 7/31; withdrawn 3/40; G Vidamour, Forest at an unknown date; AJ Snell, Forest (CI) 6/60; WS Le Poidevin 11/64.

Notes:
5895: Not operated by Guernsey Motors Ltd.

Disposal:
5895: Broken up by 11/68.

1967

New vehicles:

102	18262	Bedford J4EZ1	7814861	Reading	3612	B35F	4/67	*
103	18263	Bedford J4EZ1	7812333	Reading	3613	B35F	6/67	*
104	18264 [1]	Bedford J4EZ1	7812156	Reading	3614	B35F	4/67	*

Police plates:

18262 (102): 142   18263 (103): 149   18264 [1] (104): 151

Vehicles marked with an asterisk above, were transferred to Guernsey Railway Co Ltd (CI) 10/73 (qv):
18262-18263 (102-103); 18264 [1] (104).

1968

New vehicles:

105	19675 [1]	Bedford J4EZ5	7T103881	Reading	4638E	B35F	5/68	*
106	19676 [1]	Bedford J4EZ5	7T103704	Reading	4635E	B35F	2/68	*
107	19677 [1]	Bedford J4EZ5	7T103792	Reading	4636E	B35F	4/68	*
108	19678 [1]	Bedford J4EZ5	7T103838	Reading	4637E	B35F	3/68	*

Police plates:

19675 [1] (105): 150   19677 [1] (107): 154
19676 [1] (106): 147   19678 [1] (108): 152

Vehicles marked with an asterisk above, were transferred to Guernsey Railway Co Ltd (CI) 10/73 (qv):
19675 [1]-19678 [1] (105-108).

1969

New vehicles:

109	21901	Bedford J4EZ5	9T131199	Reading	6180G	B35F	6/69	*
110	21902	Bedford J4EZ5	9T131310	Reading	6181G	B35F	6/69	*
111	21903	Bedford J4EZ5	9T132223	Reading	6182G	B35F	7/69	*

Police plates:

21901 (109): 114   21902 (110): 226   21903 (111): 159

Vehicles marked with an asterisk above, were transferred to Guernsey Railway Co Ltd (CI) 10/73 (qv):
21901-21903 (109-111).

1970

Vehicles acquired from Guernsey Railway Co Ltd, St Peter Port (CI) 6/70:

60	9434 [1]	Albion NS3N	82050B	Reading	6159	B35F	6/60	6/70
61	9435	Albion NS3N	82052B	Reading	6160	B35F	5/60	6/70

Police plates:
9434 [1] (60): 127   9435 (61): 64

Previous histories:
9434 [1] (60): New to Guernsey Railway Co Ltd (CI) 63; withdrawn 5/69.
9435 (61): New to Guernsey Railway Co Ltd (CI) 64; withdrawn 5/69

Vehicles marked with an asterisk above, were transferred to Guernsey Railway Co Ltd (CI) 10/73 (qv):
9434 [1] (60); 9435 (61).

1972

New vehicles:

112	2493 [1]	Bedford J4EZ5	2T124550	Sparshatt	9666K	B35F	5/72	*
113	2972 [2]	Bedford J4EZ5	2T124268	Sparshatt	9667K	B35F	5/72	*

Police plates:
2493 [1] (112): 229   2972 [2] (113): 162

Vehicles marked with an asterisk above, were transferred to Guernsey Railway Co Ltd (CI) 10/73 (qv):
2493 [1] (112), 2972 [2] (113).

ANCILLARY VEHICLES

51	412	Packard E		2 ton tipper lorry	-/18	-/26	7/40
	1872	Chevrolet 27 hp	52220	25 cwt tipper lorry	-/--	-/35	-/46
13	71	Ford V8 30 hp	7162263	lorry	10/45	11/50	4/56
11	5673	Austin K3/SV	7275	3 ton lorry	4/40	8/48	*

Notes:

71 (13): New to G Staples, St Peter Port (GCI); acquired via Ash Ltd, St Peter Port (dealer).

412 (51): New as an US Army lorry; acquired from Slough Trading Depot

1872: Impressed by States of Guernsey Military Transport Services, St Peter Port (GOV) 12/41; German Military Authorities (Garrison Commander) (GOV) 12/42; returned at an unknown date.

5673 (11): New to Ash Ltd, St Peter Port (dealer); impressed by States of Guernsey Military Transport Services, St Peter Port (GOV) re-registered 443 11/41; Guernsey Fire Brigade (un-registered) at an unknown date; ran on trade plate T145 with Guernsey Motors Ltd.

Disposals:

71 (13): DG West, St Peter Port (GCI); two subsequent owners; scrapped 12/64.

412 (51): Impressed by German Military Authorities (Garrison Commander) (GOV) 7/40.

1872: No known disposal.

Vehicles marked with an asterisk above, were transferred to Guernsey Railway Co Ltd (CI) 10/73 (qv):

5673 (11).

Other vehicles:

A fleet of taxi cars (and two hearses) of a variety of makes was operated between 1926 and 1950. Many of these were impressed during WW2.

GUERNSEY RAILWAY CO LTD

The Guernsey Railway Co Ltd had been incorporated on 18 September 1888 with objective of taking over the assets of the Guernsey Steam Tramway Co Ltd and subsequently electrifying the line. On 24 April 1895, it merged with the Guernsey Omnibus Co Ltd which gave it interests in horse-bus operation which were eventually sold off by 1911. Motor buses arrived after World War I when primitive early examples were obtained from London-based operators and ex-military sources. These provided the backbone of the fleet up to 1925.

The Railway Company had enjoyed a near monopoly of the island's transport needs since the early 1890s, but now competition from the motor car and other small bus operators was increasing. Steps were taken to buy out some of the latter operators and GW Banks {The Legion} was taken over in June 1925 followed by RC & WH Collenette {Collenette Bros / Shamrock}, St Sampson in March 1926.

Early buses carried no destination boards, but from 1928, a system of coloured lights on the front of the vehicle indicated the service:

Green	St Peter Port – L'Ancresse (via Vale Road)
Red (later purple)	St Peter Port – L'Ancresse (via St Sampson)
Yellow	St Peter Port – L'Islet (via Baubigny)
White	St Peter Port – L'Islet (via Capelles)

That year saw the last of the early double-deckers withdrawn and the arrival of the first modern saloons on Bean chassis. From the early 1930s, the company undertook to build its own bus bodies. From 1933, Vulcan chassis became the standard for a few years, primarily as tram replacements. Finances were difficult in the 1930s exacerbated by the 'Ravensdale disaster'. This was the purchase of a steam ship that had run aground in Grand Havre in 1930. The plan to repair and refloat it was far more expensive than had been envisaged and it was eventually sold at a loss of £2,800 in 1933 precipitating the resignation of the Board of Directors. The financial loss had a bearing on the decision to close the tramway which ceased on 6 June 1934.

The ability to generate electricity through its own incinerating plant had been a valuable asset and consideration was given to establishing a trolleybus operation, but nothing developed from this. In 1936 however, a Morrison electric bus was purchased, but its performance was inadequate – the battery life and its need for recharging caused problems. Its body was mounted on a conventional Vulcan chassis in the following year.

Ernest Stead who ran a small bus operation called 'La Rapide' acquired some shares in Guernsey Railway Co and in 1938 became the manager there (whilst maintaining his own operation!). He presided over new Dennis manufactured purchases in 1939/40 which were painted in a new livery of malachite green and cream which was subsequently adopted as standard.

The German occupation in 1940 saw the impressing of 16 buses (including the three new Dennis's); six were later returned by the end of the War; all were rehabilitated but were generally in very poor condition. Stead had also lost all but one of his vehicles, which he transferred to the Railway Company in 1944.

In the three years immediately after the War, 21 vehicles were obtained to replace the lost vehicles – 12 Bedford OBs with Mulliner bodywork and nine Guy Vixens, similar in appearance but with Duple bodywork. The Guys were the first vehicles in the fleet built to the new postwar maximum permitted with of 7ft (the previous maximum width had been 6ft 6in).

With the possibility of nationalization in the UK, Red & White United Transport Ltd of Chepstow had been looking at the Channel Islands for possible acquisitions. Guernsey Railway Co was by now badly under-capitalised following the depredations of the War and so negotiations were started. Ernest Stead finalised matters and from 1 July 1949, Guernsey Railway Co Ltd became part of the Red & White Group. James Davies from Newbury & District, another Red & White company, was sent to Guernsey to oversee proceedings. Another Red & White associated company, Watts Factors of Lydney, Gloucestershire, was an Albion agent and this make became the standard acquisition from 1950 to 1965 by which time 34 examples had been purchased. These were the first oil-engine vehicles in the fleet. Sarre Transport Ltd was acquired by Red & White in November 1951 with the assets being equally between both the Railway and Motors companies.

After Albion ceased manufacturing, a Bedford J4 lorry chassis converted to forward control was chosen and this became the standard up to 1972 by which time 15 had entered the fleet.

On 29 October 1973, it was decided to rationalize the two company's activities. The 54-vehicle Guernsey Motors fleet was absorbed into Guernsey Railway Co allowing Motors to concentrate on their tourism and other activities. A start was made on repainting the red Motors fleet to the Railway Company green livery.

In October 1975, a South Wales businessman, William Smith, bought out the holdings held by Red & White United Transport Ltd (now United Transport Ltd). This signalled changes in purchasing policy and following the increase in permitted maximum width to 7ft 4in, the Bedford SB was now available. Livery policy was also reversed with buses now being repainted into red livery although both red and green liveries remained on the roads for some time.

A small minibus company called Delta Tours was acquired in June 1977. This was the start of an airport and harbour transfer business that was to grow over the years (the name was later resurrected in 1980 on some coaches). The last of the old independents, Watson's Garage {The Greys} was acquired in February 1978 and seven vehicles were added to the fleet.

For many years, a 'Pay as you Leave' system of fares collection was in use. This was not an easy system to police and from February 1976, this was changed for town services to 'Pay as you Enter'. This was the start of some unrest with the employees and unions who sought better wages and conditions. During which period, William Smith fell ill. As a result of this and drivers' pay increases of 16.5% (set by arbitration), the company was offered for sale in May 1979. Before this could be completed William Smith died, but the negotiations were completed with Steiner Investments Ltd, a Scottish company under the control of Alex Smith. He immediately changed vehicle policy to Bristol SU buses and 30 of these started to arrive in 1979/80 having been refurbished in the north of Scotland by another of his companies – Kinross Plant & Construction Ltd. These purchases ushered out the old guard and an auction sale held on 27 March 1980 saw 23 buses (all but one of Albion manufacture) disposed of, many into preservation.

The company however had underlying financial troubles and on 18 November 1980, an announcement was made that the it would close after the following day. The authorities quickly put in place emergency measures and the Education Council took control of arrangements for transport to and from schools – using hired minibuses and former Guernsey Railway vehicles and staff. Time was taken to consider applications to take over the operations and in February 1981, Trafalgar Leisure International (an English company) took control and a new company, Guernseybus Ltd was formed.

1909

Vehicles acquired from Andrew's Star Omnibus Co, London (LN) 5-7/09:

1	A81	Brillie-Schneider P2	?	E & H Hora	O14/20RO	-/06	-/18
2	A82	Brillie-Schneider P2	?	E & H Hora	O14/20RO	-/06	-/18
3	A83	Brillie-Schneider P2	?	E & H Hora	O14/20RO	-/06	7/20

Previous histories:

A81 (1): New to Andrew's Star Omnibus Co (LN) (registration unknown); acquired 5/09.
A82 (2): New to Andrew's Star Omnibus Co (LN) (registration unknown); acquired 6/09.
A83 (3): New to Andrew's Star Omnibus Co (LN) (registration unknown); acquired 7/09.

Notes:

A83 (3): Re-registered 83 1919.

Disposals:

A81 (1): Chassis broken up by Guernsey Railway Co Ltd; body to 1 of 1919 5/19.
A82 (2): Chassis broken up by Guernsey Railway Co Ltd; body to 2 of 1919 5/19.
83 (ex A83) (3): Converted to a rail welding plant for the tramway 7/20.

1911

Vehicle acquired from Motor Exchange, London 6/11:

4	A48	Clement-Bayard 16 hp	?	?	B11F	-/--	6/21

Previous history:

4: Was acquired as a chassis, with a new body built by an unidentified builder in London.

Notes:

4: Re-registered 48 [1] 1919; renumbered 6 1920.

Disposal:

48 [1] (ex A48) (6, ex 4): Body to Guernsey Motors Ltd 6/21; chassis presumed scrapped.

1919

New vehicles:

1	AEC YC	32	E & H Hora	O14/20RO	2/19	9/28
2	AEC YC	15089	E & H Hora	O14/20RO	10/19	11/28

Notes:

These vehicles were a cancelled Ministry of Munitions order.

1: Fitted with the body from A81 (1) of 1909; fitted with normal air pressure tyres 2/26.
2: Fitted with the body from A82 (2) of 1909; fitted with normal air pressure tyres 2/26.

Disposals:

1: No known disposal.
2: No known disposal.

1920

Vehicles acquired from London General Omnibus Co Ltd, London SW1 (LN) 11-12/20:

3	AEC B	B1743	LGOC	2028	O16/18RO	-/--	-/--
4	AEC B	B630	LGOC	2067	O16/18RO	-/--	12/25
5	AEC B	B1275	LGOC	3862	O16/18RO	-/--	-/--

Previous histories:

3: New to London General Omnibus Co Ltd, London SW1 (LN) B1743 registered LF 8508; acquired 11/20.
4: New to London General Omnibus Co Ltd, London SW1 (LN) B630 registered LE 9177; acquired 11/20.
5: New to London General Omnibus Co Ltd, London SW1 (LN) B1275 registered LF 8055; acquired 12/20.

Notes:

The dates of withdrawal of 3 and 5 (together with 9 and 10 of 1924) are not known other than one was withdrawn in 12/28, one in 12/29, one in 12/32 and one in 9/34. Two were fitted with pneumatic tyres for summer use 1930.

3: Rebodied Baico COB25F 1/24; fitted with pneumatic tyres 10/25.
4: Rebodied Baico COB25F 12/23.
5: Rebodied Baico COB25F 2/24; fitted with normal air pressure tyres 6/25.

Disposals:

3 (ex LF 8508): No known disposal.
4 (ex LE 9177): Chassis converted to a rail welding plant for the tramway 12/25; (Baico) body to Guernsey Motors Ltd 4/27.
5 (ex LF 8055): No known disposal.

1923

New vehicles:

6		Ford Supertonna	?	Baico	COB16F	8/23	-/--
7	994	Ford Supertonna	?	Baico	COB16F	8/23	-/--
8	80	Ford Supertonna	?	Baico	COB16F	9/23	-/--

Notes:

One of these vehicles was withdrawn in 12/32 and the other two in 12/34.

Disposals:

6: No known disposal.
994 (7): No known disposal.
80 (8): No known disposal.

1924

Vehicles acquired from London General Omnibus Co Ltd, London SW1 (LN) 4/24:

9		AEC B	B1886	-		12/12	-/--
10	1216	AEC B	B1183	-		2/12	-/--

Previous histories:

9: New to London General Omnibus Co Ltd, London SW1 (LN) B1886 registered LF 8660; Associated Equipment Co Ltd, Walthamstow (dealer) 4/24 and acquired as a chassis only.

1216 (10): New to London General Omnibus Co Ltd, London SW1 (LN) B1183 registered LE 9956; Associated Equipment Co Ltd, Walthamstow (dealer) 4/24 and acquired as a chassis only.

Notes:

The dates of withdrawal of 9 and 10 (together with 3 and 4 of 1920) are not known other than one was withdrawn in 12/28, one in 12/29, one in 12/32 and one in 12/34. Two were fitted with pneumatic tyres for summer use 1930.

9: Bodied Baico COB25F before entry into service; fitted with giant pneumatic tyres 12/26.

1216 (10): Bodied Baico COB25F before entry into service; fitted with normal air pressure tyres 6/25.

Disposals:

9 (?, ex LF 8660): No known disposal.

1216 (ex LE 9956) (10): No known disposal.

1925

Vehicle acquired from GW Banks {The Legion}, St Peter Port (CI) 6/25:

11	Ford TT	?	?		Ch13	-/--	12/32

Previous history:

11: Previously with GW Banks post-1920.

Notes:

11: Rebuilt to OB11F 1/27.

Disposal:

11: No known disposal.

1926

Vehicles acquired from RC & WH Collenette {Collenette Bros / Shamrock}, St Sampson (CI) 3/26:

12	Ford TT	?	Collenette	Ch13	-/23	12/32
13	Ford TT	?	Collenette	OB—F	-/23	12/31
14	Ford TT	?	Collenette	OB—F	-/23	12/31
15	Dodge LB	?	Collenette	OB12F	-/--	12/32
16	Renault	?	Collenette	OB22F	7/24	12/39
17	Renault	?	Collenette	OB22F	7/24	12/34

Previous histories:

12: First recorded with RC & WH Collenette 1 (as OB--F).

13: First recorded with RC & WH Collenette 2.

14: First recorded with RC & WH Collenette 3.

15: First recorded with RC & WH Collenette 4 (as OB12F).

16: First recorded with RC & WH Collenette 5 (as OB24F).

17: First recorded with RC & WH Collenette 6 (as OB24F)

Notes:

12: Renumbered S1 1926; fitted with normal air pressure tyres 8/26; rebuilt by Guernsey Railway Co Ltd 1927.

13: Renumbered S2 1926; fitted with normal air pressure tyres 8/26; rebuilt by Guernsey Railway Co Ltd 1927.

14: Renumbered S3 1926; fitted with normal air pressure tyres 8/26; rebuilt by Guernsey Railway Co Ltd (shortened by 38 cm) 1927.

15: Renumbered S4 1926; rebuilt by Guernsey Railway Co Ltd 1927.

16: Renumbered S5 1926; fitted with giant pneumatic tyres on the rear only 5/27; rebuilt by Guernsey Railway Co Ltd 1927.

17: Renumbered S6 1926; rebuilt by Guernsey Railway Co Ltd 1927.

Disposals:

S1 (ex 12): No known disposal.
S2 (ex 13): No known disposal.
S3 (ex 14): No known disposal.
S4 (ex 15): No known disposal.
S5 (ex 16): No known disposal.
S6 (ex 17): No known disposal.

1928

New vehicles:

18	2227	Bean Model 11	1044/11W	Willowbrook	2157	B20F	5/28	12/38
19	2377	Bean Model 11	1573/11W	Willowbrook	2214	B20F	8/28	1/42

Notes:

2377 (19): Rebuilt by Guernsey Railway Co Ltd and lengthened as B25F 10/37.

Disposals:

2227 (18): WJ Simon, Alderney (CI) 3/40, but not registered in Alderney and probably not shipped following the outbreak of WW2.

2377 (19): Impressed by impressed by States of Guernsey Military Transport Service, St Peter Port (GOV) 1/42; German Military Authorities (Military Truck Compound) (GOV) 11/42; scrapped locally at an unknown date (or sent to France for scrapping).

Vehicle acquired from E Stead {La Rapide}, St Sampson (CI) 11/28:

4		Ford TT	?	Underhill	OB21F	5/25	7/30

Previous history:

4: New to E Stead {La Rapid}.

Disposal:

4: Chassis scrapped 7/30; body to 1389 (4) of 1931.

1930

New vehicle:

20	2751	Bean Model 14	1051/14W	Willowbrook	B26F	1/30	9/47

Police plate (from 1946):

2751 (20): 107 (not confirmed)

Disposal:

2751 (20): WP Simon {Riduna Buses}, Alderney (CI) re-registered AY   129 [1] 4/48; withdrawn 1949.

Vehicle acquired from an unidentified source 2/30:

21	441	Berliet	?	(chassis only)	-/28	12/38

Previous history:

441 (21): New to an unidentified owner and acquired as a chassis only.

Notes:

441 (21): Bodied Guernsey Railway B18F and to service 5/30.

Disposal:

441 (21): Impressed by German Military Authorities (Military Truck Compound) (GOV) 10/42; scrapped locally at an unknown date (or sent to France for scrapping).

1931

New vehicle:

4	1389	Ford AA	4488900	Underhill/Guernsey Railway B21F	7/31	7/41

Notes:

1389 (4): Underhill body was transferred from 4 (Ford TT) of 1929 and rebuilt by Guernsey Railway Co Ltd.

Disposal:

   1389 (4): Impressed by German Military Authorities (Military Truck Compound) (GOV) 10/42; scrapped locally
      at an unknown date (or sent to France for scrapping).

Vehicle acquired from HC Collenette {Paragon}, St Sampson (CI) 1931:

| 22 | 1415 | Dodge A | A302112 | FT Bennett | OB22F | 6/25 | 12/37 |

Previous history:

   1415 (22): New HC Collenette {Paragon} 2.

Disposal:

   1415 (22): No known disposal.

1932

New vehicles:

| 24 | 1473 | Morris Director | 048RP | Guernsey Railway | B25F | 5/32 | 9/49 |
| 23 | 3193 | Dodge | 8343439 | Guernsey Railway | B26F | 2/32 | 7/41 |

Police plate (from 1946):

   1473 (24): 108 (not confirmed)

Notes:

   1473 (24): Impressed by States of Guernsey Military Transport Services, St Peter Port (GOV) 7/41; returned
      to Guernsey Railway Co Ltd by3/44.

Disposals:

   1473 (24): Scrapped 4/50.
   3193 (23): Impressed by States of Guernsey Military Transport Services, St Peter Port (GOV) 7/41; German
      Military Authorities (Fortress Engineer Staff) (GOV) 11/42; scrapped locally at an unknown date
      (or sent to France for scrapping).

1933

New vehicles:

25	931	Vulcan Duchess	D59	Guernsey Railway	B29F	4/33	9/47
26	3405	Vulcan Duchess	D62	Guernsey Railway	B29F	5/33	4/41
27	3688	Vulcan Duchess	D86	Guernsey Railway	B29F	12/33	9/49

Police plates (from 1946):

   931 (25): 103 (not confirmed)   3688 (27): 104 (not confirmed)

Notes:

   931 (25): Renumbered 12 mid-1930s; impressed by States of Guernsey Military Transport Services, St Peter
      Port (GOV) 4/41; German Military Authorities (Fortress Engineer Staff) (GOV) 11/42; returned
      to Guernsey Railway Co Ltd at an unknown date.
   3405 (26): Renumbered 14 mid-1930s.
   3688 (27): Renumbered 15 mid-1930s; impressed by States of Guernsey Military Transport Services, St
      Peter Port (GOV) 8/41; German Military Authorities (Fortress Engineer Staff) (GOV) 11/42;
      returned to Guernsey Railway Co Ltd at an unknown date.

Disposals:

   931 (12, ex 25): Scrapped 1/49.
   3405 (14, ex 26): Impressed by States of Guernsey Military Transport Services, St Peter Port (GOV) 4/41;
      German Military Authorities (Fortress Engineer Staff) (GOV) 11/42; scrapped locally at an
      unknown date (or sent to France for scrapping).
   3688 (15, ex 27): Scrapped 4/50.

1934

New vehicles:

| 28 | 118 | Vulcan Duchess | D87 | Guernsey Railway | B29F | 5/34 | 9/49 |
| 29 | 4052 | Vulcan Duchess | D98 | Guernsey Railway | B29F | 10/34 | 9/50 |

Police plates (from 1946):
      118 (28): 105 (not confirmed)   4052 (29): 106 (not confirmed)

Notes:
      118 (28): Renumbered 16 mid-1930s; impressed by States of Guernsey Military Transport Services, St Peter
                Port (GOV) 4/41; German Military Authorities (Fortress Engineer Staff) (GOV) 11/42; returned
                to Guernsey Railway Co Ltd at an unknown date.
      4052 (29): Renumbered 17 mid-1930s; reseated to B32F 4/40.

Disposals:
      118 (16, ex 28): Scrapped 4/50.
      4052 (17, ex 29): Unidentified owner (minus engine) 6/51.

Vehicle acquired from Guernsey Motors Ltd, St Peter Port (CI) 9/34:

15	1295	Dodge A	A577835	FT Bennett	OB21F	4/26	12/36

Previous history:
      1295 (15): New to E Stead {La Rapide}, St Sampson (CI) 3; withdrawn 1932; Guernsey Motors Ltd (CI) 3/34.

Disposal:
      1295 (15): Scrapped 12/39.

1935

New vehicle:

2	1398	Dodge PLB	1038	Guernsey Railway	B25F	8/35	9/49

Police plate (from 1946):
      1398 (2): 98 (not confirmed)

Notes:
      1398 (2): Chassis lengthened and reseated to B29F 2/38; impressed by States of Guernsey Military
                Transport Services, St Peter Port (GOV) 7/41; returned to Guernsey Railway Co Ltd by3/44.

Disposal:
      1398 (2): WP Simon {Riduna Buses}, Alderney (CI) re-registered AY   129 [2] 1/50; withdrawn 1954.

Vehicle acquired from WJ Rugg {Wayfarer}, St Sampson (CI) 6/35:

1	1940	Ford A	3735545	Rugg / Guernsey Railway	B18F	4/32	8/41

Previous history:
      1940 (1): New to WJ Rugg {Wayfarer} 3 (as OB18F).

Notes:
      1940 (1): Was rebuilt by Guernsey Railway Co Ltd to B18F.

Disposal:
      1940 (1): Impressed by States of Guernsey Military Transport Services, St Peter Port (GOV) 8/41; German
                Military Authorities (Military Truck Compound) (GOV) 3/43; scrapped locally at an unknown date
                (or sent to France for scrapping).

Vehicle acquired from HC Collenette {Paragon}, St Sampson (CI) 12/35:

3	1845	Dodge LER	D225913	Strachan	B22F	-/30	7/41

Previous history:
      1845 (3): New to HC Collenette {Paragon} (CI) 4 (as B27F).

Disposal:
      1845 (3): Impressed by States of Guernsey Military Transport Services, St Peter Port (GOV) 7/41; German
                Military Authorities (Military Truck Compound) (GOV) 12/42; scrapped locally at an unknown
                date (or sent to France for scrapping).

1936

New vehicle:

5	1337 [1]	Morrison Electricar		Morrison/Guernsey Railway	B32F	8/36	10/37

Notes:
> 1337 [1] (5): Was a battery-powered vehicle but proved to be unsuitable.

Disposal:
> 1337 [1] (5): Chassis to Burgess & Sons, St Peter Port 12/38; body to 1337 [2] (5) 3/38.

1937

New vehicles:

7	1322	Morris CS.2.13/80	1009C30753	Guernsey Railway	B33F	7/37	8/41
6	5126	Morris CS.2.13/80	1009C30754	Guernsey Railway	B33F	5/37	5/41

Disposals:
> 1322 (7): Impressed by States of Guernsey Military Transport Service, St Peter Port (GOV) 2/41; German Military Authorities (Organisation Todt) (GOV) 7/42; scrapped locally at an unknown date (or sent to France for scrapping).
> 5126 (6): Impressed by German Military Authorities (GOV) and shipped to Granville, Manche (O-F) 5/41.

1938

Vehicles acquired from Hamilton Motors, London (dealer?) 7-9/38:

8	759	Vulcan RF	RF319	(chassis only)		-/35	2/41
5	1337 [2]	Vulcan RF	RF172	(chassis only)		-/34	9/49

Police plate (from 1946):
> 1337 [2] (5): 101 (not confirmed)

Previous histories:
> 759 (8): New as a lorry; Hamilton Motors (dealer?) 1/38 and acquired by Guernsey Railway Co Ltd as a chassis 7/38.
> 1337 [2] (5): New as a lorry; Hamilton Motors (dealer?) 1/38 and acquired by Guernsey Railway Co Ltd as a chassis 9/38.

Notes:
> 759 (8): Rebodied Guernsey Railway B35F.
> 1337 [2] (5): Fitted with the 1936 Morrisons / Guernsey Railway B32F body from 1337 [1] and reseated to B35F.

Disposals:
> 759 (8): Impressed by States of Guernsey Military Transport Services, St Peter Port (GOV) 2/41; German Military Authorities (Fortress Engineer Staff) (GOV) 11/42; scrapped locally at an unknown date (or sent to France for scrapping).
> 1337 [2] (5): Unidentified owner as a shed 8/50.

1939

New vehicle:

9	3774	Dennis Falcon	280007	Dennis	B34C	4/39	2/41

Disposal:
> 3774 (9): Impressed by States of Guernsey Civil Transport Services, St Peter Port (GOV) 2/41; States of Guernsey Military Transport Services, St Peter Port (GOV) 11/41; German Military Authorities (Garrison Commander) (GOV) 11/42; scrapped locally at an unknown date (or sent to France for scrapping).

1940

New vehicles:

10	848	Dennis Falcon	280032	Dennis	B34C	3/40	2/41
11	879	Dennis Falcon	280033	Dennis	B34C	3/40	9/53

Police plate (from 1946):
879 (11): 102

Notes:
879 (11): Impressed by States of Guernsey Military Transport Services, St Peter Port (GOV) 2/41; German Military Authorities (Garrison Commander) (GOV) 8/42 and used as a military band coach; returned to Guernsey Railway Co Ltd 6/45; rebuilt as B34F and fitted with a Bedford engine c1950.

Disposals:
848 (10): Impressed by States of Guernsey Military Transport Services, St Peter Port (GOV) 2/41; German Military Authorities (Garrison Commander) (GOV) 9/42; scrapped locally at an unknown date (or sent to France for scrapping).
879 (11): Delancey Hotel as living accommodation 9/53.

1944

Vehicle acquired from E Stead {La Rapide}, St Sampson (CI) 1/44:

1	2787	Vulcan Duchess	D190	Strachan		B29F	1/38	9/50

Previous history:
2787 (1): ; .

Disposal:
2787 (1): Unidentified owner (minus engine) 6/51.

Vehicle acquired from AE Barnes, St Helier (dealer) 11/45:

4	291	Bedford WHG	179490	?		B20F	-/--	5/47

Notes:
The origins of this vehicle are unknown, however, it may be the same as the following vehicle, new on Jersey to C Le Cornu {Links Hotel}, Gorey (CI), passing to SP Groves {Links Hotel}, Gorey (CI) at an unknown date and impressed by the German Military Authorities (GOV) 8/42:

	J 8392	Bedford WHG	179140	?		B--F	6/34	

Disposal:
291 (4): Autax, St Peter Port (XCI?) 5/47; withdrawn 11/54.

Vehicle acquired from AV Newton {Channel Island Hotel}, St Peter Port (CI) 12/45:

3	3777	Dennis GL	70631	Willmott		B26F	1/35	9/47

Previous history:
3777 (3): New to AV Newton {Channel Island Hotel} (CI) (as C13F); withdrawn 11/45.

Notes:
3777 (3): Body rebuilt to B26F by Guernsey Railway Co Ltd.

Disposal:
3777 (3): WP Simon {Riduna Buses}, Alderney (CI) re-registered AY 59 [1] 9/47; withdrawn 1951.

1946

New vehicles:

18	3117	Bedford OB	30226	Mulliner	B33F	8/46	4/55
19	3118	Bedford OB	31908	Mulliner	B33F	9/46	9/57

Police plate:
3118 (19): 96

Notes:
These vehicles were fitted with bodies to Ministry of Supply 'utility' specification.

Disposals:
> 3117 (18): Body to an unidentified owner 12/55; chassis not traced.
> 3118 (19): Body to an unidentified owner 11/57; chassis not traced.

1947

New vehicles:

6	499	Guy Vixen	LVP30912	Duple	42665	B35F	7/47	9/65
7	500	Guy Vixen	LVP30913	Duple	42666	B35F	7/47	9/67
8	501	Guy Vixen	LVP30914	Duple	42667	B35F	7/47	9/67
9	502	Guy Vixen	LVP30915	Duple	42668	B35F	7/47	9/67
10	503	Guy Vixen	LVP30916	Duple	42669	B35F	7/47	9/64
4	505	Guy Vixen	LVP30917	Duple	42670	B35F	7/47	9/66
14	506	Guy Vixen	LVP30919	Duple	42671	B35F	7/47	9/67
21	2125	Guy Vixen	LVP30918	Duple	42663	B35F	7/47	9/67
22	2126	Guy Vixen	LVP30930	Duple	42664	B35F	7/47	9/68
23	3087	Bedford OB	40851	Mulliner		B33F	1/47	9/54
25	3088	Bedford OB	40830	Mulliner		B33F	1/47	9/55
26	3089	Bedford OB	41161	Mulliner		B33F	1/47	9/56
27	3090	Bedford OB	40821	Mulliner		B33F	2/47	9/54

Police plates:

499 (6): 99	503 (10): 116	2126 (22): 144
500 (7): 58	505 (4): 115	3088 (25): 110
501 (8): 114	506 (14): 136	3090 (27): 113
502 (9): 135	2125 (21): 143	

Notes:
> The Bedford OBs were fitted with bodies to Ministry of Supply 'utility' specification.
> The Guy Vixens were the first vehicles of 7ft width.
> 499 (6): Fitted with a Bedford engine 4/50; fitted with a Perkins P6 oil engine 10/54.
> 500 (7): Fitted with a Perkins P6 oil engine 11/54.
> 501 (8): Fitted with a Perkins P6 oil engine 4/64.
> 502 (9): Fitted with a Perkins P6 oil engine 3/54.
> 503 (10): Fitted with a Perkins P6 oil engine 12/53.
> 505 (4): Fitted with a Perkins P6 oil engine 4/60.
> 506 (14): Fitted with a Perkins P6 oil engine 3/53.
> 2125 (21): Fitted with a Perkins P6 oil engine 2/53.
> 2126 (22): Fitted with a Perkins P6 oil engine 1/52.

Disposals:
> 499 (6): Unidentified owner (minus engine) 10/67.
> 500 (7): Unidentified owner, Castel (minus engine) 7/67.
> 501 (8): Dumped at Priaulx's Quarry, St Sampson 10/69.
> 502 (9): Unidentified owner near Beaucette, Vale (minus engine) 11/68.
> 503 (10): Dumped at Priaulx's Quarry, St Sampson 3/68.
> 505 (4): Unidentified owner (minus engine) 10/67.
> 506 (14): B Priaulx {Priaulx's Quarry), St Sampson as a shed 10/69.
> 2125 (21): Unidentified owner (minus engine) 11/69.
> 2126 (22): Unidentified owner (minus engine) 11/69; in a field at La Maraive, Vale until 1991 at least.
> 3087 (23): WP Simon {Riduna Buses}, Alderney (CI) re-registered AY   59 [2] 2/55; withdrawn 12/56.
> 3088 (25): WP Simon {Riduna Buses}, Alderney (CI) re-registered AY   59 [3] 1/56; withdrawn 12/57.
> 3089 (26): John Upham Ltd, Castel (dealer?) (minus engine) 11/56; used as a site hut (at the building of the Bouet garage) and as a shed at St Saviour, dates unknown.
> 3090 (27): Body to an Unidentified owner 12/55; chassis not traced.

1948

New vehicles:

3	5187	Bedford OB	70813	Mulliner	SP211	B31F	3/48	9/61
20	5188	Bedford OB	73023	Mulliner	SP212	B31F	4/48	9/61
28	5189	Bedford OB	76145	Mulliner	SP213	B31F	6/48	9/59
29	5190	Bedford OB	73174	Mulliner	SP214	B31F	6/48	9/59
31	5191	Bedford OB	84059	Mulliner	SP216	B31F	7/48	9/60
30	5192	Bedford OB	79382	Mulliner	SP215	B31F	7/48	9/62

Police plates:
5187 (3): 109
5188 (20): 108

5189 (28): 105
5190 (29): 165

5191 (31): 175
5192 (30): 168

Notes:
These vehicles were fitted with bodies to Ministry of Supply 'relaxed' specification.
5189 (28): Fitted with a Perkins P6 oil engine from 8/51 to 2/53.

Disposals:
5187 (3): St Martin's Football club (minus engine) as a changing room 9/62; site hut at Collings Road, St Peter Port 1963.
5188 (20): WP Simon {Riduna Buses}, Alderney (CI) re-registered AY   59 [7]; 3/62 (as B33F); withdrawn by2/64.
5189 (28): WP Simon {Riduna Buses}, Alderney (CI) re-registered AY   101 [3]; 2/60 (as B33F); withdrawn 1962.
5190 (29): WP Simon {Riduna Buses}, Alderney (CI) re-registered AY   59 [5]; 2/60 (as B33F); withdrawn 1961.
5191 (31): Unidentified owner (minus engine) as a shed, St Peter 10/60.
5192 (30): St Martin's Football club (minus engine) as a changing room 9/62; site hut at Collings Road, St Peter Port 1963.

Vehicle acquired from Guernsey Motors Ltd, St Peter Port (CI) 9/48:

12	4400	Guy Vixen	LVP30920	Duple	42662	B35F	7/47	9/67

Police plate:
4400 (12): 94

Previous history:
4400 (12): New to Guernsey Motors Ltd (CI) 17.

Notes:
4400 (12): Fitted with a Perkins P6 oil engine 11/52; received Police plate 154 at an unknown date.

Disposal:
4400 (12): Unidentified owner (minus engine) 10/67.

1950

New vehicles:

32	6432	Albion FT39N	72869C	Heaver	8294	B35F	3/50	9/71
33	6433	Albion FT39N	72874B	Heaver	9421	B35F	3/50	9/71
34	6434	Albion FT39N	72874C	Heaver	9422	B35F	3/50	3/75
35	6435	Albion FT39N	72874D	Heaver	9423	B35F	3/50	10/71
36	6436	Albion FT39N	72874E	Heaver	9424	B35F	4/50	11/73
37	6437	Albion FT39N	72874F	Heaver	9425	B35F	4/50	9/70

Police plates:
6432 (32): 97
6433 (33): 107

6434 (34): 103
6435 (35): 104

6436 (36): 228
6437 (37): 229

Disposals:
6432 (32): O'Toole, St Sampson (dealer) as a shed 1/72.
6433 (33): Les Vauxbelets, St Andrew as a changing room 1/72; GH Quentin, Les Vauxbelets (contractor) as a shed at an unknown date (one other vehicle, possibly 6437 (37), also passed to Les Vauxbelets 1/72 and later GH Quentin).
6434 (34): Landes du Marche 12/75.
6435 (35): E Best, Brickfield, St Andrew 2/74.
6436 (36): Converted to a towing vehicle and transferred to the service fleet 1/75 (qv).
6437 (37): No known disposal (but see note above under 6433 (33)).

1951

New vehicles:

38	6438	Albion FT39N	73004B	Heaver	9711	B35F	3/51	9/74
39	6439	Albion FT39N	73004C	Heaver	9712	B35F	3/51	10/73
40	6440	Albion FT39N	73004D	Heaver	9713	B35F	3/51	11/73

Police plates:

6438 (38): 196 6439 (39): 197 6440 (40): 198

Disposals:

6438 (38): Dean Forest Railway Preservation Society, Lydney for preservation 10/74; British Leyland Heritage, Leyland for preservation 4/78; British Commercial Vehicle Museum, Leyland for preservation 6/83; unidentified preservationist, North Yorkshire (possibly J Harrison, Rufforth) by7/97; J Wilson Milngavie for preservation by12/00; current 4/10.

6439 (39): E Best, Brickfield, St Andrew (minus engine) as a store 5/74; on a farm, Rue du Douit, Vale at an unknown date to 1991 at least.

6440 (40): E Best, Brickfield, St Andrew (minus engine) as a road works hut 5/75; scrapped at an unknown date.

Vehicles acquired from Sarre Transport Ltd, St Peter Port (CI) 11/51:

42	1560	Bedford OB	23382	Mulliner			B32F	5/46	7/58
43	1951	Bedford OB	29502	Mulliner			B32F	9/46	9/55
46	2819	Bedford OB	43097	Mulliner			B32F	3/47	9/54
45	2877 [1]	Bedford OB	43412	Mulliner			B32F	4/47	9/57
	3060	Dodge UG30	8343213	WJ Rugg			B21F	10/31	----
44	3458	Bedford OB	33376	Mulliner			B32F	9/46	9/56
41	3460	Bedford OB	31380	Mulliner			B32F	9/46	9/55
	4085	Dodge	KB228	WJ Rugg			B25F	3/35	----
50	4426	Bedford OB	108594	Mulliner	T384		B28F	7/49	9/63
47	5181	Bedford OB	70827	Mulliner	SP209		B31F	3/48	9/60
48	5182	Bedford OB	72578	Mulliner	SP205		B28F	4/48	9/62
49	5183	Bedford OB	72585	Mulliner	SP210		B31F	5/48	9/61

Police plates:

1560 (42): 125	3458 (44): 122	5181 (47): 157
1951 (43): 127	3460 (41): 126	5182 (48): 179
2819 (46): 119	4085: 121	5183 (49): 163
2877 [1] (45): 60	4426 (50): 148	

Previous histories:

1560 (42): New to Sarre Transport Ltd, St Peter-in-the-Wood (CI) 5; moved to St Peter Port (CI) at an unknown date.

1951 (43): New to Sarre Transport Ltd, St Peter-in-the-Wood (CI) 6; moved to St Peter Port (CI) at an unknown date.

2819 (46): New to Sarre Transport Ltd, St Peter-in-the-Wood (CI) 11; moved to St Peter Port (CI) at an unknown date.

2877 [1] (45): New to Sarre Transport Ltd, St Peter-in-the-Wood (CI) 10; moved to St Peter Port (CI) at an unknown date.

3060: New to WJ Rugg {Kingsway}, St Sampson (CI) (as OB22F); WJ Rugg {Wayfarer}, St Sampson (CI) 4/32; reseated to OB21F at an unknown date; transferred to States of Guernsey Civil Transport Service, St Peter Port (GOV) at some point during the period 11/40 to 6/44; Sarre Transport Ltd, St Peter-in-the-Wood (CI) 4 4/46; moved to St Peter Port (CI) at an unknown date.

3458 (44): New to Sarre Transport Ltd, St Peter-in-the-Wood (CI) 9; moved to St Peter Port (CI) at an unknown date.

3460 (41): New to Sarre Transport Ltd, St Peter-in-the-Wood (CI) 4; moved to St Peter Port (CI) at an unknown date.

4085: New to WJ Rugg {Wayfarer}, St Sampson (CI) 3; Sarre Transport Ltd, St Peter-in-the-Wood (CI) 3 4/46; moved to St Peter Port (CI) at an unknown date.

4426 (50): New to Sarre Transport Ltd, St Peter-in-the-Wood (CI) 21; moved to St Peter Port (CI) at an unknown date.

5181 (47): New to Sarre Transport Ltd, St Peter-in-the-Wood (CI) 14; moved to St Peter Port (CI) at an unknown date.

5182 (48): New to Sarre Transport Ltd, St Peter-in-the-Wood (CI) 15; moved to St Peter Port (CI) at an unknown date.

5183 (49): New to Sarre Transport Ltd, St Peter-in-the-Wood (CI) 16; moved to St Peter Port (CI) at an unknown date.

Notes:

1951 (43): Fitted with a Perkins P6 oil engine from 3/52 to 10/53.

2819 (46): Fitted with a Perkins P6 oil engine from 2/52 to 11/54.

2877 [1] (45): Fitted with a Perkins P6 oil engine from 1/52 to 1/54; reseated to B29F at an unknown date.

3060: Not operated by Guernsey Railway Co Ltd.

3458 (44): Fitted with a Perkins P6 oil engine from 1/52 to 10/53; reseated to B33F at an unknown date.

3460 (41): Fitted with a Perkins P6 oil engine from 1/52 to 2/53.

4085: Not operated by Guernsey Railway Co Ltd.

Disposals:

1560 (42): WP Simon, Alderney (CI) re-registered AY   59 [4] 10/58 (as B33F); withdrawn 1960.

1951 (43): A Martel, Delancey, St Sampson (GCI) as a mobile shop 4/56; unidentified owner, St Sampson as living accommodation 3/63.

2819 (46): Unidentified owner as a non-PSV 4/56.

2877 [1] (45): Unidentified owner (minus engine) 10/56.

3060: Scrapped 9/53.

3458 (44): Victoria Hotel, St Sampson as living accommodation 3/57; exported to Bombay (O-IND) at an unknown date.

3460 (41): FJK Reynolds {Cliffways Hotel}, St Martin (XCI) 9/55; W Laine, Vale as living accommodation 1961.

4085: Le Poidevin, St Peter Port 10/53.

4426 (50): WP Simon, Alderney (CI) re-registered AY   59 [8] 2/64; withdrawn 1965.

5181 (47): Unidentified owner, Les Vardes, St Sampson as living accommodation 1/61; at Camp du Roi 4/63; scrapped at an unknown date.

5182 (48): JT Carre, Guernsey 10/63.

5183 (49): WP Simon, Alderney (CI) re-registered AY   59 [6] 3/62 (as B33F); withdrawn 1963.

1953

New vehicles:

51	6441	Albion FT39AN	73722C	Heaver	1002	B35F		5/53	9/75
52	6442	Albion FT39AN	73722D	Heaver	1004	B35F		4/53	9/75
53	6443	Albion FT39AN	73722E	Heaver	1003	B35F		4/53	9/74

Police plates:

6441 (51): 203   6442 (52): 204   6443 (53): 205

Disposals:

6441 (51): Guernsey Airport Fire Service, Forest (XCI) 8/77; used as a training unit 1982; burnt out as a training exercise at an unknown date.

6442 (52): H Luckett & Co Ltd, Fareham (HA) 10/75; C Cowdrey {Priory Coaches}, Gosport (HA) c8/79; P Davies, Farnham for preservation 10/80; M Johns, Epsom as a mobile caravan by5/85; believed to an unidentified owner by1/96; still as a caravan, Wales 2007; N Pope, Pulborough for preservation 2007.

6443 (53): Scrapped 12/75.

1955

New vehicles:

55	6769 [1]	Albion FT39AN	73780C	Heaver		B35F	4/55	10/79
56	6770	Albion FT39AN	73780D	Heaver		B35F	4/55	10/76
54	6772	Albion FT39AN	73776C	Heaver		B35F	8/55	10/76

Police plates:

6769 [1] (55): 111   6770 (56): 125   6772 (54): 102

Notes:

6769 [1] and 6770 have both been recorded with body number 2466.

Disposals:
6769 [1] (55): D Dean {Classique Coaches}, Paisley (SC) not operated 3/80; Lister PVS (Bolton) Ltd (dealer) 4/87; Richard Cound Ltd, Gloucester (dealer) 4/87; W Ritchie, Glasgow for preservation 1988; I Walker, Renfrew for preservation by3/02; current 11/07.
6770 (56): Guernsey Airport Fire Service, Forest (XCI) as a training vehicle at an unknown date; burnt out as a training exercise at an unknown date.
6772 (54): Guernsey Airport Fire Service, Forest (XCI) as a training vehicle at an unknown date; burnt out as a training exercise at an unknown date.

1956

New vehicles:

57	2616	Albion FT39AN	73793E	Heaver		B35F	2/56	10/78
58	2636	Albion FT39AN	73793F	Heaver		B35F	2/56	10/77
59	3324	Albion FT39AN	73821C	Heaver		B35F	11/56	11/79

Police plates:
2616 (57): 110   2636 (58): 119   3324 (54): 113

Disposals:
2616 (57): Used as a bus station waiting room (1978?); John Upham Ltd, Castel (dealer?) 3/80; K Diamond, Vale for use as a playroom at an unknown date; Dr JR Young, Nottingham (dealer / preservationist) by3/92; P Alford, Tamworth as a mobile caravan 3/92.
2636 (58): Used as a bus station waiting room (1978?); John Upham Ltd, Castel (dealer?) 3/80; Guernsey Old Car Club for preservation spares at an unknown date; Guernsey Airport Fire Service, Forest (XCI) for training exercises at an unknown date.
3324 (59): N Bartlett, St Peter Port as a caravan (based at Dinan, Cotes d'Armor (O-F)) by3/81.

1957

New vehicle:

60	3338 [1]	Albion FT39AN	73821D	Heaver		B35F	1/57	10/79

Police plate:
3338 [1] (60): 112

Notes:
3338 [1] (60): Renumbered 160 8/73.

Disposals:
3338 [1] (160, ex 60): O Bailey, Castel for preservation 3/80; moved to Vale at an unknown date; Dr JR Young, Nottingham (dealer / preservationist) 1/88; AJ Curtis, Midsomer Norton (AV) for preservation by7/90; re-registered YFF 660 4/95; AJ Curtis {Riduna Buses}, Alderney (CI) re-registered AY   81 [3] 1/96; SK & DH Young {CT Coaches}, Radstock (SO) for preservation re-registered YFF 660 by8/12.

1958

New vehicles:

61	8230 [1]	Albion FT39KAN	73838A	Reading	2365	B35F	4/58	11/79
62	8231 [1]	Albion FT39KAN	73837L	Reading	2368	B35F	5/58	11/79

Police plates:
8230 [1] (61): 96   8231 [1] (62): 126

Notes:
8230 [1] (61): Renumbered 161 8/73.
8231 [1] (62): Renumbered 162 8/73.

Disposals:
8230 [1] (161, ex 61): R Perry, Bath for preservation 3/80; P Moss, Sandbach for preservation by1/82; re-registered ESV 215 9/84; last licence expired 9/85; K Mander, Great Yarmouth for preservation by4/93; M Mitcham, Burwell for preservation by12/99; current 11/15.

8231 [1] (162, ex 62): Car Exchange (Guernsey) Ltd, St Peter Port (dealer) 3/80; R Harris, Solihull for preservation 4/80; R Lolly, Solihull for preservation by2/82; KP Hill, Redditch for preservation 1994; re-registered HFO 742 10/95; unidentified preservationist 6/03; Cook (or Cooke), Leigh-on-Mendip as a caravan 3/13.

1960

New vehicles:

63	9434 [1]	Albion NS3N	82050B	Reading	6159	B35F	6/60	5/69
64	9435	Albion NS3N	82052B	Reading	6160	B35F	5/60	5/69

Police plates:

9434 [1] (63): 127   9435 (64): 64

Disposals:

9434 [1] (63): Guernsey Motors Ltd, St Peter Port (CI) 60 6/70; returned to Guernsey Railway Co Ltd (CI) 60 10/73 (qv).

9435 (64): Guernsey Motors Ltd, St Peter Port (CI) 61 6/70; returned to Guernsey Railway Co Ltd (CI) 61 10/73 (qv).

1961

New vehicles:

65	10488 [1]	Albion NS3AN	82064D	Reading	9662	B35F	8/61	*
66	10489 [1]	Albion NS3AN	82064F	Reading	9663	B35F	9/61	*

Police plates:

10488 [1] (65): 60   10489 [1] (66): 71

Notes:

10488 [1] (65): Renumbered 165 8/73.
10489 [1] (66): Renumbered 166 8/73.

Vehicles marked with an asterisk above, were withdrawn 11/80 and transferred to Guernseybus Ltd (CI) 2/81 (qv):

10488 [1]-10489 [1] (165-166, ex 65-66).

1962

New vehicles:

67	11671	Albion NS3AN	82064L	Reading	2172	B35F	4/62	*
68	11672	Albion NS3AN	82064K	Reading	2173	B35F	5/62	*
69	11673	Albion NS3AN	82065B	Reading	2174	B35F	5/62	*

Police plates:

11671 (67): 191   11672 (68): 59   11673 (69): 163

Notes:

11671 (67): Renumbered 167 8/73.
11672 (68): Renumbered 168 8/73.
11673 (69): Renumbered 169 8/73.

Vehicles marked with an asterisk above, were withdrawn 11/80 and transferred to Guernseybus Ltd (CI) 2/81 (qv):

11671-11673 (167-169, ex 67-69).

1963

New vehicles:

70	12727 [1]	Albion NS3AN	82066J	Reading	4449	B35F	4/63	*
71	12728 [1]	Albion NS3AN	82066H	Reading	4450	B35F	4/63	*

Police plates:

12727 [1] (70): 128   12728 [1] (71): 129

Notes:

12727 [1] (70): Renumbered 170 8/73.
12728 [1] (71): Renumbered 171 8/73.

Vehicles marked with an asterisk above, were withdrawn 11/80 and transferred to Guernseybus Ltd (CI) 2/81 (qv):

12727 [1]-12728 [1] (170-171, ex 70-71).

Vehicles acquired from HK Falla {Paragon}, St Sampson (CI) 1/63:

41	3810	Leyland KP3	2775	Heaver	9521	FB35F	6/34	9/67	
42	864	Leyland KP3	4143	Heaver	9731	FB35F	6/35	9/66	
43	3923	Commer Commando	17A0822	Strachan	51015	B33F	-/47	9/65	
44	3924	Commer Commando	17A0793	Strachan	51166	B33F	7/48	9/64	
45	3925	Albion SpFT3L	70693J	Strachan	50934	B31F	-/48	9/65	
46	4818	Albion FT39AB	70792B	Heaver		B33F	11/49	9/72	

Police plates:

864 (42): 149   3923 (43): 151   3925 (45): 182
3810 (41): 147   3924 (44): 173   4818 (46): 194

Previous histories:

864 (42): New to HC Collenette {Paragon}, St Sampson (CI) 2 (with a Strachan B29F body); impressed by States of Guernsey Military Transport Service, St Peter Port (GOV) 9/42; German Military Authorities (Fortress Engineer Staff) (GOV) 12/42; returned to HC Collenette {Paragon} 2 at an unknown date; HK Falla {Paragon} 2 7/48; converted to forward control and re-bodied Heaver (9731) FB35F 1951; fitted with a Perkins P6 oil engine 1953.

3810 (41): New to HC Collenette {Paragon}, St Sampson (CI) 6 (with a Strachan B29F body); impressed by States of Guernsey Civil Transport Service, St Peter Port (GOV) 2/41; States of Guernsey Military Transport Service, St Peter Port (GOV) 9/42; German Military Authorities (Fortress Engineer Staff) (GOV) 12/42; returned to HC Collenette {Paragon} 6 at an unknown date; HK Falla {Paragon} 6 7/48; converted to forward control and re-bodied Heaver (9521) FB35F 6/50; fitted with a Perkins P6 oil engine 1953.

3923 (43): New to HC Collenette {Paragon}, St Sampson (CI) 5; HK Falla {Paragon} 5 7/48; fitted with a Perkins P6 oil engine 1953.

3924 (44): New to HC Collenette {Paragon}, St Sampson (CI) 4; HK Falla {Paragon} 4 7/48; fitted with a Perkins P6 oil engine 1953.

3925 (45): New to HC Collenette {Paragon}, St Sampson (CI) 3; HK Falla {Paragon} 3 7/48; fitted with a Perkins P6 oil engine 1953.

4818 (46): New to HK Falla {Paragon} 7; fitted with an Albion oil engine at an unknown date.

Notes:

864 (42): Renumbered 25 8/63.
3810 (41): Renumbered 24 8/63.
3923 (43): Renumbered 26 8/63.
3924 (44): Renumbered 27 8/63.
3925 (45): Renumbered 28 8/63.
4818 (46): Rebuilt with a standard destination box 6/63; renumbered 29 8/63.

Disposals:

864 (25, ex 42): Unidentified owner (minus engine) 3/68.
3810 (24, ex 41): Dumped at Priaulx's Quarry, St Sampson 3/68.
3923 (26, ex 43): K Rive, St Sampson as living accommodation 9/65.
3924 (27, ex 44): No known disposal.
3925 (28, ex 45): No known disposal.
4818 (29, ex 46): F Mallett & Son Ltd, St Peter Port (GCI) as a flat bed lorry 1/73; withdrawn and scrapped 1975.

1964

New vehicles:

72	14626 [1]	Albion NS3AN	82068F	Reading	7738	B35F	5/64	*
73	14651	Albion NS3AN	82069H	Reading	7739	B35F	5/64	*

Police plates:
    14626 [1] (72): 148   14651 (73): 168

Notes:
    14626 [1] (72): Renumbered 172 8/73.
    14651 (73): Renumbered 173 8/73.

Vehicles marked with an asterisk above, were withdrawn 11/80 and transferred to Guernseybus Ltd (CI) 2/81 (qv):
    14626 [1] (172, ex 72), 14651 (173, ex 73).

1965

New vehicles:

74	16215	Albion NS3AN	82071C	Reading	0502B	B35F	6/65	*
75	16216	Albion NS3AN	82071D	Reading	0503B	B35F	5/65	*

Police plates:
    16215 (74): 77   16216 (75): 121

Notes:
    16215 (74): Renumbered 174 8/73.
    16216 (75): Renumbered 175 8/73.

Vehicles marked with an asterisk above, were withdrawn 11/80 and transferred to Guernseybus Ltd (CI) 2/81 (qv):
    16215-16216 (174-175, ex 74-75).

1966

New vehicles:

76	14857 [1]	Bedford J4EZ1	6821387	Reading	2400C	B35F	7/66	*
77	14859 [1]	Bedford J4EZ1	6822049	Reading	2401C	B35F	9/66	*
78	14867	Bedford J4EZ1	6825687	Reading	2402C	B35F	9/66	*

Police plates:
    14857 [1] (76): 67   14859 [1] (77): 116   14867 (78): 178

Notes:
    14857 [1] (76): Renumbered 176 8/73.
    14859 [1] (77): Renumbered 177 8/73.
    14867 (78): Renumbered 178 8/73.

Vehicles marked with an asterisk above, were withdrawn 11/80 and transferred to Guernseybus Ltd (CI) 2/81 (qv):
    14857 [1] (176, ex 76), 14859 [1] (177, ex 77), 14867 (178, ex 78).

1967

New vehicles:

79	18265 [1]	Bedford J4EZ1	7812714	Reading	3615	B35F	7/67	*
80	18266 [1]	Bedford J4EZ1	7812970	Reading	3616	B35F	5/67	*
81	18267 [1]	Bedford J4EZ1	7812461	Reading	3617	B35F	5/67	*

Police plates:
    18265 [1] (79): 58   18266 [1] (80): 79   18267 [1] (81): 182

Notes:
    18265 [1] (79): Renumbered 179 8/73.
    18266 [1] (80): Renumbered 180 8/73.
    18267 [1] (81): Renumbered 181 8/73.

Vehicles marked with an asterisk above, were withdrawn 11/80 and transferred to Guernseybus Ltd (CI) 2/81 (qv):
    18265 [1]-18267 [1] (179-181, ex 79-81).

1968

New vehicles:

82	19660 [1]	Bedford J4EZ5	7T103528	Reading	4634E	B35F	5/68	*
83	19661	Bedford J4EZ5	7T103612	Reading	4639E	B35F	4/68	*
84	19662 [1]	Bedford J4EZ5	7T103707	Reading	4640E	B35F	4/68	*
85	19663 [1]	Bedford J4EZ5	7T103325	Reading	4641E	B35F	5/68	*

Police plates:

19660 [1] (82): 137	19662 [1] (84): 115
19661 (83): 83	19663 [1] (85): 140

Notes:

19660 [1] (82): Its chassis number is also recorded as 7T103328 and 7T103928; renumbered 182 8/73.
19661 (83): Renumbered 183 8/73.
19662 [1] (84): Renumbered 184 8/73.
19663 [1] (85): Renumbered 185 8/73.

Vehicles marked with an asterisk above, were withdrawn 11/80 and transferred to Guernseybus Ltd (CI) 2/81 (qv):
19660 [1] (182, ex 82); 19661 (183, ex 83), 19662 [1] (184, ex 84); 19663 [1] (185, ex 85).

1969

New vehicles:

86	21904	Bedford J4EZ5	9T132423	Reading	6183G	B35F	7/69	*
87	21905	Bedford J4EZ5	9T137442	Reading	6184G	B35F	9/69	*
88	21906 [1]	Bedford J4EZ5	9T137559	Reading	6185G	B35F	7/69	*

Police plates:

21904 (86): 135	21905 (87): 161	21906 [1] (88): 139

Notes:

21904 (86): Renumbered 186 8/73.
21905 (87): Renumbered 187 8/73.
21906 (88): Renumbered 188 8/73.

Vehicles marked with an asterisk above, were withdrawn 11/80 and transferred to Guernseybus Ltd (CI) 2/81 (qv):
21904-21905 (186-187, ex 86-87), 21906 [1] (188, ex 88).

1972

New vehicles:

89	2388 [1]	Bedford J4EZ5	2T123987	Sparshatt	9668K	B35F	7/72	*
90	2634 [1]	Bedford J4EZ5	2T124061	Sparshatt	9669K	B35F	8/72	*

Police plates:

2388 [1] (89): 136	2634 [1] (90): 230

Notes:

2388 [1] (89): Renumbered 189 8/73.
2634 [1] (90): Renumbered 190 8/73.

Vehicles marked with an asterisk above, were withdrawn 11/80 and transferred to Guernseybus Ltd (CI) 2/81 (qv):
2388 [1] (189, ex 89), 2634 [1] (190, ex 90).

1973

Vehicles acquired from Guernsey Motors Ltd, St Peter Port (CI) 10/73:

68	1463 [1]	Albion FT39AN	73787C	Heaver	2753	B35F	1/56	9/79
69	1529 [1]	Albion FT39AN	73791J	Heaver		B35F	1/56	9/79
70	1982	Albion FT39AN	73791K	Heaver		B35F	12/55	9/79
71	2027	Albion FT39AN	73791L	Heaver		B35F	1/56	11/79
112	2493 [1]	Bedford J4EZ5	2T124550	Sparshatt	9666K	B35F	5/72	*
113	2972 [2]	Bedford J4EZ5	2T124268	Sparshatt	9667K	B35F	5/72	*
72	4022 [2]	Albion FT39AN	73821E	Heaver		B35F	11/56	11/79
73	4029	Albion FT39AN	73821F	Heaver		B35F	12/56	10/79
74	4038	Albion FT39AN	73821H	Heaver		B35F	12/56	10/79
75	4076	Albion FT39AN	73821J	Heaver		B35F	12/56	11/79
62	6148	Albion FT39AN	73737F	Heaver	1713	B35F	5/54	10/75
63	6173	Albion FT39AN	73740F	Heaver	1714	B35F	5/54	9/75
64	6188	Albion FT39AN	73742B	Heaver	1715	B35F	5/54	9/79
66	6768 [1]	Albion FT39AN	73779D	Heaver	2465	B35F	4/55	9/79
65	6771	Albion FT39AN	73771K	Heaver		B35F	3/55	9/79
67	6773	Albion FT39AN	73779C	Heaver		B35F	4/55	9/77
76	8226 [1]	Albion FT39KAN	73837K	Reading	2364	B35F	4/58	9/79
77	8227 [1]	Albion FT39KAN	73840H	Reading	2366	B35F	4/58	10/79
78	8228 [1]	Albion FT39KAN	73840J	Reading	2369	B35F	6/58	10/79
79	8229 [1]	Albion FT39KAN	73842E	Reading	2367	B35F	4/58	11/79
60	9434 [1]	Albion NS3N	82050B	Reading	6159	B35F	6/60	*
61	9435	Albion NS3N	82052B	Reading	6160	B35F	5/60	*
80	9436 [1]	Albion NS3N	82051C	Reading	6155	B35F	4/60	*
81	9437	Albion NS3N	82051F	Reading	6156	B35F	4/60	*
82	9438 [1]	Albion NS3N	82052C	Reading	6157	B35F	4/60	10/77
83	9439 [1]	Albion NS3N	82053B	Reading	6158	B35F	4/60	*
84	10484 [1]	Albion NS3AN	82064C	Reading	9664	B35F	7/61	*
85	10485 [1]	Albion NS3AN	82064B	Reading	9665	B35F	7/61	*
86	10486	Albion NS3AN	82064E	Reading	9666	B35F	11/61	11/79
87	10487	Albion NS3AN	82064H	Reading	9667	B35F	10/61	*
88	11674	Albion NS3AN	82065H	Reading	2175	B35F	4/62	*
89	11675 [1]	Albion NS3AN	82065J	Reading	2176	B35F	4/62	*
90	11676	Albion NS3AN	82065A	Reading	2177	B35F	5/62	*
91	12723 [1]	Albion NS3AN	82066K	Reading	4445	B35F	4/63	*
92	12724	Albion NS3AN	82067A	Reading	4446	B35F	4/63	*
93	12725	Albion NS3AN	82066L	Reading	4447	B35F	4/63	*
94	12726	Albion NS3AN	82066F	Reading	4448	B35F	4/63	*
99	14223 [1]	Bedford J4EZ1	6818558	Reading	2403C	B35F	6/66	*
100	14531 [1]	Bedford J4EZ1	6823213	Reading	2404C	B35F	6/66	*
95	14627	Albion NS3AN	82069C	Reading	7740	B35F	5/64	*
96	14628	Albion NS3AN	82069D	Reading	7741	B35F	4/64	*
101	14838 [1]	Bedford J4EZ1	6816013	Reading	2405C	B35F	7/66	*
97	16213	Albion NS3AN	82071A	Reading	0500B	B35F	5/65	*
98	16214	Albion NS3AN	82071B	Reading	0501B	B35F	5/65	*
102	18262	Bedford J4EZ1	7814861	Reading	3612	B35F	4/67	*
103	18263	Bedford J4EZ1	7812333	Reading	3613	B35F	6/67	*
104	18264 [1]	Bedford J4EZ1	7812156	Reading	3614	B35F	4/67	*
105	19675 [1]	Bedford J4EZ5	7T103881	Reading	4638E	B35F	5/68	*
106	19676 [1]	Bedford J4EZ5	7T103704	Reading	4635E	B35F	2/68	*
107	19677 [1]	Bedford J4EZ5	7T103792	Reading	4636E	B35F	4/68	*
108	19678 [1]	Bedford J4EZ5	7T103838	Reading	4637E	B35F	3/68	*
109	21901	Bedford J4EZ5	9T131199	Reading	6180G	B35F	6/69	*
110	21902	Bedford J4EZ5	9T131310	Reading	6181G	B35F	6/69	*
111	21903	Bedford J4EZ5	9T132223	Reading	6182G	B35F	7/69	*

Police plates:

1463 [1] (68): 70	2972 [2] (113): 162	6148 (62): 72
1529 [1] (69): 80	4022 [1] (72): 124	6173 (63): 73
1982 (70): 158	4029 (73): 92	6188 (64): 89
2027 (71): 61	4038 (74): 118	6768 [1] (66): 76
2493 [1] (112): 229	4076 (75): 75	6771 (65): 65

6773 (67): 87	10486 (86): 91	14838 [1] (101): 183
8226 [1] (76): 68	10487 (87): 82	16213 (97): 166
8227 [1] (77): 74	11674 (88): 88	16214 (98): 184
8228 [1] (78): 100	11675 [1] (89): 108	18262 (102): 142
8229 [1] (79): 90	11676 (90): 157	18263 (103): 149
9434 [1] (60): 127	12723 [1] (91): 69	18264 [1] (104): 151
9435 (61): 64	12724 (92): 167	19675 [1] (105): 150
9436 [1] (80): 165	12725 (93): 109	19676 [1] (106): 147
9437 (81): 106	12726 (94): 155	19677 [1] (107): 154
9438 [1] (82): 120	14223 [1] (99): 173	19678 [1] (108): 152
9439 [1] (83): 122	14531 [1] (100): 180	21901 (109): 114
10484 [1] (84): 81	14627 (95): 179	21902 (110): 226
10485 [1] (85): 175	14628 (96): 177	21903 (111): 159

Previous histories:

The previous histories of these vehicles are detailed in the previous section under Guernsey Motors Ltd.

Notes:

9435 (61): Fitted with a Bedford engine and modified front panels 1/78.

9437 (81): Fitted with a Bedford engine and modified front panels 1/78.

Disposals:

1463 [1] (68): R Perry, Bath for preservation 3/80; L Booth, Buxton for preservation by10/82; re-registered MSV 412 3/84; moved to Leek at an unknown date; Classic Buses, Four Marks for preservation by2/91; moved to Winchester by6/93; moved to Portsmouth by1/94; Black & White Motorways Ltd, Portsmouth for preservation 6/01; moved to Penton Mewsey 11/05; T Smith, Sandbach for preservation c11/15; current 8/17.

1529 [1] (69): K Rowland, St Asaph for preservation 3/80; AW & RW Jones {Jones Motor Service}, Flint for preservation by8/80; AW & RW Jones & W Towers {Jones Motor Services}, Flint for preservation 3/84; J Brenson, Little Waltham for preservation 4/96; re-registered RSJ 747 7/98; N Baldwin, Ilminster for preservation 8/99; A Levell, Staines for preservation 2/01; J Page, Rickmansworth for preservation by2/04; I Barlow, Sully for preservation 10/04; current 4/16.

1982 (70): AM Wood, St Martin 3/80; re-registered 15141 3/80; S Gelsthorpe, St Pierre-du-Bois as a caravan 5/81; N Loller, St Pierre-du-Bois 8/82; Guernsey Airport Fire Service, Forest (XCI) 1/83; Dr JR Young, Nottingham (dealer / preservationist) 4/86; B Mitchell-Luker {Lighthouse & Transport Museum}, Arran for preservation 1/87; re-registered KSU 288 11/88; A Gold, Brodick for preservation by6/12; D McKelvie, Brodick for preservation by7/12.

2027 (71): R Denning {Slim's Truck Hire}, St Peter Port 3/80; P Ryan, Farnborough for preservation 8/80; re-registered 395 DEL 2/81; C White, Harston for preservation 1/90; current 9/04.

4022 [1] (72): P Davies, Farnham for preservation 3/80; re-registered JPA 82V 3/80; C Cowdrey, Alton for preservation 4/80; W Ritchie & I Walker, Glasgow for preservation 5/06; C Logan, location unknown for preservation by6/11; advertised for sale 1/18.

4029 (73): P Davies, Farnham for preservation 3/80; re-registered JPA 81V 4/80; E Chambers, Hounslow for preservation 4/80; J Sergeant, Birmingham for preservation 11/83; re-registered LSV 748 5/84; reseated to B27F by11/84; D & A Roizer, Leicester for preservation 9/86; reseated to B31F by11/84; P Welsh, Northampton for preservation 9/99; M Tidley, Wick for preservation 11/04.

4038 (74): K Rowland, St Asaph for preservation 3/80; A Tinker, Huddersfield for preservation by4/81; re-registered MCX 402W 4/81; last licence expired 10/89; D Haigh, Slaithwaite for preservation by2/95; Crayden, Doncaster for preservation by11/05 (probably 4/96); E Williams, Porthmadog (GD) 12/05; retained as a preserved vehicle 8/11; still current 8/12.

4076 (75): B Eagles, Chandlers Ford for preservation 3/80; noted in a field near Bristol 1990; unidentified travellers as a caravan by2/92; Santi, Windsor as a caravan 5/92; (?re-registered Q147 OST 9/92?); re-registered RFO 829 1/96; unidentified owner, London as a caravan 10/98; L Nye, West Sussex as a caravan by4/03; rebuilt with a Beadle style front end at an unknown date; Retro Ceremoniewagens, Aartselaar (O-B) 4/08; last licence expired 5/08; physically shipped to Belgium c7/09; unidentified dealer (O-NL) 9/11; Qatar Museum, Doha (O-UAE) c9/11

6148 (62): Bus Station waiting room 3/78; unidentified dealer for scrap by7/84.

6173 (63): T Murray, Biggar (SC) 12/77; re-registered DS 6468 1/78; J Haining, Dalkeith for preservation by8/98; reduced to a chassis only by7/01; C Randall, Kirktown of Fetteresso for preservation spares by7/01; disposed of by7/02.

6188 (64): Martel, St Peter Port 3/80; B Bessain, Vale at an unknown date; body broken up and chassis used as a boat trailer at an unknown date.

6768 [1] (66): N Marshall, Huntingdon for preservation 3/80; re-registered 842 FUF 5/80; C Kirkham, Macclesfield for preservation by6/82; N Bagel, Southampton as a caravan 6/83; derelict at Llanpumpsaint by2/03; R Greet, Broadhempston for preservation spares by5/04; current 11/13.

6771 (65): Guernsey Old Car Club for preservation 3/80; Dr JR Young, Nottingam (dealer / preservationist) 2/86; PK Historic Omnibus Co, Hunmanby for preservation 10/86; J Sykes, Carlton (dealer) 8/88; body scrapped and chassis to Dr JR Young, Nottingham for preservation spares c1988; (there is a report of it at AJS Salvage Co Ltd, Carlton (dealer) by8/88, but it is not confirmed whether this was before or after Dr JR Young).

6773 (67): Unidentified dealer for scrap 9/77.

8226 [1] (76): P Davies, Farnham for preservation 3/80; re-registered JPA 85V 3/80; W Burt, Ludgershall for preservation 4/80; unidentified owner (possibly Hirst or Hurst), Crudwell (XWI) by12/83; Saunders, Lydney as a caravan by8/90; last licence expired 3/93; advertised for sale 10/98.

8227 [1] (77): P Davies, Farnham for preservation 3/80; re-registered JPA 83V 5/80; B Catchpole, West Kingsdown for preservation 11/80; moved to Halling by11/87; re-registered YFO 127 by7/96; M Willetts & J Collins, Hertford for preservation 1/06; M Willetts, Hertford for preservation by12/08; P Davies, Farnham for preservation by9/09; current 8/18.

8228 [1] (78): P Davies, Farnham for preservation 3/80; re-registered JPA 84V 4/80; N Marshall, Huntingdon for preservation 4/80; B Catchpole, West Kingsdown for preservation by8/80; Dr JR Young, Nottingham (dealer / preservationist) by1/82; J Nettle, Oxford as a caravan 4/92; re-registered TFO 249 5/96; J Hallett, Trowbridge for preservation by5/97; Eastbourne Auction Rooms for preservation 3/99; Intransit Ltd, St Sampson (CI) 11/13.

8229 [1] (79): R Perry, Bath for preservation 3/80; Neek, Thornbury for preservation by8/80; B Heal, Sandford for preservation by11/05; R Warren, Martock for preservation 7/14; re-registered 266 UYH 7/14.

10486 (86): Scrapped 6/80.

Vehicles marked with an asterisk above, were withdrawn 11/80 and transferred to Guernseybus Ltd (CI) 2/81 (qv):

2493 [1] (112); 2972 [2] (113); 9434 [1] (60); 9435 (61); 9436 [1] (80); 9437 (81); 9438 [1] (82) (as a withdrawn vehicle); 9439 [1] (83); 10484 [1]-10485 [1] (84-85); 10487 (87); 11674 (88); 11675 [1] (89); 11676 (90); 12723 [1] (91) 12724-12726 (92-94); 14223 [1] (99); 14531 [1] (100); 14627-14628 (95-96); 14838 [1] (101); 16213-16214 (97-98); 18262-18263 (102-103); 18264 [1] (104); 19675 [1]-19678 [1] (105-108); 21901-21903 (109-111).

1974

New vehicles:

114	25701 [1]	Bedford J6L	CW119044	Pennine	1239	B35F	5/74	*
115	25702 [1]	Bedford J6L	CW119324	Pennine	1240	B35F	5/74	*
116	25703	Bedford J6L	CW119850	Pennine	1241	B35F	5/74	*
117	25704	Bedford J6L	CW119879	Pennine	1242	B35F	5/74	*

Police plates:

25701 [1] (114): 181	25703 (116): 171
25702 [1] (115): 123	25704 (117): 169

Notes:

The Bedford model type J6L is incomplete, possibly J6LZ.

Vehicles marked with an asterisk above, were withdrawn 11/80 and transferred to Guernseybus Ltd (CI) 2/81 (qv):

25701 [1] (114), 25702 [1] (115), 25703-25704 (116-117).

1976

New vehicles:

118	28401	Bedford SB5	EW456119	Wadham Stringer	9109	B39F	4/76	*
119	28402 [1]	Bedford SB5	EW456091	Wadham Stringer	9110	B39F	5/76	*
120	28403	Bedford SB5	EW456615	Wadham Stringer	9111	B39F	5/76	*
121	28404	Bedford SB5	EW456183	Wadham Stringer	9112	B39F	6/76	*

Police plates:

28401 (118): 143	28403 (120): 198
28402 [1] (119): 194	28404 (121): 228

Vehicles marked with an asterisk above, were withdrawn 11/80 and transferred to Guernseybus Ltd (CI) 2/81 (qv):
28401 (118), 28402 [1] (118-119), 28403-28404 (120-121).

1977

New vehicles:

| 1 | 29726 | Ford Transit | BD05TR54149 | Ford | | M14 | 7/77 | * |
| 2 | 29727 | Ford Transit | BD05TR54148 | Ford | | M14 | 7/77 | * |

Police plates:
29726 (1): 197   29727 (2): 205

Vehicles marked with an asterisk above, were withdrawn 11/80 and transferred to Guernseybus Ltd (CI) 2/81 (qv):
29726-29727 (1-2).

Vehicles acquired from DV Dawes {Delta Tours}, St Peter Port (CI) 7/77:

3	12614	Volkswagen LT31	2862511735	Devon Conversions		M16	7/76	*
				26003LF				
4	25912	Volkswagen Microbus		Devon Conversions		M9	7/76	*
			2352132252	050232K				

Police plates:
12614 (3): 203   25912 (4): 204

Previous histories:
12614 (3): New to St Brelade's College, St Brelade (XCI) registered J 57640; DV Dawes {Delta Tours} (CI) 3/77.
25912 (4): New to DV Dawes {Delta Tours} (CI).

Vehicles marked with an asterisk above, were withdrawn 11/80 and transferred to Guernseybus Ltd (CI) 2/81 (qv):
12614 (3); 25912 (4).

1978

New vehicles:

122	29728 [1]	Bedford SB5	GW456404	Wadham Stringer	2421	B39F	3/78	*
123	29729 [1]	Bedford SB5	GW456481	Wadham Stringer	2422	B39F	3/78	*
124	29730 [1]	Bedford SB5	GW455792	Wadham Stringer	2423	B39F	3/78	*
125	29731 [1]	Bedford SB5	GW456149	Wadham Stringer	2424	B39F	3/78	*
126	29732 [1]	Bedford SB5	GW456372	Wadham Stringer	2425	B39F	3/78	*
127	29733 [1]	Bedford SB5	GW456389	Wadham Stringer	2426	B39F	3/78	*

Police plates:
29728 [1] (122): 27   29730 [1] (124): 104   29732 [1] (126): 223
29729 [1] (123): 97   29731 [1] (125): 107   29733 [1] (127): 227

Vehicles marked with an asterisk above, were withdrawn 11/80 and transferred to Guernseybus Ltd (CI) 2/81 (qv):
29728 [1]-29733 [1] (122-127).

Vehicles acquired from Watson's Garage Ltd {The Greys}, St Martin (CI) 2/78:

24	653	Albion PH115	25026I	Reading	2908	FB32F	4/39	2/78
22	732 [2]	Albion FT3AB	70739A	Reading	5840	B36F	2/50	9/79
23	1309	Albion NS3N	82052F	Reading	7116	B36F	6/60	*
5	1559	Albion PH115	25006L	Reading	5185	FB32F	7/36	----
20	1787 [1]	Albion FT39AN	73737B	Reading	5176	B36F	6/54	9/79
25	3409	Vulcan Countess	D40	Reading		FB32F	4/33	----
21	3992	Albion FT39N	73134E	Reading	8898	B36F	5/52	9/79

Police plates:

653 (24): 133	1559 (5): 131	3992 (21): 130
732 [2] (22): 153	1787 [1] (20): 84	
1309 (23): 240	3409 (25): 132	

Previous histories:
653 (24): New to Watson Bros {The Greys} with a Heaver B29F body; Watson's Garage Ltd {The Greys} (CI) 4/46; rebodied Reading (2908) FB32F 1953 and fitted with a Perkins P6 oil engine 2/64.
732 [2] (22): New to Watson's Garage Ltd {The Greys} (CI).
1309 (23): New to Watson's Garage Ltd {The Greys} (CI).
1559 (5): New to Watson Bros {The Greys} with a Heaver B29F body; Watson's Garage Ltd {The Greys} (CI) 4/46; rebodied Reading (5185) FB32F 2/55; fitted with a Leyland Cub engine 6/58; fitted with a Morris engine 1/63.
1787 [1] (20): New to Watson's Garage Ltd {The Greys} (CI).
3409 (25): New to Watson Bros {The Greys} with a Vulcan B31F body; impressed by German Military Authorities (GOV) 11/41; returned 1942; Watson's Garage Ltd {The Greys} (CI) 4/46; fitted with a Albion petrol engine 1948/49; rebodied Reading FB32F 6/53; fitted with a Perkins P6 oil engine 5/67.
3992 (21): New to Watson's Garage Ltd {The Greys} (CI).

Notes:
1309 (23): Fitted with a Bedford engine 7/78.
1559 (5): Not operated by Guernsey Railway Co Ltd.
3409 (25): Not operated by Guernsey Railway Co Ltd.

Disposals:
653 (24): K Rowland, St Asaph for preservation 3/80; N Hirst, M Ponder & T Quinn, Coventry for preservation c4/82; re-registered DFP 496 by8/83; LT Shaw, Tamworth for preservation by9/88; M Bowring, Lydney for preservation 8/93.
732 [2] (22): A Wood, St Martin for preservation re-registered 1982 3/80; North West Transport Museum, Warrington for preservation 10/82; F Elliott & Dr JR Young, Golborne for preservation 3/85; unidentified owner, Tamworth possibly for preservation 4/92; 'Adam & Lee', location unknown as a caravan by5/93; re-registered OFF 605 by11/93; last licence expired 9/94; Fyffe, Carnoustie (dealer) for scrap c10/01.
1559 (5): J Foley, Guernsey Motor Museum for preservation 3/80; F Help, Guernsey as a caravan 1982; D & A Ridley for preservation by12/84; unidentified preservationist, Felbridge (M Verrechia?) by12/00.
1787 [1] (20): J Lidstone, Leigh-on-Sea for preservation 3/80; Tillingbourne Valley Services Ltd, Cranleigh (SR) re-registered 898 FUF 6/83; to service 7/83; F Elliott & Dr JR Young, Golborne for preservation 6/85; hired to Educational Holidays Guernsey Ltd {Island Coachways}, St Peter Port (CI) re-registered 1787 [1] 5/86-9/86; acquired by Educational Holidays Guernsey Ltd {Island Coachways}, St Peter Port (CI) 4/88; to service 5/88; Lakeland Motor Museum, Holker Hall for preservion re-registered 898 FUF 6/93; R Greet, Broadhempson for preservation 3/94; Intransit Ltd, St Peter Port (CI) 11 re-registered 1787 [1] 2/13; moved to St Sampson (CI) by9/13; fitted with a Cummins engine by3/18.
3409 (25): G Hatton, Woolston for preservation 3/80; Dr JR Young, Nottingham (dealer / preservationist) 7/84; H Glover, Nuneaton for preservation 5/96; re-registered MSJ 702 6/98; moved to Shirebrook by10/04; P Harris, Mansfield Woodhouse for preservation 9/13; D Maskell, Wilstead for preservation 4/14; T Smith, Sandbach for preservation; current 8/17.
3992 (21): B Jolly, Guernsey Old Car Club for preservation 3/80; A Tracey, London E7 for preservation 2/84; moved to Merthyr Tydfil by9/89; moved to Evesham by6/90; C White, Harston for preservation 1992; D Roizer, Leicester for preservation spares c6/93; broken up for spares 1993.

Vehicle marked with an asterisk above, was withdrawn 11/80 and transferred to Guernseybus Ltd (CI) 2/81 (qv):
1309 (23).

1979

Vehicles acquired from Western National Omnibus Co Ltd, Exeter (DN) 10/79-12/79:

128	2239 [2]	Bristol SUL4A	234.007	ECW	15981	B36F	5/66	*
129	31902	Bristol SUL4A	234.009	ECW	15983	B36F	6/66	*
130	31903	Bristol SUL4A	173.002	ECW	12036	B36F	1/61	*
131	31904	Bristol SUL4A	226.023	ECW	14721	B36F	3/65	*
133	31906 [1]	Bristol SUL4A	234.015	ECW	16005	B36F	7/66	*
135	31908 [1]	Bristol SUL4A	190.026	ECW	12755	B36F	12/61	*
136	31909 [1]	Bristol SUL4A	234.014	ECW	16004	B36F	7/66	*
139	31912 [1]	Bristol SUL4A	226.021	ECW	14719	B36F	3/65	*
152	31914 [1]	Bristol SUL4A	190.039	ECW	12886	C37F	7/62	*
153	31915 [1]	Bristol SUL4A	190.031	ECW	12882	C37F	7/62	*
154	31916 [1]	Bristol SUL4A	190.037	ECW	12877	C37F	7/62	*
155	31917 [1]	Bristol SUL4A	190.045	ECW	12892	C37F	7/62	*
156	31918 [1]	Bristol SUL4A	190.036	ECW	12885	C37F	7/62	*
141	31919 [1]	Bristol SUL4A	234.016	ECW	16006	B36F	7/66	*
157	31920 [1]	Bristol SUL4A	190.047	ECW	12894	C37F	7/62	*

Police plates:

2239 [2] (128): 103	31908 [1] (135): 85	31916 [1] (154): 92
31902 (129): 188	31909 [1] (136): 118	31917 [1] (155): 96
31903 (130): 189	31912 [1] (139): 132	31918 [1] (156): 100
31904 (131): 110	31914 [1] (152): 91	31919 [1] (141): 68
31906 [1] (133): 72	31915 [1] (153): 90	31920 [1] (157): 111

Previous histories:

These vehicles were purchased via Kinross Plant & Construction Co Ltd, Kinross, the (then) parent company of Guernsey Railway Co Ltd who prepared them for service in Guernsey.

2239 [2] (128): New to Southern National Omnibus Co Ltd, Exeter (DN) 687 registered EDV 550D; Western National Omnibus Co Ltd, Exeter (DN) 687 11/69; CF Booth Ltd, Rotherham (dealer) 6/79; Kinross Plant & Construction Co Ltd, Kinross 7/79; acquired by Guernsey Railway Co Ltd in 10/79.

31902 (129): New to Southern National Omnibus Co Ltd, Exeter (DN) 689 registered EDV 552D; Western National Omnibus Co Ltd, Exeter (DN) 689 11/69; CF Booth Ltd, Rotherham (dealer) 6/79; Kinross Plant & Construction Co Ltd, Kinross 7/79; acquired by Guernsey Railway Co Ltd in 10/79.

31903 (130): New to Western National Omnibus Co Ltd, Exeter (DN) 632 registered 346 EDV; withdrawn 4/78; W Norths (PV) Ltd, Sherburn in Elmet (dealer) 8/78; Kinross Plant & Construction Co Ltd 7/79; acquired by Guernsey Railway Co Ltd in 11/79.

31904 (131): New to Western National Omnibus Co Ltd, Exeter (DN) 672 registered BDV 253C; W Norths (PV) Ltd, Sherburn in Elmet (dealer) 8/78; Fr DJ Green, Weymouth (dealer) 9/78; Kinross Plant & Construction Co Ltd 7/79; acquired by Guernsey Railway Co Ltd in 11/79.

31906 [1] (133): New to Western National Omnibus Co Ltd, Exeter (DN) 683 registered EDV 538D; CF Booth Ltd, Rotherham (dealer) 7/79; Kinross Plant & Construction Co Ltd 7/79; acquired by Guernsey Railway Co Ltd by12/79.

31908 [1] (135): New to Southern National Omnibus Co Ltd, Exeter (DN) 661 registered 430 HDV; entered service 3/62; Western National Omnibus Co Ltd, Exeter (DN) 661 11/69; CF Booth Ltd, Rotherham (dealer) 6/79; Kinross Plant & Construction Co Ltd 7/79; acquired by Guernsey Railway Co Ltd in 12/79.

31909 [1] (136): New to Western National Omnibus Co Ltd, Exeter (DN) 682 registered EDV 537D; CF Booth Ltd, Rotherham (dealer) 6/79; Kinross Plant & Construction Co Ltd 7/79; acquired by Guernsey Railway Co Ltd in 12/79.

31912 [1] (139): New to Western National Omnibus Co Ltd, Exeter (DN) 670 registered BDV 251C; W Norths (PV) Ltd, Sherburn in Elmet (dealer) 7/78; Fr DJ Green, Weymouth (dealer) 9/78; Kinross Plant & Construction Co Ltd 7/79; acquired by Guernsey Railway Co Ltd in 11/79.

31914 [1] (152): New to Western National Omnibus Co Ltd, Exeter (DN) 422 registered 272 KTA (as C33F); renumbered 1222 6/71; reseated to C37F 1973; Fr DJ Green, Weymouth (dealer) 11/79; Kinross Plant & Construction Co Ltd 12/79; acquired by Guernsey Railway Co Ltd in 12/79.

31915 [1] (153): New to Western National Omnibus Co Ltd, Exeter (DN) 418 registered 268 KTA (as C33F); renumbered 1218 6/71; reseated to C37F 1973; Fr DJ Green, Weymouth (dealer) 11/79; Kinross Plant & Construction Co Ltd, Kinross 12/79; acquired by Guernsey Railway Co Ltd in 12/79.

31916 [1] (154): New to Southern National Omnibus Co Ltd, Exeter (DN) 434 registered 286 KTA (as C33F); Western National Omnibus Co Ltd, Exeter (DN) 434 11/69; renumbered 1234 6/71; reseated to C37F 1973; Fr DJ Green, Weymouth (dealer) 11/79; Kinross Plant & Construction Co Ltd 12/79; acquired by Guernsey Railway Co Ltd in 12/79.

31917 [1] (155): New to Western National Omnibus Co Ltd, Exeter (DN) 428 registered 278 KTA (as C33F); renumbered 1228 6/71; reseated to C37F 1973; Fr DJ Green, Weymouth (dealer) 11/79; Kinross Plant & Construction Co Ltd 12/79; acquired by Guernsey Railway Co Ltd in 12/79.

31918 [1] (156): New to Western National Omnibus Co Ltd, Exeter (DN) 421 registered 271 KTA (as C33F); renumbered 1221 6/71; reseated to C37F 1973; Fr DJ Green, Weymouth (dealer) 11/79; Kinross Plant & Construction Co Ltd 11/79; acquired by Guernsey Railway Co Ltd in 11/79.

31919 [1] (141): New to Western National Omnibus Co Ltd, Exeter (DN) 684 registered EDV 539D; CF Booth Ltd, Rotherham (dealer) 6/79; Kinross Plant & Construction Co Ltd 7/79; acquired by Guernsey Railway Co Ltd by12/79.

31920 [1] (157): New to Western National Omnibus Co Ltd, Exeter (DN) 430 registered 280 KTA (as C33F); renumbered 1230 6/71; reseated to C37F 1973; CF Booth Ltd, Rotherham (dealer) 11/79; Kinross Plant & Construction Co Ltd 12/79; acquired by Guernsey Railway Co Ltd in 12/79.

Notes:
2239 [2] (ex EDV 550D) (128): Re-registered 31901 and to service 4/80.

31902 (ex EDV 552D) (129): Painted in an advertising livery for Dan Air (becoming Guernsey's first advertising livery) and to service 4/80.

31903 (ex 346 EDV) (130): To service 4/80.

31904 (ex BDV 253C) (131): To service 4/80.

31906 [1] (ex EDV 538D) (133): To service 4/80.

31908 [1] (ex 430 HDV) (135): To service 4/80.

31909 [1] (ex EDV 537D) (136): To service 4/80.

31912 [1] (ex BDV 251C) (139): To service 4/80.

31914 [1] (ex 272 KTA) (152): Was numbered 142 in error for a few days after entering service in 5/80.

31915 [1] (ex 268 KTA) (153): To service 6/80.

31916 [1] (ex 286 KTA) (154): To service 6/80.

31917 [1] (ex 278 KTA) (155): To service 6/80.

31918 [1] (ex 271 KTA) (156): To service 7/80.

31919 [1] (ex EDV 539D) (141): To service 8/80.

31920 [1] (ex 280 KTA) (157): To service 10/80.

Vehicles marked with an asterisk above, were withdrawn 11/80 and transferred to Guernseybus Ltd (CI) 2/81 (qv):
31901 (ex 2239 [2], EDV 550D) (128); 31902 (ex EDV 552D); 31903 (ex 346 EDV) (130); 31904 (ex BDV 253C) (131); 31906 [1] (ex EDV 538D) (133); 31908 [1] (ex 430 HDV) (135); 31909 [1] (ex EDV 537D) (136); 31912 [1] (ex BDV 251C) (139); 31914 [1] (ex 272 KTA) (152); 31915 [1] (ex 268 KTA) (153); 31916 [1] (ex 286 KTA) (154); 31917 [1] (ex 278 KTA) (155); 31918 [1] (ex 271 KTA) (156); 31919 [1] (ex EDV 539D) (141); 31920 [1] (ex 280 KTA) (157).

Vehicles acquired from AC Bickers, Coddenham (SK) 10/79-12/79:

| 132 | 31905 | Bristol SUL4A | 190.013 | ECW | 12760 | B36F | 11/61 | * |
| 134 | 31907 [1] | Bristol SUL4A | 173.016 | ECW | 12046 | B36F | 4/61 | * |

Police plates:
31905 (132): 87   31907 [1] (134): 119

Previous histories:
31905 (132): New to Western National Omnibus Co Ltd, Exeter (DN) 648 registered 417 HDV; Tillingbourne Bus Co Ltd, Guildford (SR) 12/72; moved to Gomshall (SR) 6/74; AC Bickers 7/75; Fr D Green, Weymouth (dealer) 10/79; acquired by Guernsey Railway Co Ltd 12/79.

31907 [1] (134): New to Western National Omnibus Co Ltd, Exeter (DN) 642 registered 356 EDV; Fr DJ Green, Weymouth (dealer) 9/76; AC Bickers 11/76; Fr DJ Green, Weymouth (dealer) 10/79; acquired by Guernsey Railway Co Ltd 10/79.

Notes:
31905 (ex 417 HDV) (132): To service 4/80.

31907 (ex 356 EDV) (134): To service 4/80.

Vehicles marked with an asterisk above, were withdrawn 11/80 and transferred to Guernseybus Ltd (CI) 2/81 (qv):
31905 (417 HDV) (132); 31907 [1] (ex 356 EDV) (134).

Vehicle acquired from Western National Omnibus Co Ltd, Exeter (DN) by12/79:

358 EDV	Bristol SUL4A	173.018	ECW	12048	B36F	3/61	----

Previous history:
358 EDV: New to Western National Omnibus Co Ltd, Exeter (DN) 632; CF Booth Ltd, Rotherham (dealer) 6/79; acquired by Guernsey Railway Co Ltd by12/79.

Notes:
358 EDV: Acquired for spares.

Disposal:
358 EDV: Reduced to a shell by6/80.

1980

Vehicles acquired from Western National Omnibus Co Ltd, Exeter (DN) 4/80:

137	31910 [1]	Bristol SUL4A	226.015	ECW	14713	B36F	2/65	----
138	31911 [1]	Bristol SUL4A	234.017	ECW	15985	B36F	6/66	*
140	31913 [1]	Bristol SUL4A	234.025	ECW	15989	B36F	7/66	*

Police plates:
31911 [1] (138): 70   31913 [1] (140): 80

Previous histories:
These vehicles were purchased via Kinross Plant & Construction Co Ltd, Kinross, the (then) parent company of Guernsey Railway Co Ltd who prepared them for service in Guernsey.

31910 [1] (137): New to Southern National Omnibus Co Ltd, Exeter (DN) 664 registered BDV 245C; Western National Omnibus Co Ltd, Exeter (DN) 664 11/69; W Norths (PV) Ltd, Sherburn in Elmet (dealer) 8/78; Kinross Plant & Construction Co Ltd 12/79.
31911 [1] (138): New to Southern National Omnibus Co Ltd, Exeter (DN) 691 registered EDV 554D; Western National Omnibus Co Ltd, Exeter (DN) 691 11/69; CF Booth Ltd, Rotherham (dealer) 6/79; Kinross Plant & Construction Co Ltd 7/79.
31913 [1] (140): New to Southern National Omnibus Co Ltd, Exeter (DN) 695 registered EDV 558D; Western National Omnibus Co Ltd, Exeter (DN) 695 11/69; CF Booth Ltd, Rotherham (dealer) 6/79; Kinross Plant & Construction Co Ltd 7/79.

Notes:
31910 [1] (ex BDV 245C) (137): Not operated by Guernsey Railway Co Ltd and gradually used for spares.

Vehicles marked with an asterisk above, were withdrawn 11/80 and transferred to Guernseybus Ltd (CI) 2/81 (qv):
31910 [1] (ex BDV 245C) (137) (as a withdrawn vehicle); 31911 [1] (ex EDV 554D) (138); 31913 [1] (ex EDV 558D) (140).

Vehicles acquired from Kinross Plant & Construction Co Ltd (XTE) 5/80:

6	1463 [2]	Ford Transit	BDVZUU27474	Ford	M14	10/78	*
5	1529 [2]	Ford Transit	BDVZAG28059	Ford	M14	5/80	*

Police plates:
1463 [2] (6): 89   1529 [2] (5): 124

Previous histories:
1463 [2] (6): New to Kinross Plant & Construction Co Ltd (XTE) registered ESU 953T.
1529 [2] (5): New to Kinross Plant & Construction Co Ltd (XTE) registered DES 229V.

Vehicles marked with an asterisk above, were withdrawn 11/80 and transferred to Guernseybus Ltd (CI) 2/81 (qv):
1463 [2] (6); 1529 [2] (5).

ANCILLARY VEHICLES

	Ford TT		lorry	6/21	6/21	8/27
	Brille-Schneider P2		rail welder	-/06	7/20	-/--
	Ford TT		lorry	-/--	8/27	-/--
	AEC B		rail welder	-/--	12/25	-/--
3257	Ford A 30 cwt	AA4837671	tipper lorry	-/32	4/35	3/39
	Bean		clinker lorry	-/--	4/37	9/38
3794	Manchester	MT11069	clinker lorry	-/--	10/37	10/46
3257	Ford AA	AA4837671	tipper lorry	-/32	-/42	4/47
527	Fordson BB		clinker lorry	-/38	1/46	4/50
	Dodge		lorry	-/--	10/46	-/--
1376	Austin 12 hp	H2951	van	-/37	4/46	8/50
5673	Austin K3/SV	7275	3 ton lorry	4/40	10/73	12/74
6436	Albion FT39N	72874E	towing vehicle	4/50	1/75	5/80
2239 [1]	Ford Escort	BBAVWS868510	van	8/79	1/80	*
5597 [1]	Bedford TK	2T129995	breakdown tender	6/72	5/80	*

Notes:

The clinker lorries were used for transporting hot clinker from the company's incinerator to the nearby clinker field. As they only operated 'off-road' and were not required to be registered (and may have been vehicles that had officially been recorded as scrapped). A reinforced body was transferred from one chassis to another.

AEC B and Brille-Schneider rail welders: Were numbered 4 (originally registered LE 9177) and 3 in the PSV fleet (registered A83).

Bean clinker lorry: Was acquired from Leale Ltd, St Sampson.

527: Acquired from the War Department (GOV) (having been captured from the German Army – its original owner/identity is unknown).

2239 [1]: New to Kinross Plant & Construction Co Ltd (GTE) registered AMS 784V.

3257: Was new to FR Norman, Guernsey (GCI) and was acquired via O Le Lacheur, St Peter Port (dealer). It was re-acquired from Burgess Engineering, St Peter Port (GCI) in 1942.

5597 [1]: New to Strathorne Springs, Forfar (GAS) registered WSR 923K; Kinross Plant & Construction Co Ltd (GTE) at an unknown date.

5673: Transferred from Guernsey Motors Ltd (GCI) 11.

6436: Was numbered 36 in the PSV fleet; its wheelbase and body were considerably shortened before entering service as a towing vehicle.

Disposals:

The only known disposals are for the following vehicles:

527: F Palzeaird, Castel (GCI) 4/50; scrapped 1/65.

1376: E Palzeaird, Castel 8/50; various other Guernsey owners; scrapped by6/56.

3257: Unidentified owner, Herm 4/47 (there are no made up roads on the island and hence no motor vehicle laws; possibly used in the postwar reconstruction of the island).

6436: PF Ryan, Farnborough for preservation 8/80; P Davies, Farnham for preservation by10/80; unidentified owner for preservation, Ascot by1/82; A Hazell, Wellington for preservation 3/82; G Anderson, South Moulton as a caravan 1983; re-registered Q402 JDV 7/85; S Smith, South Moulton as a caravan by10/93; R & R Hart, Bodmin for preservation by12/93; re-registered RFO 375 10/96; reseated to B8F by9/99; still current 9/12.

Vehicle marked with an asterisk above, was withdrawn 11/80 and transferred to Guernseybus Ltd (CI) 2/81 (qv):
2239 [1] (ex AMS 784V); 5597 [1] (ex WSR 923K).

GUERNSEYBUS LTD

Guernseybus Ltd started in February 1981 by Ken Bates, better known for his connections to Chelsea FC. The company acquired the fleet and took on many of the employees of Guernsey Railway Co Ltd. A start was made on repainting vehicles into a white livery blue and orange relief. This rather plain livery was adopted with a view to implementing advertising liveries which started appearing from June in that year. A reshuffling and changes to routes reduced vehicle requirements slightly but broadly, the new company served the same areas as its predecessor.

As a successor to the SUs, Bristol LHs started to appear in December 1983, many originating from London. These were 7ft 6in wide, taking advantage of recent legislation changes applying to service buses. These saw off the remaining Albions apart from two which were used on Airport services.

More route developments and experiments were undertaken but the company sustained losses and it was not until 1986 that profits started to be recorded.

A new development in early 1990 was the formation of Central Transfers. This was a joint venture with Educational Holidays, the major coach firm on the island, to operate airport and harbour transfers for visitors. Both companies supplied vehicles, but the partnership had broken up by January 1991 from whence it was operated solely by Guernseybus. From 1995, a new independent company – Central Transfers Ltd was established to take over the operations.

Bristol LHs continued to be purchased from a variety of sources up until 1994 – a total of 67 were acquired in total, 19 of them coach versions but finances continued to be tight particularly when it came to vehicle replacements. In September 1992, the winter timetable for 1992/93 was presented and the States Traffic Committee expressed concern that services were falling short of the desired level. It was proposed was that the States should take ownership the vehicles which in turn would be leased back to the operators. This was not taken up at the time, but the States did agree to support public transport with funding of £1.5mn. In return, Guernseybus and Educational Holidays were invited to tender for roughly three equal groups of bus routes. After a lot of discussion and negotiation, the Holidays company secured one package and Guernseybus the other two. A condition was that both operators committed to purchase newer vehicles than hitherto and as a result, the era of midi-buses was ushered into Guernsey.

In July 1996, Ken Bates resigned as Chairman and control was assumed by a Board of Directors which included Garry Bougourd as General Manager. In January 1997, Bougourd purchased Guernseybus and was appointed Managing Director. The next few years continued to be rocky; services continued to be cut and other economies made and with his health declining in 2000, Garry Bougourd decided to close the company. Perhaps mindful of the situations caused by the closure of the Railway Company some 20 years previously, careful planning took place with the States and Educational Holidays, to ensure bus services were maintained. It was agreed that the States would purchase vehicles and lease these back to Educational Holidays – the latter changing its name to Island Coachways Ltd, which had long been its trading style. 23 Optare Metrorider midi-buses and the 15 remaining Bristol LHs were made available to the new company from 28 November 2000. The remaining vehicles owned by Guernseybus were sold off.

1981

Vehicles transferred from Guernsey Railway Co Ltd, St Peter Port (CI) 2/81:

23	1309	Albion NS3N	82052F	Reading	7116	B36F	6/60	12/83
6	1463 [2]	Ford Transit	BDVZUU27474	Ford		M14	11/78	9/85
5	1529 [2]	Ford Transit	BDVZAG28059	Ford		M14	5/80	9/85
189	2388 [1]	Bedford J4EZ5	2T123987	Sparshatt	9668K	B35F	7/72	9/87
112	2493 [1]	Bedford J4EZ5	2T124550	Sparshatt	9666K	B35F	5/72	-/88
190	2634 [1]	Bedford J4EZ5	2T124061	Sparshatt	9669K	B35F	8/72	9/87
113	2972 [2]	Bedford J4EZ5	2T124268	Sparshatt	9667K	B35F	5/72	-/88
60	9434 [1]	Albion NS3N	82050B	Reading	6159	B35F	6/60	----
61	9435	Albion NS3N	82052B	Reading	6160	B35F	5/60	----
80	9436 [1]	Albion NS3N	82051C	Reading	6155	B35F	4/60	-/82
81	9437	Albion NS3N	82051F	Reading	6156	B35F	4/60	----
82	9438 [1]	Albion NS3N	82052C	Reading	6157	B35F	4/60	----
83	9439 [1]	Albion NS3N	82053B	Reading	6158	B35F	4/60	----
84	10484 [1]	Albion NS3AN	82064C	Reading	9664	B35F	7/61	----
85	10485 [1]	Albion NS3AN	82064B	Reading	9665	B35F	7/61	----
87	10487	Albion NS3AN	82064H	Reading	9667	B35F	10/61	----
165	10488 [1]	Albion NS3AN	82064D	Reading	9662	B35F	8/61	4/84
166	10489 [1]	Albion NS3AN	82064F	Reading	9663	B35F	9/61	-/--

167	11671	Albion NS3AN	82064L	Reading	2172	B35F	4/62	8/85
168	11672	Albion NS3AN	82064K	Reading	2173	B35F	5/62	----
169	11673	Albion NS3AN	82065B	Reading	2174	B35F	5/62	----
88	11674	Albion NS3AN	82065H	Reading	2175	B35F	4/62	-/84
89	11675 [1]	Albion NS3AN	82065J	Reading	2176	B35F	4/62	11/81
90	11676	Albion NS3AN	82065A	Reading	2177	B35F	5/62	9/84
3	12614	Volkswagen LT31	2862511735	Devon Conversions 26003LF		M16	9/76	-/86
91	12723 [1]	Albion NS3AN	82066K	Reading	4445	B35F	4/63	----
92	12724	Albion NS3AN	82067A	Reading	4446	B35F	4/63	-/85
93	12725	Albion NS3AN	82066L	Reading	4447	B35F	4/63	----
94	12726	Albion NS3AN	82066F	Reading	4448	B35F	4/63	-/85
170	12727 [1]	Albion NS3AN	82066J	Reading	4449	B35F	4/63	-/82
171	12728 [1]	Albion NS3AN	82066H	Reading	4450	B35F	4/63	-/82
99	14223 [1]	Bedford J4EZ1	6818558	Reading	2403C	B35F	6/66	9/85
100	14531 [1]	Bedford J4EZ1	6823213	Reading	2404C	B35F	6/66	9/85
172	14626 [1]	Albion NS3AN	82068F	Reading	7738	B35F	5/64	-/82
95	14627	Albion NS3AN	82069C	Reading	7740	B35F	5/64	6/84
96	14628	Albion NS3AN	82069D	Reading	7741	B35F	4/64	-/85
173	14651	Albion NS3AN	82069H	Reading	7739	B35F	5/64	12/82
101	14838 [1]	Bedford J4EZ1	6816013	Reading	2405C	B35F	7/66	9/86
176	14857 [1]	Bedford J4EZ1	6821387	Reading	2400C	B35F	7/66	9/85
177	14859 [1]	Bedford J4EZ1	6822049	Reading	2401C	B35F	9/66	9/86
178	14867	Bedford J4EZ1	6825687	Reading	2402C	B35F	9/66	-/85
97	16213	Albion NS3AN	82071A	Reading	0500B	B35F	5/65	-/85
98	16214	Albion NS3AN	82071B	Reading	0501B	B35F	5/65	4/84
174	16215	Albion NS3AN	82071C	Reading	0502B	B35F	6/65	-/84
175	16216	Albion NS3AN	82071D	Reading	0503B	B35F	5/65	-/84
102	18262	Bedford J4EZ1	7814861	Reading	3612	B35F	4/67	3/86
103	18263	Bedford J4EZ1	7812333	Reading	3613	B35F	6/67	-/88
104	18264 [1]	Bedford J4EZ1	7812156	Reading	3614	B35F	4/67	-/87
179	18265 [1]	Bedford J4EZ1	7812714	Reading	3615	B35F	7/67	-/88
180	18266 [1]	Bedford J4EZ1	7812970	Reading	3616	B35F	5/67	9/87
181	18267 [1]	Bedford J4EZ1	7812461	Reading	3617	B35F	5/67	9/87
182	19660 [1]	Bedford J4EZ5	7T103528	Reading	4634E	B35F	5/68	9/87
183	19661	Bedford J4EZ5	7T103612	Reading	4639E	B35F	4/68	6/88
184	19662 [1]	Bedford J4EZ5	7T103707	Reading	4640E	B35F	4/68	-/88
185	19663 [1]	Bedford J4EZ5	7T103325	Reading	4641E	B35F	5/68	9/87
105	19675 [1]	Bedford J4EZ5	7T103881	Reading	4638E	B35F	5/68	6/88
106	19676 [1]	Bedford J4EZ5	7T103704	Reading	4635E	B35F	2/68	4/88
107	19677 [1]	Bedford J4EZ5	7T103792	Reading	4636E	B35F	4/68	9/87
108	19678 [1]	Bedford J4EZ5	7T103838	Reading	4637E	B35F	3/68	10/85
109	21901	Bedford J4EZ5	9T131199	Reading	6180G	B35F	6/69	-/87
110	21902	Bedford J4EZ5	9T131310	Reading	6181G	B35F	6/69	-/87
111	21903	Bedford J4EZ5	9T132223	Reading	6182G	B35F	7/69	6/88
186	21904	Bedford J4EZ5	9T132423	Reading	6183G	B35F	7/69	-/85
187	21905	Bedford J4EZ5	9T137442	Reading	6184G	B35F	9/69	9/85
188	21906 [1]	Bedford J4EZ5	9T137559	Reading	6185G	B35F	7/69	-/88
114	25701 [1]	Bedford J6L	CW119239	Pennine	1239	B35F	5/74	1/94
115	25702 [1]	Bedford J6L	CW119324	Pennine	1240	B35F	5/74	1/92
116	25703	Bedford J6L	CW119850	Pennine	1241	B35F	5/74	7/91
117	25704	Bedford J6L	CW119879	Pennine	1242	B35F	5/74	1/94
4	25912	Volkswagen Microbus	2352132252	Devon Conversions 050232K		M9	7/76	-/87
118	28401	Bedford SB5	EW456119	Wadham Stringer	9109	B39F	4/76	9/87
119	28402 [1]	Bedford SB5	EW456091	Wadham Stringer	9110	B39F	5/76	9/84
120	28403	Bedford SB5	EW456615	Wadham Stringer	9111	B39F	5/76	-/89
121	28404	Bedford SB5	EW456183	Wadham Stringer	9112	B39F	6/76	-/89
1	29726	Ford Transit	BD05TR54149	Ford		M14	7/77	-/86
2	29727	Ford Transit	BD05TR54148	Ford		M14	7/77	8/86
122	29728 [1]	Bedford SB5	GW456404	Wadham Stringer	2421	B39F	3/78	9/89
123	29729 [1]	Bedford SB5	GW456481	Wadham Stringer	2422	B39F	3/78	7/89
124	29730 [1]	Bedford SB5	GW455792	Wadham Stringer	2423	B39F	3/78	9/89
125	29731 [1]	Bedford SB5	GW456149	Wadham Stringer	2424	B39F	3/78	3/90

126	29732 [1]	Bedford SB5	GW456372	Wadham Stringer	2425	B39F	3/78	7/89
127	29733 [1]	Bedford SB5	GW456389	Wadham Stringer	2426	B39F	3/78	9/89
128	31901	Bristol SUL4A	234.007	ECW	15981	B36F	5/66	9/84
129	31902	Bristol SUL4A	234.009	ECW	15983	B36F	6/66	12/85
130	31903	Bristol SUL4A	173.002	ECW	12036	B36F	1/61	3/85
131	31904	Bristol SUL4A	226.023	ECW	14721	B36F	3/65	3/85
132	31905	Bristol SUL4A	190.013	ECW	12760	B36F	11/61	7/85
133	31906 [1]	Bristol SUL4A	234.015	ECW	16005	B36F	7/66	9/84
134	31907 [1]	Bristol SUL4A	173.016	ECW	12046	B36F	4/61	9/84
135	31908 [1]	Bristol SUL4A	190.026	ECW	12755	B36F	12/61	9/84
136	31909 [1]	Bristol SUL4A	234.014	ECW	16004	B36F	7/66	9/84
137	31910 [1]	Bristol SUL4A	226.015	ECW	14713	B36F	2/65	----
138	31911 [1]	Bristol SUL4A	234.017	ECW	15985	B36F	6/66	9/84
139	31912 [1]	Bristol SUL4A	226.021	ECW	14719	B36F	3/65	9/84
140	31913 [1]	Bristol SUL4A	234.025	ECW	15989	B36F	7/66	9/84
152	31914 [1]	Bristol SUL4A	190.039	ECW	12886	C37F	7/62	9/86
153	31915 [1]	Bristol SUL4A	190.031	ECW	12882	C37F	7/62	9/86
154	31916 [1]	Bristol SUL4A	190.037	ECW	12877	C37F	7/62	9/86
155	31917 [1]	Bristol SUL4A	190.045	ECW	12892	C37F	7/62	8/85
156	31918 [1]	Bristol SUL4A	190.036	ECW	12885	C37F	7/62	9/84
141	31919 [1]	Bristol SUL4A	234.016	ECW	16006	B36F	7/66	9/84
157	31920 [1]	Bristol SUL4A	190.047	ECW	12894	C37F	7/62	5/86

Public Service Omnibus plates:

Public Service Omnibus plates were introduced after Guernsey Railway Co Ltd closed. For most of the fleet acquired, it is not known whether these were the same or different numbers as the previous Police plate ones.

1463 [2] (6): 47
1529 [2] (5): 44
12614 (3): 49

25701 [1] (114): 31
25702 [1] (115): 32
25703 (116): 33

25704 (117): 34
25912 (4): 46
29727 (2): 50

Previous histories:

The previous histories of these vehicles are detailed in the previous section under Guernsey Railway Co Ltd, (with whom they were withdrawn 11/80).

1463 [2] (6): Originally registered ESU 953T.
1529 [2] (5): Originally registered DES 229V.
31901 (128): Previously registered 2239 [2], originally EDV 550D.
31902 (129): Originally registered EDV 552D.
31903 (130): Originally registered 346 EDV.
31904 (131): Originally registered BDV 253C.
31905 (132): Originally registered 417 HDV.
31906 [1] (133): Originally registered EDV 538D.
31907 [1] (134): Originally registered 356 EDV.
31908 [1] (135): Originally registered 430 HDV.
31909 [1] (136): Originally registered EDV 537D.
31910 [1] (137): Originally registered BDV 245C.
31911 [1] (138): Originally registered EDV 554D.
31912 [1] (139): Originally registered BDV 251C.
31913 [1] (140): Originally registered EDV 558D.
31914 [1] (152): Originally registered 272 KTA.
31915 [1] (153): Originally registered 268 KTA.
31916 [1] (154): Originally registered 286 KTA.
31917 [1] (155): Originally registered 278 KTA.
31918 [1] (156): Originally registered 271 KTA.
31919 [1] (141): Originally registered EDV 539D.
31920 [1] (157): Originally registered 280 KTA.

Notes:

The Bedford model type J6L is incomplete, possibly J6LZ.

1309 (23): Re-registered 31235 [1] 8/82.
1463 [2] (ex ESU 953T) (6): Re-registered 25278 8/82.
1529 [2] (ex DES 229V) (5): Re-registered 16938 8/82.
9434 [1] (60): Did not operate for Guernseybus Ltd.
9435 (61): Did not operate for Guernseybus Ltd.
9437 (81): Did not operate for Guernseybus Ltd.
9438 [1] (82): Did not operate for Guernseybus Ltd.
9439 [1] (83): Did not operate for Guernseybus Ltd.
10484 [1]-10485 [1] (84-85): Did not operate for Guernseybus Ltd.
10487 (87): Did not operate for Guernseybus Ltd; retained as a racing car transporter.
11671 (167): Reseated to B22F with a luggage compartment and renumbered 93 3/85; reverted to B35F 1985.
11672 (168): Did not operate for Guernseybus Ltd.
11673 (169): Did not operate for Guernseybus Ltd; used as a bus station waiting room.
12614 (3): Re-registered 5579 [1] 9/81.
12723 [1] (91): Did not operate for Guernseybus Ltd.
12724 (90): Reseated to B20F with a luggage compartment 4/82.
12725 (92): Did not operate for Guernseybus Ltd.
14857 [1] (176): Used as a mobile waiting room from 3/86.
19660 [1]: Its chassis number is also recorded as 7T103328 and 7T103928;
25704: Re-registered 3338 [2] 8/92.
29731 [1] (125): Re-registered 21906 [2] 1989.
31910 [1] (ex BDV 245C) (137): Did not operate for Guernseybus Ltd and was gradually used for spares.
31918 [1] (ex 271 KTA) (156): Re-registered 10558 4/85.

Disposals:

2388 [1] (189): AJS Salvage Co Ltd, Carlton (dealer) for scrap 1/88.
2493 [1] (112): D Stevenson, Worcester for preservation 7/88.
2634 [1] (190): AJS Salvage Co Ltd, Carlton (dealer) for scrap 1/88.
2972 [2] (113): No known disposal.
3338 [2] (ex 25704) (117): ND MacDonald {Riduna Buses}, Alderney (CI) re-registered AY   593 [2] 6/94; to service 7/94; AJ Curtis {Riduna Buses}, Alderney (CI) 1/96; Wacton Trading / Coach Sales, Bromyard (dealer) 3/97.
5579 [1] (ex 12614) (3): B Ceillam, Guernsey as a shed 1986.
9434 [1] (60): B Spears, St Peter Port for preservation re-registered 18718 (not carried) 7/84; GP Ripley, Carlton (dealer) for scrap 9/89.
9435 (61): Unidentified dealer, Guernsey for scrap 1983.
9436 [1] (80): Unidentified dealer, Guernsey for scrap 1983.
9437 (81): Unidentified dealer, Guernsey for scrap 1983.
9438 [1] (82): Flying Dutchman Hotel, St Peter Port as a store 9/83; Dr JR Young, Nottingham (dealer / preservationist) 10/87; A Hardwick, Carlton (dealer) for scrap by4/88.
9439 [1] (83): Unidentified dealer, Guernsey for scrap 1983.
10484 [1] (84): Unidentified dealer, Guernsey for scrap 1983.
10485 [1] (85): Unidentified dealer, Guernsey for scrap 1983.
10487 (87): AJS Salvage Co Ltd, Carlton (dealer) for scrap 4/86.
10488 [1] (165): Dr JR Young, Nottingham (dealer / preservationist) 4/84; re-registered LSV 201 by8/93; D Knapman, Lincoln as a caravan 3/94; The Curry Bus, Bridport (XDT) 9/10.
10489 [1] (166): No known disposal.
10558 (ex 31918 [1], 271 KTA) (156): F Elliott, Golborne for preservation re-registered 271 KTA 3/87 (as C33F); loaned to Ashtree Coaches Ltd, Edenfield (LA) 8/87-10/88; F Elliott {Memory Lane Coaches}, Golborne (GM) 10/88; loaned to M Hayton, Dumfries for preservation by9/92-5/05; W Staniforth, Birmingham for preservation by9/05; A Brown {Chelveston Preservation Society}, Rushden for preservation by10/05; N Helliker, Stroud for preservation 3/09.
11671 (93, ex 167): AJS Salvage Co Ltd, Carlton (dealer) for scrap 4/86.
11672 (168): Guernsey Airport, Forest (XCI) as a training unit 11/83.
11673 (169): Unidentified dealer, Guernsey for scrap 1983.
11674 (88): AJS Salvage Co Ltd, Carlton (dealer) for scrap 4/86.
11675 [1] (89): Unidentified dealer, Guernsey for scrap 1983.
11676 (90): Total (Sarnia) Ltd, Vale 9/84; Dr JR Young, Nottingham (dealer / preservationist) 12/86; A Hardwick, Carlton (dealer) for scrap 10/87.
12723 [1] (91): Unidentified dealer, Guernsey for scrap 1983.

12724 (92): AJS Salvage Co Ltd, Carlton (dealer) for scrap 4/86.

12725 (93): Flying Dutchman Hotel, St Peter Port as an outdoor dining room 1984; Dr JR Young, Nottingham (dealer / preservationist) 10/87; K Smith, Salisbury as a mobile caravan 4/90; re-registered to an unknown registration by1/98.

12726 (94): Dr JR Young, Nottingham (dealer / preservationist) by9/86; PK Historic Omnibus, Hunmanby for preservation 10/86; J Sykes, Carlton (dealer) 8/88; body scrapped; chassis to Dr JR Young, Nottingham for spares probably 1988 (some parts donated to Salter, Wareham for EBW 112B (ex 14651).

12727 [1] (170): Unidentified dealer, Guernsey for scrap 1983.

12728 [1] (171): Unidentified dealer, Guernsey for scrap 1983.

14223 [1] (99): Dr JR Young, Nottingham (dealer / preservationist) 1/88; M Clay, Breedon-on-the-Hill as a mobile caravan by2/92; re-registered JFL 93D 11/93; believed still current 2019.

14531 [1] (100): AJS Salvage Co Ltd, Carlton (dealer) for scrap 1/88.

14626 [1] (172): Unidentified dealer, Guernsey for scrap 1983.

14627 (95): Converted to a mobile commentary bus 6/84 (qv).

14628 (96): AJS Salvage Co Ltd, Carlton (dealer) for scrap 4/86.

14651 (173): M Swain (Whitefield-Fishponds School), Bristol (XAV) 12/83; R Scard, Ash Vale for preservation 10/86; D Priddle, Godalming for preservation 5/87; A & T Salter, High Wycombe for preservation by3/89; moved to Wareham at an unknown date; re-registered EBW 112B 8/89; P Longdon, Sandown for preservation 3/08; current 9/10.

14838 [1] (101): Dr JR Young, Nottingham (dealer / preservationist) 1986; last licence expired 8/90; H Tidley, Lutterworth for preservation 12/03; J Pye, Nottingham for preservation by11/09; S Keeling, Nottingham for preservation 12/09;

14857 [1] (176): AJS Salvage Co Ltd, Carlton (dealer) for scrap 1/88.

14859 [1] (177): Dr JR Young, Nottingham (dealer / preservationist) 1/88; J Walters, Newark as a mobile caravan 7/91; re-registered HFW 391D by12/91; last licence expired 3/99.

14867 (178): M Harris, Broad Town for preservation 3/87; re-registered VHO 462 6/88; moved to Swindon by10/93; Hurst (or Hirst), Crudwell (XWI / dealer) by12/96; M Cottrell, Goring Heath for preservation c2004; L Cox, Reading (dealer) by3/13; S Gravett, Great Torrington for preservation 4/13.

16213 (97): AJS Salvage Co Ltd, Carlton (dealer) for scrap 4/86.

16214 (98): AJS Salvage Co Ltd, Carlton (dealer) for scrap 4/86.

16215 (174): AJS Salvage Co Ltd, Carlton (dealer) for scrap 4/86.

16216 (175): East Somerset Railway, Cranmore for preservation 4/84; Dr JR Young, Nottingham (dealer / preservationist) by12/86; D Stevenson, Worcester for preservation 7/88; re-registered JNP 590C 9/88; Wacton Trading / Coach Sales, Bromyard (dealer) c1995; A Dixon, Annfield Plain for preservation c8/97; T Smith, Sandbach for preservation by8/15; current 8/17.

16938 (ex 1529 [2], DES 229V): Unidentified dealer, London 4/86; last licence expired 12/92.

18262 (102): Converted to a mobile commentary bus 3/86 (qv).

18263 (103): No known disposal.

18264 [1] (104): GP Ripley, Carlton (dealer) for scrap 6/88.

18265 [1] (179): No known disposal.

18266 [1] (180): AJS Salvage Co Ltd, Carlton (dealer) for scrap 1/88.

18267 [1] (181): AJS Salvage Co Ltd, Carlton (dealer) for scrap 1/88.

19660 [1] (182): AJS Salvage Co Ltd, Carlton (dealer) for scrap 1/88.

19661 (183): GP Ripley, Carlton (dealer) for scrap 6/88.

19662 [1] (184): No known disposal.

19663 [1] (185): AJS Salvage Co Ltd, Carlton (dealer) for scrap 1/88.

19675 [1] (105): GP Ripley, Carlton (dealer) for scrap 6/88.

19676 [1] (106): Dr JR Young, Nottingham (dealer / preservationist) 4/88; PK Motors, location unknown for scrap by12/05.

19677 [1] (107): AJS Salvage Co Ltd, Carlton (dealer) for scrap 1/88.

19678 [1] (108): Broken up by Guernseybus Ltd 1986.

21901 (109): AJS Salvage Co Ltd, Carlton (dealer) for scrap 1/88.

21902 (110): GP Ripley, Carlton (dealer) for scrap 6/88.

21903 (111): GP Ripley, Carlton (dealer) for scrap 6/88.

21904 (186): Broken up by Guernseybus Ltd 1986.

21905 (187): Broken up by Guernseybus Ltd 1986.

21906 [1] (188): No known disposal.

21906 [2] (ex 29731 [1]) (125): GP Ripley, Carlton (dealer) for scrap 4/90.

25278 (ex 1463 [2], ESU 953T) (6): Unidentified dealer, London 4/86.

25701 [1] (114): A Hardwick, Carlton (dealer) for scrap 10/94.

25702 [1] (115): Wacton Trading / Coach Sales, Bromyard (dealer) 1/92.

25703 (116): Converted to a mobile commentary bus 8/91 (qv).

25912 (4): No known disposal.

28401 (118): No known disposal.

28402 [1] (119): Broken up by Guernseybus Ltd 1987.

28403 (120): No known disposal.

28404 (121): No known disposal.

29726 (1): No known disposal.

29727 (2): R Hamel, location unknown 8/86.

29728 [1] (122): GP Ripley, Carlton (dealer) for scrap 9/89.

29729 [1] (123): GP Ripley, Carlton (dealer) for scrap 9/89.

29730 [1] (124): Converted to a mobile commentary bus 9/89 (qv).

29732 [1] (126): No known disposal.

29733 [1] (127): GP Ripley, Carlton (dealer) for scrap 9/89.

31235 [1] (ex 1309) (23): Dr JR Young, Nottingham (dealer / preservationist) 1/85; M Tidley, Wick for preservation 12/03; re-registered 210 UXO 8/05.

31901 (ex 2239 [2], EDV 550D) (128): AJS Salvage Co Ltd, Carlton (dealer) for scrap 4/86.

31902 (ex EDV 552D) (129): AJS Salvage Co Ltd, Carlton (dealer) for scrap 4/86.

31903 (ex 346 EDV) (130): AJS Salvage Co Ltd, Carlton (dealer) for scrap 5/86.

31904 (ex BDV 253C) (131): G Jones {Carlton Metals}, Carlton (dealer) for scrap 4/86.

31905 (ex 417 HDV) (132): Unidentified dealer, Carlton for scrap 5/86.

31906 [1] (ex EDV 538D) (133): AJS Salvage Co Ltd, Carlton (dealer) for scrap 4/86.

31907 [1] (ex 356 EDV) (134): AJS Salvage Co Ltd, Carlton (dealer) for scrap 5/86.

31908 [1] (ex 430 HDV) (135): AJS Salvage Co Ltd, Carlton (dealer) for scrap 4/86.

31909 [1] (ex EDV 537D) (136): AJS Salvage Co Ltd, Carlton (dealer) for scrap 5/86.

31910 [1] (ex BDV 245C) (137): Broken up by Guernseybus Ltd c1986.

31911 [1] (ex EDV 554D) (138): Seagrove Hotel, St Brelade (XCI) re-registered J 26896 by3/85; Holiday Tours Ltd, St Peter (CI) for spares 6/87; scrapped c1987.

31912 [1] (ex BDV 251C) (139): AJS Salvage Co Ltd, Carlton (dealer) for scrap 3/85.

31913 [1] (ex EDV 558D) (140): AJS Salvage Co Ltd, Carlton (dealer) for scrap 4/86.

31914 [1] (ex 272 KTA) (152): D Wormersley, London possibly for preservation 5/87; re-registered 272 KTA c5/87; advertised for sale 9/87; unidentified dealer, East London (for scrap?) by8/91 (but probably much earlier).

31915 [1] (ex 268 KTA) (153): Dr JR Young, Nottingham (dealer / preservationist) 5/87; J Widdesden (or Widdowson or Widdesen), Sheffield as mobile caravan 4/92; re-registered 268 KTA by4/93; R Wright, Nottingham as a mobile caravan at an unknown date; last licence expired 10/02; possibly to C Billington, Maidenhead (dealer / preservationist) by12/02 (but not confirmed); W Staniforth, Birmingham for preservation by12/02; A Brown {Chelveston Preservation Society}, Rushden for preservation by10/04; scrapped 9/06.

31916 [1] (ex 286 KTA) (154): C Billington, Maidenhead for preservation 3/87; re-registered 286 KTA 5/87; current 9/18.

31917 [1] (ex 278 KTA) (155): Beard, St Albans probably as a mobile caravan 5/87.

31919 [1] (ex EDV 539D) (141): Unidentified dealer, Carlton for scrap 3/85.

31920 [1] (ex 280 KTA) (157): Dr JR Young, Nottingham (dealer / preservationist) 4/87; C Billington, Maidenhead for preservation 9/91; reseated to DP33F by1/95; re-registered 280 KTA by1/95; Tillingbourne Bus Co Ltd, Cranleigh (SR) 1/95; P Webb, Cardington for preservation by5/00; advertised for sale 4/03; last licence expired 5/03.

Vehicle acquired from AC Bickers, Coddenham (EX) 10/81:

142	31910 [2]	Bristol SUL4A	226.014	ECW	14712	B36F	2/65	8/84

Public Service Omnibus plate:

31910 [2] (142):

Previous history:

31910 [2] (142): New to Southern National Omnibus Co Ltd, Exeter (DN) 663 registered BDV 244C; Western National Omnibus Co Ltd, Exeter (DN) 663; AC Bickers (EX) 1/77.

Notes:

31910 [2] (ex BDV 244C) (142): To service 11/81; withdrawn following an accident 8/84.

Disposal:

31910 [2] (ex BDV 244C) (142): Broken up by Guernseybus Ltd 2/85.

1982

Vehicle acquired from Kinross Plant & Construction Co Ltd (XTE) 12/82:

143	6351	Bristol SUS4A	157.012	ECW	11389	B36F	5/60	by6/85

Public Service Omnibus plate:
6351 (143):

Previous history:
6351 (143): New to Southern National Omnibus Co Ltd, Exeter (DN) 614 registered 670 COD (as B30F); Western National Omnibus Co Ltd, Exeter (DN) 614 11/69; Greenslades Tours Ltd, Exeter (DN) 7/70; Western National Omnibus Co Ltd, Exeter (DN) 614 9/73; Kinross Plant & Construction Co Ltd (XTE) 9/80; reseated to B32F 1982.

Notes:
6351 (ex 670 COD) (143): To service 5/83.

Disposal:
6351 (ex 670 COD) (143): AJS Salvage Co Ltd, Carlton (dealer) for scrap 4/86.

1983

Vehicle acquired from London Transport Executive, London SW1 (LN) 12/83:

61	9439 [2]	Bristol LH6L	LH-1285	ECW	21898	B41F	8/76	8/96

Public Service Omnibus plates:
9439 [2] (61): 10

Previous history:
9439 [2] (61): New to London Transport Executive (LN) BL43 registered OJD 43R (as B39F).

Notes:
9439 [2] (ex OJD 43R): Re-registered 54327 8/92.

Disposal:
54327 (ex 9439 [2], OJD 43R) (61): Broken up by Guernseybus Ltd 8/96.

1984

Vehicles acquired from London Transport Executive, London SW1 (LN) 1984:

72	10488 [2]	Bristol LH6L	LH-1322	ECW	21922	B41F	1/77	11/00
62	31921 [1]	Bristol LH6L	LH-1294	ECW	21907	B41F	10/76	by10/98
63	31922 [1]	Bristol LH6L	LH-1236	ECW	21858	B41F	4/76	by11/00
64	31923 [1]	Bristol LH6L	LH-1265	ECW	21880	B41F	6/76	by11/00
65	31924 [1]	Bristol LH6L	LH-1353	ECW	21945	B41F	4/77	8/99
66	31925 [1]	Bristol LH6L	LH-1292	ECW	21905	B41F	9/76	2/95
67	31926	Bristol LH6L	LH-1329	ECW	21929	B41F	1/77	by5/00
68	31927 [1]	Bristol LH6L	LH-1277	ECW	21892	B41F	7/76	8/96
69	31928	Bristol LH6L	LH-1250	ECW	21872	B41F	9/76	11/00
70	31929	Bristol LH6L	LH-1270	ECW	21885	B41F	7/76	by11/00
71	31930 [1]	Bristol LH6L	LH-1272	ECW	21887	B41F	7/76	8/96
	KJD 424P	Bristol LH6L	LH-1264	ECW	21879	B39F	4/76	----
	OJD 70R	Bristol LH6L	LH-1325	ECW	21925	B39F	1/77	----

Public Service Omnibus plates:

10488 [2] (72): 19	31924 [1] (65): 52	31928 (69): 16
31921 [1] (62): 11	31925 [1] (66): 13	31929 (70): 17
31922 [1] (63): 53	31926 (67): 14	31930 [1] (71): 18
31923 [1] (64): 12	31927 [1] (68): 15	

Previous histories:
10488 [2] (72): New to London Transport Executive (LN) BL67 registered OJD 67R (as B39F); acquired by Guernseybus Ltd 11/84.
31921 [1] (62): New to London Transport Executive (LN) BL52 registered OJD 52R (as B39F); acquired by Guernseybus Ltd 2/84.
31922 [1] (63): New to London Transport Executive (LN) BL3 registered KJD 403P (as B39F); acquired by Guernseybus Ltd 2/84.

31923 [1] (64): New to London Transport Executive (LN) BL25 registered KJD 425P (as B39F); acquired by Guernseybus Ltd 2/84.

31924 [1] (65): New to London Transport Executive (LN) BL90 registered OJD 90R (as B39F); acquired by Guernseybus Ltd 2/84.

31925 [1] (66): New to London Transport Executive (LN) BL50 registered OJD 50R (as B39F); acquired by Guernseybus Ltd 3/84.

31926 (67): New to London Transport Executive (LN) BL74 registered OJD 74R (as B39F); acquired by Guernseybus Ltd 6/84.

31927 [1] (68): New to London Transport Executive (LN) BL37 registered KJD 437P (as B39F); acquired by Guernseybus Ltd 6/84.

31928 (69): New to London Transport Executive (LN) BL17 registered KJD 417P (as B39F); acquired by Guernseybus Ltd 6/84.

31929 (70): New to London Transport Executive (LN) BL30 registered KJD 430P (as B39F); acquired by Guernseybus Ltd 7/84.

31930 [1] (71): New to London Transport Executive (LN) BL32 registered KJD 432P (as B39F); acquired by Guernseybus Ltd 10/84.

KJD 424P: New to London Transport Executive (LN) BL24; acquired by Guernseybus Ltd 11/84.

OJD 70R: New to London Transport Executive (LN) BL70; acquired by Guernseybus Ltd 11/84.

Notes:

10488 [2] (ex OJD 67R) (72): To service 1/85; re-registered 5579 [2] 4/92; re-registered 24018 by12/96; renumbered 51 12/96.

31921 [1] (ex OJD 52R) (62): To service 3/84; re-registered 3338 [4] 5/96.

31922 [1] (ex KJD 403P) (63): To service 4/84; re-registered 19675 [3] 8/94.

31923 [1] (ex KJD 425P) (64): To service 4/84; re-registered 31925 [2] and renumbered 66 4/92 (ie exchanged identities with 31925 [1] (ex OJD 50R).

31924 [1] (ex OJD 90R) (65): To service 3/85; re-registered 31906 [4] 8/94; renumbered 64 10/98.

31925 [1] (ex OJD 50R) (66): To service 5/84; re-registered 31923 [2] and renumbered 64 4/92 (ie exchanged identities with 31923 [1] (ex KJD 425P).

31926 (ex OJD 74R) (67): To service 7/84; renumbered 63 10/98.

31927 [1] (ex KJD 437P) (68): To service 7/84.

31928 (ex KJD 417P) (69): To service 9/84; renumbered 61 10/98.

31929 (ex KJD 430P) (70): To service 7/84.

31930 [1] (ex KJD 432P) (71): To service 12/84.

KJD 425P: Acquired for spares.

OJD 70R: Acquired for spares.

Disposals:

3338 [4] (ex 31921 [1], OJD 52R) (62): Cannibalised for spares; shell to Airport Fire Service, Forest for training exercises 10/98.

19675 [3] (ex 31922 [1], KJD 403P) (63): No known disposal.

24018 (ex 5579 [2], 10488 [2], OJD 67R) (51, ex 72): Exported to an unidentified dealer for scrap 12/00.

31906 [4] (ex 31924 [1], OJD 90R) (64, ex 65): Scrapped 8/99.

31923 [2] (ex 31925 [1], OJD 50R) (64 ex 66): Broken up by Guernseybus Ltd 2/95.

31925 [2] (ex 31923 [1], KJD 425P) (66 ex 64): No known disposal.

31926 (ex OJD 74R) (63, ex 67): Cannibalised for spares; shell to Airport Fire Service, Forest for training exercises 5/00.

31927 [1] (ex KJD 437P) (68): Broken up by Guernseybus Ltd 8/96.

31928 (ex KJD 417P) (61, ex 69): M Nash, Weybridge (dealer) 10/00; Tally Ho! Coaches Ltd, Kingsbridge (DN) for spares 12/00; unidentified dealer for scrap by6/02.

31929 (ex KJD 430P) (70): No known disposal.

31930 [1] (ex KJD 432P) (71): Broken up by Guernseybus Ltd 8/96.

KJD 424P: Broken up by Guernseybus Ltd 6/90.

OJD 70R: Broken up by Guernseybus Ltd 1985.

Vehicle acquired from Chelsea Football Club, London SW6 (XLN) 5/84:

7	10489 [2]	Mercedes Benz 307D WDB60236728233466	Devon Conversions	M16	9/82	12/89

Public Service Omnibus plate:

10489 [2] (7): 41

Previous history:

10489 [2]: New to Chelsea Football Club (XLN) registered JGH 431Y.

Disposal:
10489 [2] (ex JGH 431Y) (7): Transferred to the ancillary fleet 12/89 (qv).

Vehicle acquired from Martin, Rothwell (LE) 9/84:

8	11675 [2]	Ford Transit	BDVVAB461440	Dormobile	6042	B16F	4/80	6/88

Public Service Omnibus plate:
11675 [2] (8): 42

Previous history:
11675 [2] (8): New to Martin, Rothwell (LE) registered KBC 258V.

Disposal:
11675 [2] (ex KBC 258V) (8): GP Ripley, Carlton (dealer) 6/88; P Winstanley, D Cox & B Kirk {3Bs}, Tamworth (ST) 7/88; G Evans {Gordon's Minibus Service}, Cefn Coed (MG) c1/91; unidentified owner by3/94; last licence expired 7/96.

Vehicles acquired from Devon General Ltd, Exeter (DN) 11-12/84:

164	12723 [2]	Bristol LH6L	LH-1120	Plaxton	7510BC017S	C45F	7/75	11/00
165	12727 [2]	Bristol LH6L	LH-1121	Plaxton	7510BC018S	C45F	8/75	11/00

Public Service Omnibus plates:
12723 [2] (164): 60   12727 [2] (165): 38

Previous histories:
12723 [2] (164): New to Greenslades Tours Ltd, Exeter (DN) 327 registered JFJ 507N; National Travel (South West) Ltd, Cheltenham (GL) 327 6/78; Western National Omnibus Co Ltd, Exeter (DN) 327 5/81; Devon General Ltd (DN) 327 1/83; acquired by Guernseybus Ltd 11/84.
12727 [2] (165): New to Greenslades Tours Ltd, Exeter (DN) 328 registered JFJ 508N; National Travel (South West) Ltd, Cheltenham (GL) 328 6/78; Western National Omnibus Co Ltd, Exeter (DN) 328 5/81; Devon General Ltd (DN) 328 1/83; acquired by Guernseybus Ltd 12/84.

Notes:
12723 [2] (ex JFJ 507N) (164): To service 12/84; re-registered 31914 [3] 7/90.
12727 [2] (ex JFJ 508N) (165): To service 1/85; re-registered 31915 [3] 7/90.

Disposals:
31914 [3] (ex 12723 [2], JFJ 507N) (164): Transferred to the States of Guernsey, St Peter Port 11/00; C Billington, Maidenhead (dealer / preservationist) 3/01; J Pratt & M Locke, Torquay for preservation re-registered JFJ 507N by7/02; K & J Stafford, Bedford for preservation 5/04; (probably) current 2017.
31915 [3] (ex 12727 [2], JFJ 508N) (165): Transferred to the States of Guernsey, St Peter Port 11/00; C Billington, Maidenhead (dealer / preservationist) 3/01; Gray, Andrews & Allen, South Devon for preservation 1/02.

Vehicle acquired from Rennie's of Dunfermline Ltd, Dunfermline (FE) 10/84:

73	14626 [2]	Bristol LHS6L	LHS-279	ECW	22916	B37F	11/77	3/96

Public Service Omnibus plates:
14626 [2] (73): 20

Previous history:
14626 [2] (73): New to London Country Bus Services Ltd, Reigate (SR) BN63 registered TPJ 63S; Rennie's of Dunfermline Ltd (FE) 7/83.

Disposal:
14626 [2] (73): Dr JR Young, Nottingham (dealer / preservationist) 3/96; probably to an unidentified dealer for scrap.

Vehicle acquired from Moat Mount School, London NW7 (XLN) 1984:

SPK 118M	Bristol LHS6L	LHS-151	ECW		20457	B35F	10/73	----

Previous history:
SPK 118M: New to London Country Bus Services Ltd, Reigate (SR) BL18; Moat Mount School (XLN) 1/81.

Notes:
SPK 118M: Acquired for spares.

Disposal:
SPK 118M: Broken up by Guernseybus Ltd at an unknown date.

Vehicle on hire from Channel Hire Cars (Gsy) Ltd, St Peter Port (XCI) 5/84.

6	34740	Ford Transit	BDVZAY288530	Ford		M14	12/80

Notes:
34740 (6): Returned 6/84.

1985

Vehicles acquired from Devon General Ltd, Exeter (DN) 1/85:

76	5597 [2]	Bristol LHS6L	LHS-122	Marshall	30853	B33F	2/72	5/90
75	9436 [2]	Bristol LHS6L	LHS-121	Marshall	30852	B33F	2/72	9/90
74	12728 [2]	Bristol LHS6L	LHS-120	Marshall	30851	B33F	2/72	6/90
77	31235 [2]	Bristol LHS6L	LHS-126	Marshall	30857	B33F	2/72	3/90

Public Service Omnibus plates:

5597 [2] (76): 7	12728 [2] (74): 54
9436 [2] (75): 6	31235 [2] (77): 51

Previous histories:
5597 [2] (76): New to Western National Omnibus Co Ltd, Exeter (DN) 90 registered VOD 90K; Devon General Ltd (DN) 90 1/83; withdrawn 9/84.
9436 [2] (75): New to Western National Omnibus Co Ltd, Exeter (DN) 89 registered VOD 89K; Devon General Ltd (DN) 89 1/83; withdrawn 9/84.
12728 [2] (74): New to Western National Omnibus Co Ltd, Exeter (DN) 88 registered VOD 88K; Devon General Ltd (DN) 88 1/83; withdrawn 9/84.
31235 [2] (77): New to Western National Omnibus Co Ltd, Exeter (DN) 1250 registered VOD 120K; Devon General Ltd (DN) 1250 1/83; withdrawn 9/84.

Notes:
5597 [2] (ex VOD 90K) (76): To service 4/85.
9436 [2] (ex VOD 89K) (75): To service 3/85.
12728 [2] (ex VOD 88K) (74): To service 3/85.
31235 [2] (ex VOD 120K) (77): To service 4/85.

Disposals:
5597 [2] (ex VOD 90K) (76): Aurigny Air Service, Jersey Airport (XCI) A1 5/90 (as B27F with perimeter seating); unidentified owner by11/00.
9436 [2] (ex VOD 89K) (75): Converted to a mobile commentary bus and transferred to the service fleet 9/90.
12728 [2] (ex VOD 88K) (74): Aurigny Air Service, Jersey Airport (XCI) A2 6/90 (as B25F with perimeter seating); A Keogh, Exeter for preservation 11/98; re-registered VOD 88K at an unknown date; K Staddon and A Lees, Honiton for preservation 10/00; T Bennett, Sherborne for preservation 2/05; current 7/14.
31235 [2] (ex VOD 120K) (77): Converted to a mobile commentary bus and transferred to the service fleet 3/90.

Vehicles acquired from Devon General Ltd, Exeter (DN) 2-3/85:

169	31907 [2]	Bristol LH6L	LH-1069	Plaxton	7510BC011S	C43F	7/75	11/00
160	31910 [3]	Bristol LH6L	LH-1115	Plaxton	7510BC013S	C45F	7/75	by12/99
161	31911 [2]	Bristol LH6L	LH-1116	Plaxton	7510BC014S	C45F	8/75	11/00
162	31912 [2]	Bristol LH6L	LH-1117	Plaxton	7510BC015S	C45F	8/75	11/00
163	31913 [2]	Bristol LH6L	LH-1119	Plaxton	7510BC016S	C45F	7/75	11/00
168	31919 [2]	Bristol LH6L	LH-1114	Plaxton	7510BC012S	C43F	7/75	11/00

Public Service Omnibus plates:

31907 [2] (169): 61	31911 [2] (161): 55	31919 [2] (168): 40
31910 [3] (160): 35	31913 [2] (163): 37	

Previous histories:

31907 [2] (169): New to Greenslades Tours Ltd, Exeter (DN) 322 registered JFJ 502N; Western National Omnibus Co Ltd, Exeter (DN) 1337 5/78; Devon General Ltd (DN) 337 1/83; shortened to 32ft and reseated to C43F by Herald Engineering, Plymouth (in order to comply with maximum legal length on Guernsey) prior to importation; acquired by Guernseybus Ltd 3/85.

31910 [3] (160): New to Greenslades Tours Ltd, Exeter (DN) 323 registered JFJ 503N; National Travel (South West) Ltd, Cheltenham (GL) 323 3/78; Western National Omnibus Co Ltd, Exeter (DN) 323 5/81; Devon General Ltd (DN) 323 1/83; acquired by Guernseybus Ltd 2/85.

31911 [2] (161): New to Greenslades Tours Ltd, Exeter (DN) 324 registered JFJ 504N; National Travel (South West) Ltd, Cheltenham (GL) 324 3/78; Western National Omnibus Co Ltd, Exeter (DN) 324 5/81; Devon General Ltd (DN) 324 1/83; acquired by Guernseybus Ltd 2/85.

31912 [2] (162): New to Greenslades Tours Ltd, Exeter (DN) 325 registered JFJ 505N; National Travel (South West) Ltd, Cheltenham (GL) 325 3/78; Western National Omnibus Co Ltd, Exeter (DN) 325 5/81; Devon General Ltd (DN) 325 1/83; acquired by Guernseybus Ltd 2/85.

31913 [2] (163): New to Greenslades Tours Ltd, Exeter (DN) 326 registered JFJ 506N; National Travel (South West) Ltd, Cheltenham (GL) 326 3/78; Western National Omnibus Co Ltd, Exeter (DN) 326 5/81; Devon General Ltd (DN) 326 1/83; acquired by Guernseybus Ltd 3/85.

31919 [2] (168): New to Greenslades Tours Ltd, Exeter (DN) 321 registered JFJ 501N; Western National Omnibus Co Ltd, Exeter (DN) 1336 5/78; reseated to C43F by12/79; Devon General Ltd (DN) 336 1/83; shortened to 32ft by Herald Engineering Ltd, Plymouth (in order to comply with maximum legal length on Guernsey) 2/85; acquired by Guernseybus Ltd 3/85.

Notes:

31907 [2] (ex JFJ 502N) (169): To service 7/85; reseated to C45F by7/90; re-registered 31919 [3] 7/90.

31910 [3] (ex JFJ 503N) (160): To service 4/85.

31911 [2] (ex JFJ 504N) (161): To service 4/85.

31912 [2] (ex JFJ 505N) (162): To service 4/85.

31913 [2] (ex JFJ 506N) (163): To service 4/85.

31919 [2] (ex JFJ 501N) (168): To service 6/85; re-registered 31918 [3] reseated to C45F 7/90.

Disposals:

31910 [3] (ex JFJ 503N) (160): Scrapped by12/99.

31911 [2] (ex JFJ 504N) (161): Transferred to the States of Guernsey, St Peter Port 11/00; C Billington, Maidenhead (dealer / preservationist) 3/01; re-registered JFJ 504N by9/03; J Pratt, Exeter for preservation by 9/04; T Partridge, Saltash for preservation 3/05; Woods, Crediton (dealer) for scrap 9/05.

31912 [2] (ex JFJ 505N) (162): Transferred to the States of Guernsey, St Peter Port 11/00; C Billington, Maidenhead (dealer / preservationist) 3/01; unidentified owner, Birmingham for preservation and re-registered JFJ 505N by6/02; unidentified owner for conversion to exhibition unit, Weymouth by10/03; unidentified owners 6/05 and 12/15.

31913 [2] (ex JFJ 506N) (163): Transferred to the States of Guernsey, St Peter Port 11/00; C Billington, Maidenhead (dealer / preservationist) 3/01; Chelveston Preservation Group for preservation 4/01; B Heginbotham, Irthlingborough for preservation by12/01; re-registered JFJ 506N by12/01; B Smith, Kettering for preservation by1/11; Hamilton Greys (Devon) Ltd, Exeter (DN) 1/17; withdrawn 11/18.

31918 [3] (ex 31919 [2], JFJ 501N) (168): Transferred to the States of Guernsey, St Peter Port and leased to Island Coachways Ltd, St Peter Port (CI) 168 11/00; C Billington, Maidenhead (dealer / preservationist) 3/01; Rexquote Ltd, Bishops Lydeard (SO) (not operated) 11/01; Quantock Motor Services Ltd, Wiveliscombe (SO) (not operated) 3/04; unidentified owner, Semington by11/04.

31919 [3] (ex 31907 [2], JFJ 502N) (169): Transferred to the States of Guernsey, St Peter Port 11/00; C Billington, Maidenhead (dealer / preservationist) 3/01; Mrs B Cainey {Mike's Travel}, Thornbury (GL) (not operated) 4/01; allocated fleet number 19 but not carried; re-registered JFJ 502N by5/02; T Ward, Drybrook for preservation 9/09; last licence expired 8/14.

Vehicles acquired from North Devon Ltd {Red Bus}, Barnstaple (DN) 3/85:

166	31906 [2]	Bristol LH6L	LH-1064	Plaxton	7510BC009S	C43F	7/75	11/00
167	31918 [2]	Bristol LH6L	LH-1068	Plaxton	7510BC010S	C43F	7/75	11/00

Public Service Omnibus plates:

31906 [2] (166): 57   31918 [2] (167): 39

Previous histories:

31906 [2] (166): New to Greenslades Tours Ltd, Exeter (DN) 319 registered JFJ 499N (as C45F); Western National Omnibus Co Ltd, Exeter (DN) 1334 5/78; reseated to C43F 6/79; North Devon Ltd {Red Bus} (DN) 1334 1/83; shortened to 32ft by Herald Engineering Ltd, Plymouth (in order to comply with maximum legal length on Guernsey) 2/85.

31918 [2] (167): New to Greenslades Tours Ltd, Exeter (DN) 320 registered JFJ 500N (as C45F); Western National Omnibus Co Ltd, Exeter (DN) 1335 5/78; reseated to C43F by12/79; North Devon Ltd {Red Bus} (DN) 1335 1/83; shortened to 32ft by Herald Engineering Ltd, Plymouth (in order to comply with maximum legal length on Guernsey) 2/85.

Notes:

31906 [2] (ex JFJ 499N) (166): To service 5/85; re-registered 31916 [3] and reseated to C45F 7/90.

31918 [2] (ex JFJ 500N) (167): To service 4/85; re-registered 31917 [3] and reseated to C45F 7/90.

Disposals:

31916 [3] (ex 31906 [2], JFJ 499N) (166): Transferred to the States of Guernsey, St Peter Port 11/00; C Billington, Maidenhead (dealer / preservationist) 3/01; probably to an unidentified dealer for scrap 4/01.

31917 [3] (ex 31918 [2], JFJ 500N) (167): Transferred to the States of Guernsey, St Peter Port 11/00; C Billington, Maidenhead (dealer / preservationist) 3/01; Rexquote Ltd, Bishops Lydeard (SO) (not operated) 11/01; C Shears, Winkleigh for preservation 12/02; T Partridge, Saltash for preservation 9/05; T Wigley & Son (Bus) Ltd, Carlton (dealer) by10/07.

Vehicles on hire from TL Car Sales {Hertz Rent a Car}, St Peter Port (XCI) 5-6/85:

6	10633	Renault Master	?	Holdsworth		M11	4/84
5	12162	Renault Master	?	Holdsworth		M11	4/84

Notes:

10633 (6): New to a Jersey owner registered J 68771; on hire from 6/85 carrying registration 10663 in error; returned 9/85.

12162 (5): New to a Jersey owner registered J 68770; on hire from 5/85; returned 9/85.

1986

Vehicles on hire from BB Hire Cars Ltd, St Peter Port (XCI) 4-5/86:

9	23172	Ford Transit	BDVZGJ29017	Ford	M14	5/86
3	43234	Ford Transit	BDVZGS23773	Ford	M11	4/86
5	44850	Ford Transit	BDVZGS23772	Ford	M11	4/86
6	45038	Ford Transit	BDVZGS23771	Ford	M11	5/86
10	45260	Ford Transit	BDVZGJ29015	Ford	M14	5/86

Notes:

23172 (9): On hire from 5/86; returned 11/86 (exported to the UK as C649 JUH).

43234 (3): On hire from 4/86; returned 9/86 (exported 12/86).

44850 (5): On hire from 4/86; returned 9/86 (exported 12/86).

45038 (6): On hire from 5/86; returned 10/86 (exported 1/87).

45260 (10): On hire from 5/86; returned 11/86 (to J Main {Riduna Buses}, Alderney (CI) as AY 2153 1/88 (qv)).

1987

Vehicles acquired from Jacksons Garage, Forest (XCI) 3/87:

5	48701	Mercedes Benz 310 WDB6020672O610511	Devon Conversions		M12	-/86	3/90
6	48702	Mercedes Benz 310 WDB6020672O610002	Devon Conversions 98365D		M11	-/86	3/90

Public Service Omnibus plates:
48701 (5): 44   48702 (6): 47

Previous histories:
48701 (5): New to Jacksons Garage (XCI).
48702 (6): New to Jacksons Garage (XCI).

Disposals:
48701 (5): Central Transfers, St Peter Port (CI) 25 3/90; returned to Guernseybus Ltd, St Peter Port (CI) 5
1/91; Central Transfers Ltd, St Peter Port (CI) 25 1/95; withdrawn at an unknown date.
48702 (6): Central Transfers, St Peter Port (CI) 24 3/90; returned to Guernseybus Ltd, St Peter Port (CI) 6
1/91; Central Transfers Ltd, St Peter Port (CI) 24 1/95; Intransit Ltd, St Peter Port (CI) 6 12/96;
withdrawn 6/02.

Vehicles acquired from Tayside Regional Council, Dundee (TE) 3/87:

78	31914 [2]	Bristol LHS6L	LHS-221	ECW	21580	B27F	7/75	2/96
79	31915 [2]	Bristol LHS6L	LHS-222	ECW	21581	B27F	7/75	2/96
80	31916 [2]	Bristol LHS6L	LHS-220	ECW	21579	B27F	7/75	5/94
81	31917 [2]	Bristol LHS6L	LHS-239	ECW	21582	B27F	6/76	8/95
82	31920 [2]	Bristol LHS6L	LHS-240	ECW	21583	B27F	6/76	1/96

Public Service Omnibus plates:
31914 [2] (78) (as 12723 [3]): 21   31917 [2] (81) (as 31307 [3]): 23
31915 [2] (79) (as 12727 [3]): 51   31920 [2] (82): 24
31916 [2] (80) (as 31306 [3]): 22

Previous histories:
31914 [2]: New to West Yorkshire PTE, Wakefield (WY) 40 registered JUG 356N; Tayside Regional Council
(Planning Unit), Dundee (TE) 225 3/80.
31915 [2]: New to West Yorkshire PTE, Wakefield (WY) 41 registered JUG 357N; Tayside Regional Council
(Planning Unit), Dundee (TE) P221 3/80.
31916 [2]: New to West Yorkshire PTE, Wakefield (WY) 39 registered JUG 355N; Tayside Regional Council
(Planning Unit), Dundee (TE) 224 3/80.
31917 [2]: New to West Yorkshire PTE, Wakefield (WY) 42 registered MUA 42P; Tayside Regional Council
(Planning Unit), Dundee (TE) P222 3/80; loaned to J Duff {Central Garage}, Crieff (TE) 6/80;
returned at an unknown date.
31920 [2]: New to West Yorkshire PTE, Wakefield (WY) 43 registered MUA 43P; Tayside Regional Council
(Planning Unit), Dundee (TE) P223 3/80; Tayside Regional Council, Dundee (TE) 223 6/83.

Notes:
31914 [2] (ex JUG 356N) (78): To service 4/87; reseated to B29F 1989; re-registered 12723 [3] 7/90.
31915 [2] (ex JUG 357N) (79): To service 4/87; reseated to B29F 1989; re-registered 12727 [3] 7/90.
31916 [2] (ex JUG 355N) (80): To service 4/87; reseated to B29F 1989; re-registered 31906 [3] 7/90.
31917 [2] (ex MUA 42P) (81): To service 4/87; reseated to B29F 1989; re-registered 31907 [3] 7/90; re-
registered 24775 [1] 5/92.
31920 [2] (ex MUA 43P) (82): To service 4/87; reseated to B29F 1989; re-registered 25701 [2] 5/95.

Disposals:
12723 [3] (ex 31914 [2], JUG 356N) (78): Dr JR Young, Nottingham (dealer / preservationist) 3/96; D
Crowther, Booker (BK) re-registered JUG 356N by8/96; unidentified owner, Ammanford for
preservation by12/00; D Wita, Ammanford for preservation by12/00; C Pearce, Worthing for
preservation 4/06; undientfied owner, Shoreham as mobile caravan by7/14; Attree, Shoreham
as mobile caravan 5/15.
12727 [3] (ex 31915 [2], JUG 357N) (79): Dr JR Young, Nottingham (dealer / preservationist) 3/96; D
Crowther, Booker (BK) re-registered JUG 357N by8/96; last licence expired 8/97; W Staniforth,
Birmingham for spares by12/00; moved to Stroud by12/05; current 3/16.
24775 [1] (ex 31907 [3], 31917 [2], MUA 42P) (81): Dr JR Young, Nottingham (dealer / preservationist) 3/96.
25701 [2] (ex 31920 [2] (ex MUA 43P) (82): SK Curtis {CT Coaches}, Haydon (SO) re-registered MUA 43P
by8/96; unidentified owner by10/00; last licence expired 11/00; unidentified owner as a caravan,
Bristol 6/02.
31906 [3] (ex 31916 [2], JUG 355N) (80): Cannibalised for spares; shell sold for use as a shed 5/94.

Vehicle acquired from London Bus Preservation Group, Cobham 5/87:

14	2388 [2]	AEC Regent III	O9613476	Weymann	W1464	H30/26R	1/50	11/00

Previous history:
> 2388 [2] (14): New to London Transport Executive, London SW1 (LN) RT2494 registered KXW 123; Lesney Products Ltd {Matchbox Toys}, London E9 (XLN) 2/77; London Bus Preservation Group, Cobham (dealer) 1/83.

Notes:
> 2388 [2] (ex KXW 123) (14): Rebuilt by Guernseybus Ltd to O29/26R 5/87; to service 8/87; re-registered 54636 5/97.

Disposal:
> 2388 [2] (ex KXW 123) (14): M Nash, Weybridge (dealer) 11/00; P Cruise, Fulham for preservation 8/01; re-registered KXW 123 by7/02; current 7/06.

Vehicle acquired from Doncaster MBC Education Department (XSY) 9/87:

WNG 105H	Bristol LHS6P	LHS-119	ECW	18126	DP35F	12/69	----

Previous history:
> WNG 105H: Ordered by Luton Corporation (BD) and intended to be XXE 135H (135) but diverted to United Counties Omnibus Co Ltd, Northampton (NO) (not operated) 1/70; Eastern Counties Omnibus Co Ltd, Norwich (NK) LHS599 2/70 (as B37F); reseated to DP35F 8/78; CF Booth Ltd, Rotherham (dealer) 12/80; Doncaster Metropolitan Borough Council (XSY) by9/81.

Notes:
> WNG 105H: Acquired for spares.

Disposal:
> WNG 105H: E Littlewood & Co Ltd, St Sampson (contractor) as a site office by7/90.

Vehicles on hire from BB Hire Cars Ltd, St Peter Port (XCI) 4-8/87:

4	29110	Ford Transit	BDVZHS97193	Ford	M14	8/87
2	49192	Ford Transit	BDVZHC65128	Ford	M11	4/87
9	49193	Ford Transit	BDVZHC65352	Ford	M14	5/87
10	49195	Ford Transit	BDVZHZ77961	Ford	M14	5/87
3	50188	Ford Transit	BDVZHE80310	Ford	M11	6/87

Notes:
> 29110 (4): On hire from 8/87; returned 11/88.
> 49192 (2): On hire from 4/87; returned 9/87.
> 49193 (9): On hire from 5/87; returned 10/87 (exported to the UK 2/88 as D823 EBJ).
> 49195 (10): On hire from 5/87; returned 10/87.
> 50188 (3): On hire from 6/87; returned 5/88 (exported to the UK 6/88 as D449 FRF).

1988

Vehicles acquired from National Welsh Omnibus Services Ltd, Cardiff (SG) 1/88:

83	19660 [2]	Bristol LHS6L	LHS-377	ECW	24706	B27F	11/80	10/95
84	19663 [2]	Bristol LHS6L	LHS-378	ECW	24707	B27F	11/80	4/92
85	19677 [2]	Bristol LHS6L	LHS-401	ECW	25062	B27F	7/81	-/--
86	19678 [2]	Bristol LHS6L	LHS-402	ECW	25063	B27F	7/81	3/95

Public Service Omnibus plates:

19660 [2] (83): 25	19677 [2] (85) (as 19675 [2]): 27
19663 [2] (84): 26	19678 [2] (86) (as 19676 [2]): 28

Previous histories:
> 19660 [2] (83): New to National Welsh Omnibus Services Ltd (SG) MD8023 registered GTX 758W (as DP27F); renumbered MD1391 1/83; renumbered MD391 2/86.
> 19663 [2] (84): New to National Welsh Omnibus Services Ltd (SG) MD8024 registered GTX 759W (as DP27F); renumbered MD1392 1/83; renumbered MD392 2/86.
> 19677 [2] (85): New to National Welsh Omnibus Services Ltd (SG) MD8114 registered KWO 568X (as DP27F); renumbered MD1397 1/83; renumbered MD397 2/86.

19678 [2] (86): New to National Welsh Omnibus Services Ltd (SG) MD8115 registered KWO 569X as DP27F); renumbered MD1398 1/83; renumbered MD398 2/86.

Notes:
19660 [2] (ex GTX 758W) (83): To service 4/88; reseated to B29F 1989.
19663 [2] (ex GTX 759W) (84): To service 4/88; reseated to B29F 1989.
19677 [2] (ex KWO 568X) (85): To service 4/88; reseated to B29F 1989; re-registered 19675 [2] 7/90.
19678 [2] (ex KWO 569X) (86): To service 4/88; reseated to B29F 1989; re-registered 19676 [2] 7/90.

Disposals:
19660 [2] (ex GTX 758W) (83): RS Brown {Shaftsbury & District Motor Services}, Motcombe (DT) re-registered GTX 758W 10/95; LV Carter, Colchester (EX) 2/96; LV Carter, East Bergholt (SK) by12/96; LV Carter, Ipswich (SK) 1/98; WP Woodrow {Plymouth & District}, Plymouth (DN) 7/99 and as a preserved vehicle 7/09.
19663 [2] (ex GTX 759W) (84): AJ Curtis, Midsomer Norton (SO) 5/92; Meehan, Newton Ferrers (DN) 4/94; LV Carter, East Bergholt (SK) for spares 3/97; LV Carter, Ipswich (SK) for spares 1/98; DJ Spall Recycling Ltd, Dallinghoo (dealer) for scrap by4/99.
19675 [2] (ex 19677 [2], KWO 568X) (85): No known disposal,
19676 [2] (ex 19678 [2], KWO 569X) (86): AJ Curtis, Midsomer Norton (SO) 3/95; A Hewlett, Bradley Stoke for preservation by9/01; Britishbus Preservation Group for preservation 2/02; destroyed in a banger racing meeting at Aldershot 8/13.

Vehicle acquired from Hampton Cars, Poole (XDT) 3/88:

4	14223 [2]	Mercedes Benz 307D	?		M10	11/83	3/90
		WDB??????2O590798					

Public Service Omnibus plate:
14223 [2] (4): 46

Previous history:
14223 [2] (4): New to Hampton Cars (XDT) registered A167 OOT; withdrawn 12/87.

Disposal:
14223 [2] (ex A167 OOT) (4): Central Transfers, St Peter Port (CI) 26 3/90; Guernseybus Ltd, St Peter Port (CI) 4 1/91; transferred to the service fleet 12/92 (qv).

Vehicle acquired from London Country Bus (North East) Ltd, Hertford (HT) 3/88:

RPH 103L	Bristol LHS6L	LHS-136	ECW	20442	B35F	10/73	----

Previous history:
RPH 103L: New to London Country Bus Services Ltd, Reigate (SR) BL3; used as a driver tuition vehicle from 4/80; London Country Bus (North East) Ltd BL3 as a driver tuition vehicle 9/86; withdrawn 12/86; J Sykes, Carlton (dealer) 2/88.

Notes:
RPH 103L: Acquired for spares.

Disposal:
RPH 103L: Broken up by Guernseybus Ltd by7/90.

Vehicle acquired from London Transport Executive, London SW1 (LN) 5/88:

59	14859 [2]	Bristol LH6L	LH-1327	ECW	21927	B41F	1/77	11/00

Public Service Omnibus plates:
14859 [2] (59): 8

Previous history:
14859 [2] (59): New to London Transport Executive, London SW1 (LN) BL72 registered OJD 72R.

Notes:
14859 [2] (OJD 72R) (59): Acquired in an accident damaged condition; to service 2/90.

Disposal:
14859 [2] (OJD 72R) (59): Unidentified dealer for scrap 12/00.

Vehicle acquired from Martyrs Memorial Church, Belfast (XAM) 6/88:

GPD 312N	Bristol LHS6L		LHS-179	ECW		21392	B35F	11/74	----

Previous history:

GPD 312N: New to London Country Bus Services Ltd, Reigate (SR) BN44 (originally allocated registration XPD 144N); Amalgamated Passenger Transport Ltd, Bracebridge Heath (dealer) 11/82; Martyrs Memorial Church, Belfast (XAM) 12/83.

Notes:

GPD 312N: Acquired for spares.

Disposal:

GPD 312N: Broken up by Guernseybus Ltd by7/90.

Vehicle acquired from Dr JR Young, Nottingham (dealer / preservationist) 7/88:

15	2634 [2]	AEC Regent III	O9613815	Weymann		L2241	H30/26RD	6/50	11/00

Public Service Omnibus plates:

2634 [2] (15): 56

Previous history:

2634 [2] (15): New to London Transport Executive, London SW1 (LN) RT1377 registered KXW 476 (as H30/26R); rebuilt to H30/26RD at an unknown date; Greater London Coucil, Wandsworth (XLN) as a playbus 3/73; Brakell Omnibus Sales (London) Ltd, Cheam (dealer) 11/79; RA Bluffield, Woburn Sands for a trip to New Zealand 8/80; Docklands Road Transport Museum for preservation by1986; London Passenger Transport League, Docklands Road Transport Museum for use as a tender 2/87; Dr JR Young, Nottingham 10/87.

Notes:

2634 [2] (ex KXW 476) (15): Rebuilt by Guernseybus Ltd to O29/26R 7/88; re-registered 58651 4/97.

Disposal:

58651 (ex 2634 [2], KXW 476) (15): M Nash, Weybridge (SR) 11/00; Island FM (radio station publicity vehicle), St Sampson (XCI) re-registered 65161 by12/01; S Munden {Bristol Bus & Coach Sales}, Bristol (dealer) 6/07; Zinnu Bus & Coach Works, Luqa (O-M) 10/08; undergoing refurbishment 5/09.

Vehicle acquired from P Day, St Saviour (XCI) 7/88:

87	18267 [2]	Bristol LHS6L		LHS-296	ECW		22044	B29F	12/76	3/96

Public Service Omnibus plate:

18267 [2] (87) (as 19677 [3]): 29

Previous history:

18267 [2] (87): New to London Transport Executive, London SW1 (LN) BS12 registered OJD 12R; P Day, St Saviour (XCI) re-registered J 29184 5/82 (and hired b to BBC during the making of the TV series 'Bergerac').

Notes:

18267 [2] (ex OJD 12R) (87): To service 10/88; re-registered 19677 [3] 7/90.

Disposal:

19677 [2] (ex 18267 [2], OJD 12R) (87): Dr JR Young, Nottingham (dealer / preservationist) 3/96; probably to an unidentified dealer for scrap 3/96.

Vehicle acquired from Logicrose Ltd, Slough (XBE) 8/88:

60	14857 [2]	Bristol LH6L		LH-1289	ECW		21902	B41F	7/76	10/00

Public Service Omnibus plates:

14857 [2] (60): 9

Previous history:
14857 [2] (60): New to London Transport Executive, London SW1 (LN) BL47 registered OJD 47R; DE Allmey {Allco}, Eastcote (dealer) by11/83; Logicrose Ltd (XBE) as a mobile exhibition unit 11/83.

Notes:
14857 [2] (ex OJD 47R) (60): To service 9/88.

Disposal:
14857 [2] (ex OJD 47R) (60): M Nash, Weybridge (dealer) 10/00; Harris, Portsmouth as a mobile caravan 12/00; re-registered OJD 47R by11/05; P McDonald, Portsmouth for preservation by1/06; last licence expired 6/06; advertised for sale 8/06; unidentified owner by12/10.

Vehicles acquired from Tentrek Expeditions Ltd {Transcity}, Sidcup (KT) 12/88:

57	14531 [2]	Bristol LH6L	LH-756	Marshall	35106	DP39F	8/73	12/90
58	14838 [2]	Bristol LH6L	LH-765	Marshall	35111	DP39F	4/74	12/90

Previous histories:
14531 [2] (57): New to Western National Omnibus Co Ltd, Exeter (DN) 1316 registered BDV 316L (as C39F); reseated to C37F 2/79; Southern National Ltd, Taunton (SO) 1316 1/83; withdrawn 12/86; Ensign (Bus Sales) Ltd, Purfleet (dealer) 3/87; Tentrek Expeditions Ltd {Transcity}, Sidcup (KT) 4/87.
14838 [2] (58): New to Western National Omnibus Co Ltd, Exeter (DN) 1322 registered NTT 322M (as C39F); reseated to C37F 3/79; Southern National Ltd, Taunton (SO) 1322 1/83; Ensign (Bus Sales) Ltd, Purfleet (dealer) 4/87; Tentrek Expeditions Ltd {Transcity}, Sidcup (KT) 4/87; withdrawn 10/88.

Notes:
14531 [2] (ex BDV 316L) (57): To service 7/89.
14838 [2] (ex NTT 322M) (58): To service 9/89.

Disposals:
14531 [2] (ex BDV 316L) (57): Western National Ltd, Truro (CO) 9500 as a driver trainer re-registered BDV 316L 1/91; withdrawn 7/94; A Hardwick, Carlton (dealer) for scrap 3/95.
14838 [2] (ex NTT 322M) (58): Western National Ltd, Truro (CO) 9501 as a driver trainer re-registered NTT 322M 1/91; withdrawn 4/97; unidentified dealer for scrap by12/00.

Vehicles acquired from Busways Travel Services Ltd, Newcastle upon Tyne (TW) 12/88:

54	29731 [2]	Bristol LH6L	LH-1240	ECW	21862	B41F	4/76	11/00
55	29732 [2]	Bristol LH6L	LH-1328	ECW	21928	B41F	1/77	11/00

Public Service Omnibus plates:
29731 [2] (54): 3   29732 [2] (55): 4

Previous histories:
29731 [1] (54): New to London Transport Executive, London SW1 (LN) BL7 registered KJD 407P; Busways Travel Services Ltd, Newcastle upon Tyne (TW) 1811 1/87; renumbered 1701 6/87; withdrawn 10/88.
29732 [2] (55): New to London Transport Executive, London SW1 (LN) BL73 registered OJD 73R; Busways Travel Services Ltd, Newcastle upon Tyne (TW) 1812 1/87; renumbered 1702 6/87; withdrawn 12/88.

Notes:
29731 [1] (ex KJD 407P) (54): To service 11/89.
29732 [2] (ex OJD 73R) (55): To service 11/89.

Disposals:
29731 [1] (ex KJD 407P) (54): M Nash, Weybridge (dealer) 10/00; Tally Ho! Coaches Ltd, Kingsbridge (DN) for spares 11/00; unidentified dealer for scrap by6/02.
29732 [2] (ex OJD 73R) (55): M Nash, Weybridge (dealer) 10/00; Production Cars, Streatham for film work (XLN) 12/00.

Vehicle acquired from Dr JR Young, Nottingham (dealer / preservationist) 12/88:

16	2493 [2]	Leyland PS1/1	500330	Reading	7939	B34F	5/51	11/00

Public Service Omnibus plates:
> 2493 [2] (16): 59

Previous history:
> 2493 [2] (16): New to Jersey Motor Transport Co Ltd, St Helier (CI) 44 registered J 5567; JMT Ltd, St Helier (CI) 44 3/73; withdrawn 10/74; J Le Gresley, La Rocque 11/75; Dr JR Young for preservation 10/83.

Notes:
> 2493 [2] (ex J 5567) (16): Rebodied by Guernseybus Ltd as OB35F 1989; to service 7/89; re-registered 12523 by5/98.

Disposal:
> 12523 (ex 2493 [2], J 5567) (16): M Nash, Weybridge (dealer) 11/00; Dewar {Mac Tours}, Cockenzie (LO) 16 2/01; re-registered YSL 334 7/01; Mac Tours Ltd, Cockenzie (LO) 22 4/02; re-registered 840 XUJ 2/09; Ensign Bus & Coach Co Ltd, Purfleet 22 for preservation 2/09; P Talbot {Char A Banc}, St Helier (CI) re-registered J 1942 2/12 (as OB34F) (on loan 2/12-2/14).

Vehicles on hire from BB Hire Cars Ltd, St Peter Port (XCI) 5-7/88:

1	39121	Ford Transit	Ford		M11	5/88
		SFAZXXBDVZJA38031				
9	44525	Ford Transit	Ford		M14	5/88
		SFAZXXBDVZJG42274				
2	45144	Ford Transit	Ford		M11	6/88
		SFAZXXBDVZJG38989				
10	46088	Ford Transit	Ford		M14	6/88
		SFAZXXBDVZJG42272				
8	46921	Ford Transit	Ford		M14	7/88
		SFAZXXBDVZJG42273				

Notes:
> 39121 (1): On hire from 5/88; returned 10/88 (exported 10/88).
> 44525 (9): On hire from 5/88; returned 10/88 (to Central Taxis Ltd, St Peter Port (CI) 12/88 (qv)).
> 45144 (2): On hire from 6/88; returned 10/88 (exported to the UK 11/88 as E531 NFA).
> 46088 (10): On hire from 6/88; returned 10/88 (exported to the UK 11/88 as E538 NFA).
> 46921 (8): On hire from 7/88; returned 10/88 (exported to the UK 11/88 as E533 NFA).

1989

Vehicle acquired from J Sykes, Carlton (dealer) 2/89:

	GTB 906	Leyland PD1	460833	(chassis only)	7/46	----

Previous history:
> GTB 906: New to Lytham St Annes Corporation (LA) 16 (with a Leyland H30/26R body); Cross, St Annes 6/71; Lytham St Annes Society for Mentally Handicapped Children (XLA) 10/71; GR Cunliffe & DN Hamilton, St Annes for preservation 5/74; PK Historic Omnibus, Hunmanby for preservation by11/86; J Sykes (dealer) 7/88; body broken up by Sykes 2/89.

Notes:
> GTB 906: Acquired for spares.

Disposal:
> GTB 906: Chassis broken up by Guernseybus c1989.

Vehicle acquired from A & R Millman, Buckfastleigh (DN) 7/89:

159	31909 [2]	Bristol LHS6L	LHS-215	Plaxton	758BC021S	C37F	-/75	11/00

Public Service Omnibus plate:
> 31909 [2] (159): 64

Previous history:
31909 [2] (159): New to Soudley Valley Coaches Ltd, Soudley (GL) registered JFH 473N; A & R Millman (DN) at an unknown date.

Notes:
31909 [2] (ex JFH 473N) (159): Renumbered 157 1/91; re-registered 31907 [4] 5/92.

Disposal:
31907 [4] (ex 31909 [2], JFH 473N) (157, ex 159): M Nash, Weybridge (dealer) 11/00; EJ & JKD Deeble {Caradon Riviera}, Upton Cross (not operated) (CO) 2/01; unidentified owner by8/08.

Vehicle acquired from Country Bus Co, Atherington (DN) 8/89:

56	29733 [2]	Bristol LH6L	LH-1251	ECW	21873	B41F	5/76	11/00

Public Service Omnibus plate:
29733 [2] (56): 5

Previous history:
29733 [2] (56): New to London Transport Executive, London SW1 (LN) BL18 registered KJD 418P; Country Bus Co c10/86.

Notes:
29733 [2] (ex KJD 418P) (56): To service 9/89.

Disposal:
29733 [2] (ex KJD 418P) (56): M Nash, Weybridge (dealer) 12/00; Silver Star Coach Holidays Ltd, Caernarfon (GD) for spares 9/01; scrapped by8/03.

Vehicle acquired from JA Redford {Blue Lake}, Chichester (WS) 11/89:

88	2972 [3]	Bristol LHS6L	LHS-169	ECW	21384	B37F	2/75	3/96

Public Service Omnibus plate:
2972 [3] (88) (as 19678 [3]): 30

Previous history:
2972 [3] (88): New to London Country Bus Services Ltd, Reigate (SR) BN36 registered GPD 304N (originally allocated registration XPD 136N) (as B35F); Rennie's of Dunfermline Ltd, Dunfermline (FE) 5/83; G Davies, Ebbw Vale (GT) 6/84; MP Ash {Martin's Transport}, High Wycombe (BK) 10/86; JA Redford {Blue Lake} 3/87.

Notes:
2972 [3] (ex GPD 304N) (88): To service 2/90; re-registered 19678 [3] 7/90.

Disposal:
19678 [3] (ex 2972 [3], GPD 304N) (88): Dr JR Young, Nottingham (dealer / preservationist) 3/96; DH Crowther {Classic Coaches}, Booker (BK) re-registered GPD 304N by8/96; last licence expired 11/99; probably to an unidentified dealer for scrap by2/01.

Vehicle acquired from Dr JR Young, Nottingham (dealer / preservationist) 12/89:

17	9434 [2]	Leyland PS1/1	500330	Reading	7939	B34F	5/51	11/00

Previous history:
9434 [2] (17): New to Jersey Motor Transport Co Ltd, St Helier (CI) 49 registered J 5660; JMT Ltd, St Helier (CI) 49 3/73; withdrawn 10/74; J Le Gresley, La Rocque 11/75; Dr JR Young for preservation 10/83.

Notes:
9434 [2] (ex J 5660) (17): Rebodied by Guernseybus Ltd as B35F (with a sliding sun-roof) 1992; reseated to B33F before entering service; to service 8/92; re-registered 28231 by3/97.

Disposal:

    28231 (ex 9434 [2], J 5660) (17): M Nash, Weybridge (dealer) 11/00; Dewar {Mac Tours}, Cockenzie (EL) 17 12/00; re-registered OAS 624 2/03; Mac Tours Ltd, Cockenzie (EL) 23 4/02; re-registered 839 XUJ 2/09; Ensign Bus & Coach Co Ltd, Purfleet 22 for preservation (as B31F) 2/09; Belfast Duck Tours Ltd {Belfast City Sightseeing} (AM) 11/12; advertised for sale 1/19.

Vehicles on hire from BB Hire Cars Ltd, St Peter Port (XCI) 5-7/88:

8	15872	Ford Transit SFAZXXBDVZJT93916	Ford	M11	6/89
3	53499	Ford Transit SFAZXXBDVZKJ97070	Ford	M14	5/89
2	53515	Ford Transit SFAZXXBDVZKJ97069	Ford	M14	5/89
1	53516	Ford Transit SFAZXXBDVZKJ97068	Ford	M14	5/89

Notes:

    15872 (8): On hire from 5/89; returned 11/89 (exported to the UK 11/89 as F799 WBF).
    53499 (3): On hire from 5/89; returned 10/89 (exported to the UK 11/89 as F797 WBF).
    53515 (2): On hire from 5/89; returned 10/89 (exported to the UK 11/89 as F795 WBF).
    53516 (1): On hire from 5/89; returned 10/89 (exported to the UK 11/89 as F796 WBF).

1990

Vehicles acquired from Tally Ho! Coaches Ltd, Kingsbridge (DN) 3/90:

51	29728 [2]	Bristol LH6L	LH-1290	ECW	21903	B39F	9/76	8/96
52	29729 [2]	Bristol LH6L	LH-1306	ECW	21919	B39F	1/77	11/98
53	29730 [2]	Bristol LH6L	LH-1367	ECW	21949	B39F	-/77	10/00

Public Service Omnibus plates:

    29728 [2] (51): 1   29729 [2] (52): 48   29730 [2] (53): 2

Previous histories:

    29728 [2] (51): New to London Transport Executive, London SW1 (LN) BL48 registered OJD 48R (as B39F); Davies Bros (Pencader) Ltd (DD) 139 1/83; reseated to B43F and to service 3/83; Thamesdown Transport, Swindon (WI) 45 10/84; Tyne & Wear Omnibus Co Ltd, Gateshead (TW) 2/89; Coolfirm Ltd {Go-Ahead Northern}, Gateshead (TW) 11/89; reseated to B39F at an unknown date; Lister PVS (Bolton) Ltd (dealer) 3/90; Tally Ho! Coaches Ltd (DN) (not operated) 3/90.
    29729 [2] (52): New to London Transport Executive, London SW1 (LN) BL64 registered OJD 64R; Ensign Bus Co Ltd, Purfleet (dealer) 11/82; Rhymney Valley District Council, Caerphilly (MG) 32 1/83; Inter Valley Link Ltd, Caerphilly (MG) 13 10/86; Trimdon Motor Services Ltd, Trimdon Grange (DM) (not operated) 5/87; Tyne & Wear Omnibus Co Ltd, Gateshead (TW) 7/87; Coolfirm Ltd {Go-Ahead Northern}, Gateshead (TW) 11/89; Lister PVS (Bolton) Ltd (dealer) 2/90; Tally Ho! Coaches Ltd (DN) (not operated) 3/90.
    29730 [2] (53): New to London Transport Executive, London SW1 (LN) BL94 registered OJD 94R; Tyne & Wear Omnibus Co Ltd, Gateshead (TW) 7/88; Coolfirm Ltd {Go-Ahead Northern}, Gateshead (TW) 11/89; Lister PVS (Bolton) Ltd (dealer) 2/90; Tally Ho! Coaches Ltd (DN) (not operated) 3/90.

Notes:

    29728 [2] (ex OJD 48R) (51): To service 7/90.
    29729 [2] (ex OJD 64R) (52): To service 5/90.
    29730 [2] (ex OJD 94R) (53): To service 5/90.

Disposals:

    29728 [2] (ex OJD 48R) (51): Broken up by Guernseybus Ltd 8/96.
    29729 [2] (ex OJD 64R) (52): Cannibalised for spares; shell to Airport Fire Service, Forest for training exercises 5/00.
    29730 [2] (ex OJD 94R) (53): M Nash, Weybridge (dealer) 10/00; A Austin, Strood as a caravan 3/01.

Vehicles acquired from Midland Red (North) Ltd, Cannock (WM) 7/90:

7	18264 [2]	Freight Rover	AN268523	Dormobile	6843	B16F	8/86	4/96
8	18265 [2]	Freight Rover	AN268524	Dormobile	6844	B16F	8/86	5/95
9	18266 [2]	Freight Rover	AN267116	Dormobile	6841	B16F	8/86	-/--
10	18267 [3]	Freight Rover	AN268269	Dormobile	6849	B16F	8/86	5/96

Public Service Omnibus plates:

18264 [2] (7): 41   18266 [2] (9): 43
18265 [2] (8): 42   18267 [3] (10): 45

Previous histories:

18264 [2] (7): New to Midland Red (North) Ltd (ST) 66 registered D 66 YRF; Lloyd, Stafford (dealer) 7/90.
18265 [2] (8): New to Midland Red (North) Ltd (ST) 67 registered D 67 YRF; Lloyd, Stafford (dealer) 7/90.
18266 [2] (9): New to Midland Red (North) Ltd (ST) 64 registered D 64 YRF; Lloyd, Stafford (dealer) 7/90.
18267 [3] (10): New to Midland Red (North) Ltd (ST) 72 registered D 72 YRF; Lloyd, Stafford (dealer) 7/90.

Notes:

18264 [2] (ex D 66 YRF) (7): Re-registered 3338 [3] 2/95; renumbered 12 3/96.
18266 [2] (ex D 64 YRF) (9): Renumbered 13 3/96.

Disposals:

3338 [3] (ex 18264 [2], D 66 YRF) (12, ex 7): Broken up by Guernseybus Ltd 4/96.
18265 [2] (ex D 67 YRF) (8): Broken up by Guernseybus Ltd 5/95.
18266 [2] (ex D 64 YRF) (13, ex 9): No known disposal (probably broken up by Guernseybus Ltd).
18267 [3] (ex D 72 YRF) (10): Broken up by Guernseybus Ltd 5/96.

Vehicle acquired from Darley Dale Bus Co {Dodsley}, Ripley (DE) 7/90:

18	2972 [4]	AEC Regent III	O9615574	Weymann	W1403	H30/26RD	2/51	11/00

Previous history:

2972 [4] (18): New to London Transport Executive, London SW1 (LN) RT4037 registered LUC 196; Kettering Tyre Co Ltd, Ripley (XDE) re-registered ACH 845A 1/80; Darley Dale Bus Co {Dodsley} (DE) at an unknown date; last licence expired 7/90.

Notes:

2972 [4] (ex LUC 196) (18): Rebuilt by Guernseybus Ltd to O30/26R from 7/90; to service 7/94.

Disposal:

2972 [4] (ex LUC 196) (18): M Nash, Weybridge (SR) 11/00; Dansk Veteranbil Udlejning, Hillerod (O-DK) 9/01.

Vehicles on hire from BB Hire Cars Ltd, St Peter Port (XCI) 5-7/88:

1	35698	Ford Transit	Ford	M14	2/90
		SFAZXXBDVZLL79819			
2	42896	Ford Transit	Ford	M14	3/90
		SFAZXXBDVZLL79453			
3	45093	Ford Transit	Ford	M14	3/90
		SFAZXXBDVZLL79818			
4	45833	Ford Transit	Ford	M14	3/90
		SFAZXXBDVZLL79817			

Notes:

35698 (1): On hire from 2/90; returned 7/90 (exported to the UK 7/90 as G124 FRE).
42896 (2): On hire from 3/90; returned 7/90.
45093 (3): On hire from 3/90; returned 7/90.
45833 (4): On hire from 3/90; returned 7/90.

1991

Vehicles acquired from Western National Ltd, Truro (CO) 1/91:

74	12728 [3]	Bristol LHS6L	LHS-226	ECW		21575	B35F	7/75	1/96
75	14531 [3]	Bristol LHS6L	LHS-353	ECW		23612	B35F	12/79	7/95
76	14838 [3]	Bristol LHS6L	LHS-354	ECW		23613	B35F	12/79	by3/00
158	31908 [2]	Bristol LH6L	LH-1060	Plaxton	7510BC007S		C43F	6/75	11/00
159	31909 [3]	Bristol LH6L	LH-1063	Plaxton	7510BC008S		C43F	7/75	11/00

Public Service Omnibus plates:

14531 [3] (75): 6   31908 [2] (158): 69
14838 [3] (76): 7   31909 [3] (159):

Previous histories:

12728 [3] (74): New to Southern Vectis Omnibus Co Ltd, Newport (IW) 839 registered HDL 415N; United Automobile Services Ltd, Darlington (DM) 1455 6/84; Western National Ltd, Truro (CO) 1570 1988.

14531 [3] (75): New to Western National Omnibus Co Ltd, Exeter (DN) 1560 registered FDV 790V; Western National Ltd, Truro (CO) 1560 1/83; withdrawn 10/90.

14838 [3] (76): New to Western National Omnibus Co Ltd, Exeter (DN) 1561 registered FDV 791V; Western National Ltd, Truro (CO) 1561 1/83; withdrawn 10/90.

31908 [2] (158): New to Greenslades Tours Ltd, Exeter (DN) 317 registered JFJ 497N; Western National Omnibus Co Ltd, Exeter (DN) 1332 5/78; reseated to C43F 6/79; Western National Ltd, Truro (CO) 1332 1/83.

31909 [3] (159): New to Greenslades Tours Ltd, Exeter (DN) 318 registered JFJ 498N; Western National Omnibus Co Ltd, Exeter (DN) 1333 5/78; reseated to C43F 6/79; Western National Ltd, Truro (CO) 1333 1/83.

Notes:

12728 [3] (ex HDL 415N) (74): To service 2/91; re-registered 19662 [2] and reseated to B37F 3/91.

14531 [3] (ex FDV 790V) (75): To service 2/91.

14838 [3] (ex FDV 791V) (76): To service 2/91; renumbered 73 9/96; renumbered 58 12/97.

31908 [2] (ex JFJ 497N) (158): Shortened to 32ft Guernseybus Ltd (in order to comply with maximum legal length on Guernsey) prior to entry into service; to service 9/93.

31909 [3] (ex JFJ 498N) (159): Shortened to 32ft Guernseybus Ltd (in order to comply with maximum legal length on Guernsey) prior to entry into service; to service 5/92.

Disposals:

14531 [3] (ex FDV 790V) (75): Dr JR Young, Nottingham (dealer / preservationist) 3/96; C Billington, Maidenhead (dealer / preservationist) re-registered FDV 790V 3/96; current 9/18.

14838 [3] (ex FDV 791V) (58, ex 73, 76): In use as a shed by3/00.

19662 [2] (ex 12728 [3], HDL 415N) (74): Dr JR Young, Nottingham (dealer / preservationist) 3/96; probably to an unidentified dealer for scrap 3/96.

31908 [2] (ex JFJ 497N) (158): Transferred to the States of Guernsey, St Peter Port 11/00; C Billington, Maidenhead (dealer / preservationist) 3/01; Rexquote Ltd, Bishops Lydeard (SO) (not operated) 11/01; used for spares from 12/02; unidentified dealer for scrap 12/02.

31909 [3] (ex JFJ 498N) (159): Transferred to the States of Guernsey, St Peter Port 11/00; C Billington, Maidenhead (dealer / preservationist) 3/01; Exeter LH Group for preservation 10/01; T Partridge, Saltash for preservation for spares 9/05; T Wigley & Son (Bus) Ltd, Carlton (dealer) for scrap 4/06.

Vehicles acquired from Central Transfers, St Peter Port (CI) 1/91:

4	14223 [2]	Mercedes Benz 307D		?		M10	11/83	12/92
		WDB??????2O590798					
3	44525	Ford Transit		Ford		M14	5/88	1/95
		SFAZXXBDVZJG42274					
5	48701	Mercedes Benz 310		Devon Conversions		M12	-/86	1/95
		WDB6020672O610511					
6	48702	Mercedes Benz 310		Devon Conversions		M11	-/86	1/95
		WDB6020672O610002			98365D		
2	49377	Ford Transit	BDVZHJ6L9140	Ford		M14	12/87	1/95

Public Service Omnibus plates:

44525 (3): 50   49377 (2): 49

Previous histories:
14223 [2] (4): New to Hampton Cars, Poole (XDT) registered A167 OOT; withdrawn 12/87; Guernseybus Ltd, St Peter Port (CI) 4 3/88; Central Transfers, St Peter Port (CI) 26 3/90.

44525 (3): New to BB Hire Cars Ltd, St Peter Port (XCI); hired to Guernseybus Ltd (CI) 9 5/88-10/88; Central Taxis Ltd, St Peter Port (CI) 12/88; Educational Holidays Guernsey Ltd {Island Coachways} (CI) 10/89; Central Transfers, St Peter Port (CI) 22 3/90.

48701 (5): New to Jacksons Garage, Forest (XCI); Guernseybus Ltd, St Peter Port (CI) 5 3/87; Central Transfers, St Peter Port (CI) 25 3/90.

48702 (6): New to Jacksons Garage, Forest (XCI); Guernseybus Ltd, St Peter Port (CI) 6 3/87; Central Transfers, St Peter Port (CI) 24 3/90.

49377 (2): New to Central Taxis Ltd, St Peter Port (CI); Educational Holidays Guernsey Ltd {Island Coachways} (CI) 10/89; Central Transfers, St Peter Port (CI) 21 3/90.

Disposals:
14223 [2] (4): Transferred to the service fleet 12/92 (qv).

44525 (3): Central Transfers Ltd, St Peter Port (CI) 3 1/95; Intransit Ltd, St Peter Port (CI) 3 12/96; withdrawn 9/03.

48701 (5): Central Transfers Ltd, St Peter Port (CI) 5 1/95; withdrawn at an unknown date.

48702 (6): Central Transfers Ltd, St Peter Port (CI) 6 1/95; Intransit Ltd, St Peter Port (CI) 6 12/96; withdrawn 6/02.

49377 (2): Central Transfers Ltd, St Peter Port (CI) 2 1/95; withdrawn at an unknown date.

Vehicle acquired from Manchester Minibuses Ltd {Bee Line Buzz Co} (GM) 6/91:

11	29694	Freight Rover	271133	Carlyle	CFL552	B20F	1/87	by5/98

Previous history:
29694 (11): New to Manchester Minibuses Ltd {Bee Line Buzz Co} (GM) registered D126 NON; Ribble Motor Services Ltd, Preston (LA) 3126 9/88; Bee Line Buzz Co Ltd, Stockport (CH) 3126 9/89; Carlyle Works Ltd, Birmingham (dealer) 5/91.

Disposal:
29694 (ex D126 NON) (11): No known disposal.

1992

Vehicle acquired from MJ Perry {Bromyard Omnibus Co}, Bromyard (HW) 1/92:

50	31908 [3]	Bristol LH6L	LH-1288	ECW	21901	B39F	9/76	10/00

Previous history:
31908 [3] (50): New to London Transport Executive, London SW1 (LN) BL46 registered OJD 46R; Grampian PTE, Aberdeen (GN) 46 12/82; hired to Mair, Dyce (GN) 10-12/87; Mair, Dyce (GN) 12/88; Wacton Trading / Coach Sales, Bromyard (dealer) 12/91; MJ Perry {Bromyard Omnibus Co} 46 (named 'Douglas') 12/91.

Notes:
31908 [3] (ex OJD 46R) (50): To service 6/92; re-registered 25702 [2] 10/93.

Disposal:
25702 [2] (ex 31908 [3], OJD 46R) (50): M Nash, Weybridge (dealer) 10/00; Tally Ho! Coaches Ltd, Kingsbridge (DN) for spares 12/00; unidentified dealer for scrap by6/02.

Vehicle acquired from Smith's (Buntingford) Ltd (HT) 1/92:

57	28402 [2]	Bristol LH6L	LH-1278	ECW	21893	B41F	8/76	10/00

Public Service Omnibus plates:
28402 [2] (as 10026) (57): 27.

Previous history:
28402 [2] (57): New to London Transport Executive, London SW1 (LN) BL38 registered KJD 438P; Smith's (Buntingford) Ltd 7/83.

Notes:
28402 [2] (ex KJD 438P) (57): Re-registered 10026 and to service 2/94.

Disposal:
  10026 (ex 28402 [2], KJD 438P): M Nash, Weybridge (dealer) 10/00; Tally Ho! Coaches Ltd, Kingsbridge
  (DN) for spares 12/00; unidentified dealer for scrap by6/02.

1993

Vehicles acquired from Western National Ltd, Truro (CO) 1/93:

170	31920 [3]	Bristol LH6L	LH-1573	Plaxton	7910BXM515S	C41F	9/79	11/00
171	31921 [2]	Bristol LH6L	LH-1576	Plaxton	7910BXM518S	C41F	10/79	11/00

Public Service Omnibus plates:
  31920 [3] (170): 41   31921 [2] (171): 42

Previous histories:
  31920 [3] (170): New to Western National Ltd (CO) 3313 registered AFJ 733T.
  31921 [2] (171): New to Western National Ltd (CO) 3316 registered AFJ 736T.

Notes:
  31920 [3] (ex AFJ 733T) (170): Shortened to 32ft Guernseybus Ltd (in order to comply with maximum legal
  length on Guernsey) prior to entry into service; to service 5/95.
  31921 [2] (ex AFJ 736T) (171): Shortened to 32ft Guernseybus Ltd (in order to comply with maximum legal
  length on Guernsey) prior to entry into service; to service 5/96.

Disposal:
  31920 [3] (ex AFJ 733T) (170): Transferred to the States of Guernsey, St Peter Port 11/00.
  31921 [2] (ex AFJ 736T) (171): Transferred to the States of Guernsey, St Peter Port 11/00 and leased to
  Island Coachways Ltd, St Peter Port (CI) 171 12/00; Rexquote Ltd, Bishops Lydeard (SO) (not
  operated) 11/01; A Goddard, West Ewell for preservation 3/03; re-registered AFJ 736T by6/18;
  P Emery, Chase Terrace for preservation 6/18.

Vehicle on demonstration from Bougourd, St Peter Port (dealer) 1/93:

20	35940	FIAT 59.12	2002453	Marshall	C31.001	B29F	-/--	

Public Service Omnibus plate:
  35940: 84

Notes:
  35940: Returned 2/93.

Vehicle on demonstration from Mercedes-Benz, Tankersley 7/93:

30938	Mercedes Benz 811D		Plaxton	928.5MLV1094	B31F	11/92
	WDB6703032P234791					

Notes:
  30938: New as a demonstrator with Mercedes Benz registered K455 EDT; returned 7/93.

1994

Vehicles acquired from Tantivy Holiday Coach Tours Ltd, St Helier (CI) 7/94:

172	31922 [2]	Bristol LH6L	LH-1532	Plaxton	7810BXM514S	C45F	4/79	-/95
174	31923 [3]	Bristol LH6L	LH-1537	Plaxton	7810BXM517S	C45F	4/79	11/00
173	31924 [2]	Bristol LH6L	LH-1564	Plaxton	7910BXM511S	C45F	6/79	11/00

Public Service Omnibus plates:
  31922 [2] (172):   31923 [3] (173): 66   31924 [2]) 174): 65

Previous histories:
  31922 [2] (172): New to Western National Omnibus Co Ltd, Exeter (DN) 3302 registered AFJ 722T (as C43F);
  North Devon Ltd, Barnstaple (DN) 3302 1/83; Holiday Tours Ltd {Holiday Coach Tours}, St Peter
  (CI) 6 re-registered J 28766 3/87; Tantivy Holiday Coach Tours Ltd 6 1/93.
  31923 [3] (174): New to Western National Omnibus Co Ltd, Exeter (DN) 3323 registered AFJ 743T (as C41F);
  Devon General Ltd, Exeter (DN) 3323 1/83; Holiday Tours Ltd {Holiday Coach Tours}, St Peter
  (CI) 69 re-registered J 11791 5/89; Tantivy Holiday Coach Tours Ltd 9 1/93.

31924 [2] (173): New to Western National Omnibus Co Ltd, Exeter (DN) 3305 registered AFJ 725T (as C43F); North Devon Ltd, Barnstaple (DN) 3305 1/83; Holiday Tours Ltd {Holiday Coach Tours}, St Peter (CI) 3 re-registered J 18313 6/87; Tantivy Holiday Coach Tours Ltd 3 1/93.

Notes:
31922 [2] (ex J 28766, AFJ 722T) (172): To service 9/94; withdrawn following an accident 1995.
31923 [3] (ex J 11791, AFJ 743T) (174): To service 9/94.
31924 [2] (ex J 18313, AFJ 725T) (173): To service 5/95.

Disposals:
31922 [2] (ex J 28766, AFJ 722T) (172): Scrapped 1998.
31923 [3] (ex J 11791, AFJ 743T) (174): Transferred to the States of Guernsey, St Peter Port 11/00; Taw & Torridge, Merton (DN) for spares by6/02; unidentified dealer, Bideford for scrap by2/06.
31924 [2] (ex J 18313, AFJ 725T) (173): Transferred to the States of Guernsey, St Peter Port 11/00; RS Brown {Shaftsbury & District Motor Services}, Motcombe (DT) (not operated) 5/01; Shaftsbury & District Motor Services Ltd, Motcombe (DT) (not operated) 12/02; L Burt, Shaftesbury for preservation 12/02; Shaftsbury & District Motor Services Ltd, Motcombe (DT) for spares by2/09.

Vehicles acquired from Dr JR Young, Nottingham (dealer / preservationist) 10/94:

19	995	Leyland 7RT	502098	Park Royal	L1544	H--/--RD	7/50	11/00
20	LLU 804	AEC Regent III	O9613491	Park Royal	L3189	H30/26R	2/50	----

Public Service Omnibus plate:
995 (19): 15

Previous histories:
LLU 804 (20): Chassis: New to London Transport Executive, London SW1 (LN) RT1597 registered KLB 719; J Huxford & D Good (and also initially D Mikelas), Epsom for preservation c4/77; body burnt out 6/85. Body: New to London Transport Executive, London SW1 (LN) latterly on RT1896 (LLU 804); Gor-ray, Brakell & Lamming {RT1896 Preservation Group}, Bexley for preservation; RT1896 Group for preservation by12/84; J Huxford & D Good, Epsom for preservation spares by2/87; transferred to chassis of KLB 719 (retaining the registration LLU 804) by10/94.
995 (19): New to London Transport Executive, London SW1 (LN) RTL1004 registered KYY 647; London Borough of Lambeth (XLN) as an exhibition unit 6/67 and as a mobile safety unit 3/73; unidentified dealer, Colchester 1978; D Burton (& possibly Slater), London NW6 for preservation by4/79; Abbotts Langley Transport Circle for preservation 3/80; Dr JR Young by11/87.

Notes:
995 (ex KYY 647) (19): Rebuilt to H29/23F and to service 12/95; re-registered 47312 by3/97.
LLU 804 (ex KLB 719) (20): Rebuilt with a front-entrance but did not enter service with Guernseybus Ltd.

Disposal:
47312 (ex 995, KYY 647): M Nash, Weybridge (SR) 11/00; re-registered KYY 647 9/02; A Ullmer, Enfield for preservation 8/04; Boultbee Flight Academy Ltd, Goodwood (XWS) as an office within a hangar 8/12.
LLU 804 (ex KLB 719) (20): M Nash, Weybridge (SR) 11/00; K & S Austin, Sidcup for preservation 8/01; current 4/19.

Vehicle acquired from Thames Transit Ltd, Oxford (OX) 97 11/94:

175	31925 [3]	Bristol LH6L	LH-1561	Plaxton	7910BXM509S	C41F	6/79	----

Previous history:
31925 [3] (175): New to Western National Omnibus Co Ltd, Exeter (DN) 3321 registered AFJ 741T; Devon General Ltd, Exeter (DN) 3321 1/83; Thames Transit Ltd 97 10/87.

Notes:
31925 [3] (ex AFJ 741T) (175): Not operated by Guernseybus Ltd; the registration 31925 was allocated to 81 (ex G137 WOW) 12/97; AFJ 741T was un-registered after this date.

Disposal:
31925 [3] (ex AFJ 741T) (175): Unidentified owner by5/98.

1995

Vehicles acquired from Derby City Transport (DE) 5/95:

1	25474	Volkswagen LT55	HH012365	Optare	268	B25F	8/87	11/00
2	25845	Volkswagen LT55	HH017453	Optare	269	B25F	9/87	11/00
3	27237	Volkswagen LT55	HH021490	Optare	277	B25F	9/87	11/00
4	27308	Volkswagen LT55	HH021494	Optare	282	B25F	10/87	11/00

Previous histories:

25474 (1): New to Yorkshire Rider Ltd, Leeds (WY) 2005 registered E205 PWY; Derby City Transport 80 1/90.

25845 (2): New to Yorkshire Rider Ltd, Leeds (WY) 2006 registered E206 PWY; Derby City Transport 89 1/90.

27237 (3): New to Yorkshire Rider Ltd, Leeds (WY) 2014 registered E214 PWY; Derby City Transport 87 1/90.

27308 (4): New to Yorkshire Rider Ltd, Leeds (WY) 2019 registered E219 PWY; Derby City Transport 88 1/90.

Notes:

Whilst the original registrations of these vehicles is established, it is not confirmed that the above order that they were numbered and re-registered on Guernsey is correct.

Disposal:

25474 (ex E205 PWY) (1): Unidentified dealer for scrap 12/00.

25845 (ex E206 PWY) (4): Unidentified dealer for scrap 12/00.

27308 (ex E219 PWY) (3): Unidentified dealer for scrap 12/00.

27237 (ex E214 PWY) (2): Unidentified dealer for scrap 12/00.

1996

Vehicles acquired from Derby City Transport (DE) 2/96:

5	32751	Volkswagen LT55	HH000935	Optare	257	B25F	7/87	11/00
9	53428	Volkswagen LT55	HH012367	Optare	270	B25F	9/87	11/00
7	53467	Volkswagen LT55	HH012375	Optare	251	B25F	7/87	by12/99
8	54537	Volkswagen LT55	HH021492	Optare	280	B25F	9/87	8/99
6	55159	Volkswagen LT55	HH000857	Optare	250	B25F	7/87	11/00

Public Service Omnibus plates:

32751 (5): 20	53467 (7): 23	55159 (6): 21
53428 (9): 30	54537 (8): 24	

Previous histories:

32751 (5): New to Leicester Citybus Ltd (LE) 848 registered D848 CRY; Loughborough Coach & Bus Co Ltd (LE) M848 7/88; Derby City Transport Ltd 069 9/89.

53428 (9): New to Yorkshire Rider Ltd, Leeds (WY) 2007 registered E207 PWY; Derby City Transport 91 2/90.

53467 (7): New to Southend Transport Ltd (EX) registered E402 BHK; Derby City Transport (DE) 082 9/89.

54537 (8): New to Yorkshire Rider Ltd, Leeds (WY) 2017 registered E217 PWY; Derby City Transport 90 12/89.

55159 (6): New to Southend Transport Ltd (EX) registered E401 BHK; Derby City Transport 081 9/89.

Notes:

53428 (ex E207 PWY) (9): Renumbered 8 by8/99.

Disposals:

32751 (ex D848 CRY) (5): Unidentified dealer for scrap 12/00.

53428 (ex E207 PWY) (8, ex 9): Unidentified dealer for scrap 12/00.

53467 (ex E402 BHK) (7): Scrapped by12/99.

54537 (ex E217 BHK) (8): Scrapped 8/99.

55159 (ex E401 BHK) (6): Unidentified dealer for scrap 12/00.

Vehicle acquired from Western National Ltd, Truro (CO) 4/96:

AFJ 720T	Bristol LH6L	LH-1530	Plaxton	7810BXM512S	C43F	5/79	----

Previous history:
AFJ 720T: New to Western National Omnibus Co Ltd, Exeter (DN) 3300; Western National Ltd (CO) 3300 1/83.

Notes:
AFJ 720T: Acquired for spares.

Disposal:
AFJ 720T: No known disposal.

Vehicles acquired from Metrobus Ltd, Orpington (LN) 9-10/96:

75	19676 [3]	Optare MR03	VN1147	Optare	1147	B25F	11/91	11/00
76	19677 [4]	Optare MR03	VN1151	Optare	1151	B25F	11/91	11/00
77	19678 [4]	Optare MR03	VN1134	Optare	1134	B25F	11/91	11/00

Public Service Omnibus plates:
19676 [3]: 51   19677 [4]: 53   19678 [4]: 54

Previous histories:
19676 [3] (75): New to Kentish Bus & Coach Co Ltd, Northfleet (KT) 967 registered J967 JNL; Metrobus Ltd (LN) 12/95.
19677 [4] (76): New to Kentish Bus & Coach Co Ltd, Northfleet (KT) 971 registered J971 JNL; Metrobus Ltd (LN) 12/95.
19678 [4] (77): New to Kentish Bus & Coach Co Ltd, Northfleet (KT) 972 registered J972 JNL; Metrobus Ltd (LN) 12/95.

Notes:
19676 [3] (ex J967 JNL) (75): Acquired by Guernseybus Ltd 10/96.
19677 [4] (ex J971 JNL) (76): Acquired by Guernseybus Ltd 9/96.
19678 [4] (ex J972 JNL) (77): Acquired by Guernseybus Ltd 9/96.

Disposals:
19676 [3] (ex J967 JNL) (75): Transferred to the States of Guernsey, St Peter Port and leased to Island Coachways Ltd, St Peter Port (CI) 75 11/00; NatWest Island Games Committee (CI) 75 6-7/03; unidentified UK dealer 7/03; R Wilson, Gourock (SC) re-registered J967 JNL (not operated) 12/03; Caledonian Coach Co Ltd {Caledonia Buses / Linn Park Buses}, Glasgow (SC) 3/05; last licence expired 2/07; unidentified dealer for scrap by12/08.
19677 [4] (ex J971 JNL) (76): Transferred to the States of Guernsey, St Peter Port and leased to Island Coachways Ltd, St Peter Port (CI) 76 11/00; NatWest Island Games Committee (CI) 76 6-7/03; unidentified UK dealer 7/03; R Wilson, Gourock (SC) (not operated) 12/03; unidentified dealer for scrap by12/06.
19678 [4] (ex J972 JNL) (77): Transferred to the States of Guernsey, St Peter Port and leased to Island Coachways Ltd, St Peter Port (CI) 77 11/00; NatWest Island Games Committee (CI) 77 6-7/03; unidentified UK dealer 7/03; R Wilson, Gourock (SC) (not operated) 12/03; unidentified dealer for scrap by12/06.

1997

Vehicles acquired from Metrobus Ltd, Orpington (LN) 2-5/97:

78	19675 [4]	Optare MR03	VN1148	Optare	1148	B25F	11/91	11/00
74	29728 [3]	Optare MR03	VN1143	Optare	1143	B25F	11/91	11/00

Public Service Omnibus plates:
19675 [4] (78): 18   29728 [3] (74): 46

Previous histories:
19675 [4] (78): New to Kentish Bus & Coach Co Ltd, Northfleet (KT) 968 registered J968 JNL; Metrobus Ltd (LN) 12/95.
29728 [3] (74): New to Kentish Bus & Coach Co Ltd, Northfleet (KT) 963 registered J963 JNL; Metrobus Ltd (LN) 12/95.

Notes:
19675 [4] (ex J968 JNL) (78): Acquired by Guernseybus Ltd 5/97.
29728 [3] (ex J963 JNL) (74): Acquired by Guernseybus Ltd 2/97.

Disposals:
19675 [4] (ex J968 JNL) (78): Transferred to the States of Guernsey, St Peter Port and leased to Island Coachways Ltd, St Peter Port (CI) 78 11/00; NatWest Island Games Committee (CI) 78 6-7/03; unidentified UK dealer 7/03; R Wilson, Gourock (SC) (not operated) 12/03.

29728 [3] (ex J963 JNL) (74): Transferred to the States of Guernsey, St Peter Port and leased to Island Coachways Ltd, St Peter Port (CI) 74 11/00; NatWest Island Games Committee (CI) 74 6-7/03; unidentified UK dealer 7/03; R Wilson, Gourock (SC) (not operated) 12/03; unidentified dealer for scrap by12/06.

Vehicles acquired from Provincial Bus Co Ltd, Fareham (HA) 12/97:

81	31925 [4]	FIAT 49-10	12656	Phoenix	11586	B24F	11/89	11/00
82	31927 [2]	FIAT 49-10	11142	Phoenix	11544	B24F	5/89	11/00

Public Service Omnibus plates:

31925 [4] (81): 10   31927 [2] (82): 44

Previous histories:
31925 [4]: New to Provincial Bus Co Ltd (HA) 137 registered G137 WOW.
31927 [2]: New to Provincial Bus Co Ltd (HA) 133 registered F133 TCR.

Disposals:
31925 [4] (ex G137 WOW) (81): Vazon Bay Hotel, Castel (XCI) 11/00.
31927 [2] (ex F133 TCR) (82): Vazon Bay Hotel, Castel (XCI) 11/00.

1998

Vehicles acquired from Metrobus Ltd, Orpington (LN) 1-4/98:

71	12723 [4]	Optare MR03	VN1033	Optare	1033	B26F	12/90	11/00
70	18264 [3]	Optare MR03	VN1029	Optare	1029	B26F	12/90	11/00
79	19660 [3]	Optare MR03	VN1071	Optare	1071	B26F	5/91	11/00
80	19662 [3]	Optare MR03	VN1070	Optare	1070	B26F	5/91	11/00

Public Service Omnibus plates:

12723 [4] (71): 73   19660 [3] (79): 17
18264 [3] (70): 74   19662 [3] (80): 43

Previous histories:
12723 [4] (71): New to South East London & Kent Bus Co Ltd {Selkent}, Ilford (LN) MRL151 registered H151 UUA 9/94; moved to London SE26 (LN) 1/94; Metrobus Ltd (not operated) 1/98; acquired by Guernseybus Ltd 3/98.

18264 [3] (70): New to South East London & Kent Bus Co Ltd {Selkent}, Ilford (LN) MRL147 registered H147 UUA 9/94; East London Bus & Coach Co Ltd, Ilford (LN) 12/97; Metrobus Ltd (LN) (not operated) 1/98; acquired by Guernseybus Ltd 4/98.

19660 [3] (79): New to South East London & Kent Bus Co Ltd {Selkent}, Ilford (LN) MRL168 registered H168 WWT; moved to London SE26 (LN) 1/94; withdrawn 9/97; Metrobus Ltd (LN) (not operated) 11/97; acquired by Guernseybus Ltd 1/98.

19662 [3] (80): New to South East London & Kent Bus Co Ltd {Selkent}, Ilford (LN) MRL167 registered H167 WWT 9/94; moved to London SE26 (LN) 1/94; withdrawn 9/97; Metrobus Ltd (LN) (not operated) 11/97; acquired by Guernseybus Ltd 1/98.

Disposals:
12723 [4] (ex H151 UUA) (71): Transferred to the States of Guernsey, St Peter Port and leased to Island Coachways Ltd, St Peter Port (CI) 71 11/00; NatWest Island Games Committee (CI) 71 6-7/03; unidentified UK dealer 7/03.

18264 [3] (ex H147 UUA) (70): Transferred to the States of Guernsey, St Peter Port and leased to Island Coachways Ltd, St Peter Port (CI) 70 11/00; NatWest Island Games Committee (CI) 70 6-7/03; unidentified UK dealer 7/03.

19660 [3] (ex H168 WWT) (79): Transferred to the States of Guernsey, St Peter Port and leased to Island Coachways Ltd, St Peter Port (CI) 79 11/00; NatWest Island Games Committee (CI) 79 6-7/03; unidentified UK dealer 7/03; RJ, S & CJ Goulden {Master Travel}, Welwyn Garden City (HT) (not operated) by5/04; unidentified dealer for scrap by7/15.

19662 [3] (ex H167 WWT) (80): Transferred to the States of Guernsey, St Peter Port and leased to Island Coachways Ltd, St Peter Port (CI) 80 11/00; NatWest Island Games Committee (CI) 80 6-7/03; unidentified UK dealer 7/03; R Wilson, Gourock (SC) (not operated) 12/03.

Vehicles acquired from South East London & Kent Bus Co Ltd {Selkent}, London SE26 (LN) 2-4/98:

| 72 | 12727 [4] | Optare MR03 | VN1024 | Optare | 1024 | B26F | 11/90 | 11/00 |
| 73 | 18267 [4] | Optare MR03 | VN1156 | Optare | 1156 | B26F | 5/91 | 11/00 |

Public Service Omnibus plates:
12727 [4] (72): 76   18267 [4] (73): 75

Previous histories:
12727 [4] (72): New to South East London & Kent Bus Co Ltd {Selkent}, Ilford (LN) MRL142 registered H142 UUA 9/94; moved to London SE26 (LN) 1/94; acquired by Guernseybus Ltd 4/98.
18267 [4] (73): New to South East London & Kent Bus Co Ltd {Selkent} MRL164 registered H564 WWR 9/94; moved to London SE26 (LN) 1/94; acquired by Guernseybus Ltd 2/98.

Disposals:
12727 [4] (ex H142 UUA) (72): Transferred to the States of Guernsey, St Peter Port and leased to Island Coachways Ltd, St Peter Port (CI) 72 11/00; withdrawn c6/03.
18267 [4] (ex H564 WWR) (73): Transferred to the States of Guernsey, St Peter Port and leased to Island Coachways Ltd, St Peter Port (CI) 73 11/00; scrapped 3/01.

Vehicle acquired from Provincial Bus Co Ltd, Fareham (HA) 4/98:

| 83 | 31930 [2] | FIAT 49-10 | 11284 | Phoenix | 11548 | B24F | 5/89 | 11/00 |

Public Service Omnibus plates:
31930 [2] (83): 63

Previous histories:
31930 [2]: New to Provincial Bus Co Ltd 134 registered F134 TCR.

Disposal:
31930 [2] (ex F134 TCR) (83): Vazon Bay Hotel, Castel (XCI) 11/00.

Vehicles acquired from MTL London Northern Ltd, Harrow (LN) 9/98:

67	17314	Optare MR03	VN1161	Optare	1161	B31F	1/92	11/00
69	20716	Optare MR03	VN1165	Optare	1165	B31F	2/92	11/00
65	40527	Optare MR03	VN1155	Optare	1155	B31F	11/91	11/00
66	48161	Optare MR03	VN1159	Optare	1159	B31F	12/91	11/00
68	56206	Optare MR03	VN1163	Optare	1163	B31F	1/92	11/00

Public Service Omnibus plates:
17314 (67): 80   40527 (65): 78   56206 (68): 81
20716 (69): 82   48161 (66): 79

Previous histories:
17314 (67): New to London Buses Ltd, London SW1 (LN) MRL216 registered J216 BWU (as B26F); London Northern Bus Co Ltd, Harrow (LN) 10/94; MTL London Northern Ltd (LN) MRL216 10/95.
20716 (69): New to London Buses Ltd, London SW1 (LN) MRL220 registered J220 BWU (as B26F); London Northern Bus Co Ltd, Harrow (LN) 10/94; MTL London Northern Ltd (LN) MRL220 10/95.
40527 (65): New to London Buses Ltd, London SW1 (LN) MRL210 registered J210 BWU (as B26F); London Northern Bus Co Ltd, Harrow (LN) 10/94; MTL London Northern Ltd (LN) MRL210 10/95.
48161 (66): New to London Buses Ltd, London SW1 (LN) MRL214 registered J214 BWU (as B26F); London Northern Bus Co Ltd, Harrow (LN) 10/94; MTL London Northern Ltd (LN) MRL214 10/95.
56206 (68): New to London Buses Ltd, London SW1 (LN) MRL218 registered J218 BWU (as B26F); London Northern Bus Co Ltd, Harrow (LN) 10/94; MTL London Northern Ltd (LN) MRL218 10/95.

Disposals:
17314 (ex J216 BWU) (67): Transferred to the States of Guernsey, St Peter Port and leased to Island Coachways Ltd, St Peter Port (CI) 67 11/00; NatWest Island Games Committee (CI) 67 6-7/03; unidentified UK dealer 7/03; R Wilson, Gourock (SC) re-registered J216 BWU (not operated) 12/03; Caledonian Coach Co Ltd {Caledonia Buses / Linn Park Buses}, Glasgow (SC) 10/04; last licence expired 3/07; unidentified dealer for scrap by12/08.
20716 (ex J220 BWU) (69): Transferred to the States of Guernsey, St Peter Port and leased to Island Coachways Ltd, St Peter Port (CI) 69 11/00; NatWest Island Games Committee (CI) 69 6-7/03; unidentified UK dealer 7/03; noted disused on the premises of CR Craske, Sutton (NK) 1/05 (owner unknown).
40527 (ex J210 BWU) (65): Transferred to the States of Guernsey, St Peter Port and leased to Island Coachways Ltd, St Peter Port (CI) 65 11/00; NatWest Island Games Committee (CI) 65 6-7/03; unidentified UK dealer 7/03; RA Giles {KG Motors}, Caerphilly (MG) by10/03; re-registered J210 BWU 11/03; IA Tomlinson, Winsford (CH) by5/06; MJ Perry {Bromyard Omnibus Co}, Bromyard (HW) 5/06; re-registered J555 BUS 5/06; to service 6/06; DT Brundrit {RML Travel}, Burslem (ST) MRL210 10/06; re-registered J555 RML and named '*Gladys*' 11/06; re-registered J210 BWU 7/08; withdrawn 11/08; last licence expired 11/10; unidentified dealer for scrap c11/10.
48161 (ex J214 BWU) (66): Transferred to the States of Guernsey, St Peter Port and leased to Island Coachways Ltd, St Peter Port (CI) 66 11/00; withdrawn c6/03.
56206 (ex J218 BWU) (68): Transferred to the States of Guernsey, St Peter Port and leased to Island Coachways Ltd, St Peter Port (CI) 68 11/00; NatWest Island Games Committee (CI) 68 6-7/03; unidentified UK dealer 7/03; unidentified owner as a mobile caravan re-registered J218 BWU 8/05.

1999

Vehicles acquired from Educational Holidays Guernsey Ltd {Island Coachways}, St Peter Port (CI) 8/99:

172	38406 [2]	Leyland ST2R44C97T5LBM00331	Elme		075	C45F	5/92	11/00
160	39138 [2]	Leyland ST2R44C97T5LBM00315	Elme		068	C45F	8/91	11/00

Public Service Omnibus plates:
38406 [2] (172): 30   39138 [2] (160): 31

Previous histories:
38406 [2] (172): New to Educational Holidays Guernsey Ltd {Island Coachways} registered 8228 [5] (as C43F).
39138 [2] (160): New to Educational Holidays Guernsey Ltd {Island Coachways} registered 8225 [2] (as C43F).

Notes:
38406 [2] (ex 8228 [5] (172): To service 4/00
39138 [2] (ex 8225 [2] (160): To service 4/00.

Disposals:
38406 [2] (ex 8228 [5] (172): Island Coachways Ltd, St Peter Port (CI) 52 11/00; re-registered 8228 [5] c4/07; re-registered 26984 11/09; Sarnia Autos, St Peter Port (dealer) 11/09; Mr Pink, Portsmouth (as a caravan?) by9/12.
39138 [2] (ex 8225 [2] (160): Island Coachways Ltd, St Peter Port (CI) 53 11/00; unidentified dealer for scrap by5/07.

2000

Vehicles acquired from Cambus Ltd, Cambridge (CM) 3/00:

84	33541	Optare MR03	VN1206	Optare	1206	B29F	5/92	11/00
85	34518	Optare MR03	VN1204	Optare	1204	B29F	5/92	11/00

Public Service Omnibus plates:
33541 (84): 7   34518 (85): 11

Previous histories:
33541 (84): New to Cambus Ltd 962 registered J962 DWX.
34518 (85): New to Cambus Ltd 960 registered J960 DWX.

Notes:
33541 (ex J962 DWX) (84): To service 4/00.
34518 (ex J960 DWX) (85): To service 4/00.

Disposals:
33541 (ex J962 DWX) (84): Transferred to the States of Guernsey, St Peter Port and leased to Island
Coachways Ltd, St Peter Port (CI) 84 11/00; NatWest Island Games Committee (CI) 84 6-7/03;
unidentified UK dealer 7/03; RJ, S & CJ Goulden {Master Travel}, Welwyn Garden City (HT) 13
re-registered J962 DWX 2/06; last licence expired 2/13; unidentified dealer for scrap by5/15.
34518 (ex J960 DWX) (85): Transferred to the States of Guernsey, St Peter Port and leased to Island
Coachways Ltd, St Peter Port (CI) 85 11/00; was set aside to be transferred to the NatWest
Island Games Committee fleet 6/03, but in the event was not used; unidentified UK dealer
by7/03; R Wilson, Gourock (SC) (not operated) 12/03; unidentified dealer for scrap by12/06.

Vehicles acquired from Metrobus Ltd, Orpington (LN) 3/00:

88	24603	Optare MR03	VN1057	Optare	1057	B26F	5/91	11/00
90	24775 [2]	Optare MR03	VN1053	Optare	1053	B26F	5/91	11/00
89	47979	Optare MR03	VN1055	Optare	1055	B26F	5/91	11/00
86	61973	Optare MR01	VN1058	Optare	1058	B33F	8/91	11/00
87	62067	Optare MR01	VN1008	Optare	1008	B33F	4/90	11/00

Public Service Omnibus plates:
24603 (88): 36   47979 (89): 14   62067 (87): 48
24775 [2] (90): 84   61973 (86): 67

Previous histories:
24603 (88): New to South East London & Kent Bus Co Ltd {Selkent}, Ilford (LN) MRL165 registered H165
WWT; moved to London SE26 (LN) 1/94; Metrobus Ltd (LN) 68 11/97; renumbered 915 8/98.
24775 [2] (90): New to South East London & Kent Bus Co Ltd {Selkent}, Ilford (LN) MRL161 registered H161
WWT; moved to London SE26 (LN) 1/94; Metrobus Ltd (LN) 67 11/97; renumbered 913 8/98.
47979 (89): New South East London & Kent Bus Co Ltd {Selkent}, Ilford (LN) MRL163 registered H163 WWT;
moved to London SE26 (LN) 1/94; withdrawn 9/97; Wealden PSV Sales Ltd, Five Oak Green
(dealer) 11/97; Metrobus Ltd (LN) 11/97; numbered 914 8/98.
61973 (86): New to East Surrey Bus Services Ltd, South Godstone (SR) 26 registered J326 PPD; Metrobus
Ltd (LN) 917 6/97.
62067 (87): New East Surrey Bus Services Ltd, South Godstone (SR) 34 registered G972 WPA; Metrobus
Ltd (LN) 911 6/97.

Notes:
24603 (ex H165 WWT) (88): To service 4/00.
24775 [2] (ex H161 WWT) (90): To service 6/00.
47979 (ex H163 WWT) (89): To service 5/00.
61973 (ex J326 PPD) (86): To service 5/00.
62067 (ex G972 WPA) (87): To service 4/00.

Disposals:
24603 (ex H165 WWT) (88): Transferred to the States of Guernsey, St Peter Port and leased to Island
Coachways Ltd, St Peter Port (CI) 88 11/00; was set aside to be transferred to the NatWest
Island Games Committee fleet 6/03, but in the event was not used; unidentified UK dealer 7/03;
RJ, S & CJ Goulden {Master Travel}, Welwyn Garden City (HT) (not operated) by1/05;
unidentified dealer for scrap 6/05.
24775 [2] (ex H161 WWT) (90): Transferred to the States of Guernsey, St Peter Port and leased to Island
Coachways Ltd, St Peter Port (CI) 90 11/00; NatWest Island Games Committee (CI) 90 6-7/03;
unidentified UK dealer 7/03; R Wilson, Gourock (SC) (not operated) 12/03; unidentified dealer
for scrap by12/06.
47979 (ex H163 WWT) (89): Transferred to the States of Guernsey, St Peter Port and leased to Island
Coachways Ltd, St Peter Port (CI) 89 11/00; was set aside to be transferred to the NatWest
Island Games Committee fleet 6/03, but in the event was not used; no traced further.
61973 (ex J326 PPD) (86): Transferred to the States of Guernsey, St Peter Port and leased to Island
Coachways Ltd, St Peter Port (CI) 86 11/00; NatWest Island Games Committee (CI) 86 6-7/03;
unidentified UK dealer 7/03; R Wilson, Gourock (SC) (not operated) 12/03; unidentified dealer
for scrap by12/06.

62067 (ex G972 WPA) (87): Transferred to the States of Guernsey, St Peter Port and leased to Island Coachways Ltd, St Peter Port (CI) 87 11/00; unidentified dealer c7/03; exported to France by7/10; dumped in a field off the D62 road near Linieres-Bouton and being used for spares.

ANCILLARY VEHICLES

Former PSVs:

14627	Albion NS3AN	82069C	mobile commentary bus	5/64	6/84	3/86
18262	Bedford J4EZ1	7814861	mobile commentary bus	4/67	3/86	9/89
29730 [2]	Bedford SB5	455792	mobile commentary bus	2/78	9/89	3/90
10489 [2]	Mercedes Benz 307D		minibus	9/82	12/89	12/92
	WDB60236728233466					
25703	Bedford J6L	119850	mobile commentary bus	5/74	7/91	-/--
9436 [2]	Bristol LHS6L	LHS121	mobile commentary bus	-/72	9/90	12/90
31235 [2]	Bristol LHS6L	LHS126	mobile commentary bus	-/72	3/90	9/90
14223 [2]	Mercedes Benz 307D		minibus	11/83	12/92	-/--
	WDB??????2O590798					

Notes:

The mobile commentary buses were available for hire for shows and sporting events; they were fully mobile but lacked normal seating; some were fitted with tow-hooks to assist with breakdowns.

9436 [2]: Was originally registered VOD 89K; previously numbered 75 in the PSV fleet.
10489 [2]: Was originally registered JGH 431Y; numbered 7 in the PSV fleet.
14223 [2]: Was originally registered A167 OOT; numbered 4 in the PSV fleet.
14627: Was previously numbered 95 in the PSV fleet.
18262: Was previously numbered 102 in the PSV fleet.
25703: The Bedford model type J6L is incomplete, possibly J6LZ; was previously numbered 116 in the PSV fleet.
29730 [2]: Was previously numbered 124 in the PSV fleet.
31235 [2]: Was originally registered VOD 120K; previously numbered 77 in the PSV fleet.

Disposals:

9436 [2]: Written off in an accident 12/90; scrapped 1/91.
10489 [2]: Private owner, Guernsey 12/92.
14223 [2]: No known disposal.
14627: AJS Salvage Co Ltd, Carlton (dealer) for scrap 3/86.
18262: GP Ripley, Carlton (dealer) for scrap 9/89.
25703: No known disposal.
29730 [2]: GP Ripley, Carlton (dealer) for scrap 3/90.
31235 [2]: Broken up by Guernseybus Ltd 12/90.

Other vehicles:

	2239 [1]	Ford Escort	BBAVWS868510	van	8/79	2/81	4/81
7	5597 [1]	Bedford TK	2T129995	breakdown tender	6/72	2/81	3/86
	10346	Ford Escort		van	-/--	-/81	-/--
	10484 [2]	Volkswagen LT28		van	-/85	-/85	-/--
	10485 [2]	Ford Cortina		estate car	-/85	-/85	-/--
		Bedford TK		lorry	-/--	3/86	-/--
	52962	Citroen CX22RS		estate car	1/91	1/91	-/--

Notes:

Bedford TK: Operated on trade plate T145.
2239 [1]: Transferred from Guernsey Railway Co Ltd (qv); originally registered AMS 784V.
5597 [1] (7): Transferred from Guernsey Railway Co Ltd (qv); originally registered WSR 923K; it also operated on trade plate T145 (registration 5597 was transferred to a PSV 4/85).
10485: Was principally used as transport for management but was also licensed to carry passengers on Public Service Omnibus plate ph23.
52962: Was principally used as transport for management but was also licensed to carry passengers on Public Service Omnibus plate ph23.

Disposals:

The only known disposals are for the following vehicles:

2239 [1] (ex AMS 784V): Written off in a road accident 4/81.
5597 [1] (ex WSR 923K) (7): J Sykes, Carlton (dealer) 3/86; unidentified dealer, London at an unknown date.

Tram no. 10 dates from 1891 and was an early arrival after Guernsey Railway Co had electrified the system. It was manufactured by the Falcon Engineering & Car Works of Loughborough and was fitted with Siemens motors, the latter being involved in running the line in the early years. It seated 56. (Bus Archive)

2783, 2791-3 represented Guernsey Motors' 1930 intake of new vehicles and the first Vulcans in the fleet, a make that was to be standard for a few years. They had 19-seat Metcalfe bodies. All were impressed by the Germans in WW2. (Bus Archive)

Pictured at the harbour in St Peter Port, 5499 (26) sets off for St Sampson, a route that has been served by horse-bus and trams, as well as motor buses for 180 years. It was a 1939 Reo with a Heaver body (its second) that came to Motors with the Falla {Blue Bird} business in 1963. (The Bus Archive, Peter Henson)

3990 (29) also came to Guernsey Motors with the Blue Bird business in 1963, this being a Commer Commando with the usual Heaver bodywork, new in 1947. It is passing the Albion House Tavern in St Peter Port, reputedly the closest pub to a church on the islands or even the UK. (Geoffrey Morant, courtesy Richard Morant)

From 1966, Guernsey Motors took delivery of buses based on the Bedford J4 lorry chassis, after Albion stopped manufacturing. This type was the only one purchased until bus operations ended in 1973. 14531 [1] (100) had Reading bodywork and is at St Peter Port harbour passing the statue of Prince Albert. (The Bus Archive, Peter Henson)

A81-83 (1-3) were the first motor buses in the Guernsey Railway fleet, arriving in 1909. They had French built Brillie-Schneider chassis fitted with Hora 34-seat bodies (two of these were later fitted on 1919 deliveries, lasting until 1928). They came from Andrews Star Omnibus in London, but their original registrations are not known. (John Carman)

Guernsey Railway Co 10 was registered 1216. It was an ex-London General Omnibus AEC B that had been acquired as a chassis only in 1924 and fitted with a Baico 25-seat body. It was fitted with pneumatic tyres in 1925, but this picture predates that. (Bus Archive)

2377 was a Bean Model 11 with Willowbrook B20F bodywork new to Guersey Railway in 1928, one of a pair. It was lengthened in 1937 to seat 25 but like many others, was impressed by the German Military authorities in 1942, (Bus Archive)

1309 (23) was new to Watson's Garage in 1960 passing to Guernsey Railway in 1978 (Watson was the last old independent operator to be acquired by the one of the big two). It is seen Motors red livery after some vehicles were repainted in those colours after 1975. It was an Albion NS3N with Reading bodywork. (The Bus Archive, Roy Marshall)

506 (14) was one of nine Guy Vixens with Duple 35-seat bodywork purchased by Guernsey Railway in 1947 as part of their postwar rebuilding programme. Many of these saw a good 20-years service with the company and were the first 7ft wide vehicles to be acquired (The Bus Archive, Peter Henson).

3060 was a Dodge new to WJ Rugg and had a body built by him. It was impressed during WW2 but was later returned. Rugg sold his business to Sarre Transport in 1946 and it later saw time with Guernsey Railway in 1951. When it was scrapped in 1953, it was an impressive 22 years old. (Bus Archive)

19660 [1] (82) was a Bedford J4EZ5 with Reading B35F bodywork which was new to Guernsey Railway in 1968. It passed to Guernseybus in 1981 before eventually going for scrap in 1988. (Trevor Brookes)

After Alex Smith took over Guernsey Railway in 1979, he changed vehicle policy to Bristol manufactured buses. Considerable numbers of the SUL4A type originating with Western National were acquired including 31913 [1] (ex EDV 558D) (140), a 1966 example seen here in Guernseybus white livery. (Geoffrey Morant, courtesy Richard Morant)

14838 [2] (ex NTT 322M) (58) was another that originated from Western National although this saw later service with Tentrek of Sidcup (KT). It was a 1974 Bristol LH6L with Marshall DP39F bodywork. It came to Guernseybus in 1988 but was later repatriated back to Western National where it saw further use as a driver trainer. (Mike Penn)

31917 [3] (ex 31918 [2], JFJ 500N) (167) was a Bristol LH6L with Plaxton bodywork. It was new in the Greenslades fleet and saw service with Western National and North Devon as well. It was one of the Guernseybus arrivals in the mid-1980s that were shortened to 32ft to comply with the regulations of the day. (Geoffrey Morant, courtesy Richard Morant)

Following on from the Bristol SU, the standard service bus of the late 1980s/early 1990s was the ECW bodied Bristol LH. 29729 [2] (ex OJD 64R) ((52) was new to London Transport, but had seen service in Wales, the North East of England and the West Country before coming to Guernseybus in 1990. (The Bus Archive, Roy Marshall)

The midi-bus era arrived on Guernsey in the 1990s. An early example operated by Guernseybus was 29694 (ex D126 NON) (11), a solitary purchase from Manchester Minibuses {Bee Line Buzz} in 1991. It was a Freight Rover with 20-seat Carlyle bodywork. (The Bus Archive, Roy Marshall)

70019 was one of 33 Dennis Darts that were funded by the States of Guernsey in 2003 to renew the Island Coachways bus fleet when they took over after the demise of Guernseybus. It passed to CT Plus in 2012 after they were awarded the franchise and was only withdrawn in 2018. (Dave Arnold)

A line up of CT Plus vehicles - 70011 is a 2005 Dennis Dart / SCC, new as an airport bus in the UK, 33040 one of the 2017 intake of Wright StreetVibes and 70027 a 2003 Dennis Dart / East Lancs. (Dave Arnold)

The registration of this V & A Mallett {Blue Bird} Ford TT is not known, but it was new in 1923 and fitted with locally built F Mallett bodywork. It had left the fleet by 1926, as more modern vehicles of Reo manufacture were obtained. (Bus Archive)

Similarly, the registration of JH Miller's no. 1 is not known, but it was new in 1920 and was a Maxwell with locally built T Davies bodywork. It was one of eight vehicles that passed to Guernsey Motors in late 1921 and may have been one they rebodied to extend its life. (Bus Archive)

HC Collenette {Paragon} 99 (7) was a Dodge new in 1930 in the UK, possibly rebuilt from an earlier Graham-Dodge. It came to Guernsey in 1939 and was fitted locally with a full-front body having been converted to forward control. A year later it was impressed by the German Military and was never seen again. (Bus Archive)

WJ Rugg, a well-known prewar operator and bodybuilder operated 2799, a Bean Model 11 with a Willowbrook body new in 1930. It ended its days like many of its era, impressed by the German Authorities during the WW2 and no doubt ended up as scrap metal. (Bus Archive)

1633 was another Rugg vehicle, but one which passed to Sarre Transport in 1946. It didn't last long enough to pass to Guernsey Motors/Railway when Red & White acquired the business in 1951, but ended its days on Alderney with WP Simon re-registered AY 101 [1]. It was a Dodge with Rugg B25F bodywork new in 1934. (Bus Archive)

2711 was of uncertain ancestry. It was a 1930/1 Dodge chassis obtained from Jersey and fitted locally with a WJ Rugg body in 1938. It passed to Sarre Transport in 1946 and Guernsey Motors in 1951 who held on to it for a few years but did not operate it. (Bus Archive)

This Heaver bodied Albion PK115, 4869, was no. 5 in the Falla {Blue Bird} fleet when new in 1936. It was rebodied in 1950 with a second body similar to its first and ran for a year and a half for Guernsey Motors after the Blue Bird business had been acquired in 1963, by which time it was 28 years old. (Bus Archive)

Reynolds {Cliffways Hotel} was unusual in running a full-size coach in agreement with the Motors and Railway companies, probably due to it being situated some way from the nearest bus route. 4414, a Bedford OB / Mulliner had previously operated for Sarre Transport and Guernsey Motors and was with the hotel 1961-9. (The Bus Archive, Peter Henson)

2445 [2] (ex NVA 75L) was a Bedford / Duple C53F acquired by Educational Holidays in 2/85. It was used on a service to Manchester via the Weymouth ferry, jointly with Dean Forest, Joys Green (GL). Because it was over the maximum width allowed on Guernsey, it did not carry passengers on the island. (Dave Arnold)

20716 (ex J220 BWU) was one of a number of midi-buses originally from London, that operated for Guernseybus and then Educational Holidays in the 1990s. It last saw service on the island in 2003, when it worked for a week for the Nat West Island Games Committee, before returning to the UK. It was a 31-seat Optare MR03. (Mike Street)

Island Coachways 51 is 2609, an unusual MAN TGL10.180 with MOBIpeople (Portugal) bodywork, new to the operator in 2016. It is seen here apparently on a wedding private hire. (Chris Elkin)

Riduna Buses was the main operator on Alderney for 75 years. The registration AY 59 appeared on 17 different vehicles, seven of which were Mulliner bodied Bedford OBs, of which this was one. All originated on Guernsey. (Bus Archive)

AY 1773 operated for R Spandler {Alderney Taxi & Hire Cars} on Alderney between 1995 and 2001. Before that it had been with Educational Holidays on Guernsey registered 6768 [4] and originally with Nebard's of Wakefield (WY) as their WUA 655X. It was a FIAT 60-10 with Caetano bodywork. (Peter Tulloch)

CT PLUS GUERNSEY LTD {Buses.gg}
Les Banques, ST PETER PORT

CT Plus Guernsey Ltd, branded 'Buses.gg' were awarded the franchise for public transport in 2012. This broadly followed the model previously adopted on Jersey, but there were fundamental differences. On Jersey, the franchise awarded to Connex in 2003 was a 'minimum subsidy' model where the operator took the revenue / cost risk, chose the vehicles and set the fares, subject to Infrastructure Ministry approval.

On Guernsey, the model adopted was 'minimum cost' with the States sourcing and owning the vehicles and leasing them to the operator together with setting the service levels and fares, most routes being charged at a flat fee of £1 with school students travelling free. The States also met any shortfall between revenue and operating costs. This was adopted in Jersey in 2013 when CT Plus' 'LibertyBus' operation won the franchise there in 2013.

CT Plus took over the Island Coachways fleet of 41 Dennis Darts from April 2012.

2012

Vehicles acquired from Island Coachways Ltd, St Peter Port (CI) 4/12:

DCS10	70011	Dennis Dart SLF SFD6BACR43GWA7609	SCC	4465	B28F	1/05	#
DM1	70012	Dennis Dart SFD SFD1BACR32GWA6943	East Lancs	43902	B35F	12/02	7/17
DM2	70013	Dennis Dart SFD SFD1BACR32GWA6942	East Lancs	43901	B35F	12/02	7/17
DM3	70014	Dennis Dart SFD SFD1BACR32GWA6944	East Lancs	43903	B35F	1/03	9/18
DM4	70015	Dennis Dart SFD SFD1BACR32GWA6946	East Lancs	43905	B35F	1/03	7/17
DM5	70016	Dennis Dart SFD SFD1BACR32GWA6945	East Lancs	43904	B35F	1/03	10/18
DM6	70017	Dennis Dart SFD SFD1BACR32GWA7064	East Lancs	43911	B35F	2/03	10/18
DM7	70018	Dennis Dart SFD SFD1BACR32GWA7061	East Lancs	43908	B35F	2/03	10/18
DM8	70019	Dennis Dart SFD SFD1BACR32GWA7060	East Lancs	43907	B35F	2/03	9/18
DM9	70020	Dennis Dart SFD SFD1BACR32GWA7074	East Lancs	43915	B35F	2/03	10/18
DM10	70021	Dennis Dart SFD SFD1BACR33GWA7107	East Lancs	43916	B35F	2/03	by4/17
DM11	70022	Dennis Dart SFD SFD1BACR32GWA7072	East Lancs	43913	B35F	3/03	9/18
DM12	70023	Dennis Dart SFD SFD1BACR32GWA7063	East Lancs	43910	B35F	3/03	9/18
DM13	70024	Dennis Dart SFD SFD1BACR33GWA7116	East Lancs	43920	B35F	3/03	9/18
DM14	70025	Dennis Dart SFD SFD1BACR32GWA7065	East Lancs	43912	B35F	3/03	9/18
DM15	70026	Dennis Dart SFD SFD1BACR32GWA7059	East Lancs	43906	B35F	3/03	#
DM16	70027	Dennis Dart SFD SFD1BACR32GWA7073	East Lancs	43914	B35F	3/03	10/18
DM17	70028	Dennis Dart SFD SFD1BACR33GWA7117	East Lancs	43921	B35F	3/03	7/17
DM18	70029	Dennis Dart SFD SFD1BACR33GWA7119	East Lancs	43923	B35F	3/03	10/18
DM19	70030	Dennis Dart SFD SFD1BACR33GWA7108	East Lancs	43917	B35F	3/03	7/17
DM20	70031	Dennis Dart SFD SFD1BACR33GWA7137	East Lancs	43927	B35F	3/03	7/17
DM21	70032	Dennis Dart SFD SFD1BACR33GWA7130	East Lancs	43925	B35F	3/03	10/18
DM22	70033	Dennis Dart SFD SFD1BACR33GWA7118	East Lancs	43922	B35F	3/03	7/17

DM23	70034	Dennis Dart SFD SFD1BACR33GWA7136	East Lancs	43926	B35F	3/03	7/17
DM24	70035	Dennis Dart SFD SFD1BACR33GWA7138	East Lancs	43928	B34F	3/03	2/19
DM25	70036	Dennis Dart SFD SFD1BACR32GWA7062	East Lancs	43909	B34F	4/03	11/18
DM26	70037	Dennis Dart SFD SFD1BACR33GWA7110	East Lancs	43919	B34F	4/03	7/17
DM27	70038	Dennis Dart SFD SFD1BACR33GWA7150	East Lancs	43931	B34F	4/03	by4/17
DM28	70039	Dennis Dart SFD SFD1BACR33GWA7129	East Lancs	43924	B34F	4/03	9/18
DM29	70040	Dennis Dart SFD SFD1BACR33GWA7109	East Lancs	43918	B34F	5/03	9/18
DM30	70041	Dennis Dart SFD SFD1BACR33GWA7149	East Lancs	43930	B34F	5/03	9/18
DM31	70042	Dennis Dart SFD SFD1BACR33GWA7139	East Lancs	43929	B34F	5/03	9/18
DM32	70043	Dennis Dart SFD SFD1BACR33GWA7151	East Lancs	43932	B34F	5/03	10/18
DM33	70044	Dennis Dart SFD SFD1BACR33GWA7152	East Lancs	43933	B34F	5/03	7/17
DCS11	70055	Dennis Dart SLF SFD6BACR43GWA7639	SCC	4483	B28F	1/05	#
DCS13	70066	Dennis Dart SLF SFD6BACR43GWA7625	SCC	4481	B28F	1/05	#
DCS14	70077	Dennis Dart SLF SFD6BACR43GWA7624	SCC	4482	B28F	4/05	#
DCS15	70088	Dennis Dart SLF SFD6BACR43GWA7611	SCC	4486	B28F	3/05	#
DCS17	70099	Dennis Dart SLF SFD6BACR43GWA7623	SCC	4487	B28F	3/05	#
DCS12	77056	Dennis Dart SLF SFD6BACR43GWA7640	SCC	4480	B28F	12/04	#
DCS16	77091	Dennis Dart SLF SFD6BACR43GWA7641	SCC	4479	B28F	12/04	#

Vehicles marked # were still in service at the date of this Fleet History.

Public Service Omnibus plates:

70011 (DCS10): 34	70025 (DM14): 14	70039 (DM28): 28
70012 (DM1): 1	70026 (DM15): 15	70040 (DM29): 29
70013 (DM2): 2	70027 (DM16): 16	70041 (DM30): 30
70014 (DM3): 3	70028 (DM17): 17	70042 (DM31): 31
70015 (DM4): 4	70029 (DM18): 18	70043 (DM32): 32
70016 (DM5): 5	70030 (DM19): 19	70044 (DM33): 33
70017 (DM6): 6	70031 (DM20): 20	70055 (DCS11): 35
70018 (DM7): 7	70032 (DM21): 21	70066 (DCS13): 36
70019 (DM8): 8	70033 (DM22): 22	70077 (DCS14): 37
70020 (DM9): 9	70034 (DM23): 23	70088 (DCS15): 38
70021 (DM10): 10	70035 (DM24): 24	70099 (DCS17): 39
70022 (DM11): 11	70036 (DM25): 25	77056 (DCS12): 40
70023 (DM12): 12	70037 (DM26): 26	77091 (DCS16): 41
70024 (DM13): 13	70038 (DM27): 27	

Previous histories:

70011 (DCS10): New to National Car Parks, Paisley (SC) registered AE54 MWF (as B23F); Island Coachways Ltd 11 3/08 (as B28F).

70012-70034 (DM1-23): New to Island Coachways Ltd 12-34 (as B35F); reseated to B34F before or shortly afterward entering service.

70035-70044 (DM24-33): New to Island Coachways Ltd 35-44.

70055 (DCS11): New to National Car Parks, Paisley (SC) registered AE54 NUB (as B23F); Island Coachways Ltd 55 3/08 (as B28F).

70066 (DCS13): New to EMA Carparks, Nottingham East Midlands Airport (LE) 3 registered MV 54 EEM; Nottingham East Midlands Airport, Castle Donington (LE) 3 1/06; Manchester Airport (GM) 12/06; National Car Parks, Luton Airport (BD) 2/08; Island Coachways Ltd 66 8/08.

70077 (DCS14): New to EMA Carparks, Nottingham East Midlands Airport (LE) 2 registered FJ 05 HYM; Nottingham East Midlands Airport, Castle Donington (LE) 2 1/06; Manchester Airport (GM) 12/06; National Car Parks, Luton Airport (BD) 7/07; Island Coachways Ltd 77 8/08.

70088 (DCS15): New to EMA Carparks, Nottingham East Midlands Airport (LE) 6 registered FJ 05 HYK; Nottingham East Midlands Airport, Castle Donington (LE) 6 1/06; Manchester Airport (GM) 12/06; National Car Parks, Luton Airport (BD) 7/07; Island Coachways Ltd 88 8/08.

70099 (DCS17): New to EMA Carparks, Nottingham East Midlands Airport (LE) 1 registered FJ 05 HYL; Nottingham East Midlands Airport, Castle Donington (LE) 1 1/06; Manchester Airport (GM) 12/06; National Car Parks, Luton Airport (BD) 6/07; Island Coachways Ltd 99 8/08.

77056 (DCS12): New to National Car Parks, Paisley (SC) registered AE54 MWC (as B23F); Hansar Finance Ltd, Cheadle Hulme (dealer) by10/07; O'Hara {Row Travel}, Clifton (GM) 12/07; M Travel, Old Trafford (GM) 9/08; Hansar Finance Ltd, Cheadle Hulme (dealer) 11/08; Island Coachways Ltd 56 4/09.

77091 (DCS16): New to National Car Parks, Paisley (SC) registered AE54 MWD (as B23F); Hansar, Cheadle Hulme (dealer) by10/07; O'Hara {Row Travel}, Clifton (GM) 12/07; Hansar Finance Ltd, Cheadle Hulme (dealer) 9/08; Island Coachways Ltd 91 4/09.

Notes:

These vehicles were owned from new by the States of Guernsey and were leased to Island Coachways Ltd and from 4/12, CT Plus Guernsey Ltd.

70011 (ex AE54 MWF) (DCS10): Renumbered 214 4/17; renumbered 1114 10/18.
70012-70020 (DM1-9): Renumbered 419-427 4/17.
70021 (DM10): Was being used for spares by4/17; renumbered 428 (not carried, on paper only) 4/17.
70022-70025 (DM11-14): Renumbered 429-432 4/17.
70026 (DM15): Renumbered 433 4/17; retained for use as a driver training vehicle 2019.
70027-70034 (DM16-23): Renumbered 434-441 4/17.
70035 (DM24): Renumbered 442 4/17; retained for use as a driver training vehicle 2/19.
70036-70037 (DM25-26): Renumbered 443-444 4/17.
70038 (DM27): Was being used for spares by4/17; renumbered 445 (not carried, on paper only) 4/17.
70039-70044 (DM28-33): Renumbered 446-451 4/17.
70055 (ex AE54 NUB) (DCS11): Renumbered 215 4/17; renumbered 1115 10/18.
70066 (ex MV54 EEM) (DCS13): Renumbered 216 4/17; renumbered 1116 10/18.
70077 (ex FJ05 HYM) (DCS14): Renumbered 217 4/17; renumbered 1117 10/18.
70088 (ex FJ05 HYK) (DCS15): Renumbered 218 4/17; renumbered 1118 10/18.
70099 (ex FJ05 HYL) (DCS17): Renumbered 219 4/17; renumbered 1119 10/18.
77056 (ex AE54 MWC) (DCS12): Renumbered 220 4/17; renumbered 1120 10/18.
77091 (ex AE54 MWD) (DCS16): Renumbered 221 4/17; renumbered 1121 10/18.

Disposals:

70012 (419, ex DM1): Unidentified dealer by10/18.
70013 (420, ex DM2): Unidentified UK dealer 9/17.
70014 (421, ex DM3): Unidentified dealer by10/18.
70015 (422, ex DM4): Unidentified dealer by10/18.
70016 (423, ex DM5): Unidentified dealer 10/18.
70017 (424, ex DM6): Unidentified dealer 10/18.
70018 (425, ex DM7): Unidentified dealer by11/18.
70019 (426, ex DM8): Unidentified dealer by10/18.
70020 (427, ex DM9): Unidentified dealer 10/18.
70021 (428, ex DM10): Unidentified dealer for scrap 7/17.
70022 (429, ex DM11): Unidentified dealer by10/18.
70023 (430, ex DM12): Unidentified dealer by10/18.
70024 (431, ex DM13): Unidentified dealer by10/18.
70025 (432, ex DM14): Unidentified dealer by10/18.
70027 (434, ex DM16): Unidentified dealer 10/18.
70028 (435, ex DM17): Unidentified UK dealer 9/17.
70029 (436, ex DM18): Unidentified dealer 10/18.
70030 (437, ex DM19): Unidentified dealer by10/18.
70031 (438, ex DM20): Unidentified dealer by10/18.
70032 (439, ex DM21): Unidentified dealer 10/18.
70033 (440, ex DM22): Unidentified dealer by10/18.

70034 (441, ex DM23): Unidentified dealer by11/18.
70036 (443, ex DM25): Unidentified dealer 11/18.
70037 (444, ex DM26): Unidentified dealer 9/17.
70038 (445, ex DM27): Unidentified dealer for scrap 7/17.
70039 (446, ex DM28): States Airport, Forest (XCI) 9/18.
70040 (447, ex DM29): Unidentified dealer by10/18.
70041 (448, ex DM30): Unidentified dealer by10/18.
70042 (449, ex DM31): Unidentified dealer by1/19.
70043 (450, ex DM32): Unidentified dealer 10/18.
70044 (451, ex DM33): Unidentified UK dealer 9/17.

2015

Vehicle acquired from Evobus, Coventry (dealer) by5/15:

29333	Mercedes Benz City 45 WDB9066572S812863	Mercedes Benz	M13	6/14	#

Vehicles marked # were still in service at the date of this Fleet History.

Previous history:
New as a demonstration vehicle with Evobus registered BU14 SZC.

Notes:
29333 (ex BU14 SZC): To service 7/15; numbered 108 4/17.

2016

Vehicles acquired from CT Plus Community Interest Co, Bristol (GL) 9/16:

9901	BL64 HJD	Mercedes Benz Sprinter 45 WDB9066572S971255	Mercedes Benz	M13	1/15	7/17
9902	BL64 HJE	Mercedes Benz Sprinter 45 WDB9066572S974392	Mercedes Benz	M13	1/15	3/18

Public Service Omnibus plates:
BL64 HJD: 43   BL64 HJE: 44

Previous histories:
BL64 HJD (9901): New to CT Plus Community Interest Co (GL).
BL64 HJE (9902): New to CT Plus Community Interest Co (GL).

Notes:
These vehicles were on loan from CT Plus Community Interest Co, Bristol (GL) and were not registered on Guernsey.

Disposals:
BL64 HJD (9901): CT Plus Community Interest Co, Bristol (GL) MS36 3/18; renumbered 5310 by1/19.
BL64 HJE (9902): CT Plus Community Interest Co, Bristol (GL) MS37 3/18; renumbered 5311 by1/19

2017

New vehicles:

351	26943	Wright StreetVibe SA9NSRVXX17360018	Wright	AN898	B31F	6/17	#
352	27718	Wright StreetVibe SA9NSRVXX17360019	Wright	AN899	B31F	6/17	#
353	29090	Wright StreetVibe SA9NSRVXX17360020	Wright	AN900	B31F	7/17	#
354	29191	Wright StreetVibe SA9NSRVXX17360021	Wright	AN901	B31F	7/17	#
355	33040	Wright StreetVibe SA9NSRVXX17360022	Wright	AN902	B31F	7/17	#
356	34516	Wright StreetVibe SA9NSRVXX17360023	Wright	AN903	B31F	7/17	#
357	34857	Wright StreetVibe SA9NSRVXX17360024	Wright	AN904	B31F	7/17	#

358	35295	Wright StreetVibe	Wright	AN905	B31F	7/17	#
		SA9NSRVXX17360025					
359	35694	Wright StreetVibe	Wright	AN906	B31F	7/17	#
		SA9NSRVXX17360026					
360	40631	Wright StreetVibe	Wright	AN907	B31F	7/17	#
		SA9NSRVXX17360027					
361	42625	Wright StreetVibe	Wright	AN908	B31F	7/17	#
		SA9NSRVXX17360028					
362	46893	Wright StreetVibe	Wright	AN909	B31F	7/17	#
		SA9NSRVXX17360029					

Vehicles marked # were still in service at the date of this Fleet History.

Public Service Omnibus plates:

26943 (351): 27	33040 (355): 4	35694 (359): 2
27718 (352): 10	34516 (356): 19	40631 (360): 43
29090 (353): 26	34857 (357): 44	42625 (361): 33
29191 (354): 17	35295 (358): 1	46893 (362): 22

Notes:

26943 (351): Renumbered 1951 10/18.
27718 (352): Renumbered 1952 10/18.
29090 (353): Renumbered 1953 10/18.
29191 (354): Renumbered 1954 10/18.
33040 (355): Renumbered 1955 10/18.
34516 (356): Renumbered 1956 10/18.
34857 (357): Renumbered 1957 10/18.
35295 (358): Renumbered 1958 10/18.
35694 (359): Renumbered 1959 10/18.
40631 (360): Received Public Service Omnibus plate 23 9/17; renumbered 1960 10/18.
42625 (361): Renumbered 1961 10/18.
46893 (362): Renumbered 1962 10/18.

2018

New vehicles:

1963	29131	Wright StreetVibe	Wright	AQ972	B31F	9/18	#
		SA9NSRVXX18360030					
1964	32758	Wright StreetVibe	Wright	AQ973	B31F	9/18	#
		SA9NSRVXX18360031					
1965	35428	Wright StreetVibe	Wright	AQ974	B31F	9/18	#
		SA9NSRVXX18360032					
1966	40869	Wright StreetVibe	Wright	AQ975	B31F	10/18	#
		SA9NSRVXX18360033					
1967	44925	Wright StreetVibe	Wright	AQ976	B31F	10/18	#
		SA9NSRVXX18360034					
1968	47878	Wright StreetVibe	Wright	AQ977	B31F	10/18	#
		SA9NSRVXX18360035					
1969	48032	Wright StreetVibe	Wright	AQ978	B31F	9/18	#
		SA9NSRVXX18360036					
1970	49641	Wright StreetVibe	Wright	AQ979	B31F	9/18	#
		SA9NSRVXX18360037					
1971	49679	Wright StreetVibe	Wright	AQ980	B31F	10/18	#
		SA9NSRVXX18360038					
1972	51668	Wright StreetVibe	Wright	AQ981	B31F	10/18	#
		SA9NSRVXX18360039					
1973	51735 [2]	Wright StreetVibe	Wright	AQ982	B31F	9/18	#
		SA9NSRVXX18360040					
1974	56302	Wright StreetVibe	Wright	AQ983	B31F	10/18	#
		SA9NSRVXX18360041					
1975	60317	Wright StreetVibe	Wright	AQ984	B31F	9/18	#
		SA9NSRVXX18360042					
1976	63798	Wright StreetVibe	Wright	AQ985	B31F	9/18	#
		SA9NSRVXX18360043					

1977	64098	Wright StreetVibe SA9NSRVXX18360044	Wright	AQ986	B31F	9/18	#
1978	64153	Wright StreetVibe SA9NSRVXX18360045	Wright	AQ987	B31F	9/18	#
1979	64189	Wright StreetVibe SA9NSRVXX18360046	Wright	AQ988	B31F	10/18	#
1980	64193	Wright StreetVibe SA9NSRVXX18360047	Wright	AQ989	B31F	10/18	#
1981	64195	Wright StreetVibe SA9NSRVXX18360048	Wright	AQ990	B31F	9/18	#
1982	64198	Wright StreetVibe SA9NSRVXX18360049	Wright	AQ991	B31F	11/18	#
1983	64202	Wright StreetVibe SA9NSRVXX18360050	Wright	AQ992	B31F	11/18	#

Vehicles marked # were still in service at the date of this Fleet History.

Public Service Omnibus plates:

29131 (1963): 8	49641 (1970): 11	64098 (1977): 31
32758 (1964): 28	49679 (1971): 5	64153 (1978): 3
35428 (1965): 12	51668 (1972): 9	64189 (1979): 32
40869 (1966): 6	51735 [2] (1973): 13	64193 (1980): 18
44925 (1967): 21	56302 (1974): 7	64195 (1981): 30
47878 (1968): 16	60317 (1975): 14	64198 (1982): 23
48032 (1969): 49	63798 (1976): 29	64202 (1983): 25

2019

<u>New vehicle:</u>

1984	64203	Wright StreetVibe SA9NSRVXX18360051	Wright	AQ993	B31F	2/19	#

Vehicles marked # were still in service at the date of this Fleet History.

Public Service Omnibus plate:

64203 (1984): 24

ANCILLARY VEHICLES

Former PSVs:

	32057	Renault Master	mobile staff canteen	2/04	12/14	by10/18
		VF1UDCUK629831210				
953	60174	Volkswagen Transporter	minibus	1/10	7/17	#
		WV1ZZZ7HZ9H135780				

Vehicles marked # were still in service at the date of this Fleet History.

Notes:

32057: New to West Hull Community Transport, Kingston-upon-Hull (XEY) WHCT3 registered GN53 UJU (its body was by Rohill and it had a B15F capacity); numbered 107 4/17.

60174: New to CT Plus Community Interest Co, London E8 (LNx) registered LJ59 NFA. It is fitted with a Stanford M7L body.

Disposal:

32057 (107): Unidentified dealer for scrap by10/18.

GUERNSEY INDEPENDENT OPERATORS

AIRLINES (JERSEY) LTD {Jersey Airlines}

Fountain Street, ST PETER PORT & States Airport, La Villiaze, FOREST

Airlines (Jersey) Ltd ran a transfer service from St Peter Port to the Airport, in conjunction with flights.

| 7798 | Volkswagen Microbus | 138905 | Volkswagen | M10 | 4/56 | 4/56 | 1/60 |
| 7799 | Volkswagen Microbus | 172355 | Volkswagen | M10 | 5/56 | 5/56 | 5/60 |

Police plates:
7798: 201   7799: 208

Disposals:
7798: Exported 1/60.
7799: Exported 5/60.

ULRIC UNDERWOOD ASH   Brock Road, ST PETER PORT

Ulric Ash was the major coach operator of the early 1920s running excursions and tours from The Quay, St Peter Port. He also acted as a dealer and broker. A number of bus services and vehicles passed through his hands and which were passed on to Guernsey Motors Ltd. His taxi and coach business passed to the Motors Company on 1 November 1931 and he and (later) his son became directors of that business. The motor garage side of the business was not included in the sale and continued for many years. He also was a distributor of Vulcan, Dennis and later Austin vehicles. A limited company, Ash Ltd, was formed in May 1933.

	Willys-Overland 25 cwt	?	?	Ch18	-/--	-/--	11/31
671	Pierce-Arrow	?	?	Ch--	-/--	-/--	-/--
	Maxwell 30 cwt	?	?	Ch20	by4/22	4/22	11/31
	Acason 3 ton	?	Baico	Ch28	by8/22	8/22	11/31
885	Vulcan 30 cwt	?	?	Ch20	-/24	5/24	11/31
987	Vulcan 3 ton	?	?	Ch28	-/24	5/24	11/31
48 [2]	Maxwell 30 cwt	?	?	Ch22	6/23	-/--	11/31
2220	Vulcan Duke	3XS06	Spicer	Ch20	11/27	3/28	11/31
2840	Vulcan Duke	3XS65	?	Ch23	4/31	4/31	11/31
2965	Vulcan Duke	3XS70	?	Ch23	-/31	-/31	11/31

Previous histories:
The origins of these vehicles are unknown apart from:

48 [2]: New to WT Robilliard {Reindeer}, St Peter Port (CI) (as Ch20).
885: New to WN Priaulx / Ozanne Bros {Primrose}, Forest (CI) named 'Queen of the Isles'.
987: New to WN Priaulx / Ozanne Bros {Primrose}, Forest (CI) named 'Princess Ena'.
2220: Probably new as a demonstrator with Vulcan Motors Ltd, Southport registered WM 1405 (it was also recorded as registered GD 9128 12/27).

Notes:
Willys-Overland: Operated on contract to the Richmond Hotel.
2220: Named 'Rambler'.

Disposals:
Acason: Guernsey Motors Ltd, St Peter Port (CI) 62 10/31 (as Ch26); withdrawn by1933.
Maxwell: Guernsey Motors Ltd, St Peter Port (CI) 64 10/31 (as Ch18); withdrawn by1941.
Willys-Overland: Guernsey Motors Ltd, St Peter Port (CI) 65 10/31; withdrawn by1937.
48 [2]: Guernsey Motors Ltd, St Peter Port (CI) 63 10/31 (as Ch18); impressed by German Military Authorities (Military Truck Compound) (GOV) 10/42; scrapped locally at an unknown date (or sent to France for scrapping).
671: No known disposal.
885: Guernsey Motors Ltd, St Peter Port (CI) 60 10/31 (as Ch19); impressed by German Military Authorities (Military Truck Compound) (GOV) 10/42; scrapped locally at an unknown date (or sent to France for scrapping).
987: Guernsey Motors Ltd, St Peter Port (CI) 61 10/31; impressed by German Military Authorities (Military Truck Compound) (GOV) 10/42; scrapped locally at an unknown date (or sent to France for scrapping).

2220 (ex WM 1405): Guernsey Motors Ltd, St Peter Port (CI) 59 10/31 (as Ch19); impressed by German Military Authorities (Military Truck Compound) (GOV) 10/42; scrapped locally at an unknown date (or sent to France for scrapping).

2840: Guernsey Motors Ltd, St Peter Port (CI) 58 10/31; withdrawn 9/50; scrapped 1/55.

2965: Guernsey Motors Ltd, St Peter Port (CI) 18 10/31; withdrawn 9/49; Ash Ltd, St Peter Port (dealer) for scrap 11/49.

GW BANKS {The Legion}   Grand Bouet, ST PETER PORT

Banks ran a route between St Peters Port and St Sampson's Bridge which he sold to Guernsey Railway in June 1925. He was also a coal dealer.

	Ford TT	? ?	Ch13	-/--	-/--	6/25

Disposal:
Ford: Guernsey Railway Co Ltd, St Peter Port (CI) 11 6/25; rebuilt to OB11F 1/27; withdrawn 12/32.

BARNABE Ltd   Market Street, ST PETER PORT

Barnable Ltd operates a Land Rover Defender truck fitted with seats and a convertible roof.

32464	Land Rover Defender	? ?	M9	-/--	by-/18	#

Public Service Omnibus plate:
32464: ph45

Previous history:
32464: Its origins are unknown.

BIRD BROS   South Side, ST SAMPSON

Bird Bros also ran a route between St Peters Port and St Sampson's Bridge. They were also were coal merchants as well as ship brokers. Their vehicles had detachable coal lorry bodies which could be swapped for passenger carrying ones.

	Maxwell 25 cwt	? ?	?	1/20	1/20	-/--
	W & G du Cros	? ?	B11R	1/20	1/20	-/--
437	Vulcan	? ?	OB23R	-/--	-/--	-/--
1035	W & G du Cros	? ?	OB27R	-/--	-/--	-/--
	W & G du Cros	? F Mallett	B18R	-/--	-/--	-/26

Previous histories:
These vehicles were probably all new to Bird Bros.

Notes:
First W & G du Cros: Named 'Sarnia'.
Third W & G du Cros: Named 'Island Belle'.
437: Named 'Western Belle'.
1035: Named 'Village Belle'.

Disposals:
Maxwell: No known disposal.
First W & G du Cros: No known disposal.
Third W & G du Cros: Guernsey Motors Ltd, St Peter Port (CI) 53 1926; withdrawn c1935.
437: No known disposal.
1035: No known disposal.

BLUE BIRD

Vic & Arthur MALLETT {Blue Bird}	Albion Villa, Vale Road, ST SAMPSON
Herbert N & Harold K FALLA {Blue Bird} (11/25)	Burton Villa, Route des Coutures, VALE
Harold K FALLA {Blue Bird} (7/48)	

Services from St Sampson to L'Ancresse were operated by Blue Bird for 40 years from 1923. The operation was started by the Mallett brothers (another brother also built bodies) but was taken over by the Falla Bros on 11 November 1925. After the War, the Paragon business (which shared the L'Ancresse route) came up for sale, Harold Falla left the Blue Bird partnership to take it over. The business passed to Guernsey Motors Ltd in January 1963, the garage and taxi business remaining under the control of the Falla family until 1987. This was sold to Peter Elliot and Len Le Roi who started a minibus operation called Blue Bird Services Ltd.

1		Ford TT	?	F Mallett		OB16F	6/23	6/23	-/26
2		Chevrolet 1 ton	?	?		B13F	-/--	10/23	4/25
3	917	Ford TT	?	FT Bennett		OB20F	4/24	4/24	9/30
2	1480	Ford TT	?	F Mallett		OB22F	4/25	4/25	by10/31
4	1319	Reo Speed Wagon	?	FT Bennett		OB22F	5/26	5/26	10/31
5	2047	Reo Sprinter LWB	?	Bence		B24F	3/28	3/28	-/35
6	1765	Reo Sprinter	FAX10234	Heaver		B24F	4/29	4/29	7/33
7	2714	Reo Sprinter	FAA11138	Heaver		B22F	10/29	10/29	5/37
8	2981	Reo FAX	1691	Heaver		B27F	5/31	5/31	1/49
4	3120	Reo C	?	FT Bennett		B26F	-/32	-/32	-/37
3	2341	Commer 6TK/1	?	Heaver		B28F	-/33	-/33	10/42
6	1410	Reo TDX	?	Heaver		B29F	4/34	4/34	5/41
2	4252	Leyland KP3	?	Strachan		B29F	-/35	-/35	5/41
5	4869	Albion PK115	25011G	Heaver		FB35F	10/36	10/36	1/63
4	4879	Reo (Speed Wagon?)	5372	Heaver		FB35F	7/37	7/37	-/54
7	5499	Reo (Speed Wagon?)	909	Heaver		FB35F	4/39	4/39	1/63
2	2960	Commer Commando	17A0442	Heaver		B31F	9/46	9/46	1/63
3	2961	Commer Commando	17A0444	Heaver		B31F	10/46	10/46	1/63
6	3990	Commer Commando	17A0626	Heaver		B35F	9/47	9/47	1/63
1	5967	Albion SpFT3L	70695H	Strachan	50944	B31F	9/48	9/48	1/63

Police plates:

2960 (2): 139	3990 (6): 152	5499 (7): 140
2961 (3): 137	4869 (5): 142	5967 (1): 180
2981 (8): 138	4879 (4): 141	

Previous histories:

2 (Chevrolet): Acquired from Southern Traction, Southampton (HA).

Notes:

2 (Chevrolet): Possibly rebodied F Mallett OB20F at an unknown date (which was subsequently fitted to 1480 (2)).

1480 (2): Probably fitted with the F Mallett body from 2 (Chevrolet).

2714 (7): Fitted with a Silver Crown engine; rseated to B25F at an unknown date.

2960 (2): Fitted with a Perkins P6 oil engine 4/56.

2961 (3): Fitted with a Perkins P6 oil engine 8/52.

2981 (8): Converted to forward control, rebodied Heaver FB32F and renumbered 1 12/36; transferred to States of Guernsey Civil Transport Service, St Peter Port (GOV) 2/41; returned 5/45.

3990 (6): Fitted with a Perkins P6 oil engine 4/52.

4869 (5): Impressed by States of Guernsey Civil Transport Service, St Peter Port (GOV) 5/41; converted to gazogene propulsion 8/42; returned to HN & HK Falla {Blue Bird} 5/45; rebodied Heaver (9376) FB35F 1/50; fitted with a Perkins P6 oil engine 3/53.

4879 (4): Fitted with a Gold Crown engine; impressed by States of Guernsey Civil Transport Service, St Peter Port (GOV) 5/41; converted to gazogene propulsion 11/42; returned to HN & HK Falla {Blue Bird} 5/45.

5499 (7): Fitted with a Gold Crown engine; impressed by States of Guernsey Civil Transport Service, St Peter Port (GOV) 2/41; converted to gazogene propulsion 1/43; returned to HN & HK Falla {Blue Bird} 5/45; fitted with a Perkins P6 oil engine 3/52; rebodied Heaver (2008) FB35F 1954.

5967 (1): Fitted with a Perkins P6 oil engine 4/55.

Disposals:
1 (Ford): No known disposal.
2 (Chevrolet): Chassis to Piprell, Longstore as a lorry (GCI) c7/25; body to Guernsey Motors Ltd, St Peter Port (CI) c7/25.
917 (3): No known disposal.
1319 (4): Possibly to J Newton {The Bonnie}, Alderney (CI) 1931.
1410 (6): Impressed by German Military Authorities (GOV) and shipped to France 5/41.
1480 (2): Possibly to J Newton {The Bonnie}, Alderney (CI) 1931.
1765 (6): WJ Rugg {Wayfarer}, St Sampson (CI) 5 7/33; body rebuilt by Rugg before entering service; impressed by States of Guernsey Military Transport Service, St Peter Port (GOV) 7/41; German Military Authorities (Fortress Engineer Staff) (GOV) 7/42; scrapped locally at an unknown date (or sent to France for scrapping).
2047 (5): JW Stacey, St Peter Port (CI) 1935; impressed by German Military Authorities (Military Truck Compound) (GOV) 11/42; scrapped locally at an unknown date (or sent to France for scrapping).
2341 (3): Impressed by German Military Authorities (Military Truck Compound) (GOV) 10/42; scrapped locally at an unknown date (or sent to France for scrapping).
2714 (7): NA Lenfestey {Lorina}, Pleinmont (CI) 5/37; Guernsey Motors Ltd, St Peter Port (CI) 48 2/39; impressed by States of Guernsey Military Transport Service, St Peter Port (GOV) 11/41; German Military Authorities (Fortress Engineer Staff) (GOV) 7/42; returned at an unknown date; withdrawn 9/49.
2960 (2): Guernsey Motors Ltd, St Peter Port (CI) 27 1/63; withdrawn 10/63; scrapped 8/65.
2961 (3): Guernsey Motors Ltd, St Peter Port (CI) 28 1/63; withdrawn 4/64; unidentified owner 1/67.
2981 (1, ex 8): HK Falla {Paragon}, St Sampson (CI) 1 1/49; S Le Poidevin, St Peter Port 4/53; unidentified owner as a mobile shop (GCI) at an unknown date.
3120 (4): Mrs SE Watson {The Greys}, St Martin (CI) 1937; Watson Bros {The Greys}, St Martin (CI) at an unknown date; impressed by German Military Authorities (Military Truck Compound) (GOV) 2/43; scrapped locally at an unknown date (or sent to France for scrapping).
3990 (6): Guernsey Motors Ltd, St Peter Port (CI) 29 1/63; withdrawn 10/67; dumped at Priaulx's Quarry, St Sampson 2/68.
4252 (2): Impressed by German Military Authorities (GOV) and shipped to France 5/41.
4869 (5): Guernsey Motors Ltd, St Peter Port (CI) 25 1/63; withdrawn 10/64; dumped at Priaulx's Quarry, St Sampson 1966.
4879 (4): No known disposal.
5499 (7): Guernsey Motors Ltd, St Peter Port (CI) 26 1/63; withdrawn 10/67; scrapped 3/68.
5967 (1): Guernsey Motors Ltd, St Peter Port (CI) 30 1/63; withdrawn 10/63.

BLUE BIRD SERVICES LTD {Blue Bird Taxis}   2 Vale Avenue, VALE
South Quay, ST SAMPSON (-/--)
Braye Road Industrial Estate, VALE (8/96)
La Hure Mare Industrial Estate, VALE (by1/02)

Peter Elliott and Len Le Roi purchased the Blue Bird garage and taxi business from the Falla family in June 1987. They started a minibus service and were soon running transfers to the airport and the harbour as well as other private hire work. They sold out to Delta Taxis Ltd in 2004.

47635	Toyota Hiace	61V000254444	Dormobile		M14	5/85	8/87	by1/04
21173	Volkswagen LT28	28CH013665	Volkswagen		M15	9/82	3/88	-/89
36676	Toyota Hiace	61V00109092A	Toyota		M8	8/88	8/88	by1/04
30455	Mazda E2200	143200603683	Mazda		M8	11/88	11/88	by1/04
50414	Ford Transit	BDVZHE77962	Ford		M14	5/87	-/89	by1/04
17052	Toyota Hiace	?	Toyota		M8	3/92	3/92	by12/97
41558	Toyota Hiace	00054232	Autotrim		M8	6/93	6/93	by6/02
16697	Toyota Hiace	00064565	Autotrim		M8	4/94	4/94	by6/02
49282	Toyota HB31R	0002802	Caetano	951060	C18F	2/90	10/94	1/04
26209	LDV 400	CN950316	LDV		M16	10/94	8/95	1/04
58054	Toyota Hiace	00019497	Autotrim		M8	6/96	11/97	1/04
62812	Toyota HDB30R	0002152	Caetano	351007	C18F	6/93	9/98	1/04
64918	Mercedes Benz O814D		Plaxton	977.8MWV6547	B31F	4/97	9/00	1/04
	WDB6703732N062304							
67463	Toyota BBR50R		Caetano	051214	C27F	6/01	6/01	1/04
	TW043BB5000001644							
38293 [2]	Toyota Hiace	00014692	Central Coachcraft		M8	10/98	-/01	1/04

Public Service Omnibus plates:

16697: t98	26209: ph3	41558: t72
17052: t58	30455: t46	47635: ph77
21173: ph48	36676: t88	49282: t2
50414: ph48	62812: ph7	

Previous histories:
21173: New to Bluescare Ltd, Sittingbourne (XKT) registered VPL 819Y; withdrawn 2/88.
26209: New to Leeds Commercial Van & Taxi Hire (XWY) registered M139 UWY.
38293 [2]: Its origins are unknown.
47635: New to JP Whitworth, Ilkeston (DE) registered B287 KCH; withdrawn 6/87.
49282: New as a demonstrator with Toyota, Redhill registered G700 APB; Ardenvale Coaches Ltd, Knowle (WM) 10/90.
50414: New to Suredrive Car Rental, St Martin (XCI).
58054: New to an unidentified UK operator registered N876 PPK.
62812: New to Capital Coaches Ltd, West Drayton (LN) 26 registered K 26 VRY; Hertz Rent a Car Ltd, London SW16 (LN) 26 8/93.
64918: New to Pete's Travel Ltd, Birmingham (WM) registered P856 GRC; withdrawn 4/00.

Notes:
49282 (ex G700 APB): To service 12/94.

Disposals:
16697: Private owner, Guernsey by6/02.
17052: Private owner, Guernsey by12/97.
21173 (ex VPL 819Y): Private owner, Guernsey 1989.
26209 (ex M139 UWY): Delta Taxis Ltd, Vale (CI) 9 1/04; unidentified owner, Guernsey (XCI) 12/04.
30455: No known disposal.
36676: No known disposal.
38293 [2]: Delta Taxis Ltd, Vale (CI) 8 1/04; converted to a service van with Delta Taxis Ltd by5/09
41558: Private owner, Guernsey by6/02.
47635 (ex B287 KCH): No known disposal.
49282 (ex G700 APB): Delta Taxis Ltd, Vale (CI) 8 1/04; unidentified UK dealer 4/10.
50414: No known disposal.
58054 (ex N876 PPK): Delta Taxis Ltd, Vale (CI) 25 1/04; private owner, Guernsey 4/10.
62812 (ex K 26 VRY): Delta Taxis Ltd, Vale (CI) 7 1/04; Island Taxis Ltd, St Peter Port (CI) 4/10; unidentified owner by12/18.
64918 (ex P856 GRC): Delta Taxis Ltd, Vale (CI) 10 1/04.
67463: Delta Taxis Ltd, Vale (CI) 6 1/04; Island Taxis Ltd, St Peter Port (CI) 4/10; numbered 7 2018; being cannibalised for spares by12/18.

CENTRAL TAXIS LTD {Central / Vaudin's Taxis from 6/91}   **Weighbridge, ST PETER PORT**
Central Taxis Ltd provided transport for specialist holidays and later airport and harbour transfers. The business was sold to Delta Taxis Ltd in July 1994.

10532	Ford Transit	BDVZBE37627	Ford	M11	1/82	7/85	12/87
30715	Ford Transit	BDVZBK29322	Ford	M14	11/81	9/85	12/88
49377	Ford Transit	BDVZHJ6L9140	Ford	M14	12/87	12/87	10/89
44525	Ford Transit		Ford	M14	5/88	12/88	10/89
		SFAZXXBDVZJG42274					
34932	Toyota Hiace	60V00009946	Toyota	M14	6/84	6/91	7/94
44993	Mazda E2200	143200708730	Howletts	M8	5/91	6/91	7/94

Public Service Omnibus plates:

10532: ph55	34932: ph34	44993: t132
30715: ph95	44525: ph95	
49377: ph21		

Previous histories:
10532: New to Rank Xerox (UK) Ltd, Uxbridge (XLN) registered NJB 356X; VMW Commercials Ltd, St Peter Port (dealer) by7/85.
30715: New to Holiday Pak Ltd, St Peter Port (CI).
34932: New to RL Gaudion {L'Islet Cabs}, St Sampson (CI); Vaudin's United Taxis, St Sampson (CI) 4/88; withdrawn 6/90-4/91.
44525: New to BB Hire Cars Ltd, St Peter Port (XCI); hired to Guernseybus Ltd, St Peter Port (CI) 9 5/88-10/88.
44993: New to Vaudin's United Taxis, St Sampson (CI).

Notes:
44993: Received Public Service Omnibus plate ph1 by5/92.

Disposals:
10532 (ex NJB 356X): Private owner, Guernsey 12/87.
30715: Private owner, Guernsey 12/88.
34932: No known disposal.
44525: Educational Holidays Guernsey Ltd {Island Coachways}, St Peter Port (CI) 10/89; Central Transfers, St Peter Port (CI) 3/90; Guernseybus Ltd, St Peter Port (CI) 3 1/91; Central Transfers Ltd, St Peter Port (CI) 3 1/95; Intransit Ltd, St Peter Port (CI) 3 12/96; withdrawn 9/03.
44993: Delta Taxis Ltd, St Peter Port (CI) 7/94.
49377: Educational Holidays Guernsey Ltd {Island Coachways}, St Peter Port (CI) 10/89; Central Transfers, St Peter Port (CI) 21 3/90; Guernseybus Ltd, St Peter Port (CI) 2 1/91; Central Transfers Ltd, St Peter Port (CI) 2 1/95; withdrawn at an unknown date.

CENTRAL TRANSFERS   St George's Esplanade, ST PETER PORT
This operator was set up in 1990 as a joint enterprise between Guernseybus Ltd and Educational Holidays whereby resources were pooled in order to provide airport and harbour transfers. After January 1991, Guernseybus took over the operation in its entirety and it was later in 1995 sold off as an independent company (Central Transfers Ltd).

21	49377	Ford Transit	BDVZHJ6L9140	Ford		M14	12/87	3/90	1/91
22	44525	Ford Transit	SFAZXXBDVZJG42274	Ford		M14	5/88	3/90	1/91
25	48701	Mercedes Benz 310	WDB6020672O610511	Devon Conversions		M12	-/86	3/90	1/91
24	48702	Mercedes Benz 310	WDB6020672O610002	Devon Conversions	98365D	M11	-/86	3/90	1/91
26	14223 [2]	Mercedes Benz 307D	WDB??????2O590798	?		M10	11/83	3/90	1/91

Public Service Omnibus plates:
44525 (22): ph95   49377 (21): ph21

Previous histories:
14223 [2] (26): New to Hampton Cars, Poole (XDT) registered A167 OOT; withdrawn 12/87; Guernseybus Ltd, St Peter Port (CI) 4 3/88.
44525 (22): New to BB Hire Cars Ltd, St Peter Port (XCI); hired to Guernseybus Ltd, St Peter Port (CI) 9 5/88-10/88; Central Taxis Ltd, St Peter Port (CI) 12/88; Educational Holidays Guernsey Ltd {Island Coachways}, St Peter Port (CI) 10/89.
48701 (25): New to Jacksons Garage, Forest (XCI); Guernseybus Ltd, St Peter Port (CI) 5 3/87.
48702 (24): New to Jacksons Garage, Forest (XCI); Guernseybus Ltd, St Peter Port (CI) 6 3/87.
49377 (21): New to Central Taxis Ltd, St Peter Port (CI); Educational Holidays Guernsey Ltd {Island Coachways}, St Peter Port (CI) 10/89.

Disposals:
14223 [2] (ex A167 OOT) (26): Guernseybus Ltd, St Peter Port (CI) 4 1/91; transferred to the service fleet 12/92 (qv).
44525 (22): Guernseybus Ltd, St Peter Port (CI) 3 1/91; Central Transfers Ltd, St Peter Port (CI) 3 1/95; Intransit Ltd, St Peter Port (CI) 3 12/96; withdrawn 9/03.
48701 (25): Guernseybus Ltd, St Peter Port (CI) 5 1/91; Central Transfers Ltd, St Peter Port (CI) 5 1/95; withdrawn at an unknown date.
48702 (24): Guernseybus Ltd, St Peter Port (CI) 6 1/91; Central Transfers Ltd, St Peter Port (CI) 6 1/95; Intransit Ltd, St Peter Port (CI) 6 1/96; withdrawn 6/02.

49377 (21): Guernseybus Ltd, St Peter Port (CI) 2 1/91; Central Transfers Ltd, St Peter Port (CI) 2 1/95; withdrawn at an unknown date.

CENTRAL TRANSFERS LTD   Grand Bouet, ST PETER PORT

Central Transfers Ltd was an independent company set up by Robin Le Feuvre which was formed from the Guernseybus/Educational Holidays (later Guernseybus only) Central Transfers operation. It was sold to his sister Lauren Le Feuvre and and her partner Mark Duncan in December 1996, who changed the name to Intransit Ltd.

1	19797	Ford Transit SFAZXXBDVZHD59537	Ford	M14	9/91	1/95	12/96
3	44525	Ford Transit SFAZXXBDVZJG42274	Ford	M14	5/88	1/95	12/96
2	49377	Ford Transit BDVZHJ6L9140	Ford	M14	12/87	1/95	by12/96
5	48701	Mercedes Benz 310 WDB6020672O610511	Devon Conversions	M12	-/86	1/95	by12/96
6	48702	Mercedes Benz 310 WDB6020672O610002	Devon Conversions 98365D	M11	-/86	1/95	12/96
7	30752	LDV 400 SFAMYSFACN959596	LDV	M16	7/96	7/96	12/96

Previous histories:

19797: Its origins are unknown; Delta Taxis Ltd, St Peter Port (CI) 7/94.

44525 (3): New to BB Hire Cars Ltd, St Peter Port (XCI); hired to Guernseybus Ltd (CI) 9 5/88-10/88; Central Taxis Ltd, St Peter Port (CI) 12/88; Educational Holidays Guernsey Ltd {Island Coachways} (CI) 10/89; Central Transfers, St Peter Port (CI) 22 3/90; Guernseybus Ltd, St Peter Port (CI) 3 1/91.

48701 (5): New to Jacksons Garage, Forest (XCI); Guernseybus Ltd, St Peter Port (CI) 5 3/87; Central Transfers, St Peter Port (CI) 25 3/90; Guernseybus Ltd, St Peter Port (CI) 5 1/91.

48702 (6): New to Jacksons Garage, Forest (XCI); Guernseybus Ltd, St Peter Port (CI) 6 3/87; Central Transfers, St Peter Port (CI) 24 3/90; Guernseybus Ltd, St Peter Port (CI) 6 1/91.

49377 (2): New to Central Taxis Ltd, St Peter Port (CI); Educational Holidays Guernsey Ltd {Island Coachways} (CI) 10/89; Central Transfers, St Peter Port (CI) 21 3/90; Guernseybus Ltd, St Peter Port (CI) 2 1/91

Disposals:

19797: Intransit Ltd, St Peter Port (CI) 1 12/96; withdrawn 1998.

30752: Intransit Ltd, St Peter Port (CI) 7 12/96; withdrawn 12/01; private owner, Guernsey by6/02.

44525: Intransit Ltd, St Peter Port (CI) 3 12/96; withdrawn 9/03.

48701: No known disposal.

48702: Intransit Ltd, St Peter Port (CI) 6 12/96; withdrawn 6/02.

49377: No known disposal.

RC & WH COLLENETTE {Collenette Bros / Shamrock}   Delancey Garage, Pointues Rocques, ST SAMPSON

Collenette Bros' Shamrock operation was the largest operator covering the north of the island in the early 1920s, providing services from St Peter Port to L'Ancresse and L'Islet. The operation was sold to the Guernsey Railway Co Ltd on 12 March 1926 for £2,800 and the Collenette Bros moved on to running the Pembroke Tea Rooms.

	Humber	?	Collenette	W18	-/--	by7/22	-/--
1	Ford TT	?	Collenette	OB--F	-/--	-/23	3/26
2	Ford TT	?	Collenette	OB--F	-/--	-/23	3/26
3	Ford TT	?	Collenette	OB--F	-/--	-/23	3/26
4	Dodge LB	?	Collenette	OB12F	-/--	-/--	3/26
5	Renault	?	Collenette	OB24F	-/--	7/24	3/26
6	Renault	?	Collenette	OB24F	-/--	7/24	3/26

Previous histories:

The previous histories of these vehicles are not known, all being first recorded with RC & WH Collenette on the dates shown.

Disposals:

Humber: No known disposal.

1: Guernsey Railway Co Ltd, St Peter Port (CI) 12 3/26 (as Ch13); renumbered S1 1926; fitted with normal air pressure tyres 8/26; rebuilt 1927; withdrawn 12/32.

2: Guernsey Railway Co Ltd, St Peter Port (CI) 13 3/26; renumbered S2 1926; fitted with normal air pressure tyres 8/26; rebuilt 1927; withdrawn 12/31.

3: Guernsey Railway Co Ltd, St Peter Port (CI) 14 3/26; renumbered S3 1926; fitted with normal air pressure tyres 8/26; rebuilt (shortened by 38 cm) 1927; withdrawn 12/31.

4: Guernsey Railway Co Ltd, St Peter Port (CI) 15 3/26 (as OB12F); Renumbered S4 1926; rebuilt 1927; withdrawn 12/32.

5: Guernsey Railway Co Ltd, St Peter Port (CI) 16 3/26 (as OB22F); renumbered S5 1926; fitted with giant pneumatic tyres on the rear only 5/27; rebuilt 1927; withdrawn 12/39.

6: Guernsey Railway Co Ltd, St Peter Port (CI) 17 3/26 (as OB22F); renumbered S6 1927; withdrawn 12/34.

N CUTLER   ST PETER PORT
Cutler was granted a licence to operate the Petit Bot bus route.

| 28274 | MCW MF150/4 | MB8807 | MCW | B25F | 3/87 | 8/00 | by12/00 |

Previous history:
28274: New to West Midlands (WM) 634 registered D634 NOE.

Disposal:
28274: No known disposal.

DV DAWES {Delta Tours}   Delta House, Cornet Street, ST PETER PORT
Delta Tours provided airport and harbour transfers. It was sold to Guernsey Railway Co in 1977 and formed the start of their similar operations which later Guernseybus and Educational Holidays took on. The Delta Tours name was also used on the Railway Company's coaches for a while from 1980.

15975	Ford Transit	BCVGLP54119	Ford	M16	1/72	4/75	12/75
25912	Volkswagen Microbus	2352132252	Devon Conversions 050232K	M9	7/76	7/76	7/77
12614	Volkswagen LT31	2862511735	Devon Conversions 26003LF	M16	9/76	3/77	7/77

Police plates:
12614: ph84   15975: ph78   25912: ph78

Previous histories:
12614: New to St Brelade's College, St Brelade (XCI) registered J 57640.
15975: Its origins are unknown.

Disposals:
12614 (ex J 57640): Guernsey Railway Co Ltd, St Peter Port (CI) 3 7/77; withdrawn 11/80; Guernseybus Ltd, St Peter Port (CI) 3 2/81; re-registered 5579 [1] 9/81; withdrawn 1986; B Ceillam, Guernsey as a shed 1986.
15975: No known disposal.
29512: Guernsey Railway Co Ltd, St Peter Port (CI) 4 7/77; withdrawn 11/80; Guernseybus Ltd, St Peter Port (CI) 4 2/81; withdrawn 1987.

LA DE LA MARE   Vue de l'Eglise, FOREST
De La Mare was granted a licence to operate the Petit Bot bus route.

| 38273 | Renault Master | G0500784 | Coachwork Conversions | B12F | 6/86 | 4/93 | 10/94 |

Previous history:
38273: New to Godfrey Davis Europecar Ltd, Bushey (XHT) registered C998 VLD; Budget Rent-a-Car, St Brelade (XCI) registered J 46467 3/90; South Quay Garage, St Sampson (dealer) by11/92.

Disposal:
38273: Vale Rec Football Club, Vale (XCI) 10/94.

DELTA TAXIS LTD Les Gravees, ST PETER PORT
King's Road, ST PETER PORT (by-/97)
La Hure Mare Industrial Estate, VALE (by1/02)

DELTA TAXIS (2004) Ltd (-/04)
Delta Taxis Ltd was a substantial minibus operator who started by taking over Central / Vaudin's Taxis in 1994 and ten years later in 2004, acquired the Blue Bird Taxis business. Delta Taxis collapsed however in March 2010 and some school contracts were taken over by Island Taxis Ltd.

	19797	Ford Transit		Ford		M14	9/91	7/94	1/95
		SFAZXXBDVZHD59537							
	44993	Mazda E2200	143200708730	Howletts		M8	5/91	7/94	-/--
	56650	Renault Master	11331221	Cymric	RM94/1425	M14	7/94	7/94	2/07
	56690	Renault Master		Cymric	RM95/1537	M14	5/95	5/95	3/10
		VF1FB30AH12482772							
5	37487	Toyota Hiace	0020961	Toyota		M8	11/96	11/96	3/10
	56660	Renault Master		Cymric	RM97/2246	M14	5/97	5/97	3/10
		VF1FB30AK15537481							
1	66959	Toyota BBR50R		Caetano	951204	C27F	6/01	6/01	3/10
		TW043BB5000001549							
9	26209	LDV 400	CN950316	LDV		M16	10/94	1/04	12/04
8	38293 [2]	Toyota Hiace	00014692	Central Coachcraft		M8	10/98	1/04	by5/09
8	49282	Toyota HB31R	0002802	Caetano	951060	C18F	2/90	1/04	3/10
25	58054	Toyota Hiace	00019497	Autotrim		M8	6/96	1/04	3/10
7	62812	Toyota HDB30R		Caetano	351007	C18F	6/93	1/04	3/10
		HBB3000002152							
10	64918	Mercedes Benz O814D		Plaxton 977.8MWV6547	B31F	4/97	1/04	by3/10
		WDB6703732N062304							
6	67463	Toyota BBR50R		Caetano	051214	C27F	6/01	1/04	3/10
		TW043BB5000001644							
9	14031	Renault Master		Atlas		M16	12/04	12/04	3/10
		VF1FDCUM631836424							
	R196 LBC	Toyota BB50R	0001152	Caetano	751131	C16F	4/98	6/09	----

Public Service Omnibus plates:
14031 (9): ph3   19797: ph1   44993: t23
56650 (4): ph4   56690: ph5   66959 (1): ph9
56660: ph10   58054 (25): ph19
37487 (5): t23

Previous histories:
19797: Its origins are unknown.
26209 (9): New to Leeds Commercial Van & Taxi Hire (XWY) registered M139 UWY; Blue Bird Taxis Ltd, St Sampson (CI) 8/95; moved to Vale (CI) 8/96.
38293 [2] (8): Its origins are unknown; Blue Bird Taxis Ltd, Vale (CI) 2001.
44993: New to Vaudin's United Taxis, St Sampson (CI); Central / Vaudin's Taxis, St Peter Port (CI) 6/91.
49282 (8): New as a demonstration vehicle with Toyota, Redhill registered G700 APB; Ardenvale, Knowle (WM) 10/90; Blue Bird Taxis Ltd, St Sampson (CI) 10/94; moved to Vale (CI) 8/96.
58054 (10): New to an unidentified UK operator registered N876 PPK; Blue Bird Taxis Ltd, Vale (CI) 11/97.
62812 (7): New to Capital Coaches Ltd, West Drayton (LN) 26 registered K 26 VRY; Hertz Rent a Car Ltd, London SW16 (LN) 26 8/93; Blue Bird Taxis Ltd, Vale (CI) 9/98.
64918 (10): New to Pete's Travel Ltd, Birmingham (WM) registered P856 GRC; withdrawn 4/00; Blue Bird Taxis Ltd, Vale (CI) 9/00.
67463 (6): New to Blue Bird Taxis Ltd, Vale (CI).
R196 LBC: New to Clarke, Lower Sydenham (LN); unidentified owner 4/06; Blue Islands, St Peter Port (based at Jersey airport) (XCI) by5/07.

Notes:
14031 (9): Received Public Service Omnibus plate 204 7/09.
49282 (ex G700 APB) (8): Received Public Service Omnibus plate 202 7/09.
56650: Numbered 5 6/01.
56660: Numbered 2 6/01; received Public Service Omnibus plate 205 7/09.
56690: Numbered 3 6/01; received Public Service Omnibus plate 206 7/09.
62812 (ex K 26 VRY) (7): Received Public Service Omnibus plate 203 7/09.

66959 (1): Received Public Service Omnibus plate 200 7/09.
67463 (6): Received Public Service Omnibus plate 201 7/09.
R196 LBC: Was not registered on Guernsey; it was allocated Public Service Omnibus plate 207 7/09.

Disposals:
14031 (9): Island Taxis Ltd, St Peter Port (CI) 4/10; re-registered 11188 by5/10; re-registered 38225 10/15.
19797: Central Transfers Ltd, St Peter Port (CI) 1/95; Intransit Ltd, St Peter Port (CI) 12/96; withdrawn 1998.
26209 (ex M139 UWY) (9): Unidentified owner, Guernsey (XCI) 12/04.
37487 (5): Private owner, Guernsey 4/10.
38293 [2] (8): Converted to a service van with Delta Taxis Ltd by5/09.
44993: No known disposal.
49282 (ex G700 APB) (8): Unidentified UK dealer 4/10.
56650 (5): No known disposal.
56660 (2): Island Taxis Ltd, St Peter Port (CI) 4/10; unidentified owner by5/11.
56690 (3): Island Taxis Ltd, St Peter Port (CI) 4/10; unidentified owner by5/11.
58054 (ex N876 PPK) (25): Private owner, Guernsey 4/10.
62812 (ex K 26 VRY) (7): Island Taxis Ltd, St Peter Port (CI) 4/10; unidentified owner by12/18.
64918 (ex P856 GRC) (10): No known disposal.
66959 (1): Island Taxis Ltd, St Peter Port (CI) by5/11; numbered 5 2018.
67463 (6): Island Taxis Ltd, St Peter Port (CI) 4/10; numbered 7 2018; being cannibalised for spares by12/18.

AJ DINGLE   Ann's Place & Stanley Road, ST PETER PORT

Dingle ran a service between St Peter Port and St Sampson having taken over the service from SJC Duquemin (who subsequently drove for Dingle). A fire destroyed the Ann's Place premises in February 1913 but later in that year, he was competing with trams on Saturdays and Sundays. He wound up the business at the start of World War I.

Charron 20/30 hp	?	?	Ch--	-/--	-/13	-/--
Maudslay 30 hp	?	?		5/07	12/13	-/14
			O18/16RO			
Maudslay 30 hp	?	?		5/07	12/13	-/14
			O18/16RO			
Thornycroft 24 hp	581	?		7/06	12/13	-/14
			O18/16RO			
Thornycroft 24 hp	582	?		7/06	12/13	-/14
			O18/16RO			
Thornycroft 24 hp	583	?		7/06	12/13	-/14
			O18/16RO			
Panhard 1 ton	?	?	OB18R	-/--	-/--	-/--
Panhard 30 cwt	?	?	OB24R	-/--	-/--	-/--

Previous histories:
Charron: First recorded with SJC Duquemin, St Peter Port (CI).
Maudslays: New to Great Eastern Railway, London EC1 (LN) 19?, 21 registered F 2440, F 2442.
Thornycroft (chassis 581): New to Great Eastern Railway, London EC1 (LN) 16? registered F 1874.
Thornycroft (chassis 582): New to Great Eastern Railway, London EC1 (LN) 17? registered BJ 415.
Thornycroft (chassis 583): Acquired from Great Eastern Railway, London EC1 (LN) 18 registered BJ 416; rebodied Ch23 by an unknown builder for the summer season 7/12; the original O18/16RO body was refitted at the end of the season
Panhards: Their origins are unknown.

Notes:
Some of the registrations of these vehicles may have included 39, 127, 128 and 141.

Maudslays (ex F 2440, F 2442): Had two extra seats alongside the driver which increased their total capacity to 36.
Thornycrofts (ex F 1874, BJ 415-416): Had two extra seats alongside the driver which increased their total capacity to 36.

Disposals:
Charron: Advertised for sale 7/15; no known disposal.
Maudslays (ex F2440, F 2442): One of these to E Lander {Channel Island Motor & General Engineering Co}, St Helier (GCI) registered J 257 1/15; Lander had a second Maudslay lorry registered J 515 10/15 which may have been the other one.
Thornycrofts (ex F 1874, BJ 415-416): Advertised for sale 7/15; no known disposals.

Panhards: TW Sarre, St Peter-in-the-Wood (CI) by3/21; for sale by auction 3/21; one, possibly both of these to F Le Cheminant {Saints Bus Service}, St Martin (CI) at an unknown date.

SJC DUQUEMIN   **ST PETER PORT**

Duquemin preceded AJ Dingle with a service between St Peter Port and St Sampson which was operated up to 1913.

	Charron 20/30 hp		? ?		Ch--	-/--	-/--	-/13

Previous history:
Charron: Its origins are unknown.

Disposal:
Charron: AJ Dingle, St Peter Port (CI) 1913; withdrawn 1914; advertised for sale 7/15; no known disposal.

R ELLIOTT {Vazon Bay Hotel}   **Vazon, CASTEL**

Courtesy coach for the Vazon Bay Hotel.

6776	Toyota Hiace	RH3200015781	Toyota	M11	4/81	4/81	8/86

Public Service Omnibus plate:
6776: ph25

Disposal:
6776: Private owner, Guernsey re-registered 20582 8/86.

EXECUTIVE CAR SERVICES LTD   **Shandla, Clos des Arbres, Les Prins Estate, VALE**

2599	Ford Transit	?	Ford	M8	by2/13	by2/13	by5/16
5389	Ford Transit		Ford	M16	9/06	by9/13	#
	WF0DXXTTFD6P52088						
35888	Mercedes Benz O814D	Plaxton 028.5MAE4873	C33F	8/02	3/15	1/18
	WDB6703742N105479						
36394	Mercedes Benz 515CDI	Tawe	C19F	11/09	2/17	#
	WDB9066572S351865						
3787	Mercedes Benz 11?CDI	?	Mercedes Benz	M8	by4/17	by4/17	#
23337	Mercedes Benz O816D	Plaxton 078.5MBJ7360	C29F	3/08	12/17	#
	WDB6703742N128606						
15562	Iveco 45C15	?		M16	11/10	5/18	#
	ZCFC45A200D399563						

Vehicles marked # were still in service at the date of this Fleet History.

Public Service Omnibus plates:

2599: ph9	5389: ph7	23337: ph8
3787: ph9	15562: ph32	36394: ph14
35888: ph8?		

Previous histories:
2599: Its origins are unknown.
5389: New to North West Essex Schools Sports Partnership, Halstead (XEX) registered EO56 NTJ.
15562: New to I & KA Jardine {Darras Minibuses}, Milbourne (ND) registered YJ60 CVO.
23337: New to Nash's Coaches Ltd, Smethwick (WM) registered YN08 DLZ; Solus Travel Ltd, Tamworth (dealer) 2/15; York Pullman Bus Co Ltd, Strenshall (NY) 398 2/15; re-registered CB08 YPB 7/16; re-registered YN08 DLZ 4/17; Plaxton, Anston (dealer) 6/17.
36394: New to Coliseum Coaches Ltd, West End (HA) 190417 registered LX59 DGO; re-registered MIB 650 2/11; re-registered LX 59 DGO 1/17.
35888: New to Guideissue Ltd {Baker's Coaches}, Knypersley (ST) 19 registered 8439 RU; TD Parnell, Honiton (dealer) 3/15.

Notes:
5389 (ex EO 56 NTJ): Named '*LJ*'.
23337 (ex YN08 DLZ): Named '*Millie*'.
35888 (ex 8439 RU): Named '*Lorna May*'.
36394: Re-registered 30888 by12/17.

Disposals:
2599: No known disposal.
35888 (ex 8439 RU): Intransit Ltd, St Sampson (CI) for spares 1/18.

GALA ENTERPRISES LTD   **Fermain Hotel, Port Road, ST PETER PORT**
Gala Enterprises operated a courtesy coach for the Fermain Hotel.

12924	Volkswagen	25CH118298	Volkswagen	M11	5/82	5/82	-/--

Public Service Omnibus plate:
12924: ph66

Disposal:
12924: No known disposal.

RL GAUDION {L'Islet Cabs}   **Les Salines, ST SAMPSON**
Operated airport and harbour transfers.

34932	Toyota Hiace	60V00009946	Toyota	M14	6/84	6/84	4/88

Public Service Omnibus plate:
34932: ph97

Disposal:
34932: Vaudin's United Taxis, St Sampson (CI) 4/88; withdrawn 6/90-4/91; Central Taxis Ltd, St Peter Port (CI) 6/91; withdrawn 7/94.

HOLIDAY PAK LTD   **Les Buttes, St Pierre du Bois, ST PETER PORT**
       St George's Esplanade, ST PETER PORT (-/---)
Holiday Pak provided transport for specialist holidays.

12833	FIAT 850	?	?	M4	1/78	1/78	2/79
29776	Volkswagen Microbus		Devon Conversions	M11	2/79	2/79	12/82
		219Z047133					
29904	Volkswagen Microbus	?	?	?	3/81	3/81	11/81
30715	Ford Transit	BDVZBK29322	Ford	M14	11/81	11/81	12/82

Police plates (Public Service Omnibus plates from 1981):

12833: ph94	29904: ph95
29776: ph94	30715: ph95

Disposals:
12833: Private owner, Guernsey 2/79.
29776: Private owner, Guernsey 12/82.
29904: Private owner, Guernsey 11/81.
30715: Central Taxis Ltd, St Peter Port (CI) 9/85; private owner, Guernsey 12/88.

INTRANSIT LTD First Tower Lane, ST PETER PORT
Clock Tower, Weighbridge, ST PETER PORT (by4/02)
The Coach Depot, Les Hougues Magues Road, ST SAMPSON (by9/13)

In December 1996, the Central Transfers Ltd business was purchased by Lauren Le Feure and Mark Duncan and renamed it Intransit Ltd. Its core business was airport and harbour transfers, school contracts and tours. Over the years larger vehicles were purchased as the business expanded its operations.

No	Reg	Model / Chassis	Body	Body No	Seats	Date1	Date2	Date3
1	19797	Ford Transit SFAZXXBDVZHD59537	Ford		M14	9/91	12/96	-/98
7	30752	LDV 400 SFAMYSFACN959596	LDV		M16	7/96	12/96	12/01
3	44525	Ford Transit SFAZXXBDVZJG42274	Ford		M14	5/88	12/96	9/03
6	48702	Mercedes Benz 310 WDB6020672O610002	Devon Conversions	98365D	M11	-/86	12/96	6/02
4	34796	Peugeot 806 VF3221RB211075034	Peugeot		M8	9/95	1/97	-/99
2	58228	Ford Transit SFAZXXBDVENC25559	Ford		M10	11/92	5/97	4/05
1	54361	LDV Convoy XLRZMNFEACN931260	Pentagon	9272	M16	c12/92	4/99	9/03
3	42438	Ford Transit SFAZXXBDVESU42182	Ford		M10	6/00	6/00	5/06
5	52408	Iveco 49-10 ZCF04970005127152	?		B15F	5/97	12/00	4/09
7	11926	Ford Transit WF0FXXBDVFXL30570	Ford		M8	2/01	2/01	2/09
6	48641	Toyota HZB50R TW043PB5009000125	Caetano	451046	C21F	10/94	6/01	12/08
4	13704	LDV Convoy SEYZMYSHEDN046285	LDV		M16	3/99	4/02	8/02
4	15206	Toyota HZB50R TW043PB5009000127	Caetano	451048	C21F	10/94	4/04	-/11
1	23069	Mercedes Benz O814D WDB6703742N098086	Plaxton 018.5MZE3880		C33F	4/01	5/06	#
2	73861	Mercedes Benz 413CDI WDB9046632R230637	Ferqui		C16F	4/02	5/07	by5/17
3	76385	Ford Transit WF0LXXGBVLVB27277	Ferqui		C8F	8/97	4/08	12/10
5	50524	Iveco 40C12 ZCFC1081005601943	?		M16	7/07	9/08	#
7	26248	Toyota BB50R TW043BB5000001346	Caetano	851156	C22F	5/00	2/09	by5/17
6	26960	Toyota BB50R TW043BB5000001443	Caetano	951113	C21F	4/00	2/09	9/14
	76357	Volkswagen Transporter WV2ZZZ7HZ4X039762	Volkswagen		M8	6/04	2/10	12/11
8	74271	BMC 850 NMCRKTRD100002	BMC		C35F	6/04	5/10	4/14
3	37603	Ford Transit WF0AXXTTFA4K63784	Ferqui		C16F	9/05	12/10	5/17
8	17337	Toyota BB50R TW1FG518105500549	Caetano	F043071063	C23F	3/05	1/12	1/18
11	1787 [1]	Albion FT39AN 73737B	Reading	5176	B36F	6/54	2/13	#
4	1787 [6]	Iveco 45C14 ZCFC45A1005612425	?		C16F	5/07	2/13	#
	TFO 249	Albion FT39KAN 73840J	Reading		B35F	2/58	11/13	----
9	12034	Mercedes Benz O816D WDB6703742N136478	Plaxton 098.5MBJ8406		C33F	5/10	4/14	#
6	20234	Toyota XZB50R TW1FC518206000012	Caetano	F073071003	C21F	6/08	3/16	#
3	12045	Iveco 50C14 ZCFC50A1005610830	Stanford		C16FL	1/07	10/17	#
8	49768	Mercedes Benz O816D WDB6703742N139100	Plaxton 108.5MBJ8535		C33F	5/10	1/18	#

	35888	Mercedes Benz O814D	Plaxton 028.5MAE4873	C33F	8/02	1/18	----
		WDB6703742N105479					
7	65075	Temsa Opalin	Temsa MA0454	C35F	6/08	9/18	#
		NLTHNJ45R01000025					

Vehicles marked # were still in service at the date of this Fleet History.

Public Service Omnibus plates:

1787 [1] (11): 113	23069 (1): ph11	49768 (8): 111
1787 [6] (4): 204	26248 (7): 110	50524 (5): 120
11926 (7): ph14	26960 (6): 114	52408 (5): ph12
12034 (9): 201	30752 (7): ph14	54361 (1): ph16
12045 (3): 116	34796 (4): ph16	58228 (2): ph11
13704 (4): ph16	37603 (3): 116	65075 (7): 110
15206 (4): ph18	42438 (3): ph13	73861 (2): 112
17337 (8): 111	44525 (3): ph13	74271 (8): 201
19797 (1): ph12	48641 (6): ph20	
20234 (6): 114	48702 (6): ph15	
76357: ph32	76385 (3): 116	

Previous histories:

1787 [1] (11): New to Watson's Garage Ltd {The Greys}, St Martin (CI); Guernsey Railway Co Ltd, St Peter Port (CI) 20 2/78; withdrawn 9/79; J Lidstone, Leigh-on-Sea for preservation 4/80; Tillingbourne Valley Services Ltd, Cranleigh (SR) re-registered 898 FUF 6/83; to service 7/83; F Elliott & Dr JR Young, Golborne for preservation 6/85; hired to Educational Holidays Guernsey Ltd {Island Coachways}, St Peter Port (CI) re-registered 1787 [1] 5/86-9/86; acquired by Educational Holidays Guernsey Ltd {Island Coachways}, St Peter Port (CI) 4/88; to service 5/88; Lakeland Motor Museum, Holker Hall for preservion re-registered 898 FUF 6/93; R Greet, Broadhempson for preservation 3/94.

1787 [6] (4): New to Island Coachways Ltd, St Peter Port (CI) 8.

12034 (9): New to Weavaway Travel Ltd, Newbury (BE) registered SF10 EBV; Blythswood Motors Ltd, Glasgow (dealer) 4/13; Porterfield, Renfrew (dealer) by4/14.

12045 (3): New to Easington District Communicare, Peterlee (XDM) registered LK56 GYJ; R Laverick {Easington District Communicare}, Peterlee (DM) 8/10.

13704 (4): Its origins are unknown.

15206 (4): New to Bonas & Son Ltd {Supreme Coaches}, Coventry (WM) registered M652 FWK; Bob Vale PSV Sales Ltd, Great Kingshill (dealer) 3/98; RA Coates {Chariots}, Heald Green (GM) by4/98.

17337 (8): New to Johnson's (Henley) Ltd, Henley-in-Arden (WK) registered FJ05 HXZ (as C22F); DG, RM, CG & SS Stone & NR Russell, Bath (SO) 8/08; AC, EK, MW & NK Hillier, Foxham (WI) 6/10.

19797 (1): Its origins are unknown; Delta Taxis Ltd, St Peter Port (CI) 7/94; Central Transfers Ltd, St Peter Port (CI) 1 1/95.

20234 (6): New to Lakeside Coaches Ltd, Ellesmere (SH) registered BU08 BGF.

23069 (1): New to Burgundy Car Co Ltd, Bracknell (BE) registered Y831 HHE; Courtney Coaches Ltd, Bracknell (BE) 8/02.

26248 (7): New to PT Dawson, Tadcaster (NY) registered W314 SBC; DD Burditt {David's}, Haywards Heath (WS) by8/04; Jacobite Cruises Ltd, Inverness (HI) 11/04; re-registered 4234 NT 11/05; re-registered W314 SBC 4/07.

26960 (6): New to JMD & MH Burns, Tarves (GN) registered W244 GSE.

30752 (7): New to Central Transfers Ltd, St Peter Port (CI) 7.

34796 (4): New to a private owner, Guernsey.

35888: New to Guideissue Ltd {Baker's Coaches}, Knypersley (ST) 19 registered 8439 RU; TD Parnell, Honiton (dealer) 3/15; Executive Car Services Ltd, Vale (CI) named 'Lorna May' 3/15.

37603 (3): New to Panache Travel, Hedge End (HA) registered YN55 UJX.

42438 (3): Its origins are unknown.

44525 (3): New to BB Hire Cars Ltd, St Peter Port (XCI); hired to Guernseybus Ltd (CI) 9 5/88-10/88; Central Taxis Ltd, St Peter Port (CI) 12/88; Educational Holidays Guernsey Ltd {Island Coachways} (CI) 10/89; Central Transfers, St Peter Port (CI) 22 3/90; Guernseybus Ltd, St Peter Port (CI) 3 1/91; Central Transfers Ltd, St Peter Port (CI) 3 1/95.

48641 (6): New to Bonas & Son Ltd {Supreme Coaches}, Coventry (WM) registered M651 FWK; Bob Vale PSV Sales Ltd, Great Kingshill (dealer) 3/98; RA Coates {Chariots}, Heald Green (GM) by4/98.

48702 (6): New to Jacksons Garage, Forest (XCI); Guernseybus Ltd, St Peter Port (CI) 6 3/87; Central Transfers, St Peter Port (CI) 24 3/90; Guernseybus Ltd, St Peter Port (CI) 6 1/91; Central Transfers Ltd, St Petcr Port (CI) 6 1/95.

49768 (8): New to W Cropper, Guiseley (WY) registered YN10 ACO; D Fishwick, Colne (dealer) 9/17.

50524 (5): New to an unidentified UK owner registered MX07 VUN.
52408 (5): New to Harlequin Hire Cars, Guernsey (XCI).
54361 (1): Its origins are unknown.
58228 (2): New to Montessori School, St Peter Port (XCI).
65075 (7): New to London Borough of Lewisham, Ladywell (LN) 1583 registered YJ08 EFB.
73861 (2): New to Magic Marketing GB Ltd, West Harrow (LN) registered FY02 OTG.
74271 (8): New to J & A Brennan {Devon Mini Coaches}, Sauchie (CE) registered SF04 RHY; Swift Taxis & Private Hire Ltd, Great Yarmouth (NK) 11/05.
76357: New to a private owner, Guernsey.
76385 (3): New to Titan, Redhill (XSR) F34 registered R334 EFG; Thorne {Adelphi Travel}, Horley (SR) 9/03.
TFO 249: New to Guernsey Motors Ltd, St Peter Port (CI) 78 registered 8228 [1]; Guernsey Railway Co Ltd, St Peter Port (CI) 78 10/73; PF Davies, Farnham for preservation 3/80; re-registered JPA 84V 4/80; N Marshall, Huntingdon for preservation at an unknown date; B Catchpole, Halling for preservation at an unknown date; Dr JR Young, Nottingham (dealer / preservationist) at an unknown date; Nettle, Oxford as a caravan at an unknown date; re-registered TFO 249 6/96; Hallett, Trowbridge for preservation by5/97; Eastbourne Auction Rooms for preservation 3/99.

Notes:
1787 [1] (ex 898 FUF, 1787 [1]) (11): Fitted with a Cummins engine by3/18.
1787 [6] (4): Re-registered 55184 2/13.
11926 (7): Received Public Service Omnibus plate 113 by11/06.
15206 (ex M652 FWK): Received Public Service Omnibus plate 111 by11/06.
23069 (ex Y831 HHE): Received Public Service Omnibus plate 115 by11/06; renumbered 10 by5/17.
35888 (ex 8439 RU): Acquired for spares.
48641 (ex M651 FWK): Received Public Service Omnibus plate 114 by11/06.
52408 (5): Received Police plate 110 by11/06.
74271 (ex SF04 RHY) (8): To service 7/10; renumbered 9 by2/12.
TFO 249 (ex JPA 84V, 8228 [1]: Acquired for restoration.

Disposals:
11926 (7): Private owner, Guernsey 2/09.
13704 (4): No known disposal.
15206 (ex M652 FWK) (4): Private owner, Guernsey by12/11.
17337 (ex FJ05 HXZ) (8): Unidentified dealer for scrap 1/18.
19797 (1): No known disposal.
26248 (ex W314 SBC, 4234 NT, W314 SBC) (7): No known disposal.
26960 (ex W244 GSE) (6): No known disposal.
30752 (7): Private owner, Guernsey by6/02.
34796 (4): No known disposal.
37603 (ex YN55 UJX) (3): Unidentified dealer for scrap 5/17.
35888 (ex 8439 RU): Unidentified dealer for scrap 4/18.
42438 (3): No known disposal.
44525 (3): No known disposal.
48641 (ex M651 FWK): Scrapped by12/11.
48702 (6): No known disposal.
52408 (5): Unidentified owner as a transporter, Guernsey 4/09.
54361 (1): Private owner, Guernsey by12/03.
58228 (2): No known disposal.
73861 (ex FY02 OTG) (2): Unidentified dealer for scrap by12/17.
74241 (ex SF04 RHY): Unidentified UK dealer 5/14.
76357: Converted to a luggage van 12/11; unidentified owner by5/16.
76385 (ex R334 EFG): Scrapped 12/10.

ISLAND COACHWAYS

EDUCATIONAL HOLIDAYS GUERNSEY LTD {Island Coachways – from 10/80}   **Le Menage Hotel, CASTEL**
Hougue a la Perre, ST PETER PORT (c-/82)

ISLAND COACHWAYS LTD (10/00)

The Tram Sheds, Les Banques, ST PETER PORT (-/--)

Educational Holidays Guernsey Ltd was formed in 1976 by Lionel Miles who owned Le Menage Guest House. He also obtained an interest in Tally Ho! Cabs. Turning his establishment into a hotel with parties of school children as the guests, initially the coaches were hired from Tally Ho! but over 1977/78, these were acquired by Educational Holidays together with the private hire licences of that company. At its height, some 12,000 children visited per annum and other establishments were needed to cater for these numbers.

The early vehicles were sourced from Jersey and complied with the 7ft 4in width maximum, but such coaches were more difficult to obtain from elsewhere. In order to overcome this, Miles acquired two 8ft wide coaches and cut them down to just under 7ft 4in wide and completely refurbished them. 19 vehicles were so modified up to 1988.

The fleet name 'Ed Hols' was used for a short time in 1980, but in October of that year, Island Coachways was adopted. The livery was also changed at this time from yellow to cream. Several attempts were also made in these early years to run a bus service, but this was denied by the authorities. An interesting acquisition towards the end of 1980 were three former Greenslades AEC Reliances with Harrington bodywork which had been en-route from Jersey to Riduna Buses on Alderney. A deal was completed and these were acquired, later joined by two more of the same type. They were disposed of after it was discovered that they were slightly over the legal maximum width and co-incidently perhaps, two of them ended up on Alderney after all.

The hotel was sold in 1982 to allow full attention to be given to the growing coaching activities.

The first regular express services from the Channel Islands to the UK commenced in June 1985 taking the Sealink Ferry to Weymouth and then travelling to Manchester. This was jointly run with Dean Forest Coaches of Joys Green, Gloucestershire in 1986 (a second service to Sheffield had also been introduced) and two of their coaches were regularly seen on the island. As these (and the Island Coachways' vehicle) were over width, they were not licensed for use on Guernsey, so they only carried luggage for the first leg of the journey, the passengers being carried on approved vehicles.

From 1990, the Leyland Swift became available and this was adopted as the standard coach seated vehicle and the need to modify further second-hand coaches was avoided. A novel initiative in 1992 was the construction of a tram, the design of which was based on the original no. 3 from 1897. It was constructed on the chassis of a FIAT lorry and worked a route along the seafront in St Peter Port. Sadly however, it only lasted four seasons before being sold for further use in the UK.

A major development came in 1993 when the company's private hire licences were converted to omnibus. This meant that Educational Holidays could at last operate bus services on an even footing with Guernseybus and from the following January, four school services commenced. The company was well placed now to take advantage of the States of Guernsey's desire to improve public services and it invited tenders for the island's bus routes, roughly split into three packages. The Holidays company secured one package and Guernseybus the other two. As a result, numbers of midi-buses of a variety of types were obtained, being branded 'Roadrunner'. Sovereign Coaches was used for front-line coaches for a while from 1997.

1998 saw the death of the innovative Lionel Miles and George Boucher took over as Managing Director.

Declining passenger numbers over the next few years left the company in a parlous financial shape which was only relieved by support from the States, releasing sums of money under the terms of the services contract. There followed a period when vehicle purchases reduced and were restricted to older vehicles. On 20 October 2000, the company's name changed to Island Coachways Ltd. One month later, Guernseybus ceased operations and the outlook changed. Island Coachways took over Guernseybus's routes and contracts with their vehicles leased by the States. The States only handed over serviceable vehicles after which Island Coachways were responsible for their maintenance.

Following a study by Southern Vectis, the Isle of Wight company, the States' Traffic Committee formulated a new policy called 'A New Public Transport Strategy'. The plan was that bus services must be profitable whilst:

- Enhancing service frequencies
- Reducing bus fares
- Improving the quality of vehicles and keeping them maintained

As part of the review, changes were introduced in March 2001 - St Peter Port town services were revised and a flat fare of 50p charged. Then at the beginning of 2003, a £3.1mn investment by the States saw 33 new Dennis Darts with East Lancs bodywork arrive. With the company now in good shape, George Boucher retired and his daughter Mrs Hannah Beacom became the new Managing Director.

In 2012, the States of Guernsey put the network out to tender and CT Plus Guernsey Ltd won the contract to operate the island's bus services. The Dennis Darts were transferred to the new company where they continued to give sterling service, only being replaced in 2017-19 when a new generation of Wright StreetVibe buses were purchased to replace them.

	Reg	Chassis	Chassis No	Body	Body No	Code			
	2424	Ford Transit	BD05VV51243	Ford		M11	2/69	6/76	12/79
3	7269	Bedford SB3	77291	Plaxton	602914	C41F	3/60	7/77	9/81
	10152	Bedford J2SZ10	164897	Duple (Midland)		C19F	5/63	10/77	-/80
			CFJ2/152						
	7091 [1]	Bedford SB3	77295	Plaxton	602921	C41F	3/60	12/77	-/81
2	3989 [1]	Albion VT21L	78112K	Duple (Northern)	143/17	C41F	10/63	2/78	12/82
	11033	Bedford SBG	51496	Duple	1074/210	C37F	-/57	2/78	9/78
	11840	Bedford SBG	37194	Duple	1055/320	C38F	4/55	10/78	----
2	2445 [1]	Bedford VAM14	6834742	Duple	1205/265	C45F	6/66	11/78	-/83
1	9969 [1]	Bedford SB5	94763	Duple (Northern)	155/22	C41F	6/64	11/78	4/83
1	1787 [2]	Bedford SBG	28463	(chassis only)			5/54	5/79	-/86
	TUN 627	Bedford SB3	72055	Plaxton	592659	C37F	7/59	11/79	----
12	5260	Bedford J2LZ2	9T133208	(van)			-/69	9/80	by-/87
3	8226 [2]	Bedford SB3	91734	Duple	1159/132	C41F	3/63	11/80	10/84
4	8227 [2]	Bedford SB3	91700	Duple	1159/131	C41F	3/63	11/80	10/84
8	8228 [2]	AEC Reliance	2MU4RA4908	Harrington	2832	C41F	3/64	12/80	1/84
9	8229 [2]	AEC Reliance	2MU4RA5077	Harrington	2964	C41F	5/64	12/80	10/84
10	8230 [2]	AEC Reliance	2MU4RA5076	Harrington	2963	C41F	5/64	12/80	10/84
	MXX 481	AEC Regal IV	9821LT874	MCCW		B39F	3/53	12/80	----
11	8231 [2]	Ford Transit	BD05NA63174	Ford		M13	-/73	3/81	-/83
6	6768 [2]	AEC Reliance	2MU4RA4905	Harrington	2829	C41F	3/64	8/81	1/84
7	6769 [2]	AEC Reliance	2MU4RA4975	Harrington	2854	C41F	4/64	8/81	10/84
	510 PYB	AEC Reliance	2MU3RA4006	Duple	1149/5	C41F	5/62	6/82	----
6	7091 [2]	Bedford VAS2	1003	Duple	1154/29	C29F	5/62	11/82	by-/87
14	12859	Ford Transit	BC05LV58775	Ford		M9	3/72	1/83	7/85
5	9438 [2]	Bedford SB3	97457	Duple	1183/384	C41F	5/65	3/83	-/87
9	3989 [2]	Bedford SB3	94136	Duple	1170/253	C41F	4/64	6/83	11/89
7	5779 [1]	Bedford SB3	6819491	Duple	1207/10	C41F	5/66	3/83	11/89
8	6430 [1]	Bedford SB3	6838409	Duple	1207/41	C41F	5/66	3/83	11/89
2	8228 [3]	Bedford J2SZ10	DW112856	Caetano	75/24	C20F	6/75	6/83	10/84
10	9969 [2]	Bedford SB3	97341	Duple	1183/396	C41F	5/65	6/83	by7/88
11	6768 [3]	Ford Transit	BD05ST63237	Robin Hood		C16F	4/77	5/84	by9/88
44	4510 [1]	Austin K4/CXB	109792	Barnard	CX3	B33F	5/48	5/84	9/92
3	8226 [3]	Bedford SB5	DW451539	Duple	414/1703	C41F	8/74	10/84	4/96
4	8227 [4]	Bedford YRQ	CW453308	Duple	266/73	C45F	2/73	10/84	5/97
	9969 [3]	Bedford YRQ	CW451896	Duple	266/250	C45F	7/73	11/84	-/--
	8227 [3]	Ford R1115	BCRSER40549	Wadham Stringer	8395/84	B41F	-/84	12/84	1/85
	8228 [4]	Bedford SB3	EW452248	Duple	514/1461	C41F	7/75	1/85	11/91
	2445 [2]	Bedford YRT	CW451855	Duple	272/1004	C53F	5/73	2/85	2/85
	12359	Ford Transit	BD05SY53828	Dormobile		C16F	2/77	7/87	-/89
	1787 [3]	Bedford SB5	FW450136	Duple	614/1462	C41F	3/76	9/87	2/98
	10739 [1]	Bedford SB5	0T477559	Duple	216/25	C41F	6/70	9/87	12/89
	10797	Bedford SB5	0T476107	Duple	216/45	C41F	6/70	9/87	12/89
	J 26019	Commer Avenger	23A0687	Harrington	916	C35F	5/51	11/87	----
	6289	Austin K4/CXB	130617	Thurgood	527	B--F	1/49	-/87	----
	51735 [1]	Ford Transit	BDVZWE237470	(van)			6/79	1/88	-/--
	13456	Bedford CFL	HY614438	Reeve Burgess	11505	C17F	8/78	2/88	12/89
	1787 [1]	Albion FT39AN	73737B	Reading	5176	B36F	6/54	4/88	6/93
	9438 [3]	FIAT 60F10	300303	Caetano	181166	C18F	11/82	7/88	12/96
	6768 [4]	FIAT 60F10	300127	Caetano	181156	C18F	9/81	8/88	4/95
	56624	FIAT 242E	1077103	?		C8-	-/--	5/89	9/92
	44525	Ford Transit	SFAZXXBDVZJG42274	Ford		M14	5/88	10/89	3/90
	49377	Ford Transit	BDVZHJ6L9140	Ford		M14	12/87	10/89	3/90
	3989 [3]	Bedford VAS5	DW451223	Duple	411/1001	C29F	6/74	2/90	10/92
	5779 [2]	Leyland ST2R44C97T5	LBM0298	Elme	061	C43F	4/90	4/90	by5/07
	6430 [2]	Leyland ST2R44C97T5	LBM0292	Elme	062	C39F	3/90	3/90	5/95
	58677	Bedford VAS5	DW455890	Duple	411/1005	C28F	8/74	6/90	4/92
	8225 [2]	Leyland ST2R44C97T5	LBM0315	Elme	068	C35F	8/91	8/91	8/99

	8228 [5]	Leyland ST2R44C97T5		Elme		075	C43F	5/92	5/92	8/99
		LBM0331								
	1931	FIAT 79.14	2357656	(lorry)				5/87	6/92	10/95
	1787 [4]	Bedford SB5	2T472075	Duple	246/75		C41F	2/73	5/93	11/94
	38290	Volkswagen LT55	HH016494	Optare		267	B25F	7/87	11/93	by6/02
	38293 [1]	Volkswagen LT55	HH003038	Optare		254	B25F	7/87	1/94	by11/00
	3989 [4]	FIAT 95E18F	0002112542	Carrocerias Modernas			C42F	8/94	8/94	by1/14
	1787 [5]	Toyota HB31R	0003024	Caetano	951085		C18F	2/90	1/95	by5/07
	38327	Mercedes Benz 811D		Optare		3015	B31F	9/89	3/95	12/00
		WDB6703032O912671								
	38328	Volkswagen LT55	GH019619	Optare		110	B25F	9/86	3/95	by12/01
	38393	Mercedes Benz 811D		Optare		441	B31F	6/88	3/95	1/98
		WDB6703032O839771								
	38406 [1]	Mercedes Benz 811D		Optare		3010	B31F	4/89	6/95	5/03
		WDB6703032O951588								
	38243	Volkswagen LT55	HH003045	Optare		260	B25F	7/87	7/95	by6/02
	38296	Volkswagen LT55	HH016489	Optare		262	B25F	7/87	5/95	by11/00
	52097	Volkswagen LT55	JH009886	Optare		511	B25F	3/88	8/95	2/98
	6768 [5]	Renault PP180.10		Carrocerias Modernas			C43F	9/95	9/95	5/16
		VF6JP2P1200000082				1748				
	23196	Iveco 49-10	5062967	?			B20F	12/95	12/95	by4/09
	6430 [3]	Bedford SB3	KW451605	Duple	013/1511		C41F	5/80	1/96	3/98
	18047	Optare MR11	VN1899	Optare		1899	B31F	3/96	3/96	4/06
	24539	Optare MR11	VN1898	Optare		1898	B31F	3/96	3/96	8/08
	39138 [1]	Iveco 49-10	5061377	?			B18F	4/96	4/96	by8/08
	9438 [4]	Iveco 49-10	5061162	?			B18F	12/96	12/96	by12/06
	8227 [5]	Leyland LBM6T/2RS		Wadham Stringer			C37F	6/88	6/97	3/08
		LBM00031				2078/88				
	8226 [4]	Renault PP180	00000035	Carrocerias Modernas			C43F	7/97	7/97	#
						1996				
	8230 [5]	Renault PP180	00000061	Carrocerias Modernas			C43F	2/98	2/98	9/17
						2161				
	24493	MCW MF150/113	MB10072	MCW			B25F	11/88	5/98	by12/01
	9969 [4]	Renault PP180	00000062	LCB			B39F	7/99	7/99	#
	6430 [4]	Volkswagen LT55		Optare		120	B25F	10/86	12/99	by12/01
		WV2ZZZ29ZGH019631								
	D898 NUA	Volkswagen LT55		Optare		156	B25F	5/87	12/99	----
		WV2ZZZ29ZHH000685								
	64991	Leyland LBM6T/2RA	LBM00078	Wadham Stringer			B41F	4/89	9/00	by4/05
						2082/88				
71	12723 [4]	Optare MR03	VN1033	Optare		1033	B26F	12/90	11/00	6/03
72	12727 [4]	Optare MR03	VN1024	Optare		1024	B26F	11/90	11/00	c6/03
67	17314	Optare MR03	VN1161	Optare		1161	B31F	1/92	11/00	6/03
70	18264 [3]	Optare MR03	VN1029	Optare		1029	B26F	12/90	11/00	6/03
73	18267 [4]	Optare MR03	VN1156	Optare		1156	B26F	5/91	11/00	3/01
79	19660 [3]	Optare MR03	VN1071	Optare		1071	B26F	5/91	11/00	6/03
80	19662 [3]	Optare MR03	VN1070	Optare		1070	B26F	5/91	11/00	6/03
78	19675 [4]	Optare MR03	VN1148	Optare		1148	B25F	11/91	11/00	6/03
75	19676 [3]	Optare MR03	VN1147	Optare		1147	B25F	11/91	11/00	6/03
76	19677 [4]	Optare MR03	VN1151	Optare		1151	B25F	11/91	11/00	6/03
77	19678 [4]	Optare MR03	VN1134	Optare		1134	B25F	11/91	11/00	6/03
69	20716	Optare MR03	VN1165	Optare		1165	B31F	2/92	11/00	6/03
88	24603	Optare MR03	VN1057	Optare		1057	B26F	5/91	11/00	by6/03
90	24775 [2]	Optare MR03	VN1053	Optare		1053	B26F	5/91	11/00	6/03
74	29728 [3]	Optare MR03	VN1143	Optare		1143	B25F	11/91	11/00	6/03
84	33541	Optare MR03	VN1206	Optare		1206	B29F	5/92	11/00	6/03
85	34518	Optare MR03	VN1204	Optare		1204	B29F	5/92	11/00	by6/03
52	38406 [2]	Leyland ST2R44C97T5LBM00331		Elme		075	C45F	5/92	11/00	11/09
53	39138 [2]	Leyland ST2R44C97T5LBM00315		Elme		068	C45F	8/91	11/00	by5/07
65	40527	Optare MR03	VN1155	Optare		1155	B31F	11/91	11/00	6/03
89	47979	Optare MR03	VN1055	Optare		1055	B26F	5/91	11/00	by6/03
66	48161	Optare MR03	VN1159	Optare		1159	B31F	12/91	11/00	c6/03
68	56206	Optare MR03	VN1163	Optare		1163	B31F	1/92	11/00	6/03
86	61973	Optare MR01	VN1058	Optare		1058	B33F	8/91	11/00	6/03

87	62067	Optare MR01	VN1008	Optare	1008	B33F	4/90	11/00	by6/03
171	31921 [2]	Bristol LH6L	LH-1576	Plaxton 7910BXM518S		C41F	10/79	12/00	by12/01
46	66867	Leyland CU302		Wadham Stringer		B33FL	1/89	6/01	3/09
		SBLK4P44BLBJ11128		2095/88					
44	66868	DAF 9.13R	L040126	Wadham Stringer		B33FL	10/90	6/01	6/09
				3193/90					
43	65802	Cannon Hi-Line C100071B6AT		LCB	3427	C43F	1/02	1/02	11/18
58	6430 [5]	Leyland LBM6T/2RAO		Wadham Stringer		B37F	2/89	4/02	by6/06
		LBM00142		2486/89					
59	69101	Leyland LBM6T/2RAO		Wadham Stringer		B37F	4/89	4/02	by6/06
		LBM00150		2412/89					
12	70012	Dennis Dart SFD		East Lancs	43902	B35F	12/02	12/02	4/12
		SFD1BACR32GWA6943							
13	70013	Dennis Dart SFD		East Lancs	43901	B35F	12/02	12/02	4/12
		SFD1BACR32GWA6942							
14	70014	Dennis Dart SFD		East Lancs	43903	B35F	1/03	1/03	4/12
		SFD1BACR32GWA6944							
15	70015	Dennis Dart SFD		East Lancs	43905	B35F	1/03	1/03	4/12
		SFD1BACR32GWA6946							
16	70016	Dennis Dart SFD		East Lancs	43904	B35F	1/03	1/03	4/12
		SFD1BACR32GWA6945							
17	70017	Dennis Dart SFD		East Lancs	43911	B35F	2/03	2/03	4/12
		SFD1BACR32GWA7064							
18	70018	Dennis Dart SFD		East Lancs	43908	B35F	2/03	2/03	4/12
		SFD1BACR32GWA7061							
19	70019	Dennis Dart SFD		East Lancs	43907	B35F	2/03	2/03	4/12
		SFD1BACR32GWA7060							
20	70020	Dennis Dart SFD		East Lancs	43915	B35F	2/03	2/03	4/12
		SFD1BACR32GWA7074							
21	70021	Dennis Dart SFD		East Lancs	43916	B35F	2/03	2/03	4/12
		SFD1BACR33GWA7107							
22	70022	Dennis Dart SFD		East Lancs	43913	B35F	3/03	3/03	4/12
		SFD1BACR32GWA7072							
23	70023	Dennis Dart SFD		East Lancs	43910	B35F	3/03	3/03	4/12
		SFD1BACR32GWA7063							
24	70024	Dennis Dart SFD		East Lancs	43920	B35F	3/03	3/03	4/12
		SFD1BACR33GWA7116							
25	70025	Dennis Dart SFD		East Lancs	43912	B35F	3/03	3/03	4/12
		SFD1BACR32GWA7065							
26	70026	Dennis Dart SFD		East Lancs	43906	B35F	3/03	3/03	4/12
		SFD1BACR32GWA7059							
27	70027	Dennis Dart SFD		East Lancs	43914	B35F	3/03	3/03	4/12
		SFD1BACR32GWA7073							
28	70028	Dennis Dart SFD		East Lancs	43921	B35F	3/03	3/03	4/12
		SFD1BACR33GWA7117							
29	70029	Dennis Dart SFD		East Lancs	43923	B35F	3/03	3/03	4/12
		SFD1BACR33GWA7119							
30	70030	Dennis Dart SFD		East Lancs	43917	B35F	3/03	3/03	4/12
		SFD1BACR33GWA7108							
31	70031	Dennis Dart SFD		East Lancs	43927	B35F	3/03	3/03	4/12
		SFD1BACR33GWA7137							
32	70032	Dennis Dart SFD		East Lancs	43925	B35F	3/03	3/03	4/12
		SFD1BACR33GWA7130							
33	70033	Dennis Dart SFD		East Lancs	43922	B35F	3/03	3/03	4/12
		SFD1BACR33GWA7118							
34	70034	Dennis Dart SFD		East Lancs	43926	B35F	3/03	3/03	4/12
		SFD1BACR33GWA7136							
35	70035	Dennis Dart SFD		East Lancs	43928	B34F	3/03	3/03	4/12
		SFD1BACR33GWA7138							
36	70036	Dennis Dart SFD		East Lancs	43909	B34F	4/03	4/03	4/12
		SFD1BACR32GWA7062							
37	70037	Dennis Dart SFD		East Lancs	43919	B34F	4/03	4/03	4/12
		SFD1BACR33GWA7110							

38	70038	Dennis Dart SFD	East Lancs	43931	B34F	4/03	4/03	4/12
		SFD1BACR33GWA7150						
39	70039	Dennis Dart SFD	East Lancs	43924	B34F	4/03	4/03	4/12
		SFD1BACR33GWA7129						
40	70040	Dennis Dart SFD	East Lancs	43918	B34F	5/03	5/03	4/12
		SFD1BACR33GWA7109						
41	70041	Dennis Dart SFD	East Lancs	43930	B34F	5/03	5/03	4/12
		SFD1BACR33GWA7149						
42	70042	Dennis Dart SFD	East Lancs	43929	B34F	5/03	5/03	4/12
		SFD1BACR33GWA7139						
43	70043	Dennis Dart SFD	East Lancs	43932	B34F	5/03	5/03	4/12
		SFD1BACR33GWA7151						
44	70044	Dennis Dart SFD	East Lancs	43933	B34F	5/03	5/03	4/12
		SFD1BACR33GWA7152						
2	62417	Mercedes Benz O814D	Plaxton 058.5MAE5975		C33F	5/05	5/05	#
		WDB6703742N117427						
1	65119	Mercedes Benz O814D	Plaxton 058.5MAE5977		C33F	5/05	5/05	1/19
		WDB6703742N117428						
6	5779 [3]	Mercedes Benz O814D	Plaxton 068.5MAE6638		C29F	2/07	2/07	#
		WDB6703742N123642						
7	39138 [3]	Mercedes Benz	Plaxton 068.5MAE6709		C29F	2/07	2/07	#
		WDB6703742N123664						
8	1787 [6]	Iveco 45C14	?		C16F	5/07	5/07	2/13
		ZCFC45A1005612425						
9	9438 [5]	Iveco 45C14	?		C16F	5/07	5/07	#
		ZCFC45A1005610579						
11	70011	Dennis Dart SLF	SCC	4465	B28F	1/05	3/08	4/12
		SFD6BACR43GWA7609						
55	70055	Dennis Dart SLF	SCC	4483	B28F	1/05	3/08	4/12
		SFD6BACR43GWA7639						
66	70066	Dennis Dart SLF	SCC	4481	B28F	1/05	8/08	4/12
		SFD6BACR43GWA7625						
77	70077	Dennis Dart SLF	SCC	4482	B28F	4/05	8/08	4/12
		SFD6BACR43GWA7624						
88	70088	Dennis Dart SLF	SCC	4486	B28F	3/05	8/08	4/12
		SFD6BACR43GWA7611						
99	70099	Dennis Dart SLF	SCC	4487	B28F	3/05	8/08	4/12
		SFD6BACR43GWA7623						
56	77056	Dennis Dart SLF	SCC	4480	B28F	12/04	4/09	4/12
		SFD6BACR43GWA7640						
91	77091	Dennis Dart SLF	SCC	4479	B28F	12/04	4/09	4/12
		SFD6BACR43GWA7641						
	8225 [4]	Ford Transit	Ford		M14	7/03	8/08	by5/17
		WF0EXXGBFE3Y23282						
10	77819	Mercedes Benz O816D	Plaxton 088.5MBJ8023		C29F	5/09	5/09	#
		WDB6703742N135134						
109	50109	Mercedes Benz O816D	Plaxton 088.5MBJ8137		C33F	6/09	6/09	#
		WDB6703742N136000						
48	6430 [6]	Cannon Hi-Line C100051B6AT	LCB	2018	C40F	4/99	5/11	7/18
108	38509	Mercedes Benz O814D	Plaxton 058.5MAE6154		C29F	3/06	5/14	#
		WDB6703742N119553						
104	18109	Mercedes Benz O816D	Plaxton 088.5MBJ7942		C29F	3/10	6/14	#
		WDB6703742N134794						
51	2609	MAN TGL10.180	Mobi		C43F	5/16	5/16	#
		WMAN14ZZ9GY342086						
16B	52141	Ford Transit	Ford		M13	9/09	by5/16	#
		WF0DXXTTFD9J6L2987						
17P	59610	Ford Transit	Ford		M13	4/14	4/17	#
		WF0DXXTTFDDK85663						
52E	18221 [1]	MAN TGL10.180	Mobi		C35F	8/17	4/18	#
		WMAN15ZZ7GY346028						
53	8230 [6]	MAN TGL10.180	Mobi		C39F	5/18	5/18	#
		WMAN15ZZ2JY373841						

| 54 | 6430 [7] | MAN TGL10.180 | Mobi | C39F | 5/18 | 5/18 | # |
| | | WMAN15ZZ9JY373156 | | | | | |

Vehicles marked # were still in service at the date of this Fleet History.

Police plates (Public Service Omnibus plates from 1981):

1787 [1]: ph75	7091 [2] (6): ph93	11033: ph86
1787 [3]: ph87	7269 (3): ph81	12359: ph100
1787 [5]: ph85	8225 [2]: ph88	12859: ph98
1787 [6] (8): 85	8226 [2] {3): ph50	13456: ph100
1931: 100	8226 [3]: ph86	18047: 107
2424: ph56	8226 [4]: 96	18109 (104): 86
2445 [1] (2): ph88	8227 [2] (4): ph81	18221 [1] (52E): 43
2609 (51): 104	8227 [3]: ph70	23196: 120
3989 [1] (2): ph81	8227 [4] (4): ph70	24493: 101
3989 [2] (9): ph80	8227 [5]: 94	24539: 106
3989 [3]: ph80	8228 [2] (8): ph83	38243: 105
3989 [4]: ph86	8228 [3] (2): ph83	38290: 88
4510 [1] (44): ph15	8228 [4]: ph83	38293 [1]: 87
5260 (12): ph100	8228 [5]: ph7	38296: 91
5779 [1] (7): ph7	8229 [2] (9): ph93	38327: 90
5779 [2]: ph93	8230 [2] (10): ph87	38328: 103
5779 [3] (6): 95	8230 [5]: 92	38393: 101
6430 [1] (8): ph88	8230 [6] (53): 92	38406 [1]: 102
6430 [2]: ph92	8231 [2] (11): ph86	38509 (108): 85
6430 [3]: 97	9438 [2] (5): ph92	39138 [1]: 100
6430 [5] (58): 87	9438 [3]: ph27	39138 [3] (7): 42
6430 [6] (48): 58	9438 [5] (9): 98	44525: ph95
6430 [7] (54): 105	9969 [1] (1): ph87	49377: ph21
6768 [2] (6): ph86	9969 [2] (10): ph50	50109 (109): 107
6768 [3] (11): ph98	9969 [3]: ph50	52141: 106
6768 [4]: ph98	9969 [4]: 93	56624: ph37
6768 [5]: 104	10152: ph80	58677: ph7
6769 [2] (7): ph70	10739 [1]: ph92	59610: 46
7091 [1]: ph83	10797: ph93	59837: ph76
62417 (2): 93	70021 (21): 10	70037 (37): 26
65119 (1): 91	70022 (22): 11	70038 (38): 27
65802 (43): 60	70023 (23): 12	70039 (39): 28
66867: 90	70024 (24): 13	70040 (40): 29
66868 (44): 55	70025 (25): 14	70041 (41): 30
69101 (59): 105	70026 (26): 15	70042 (42): 31
70011 (11): 34	70027 (27): 16	70043 (43): 32
70012 (12): 1	70028 (28): 17	70044 (44): 33
70013 (13): 2	70029 (29): 18	70055 (55): 35
70014 (14): 3	70030 (30): 19	70066 (66): 36
70015 (15): 4	70031 (31): 20	70077 (77): 37
70016 (16): 5	70032 (32): 21	70088 (88): 38
70017 (17): 6	70033 (33): 22	70099 (99): 39
70018 (18): 7	70034 (34): 23	77056 (56): 40
70019 (19): 8	70035 (35): 24	77091 (91): 41
70020 (20): 9	70036 (36): 25	77819 (10): 90

Previous histories:

1787 [1]: New to Watson's Garage Ltd {The Greys}, St Martin (CI); Guernsey Railway Co Ltd, St Peter Port (CI) 20 2/78; withdrawn 9/79; J Lidstone, Leigh-on-Sea for preservation 4/80; Tillingbourne Valley Services Ltd, Cranleigh (SR) re-registered 898 FUF 6/83; to service 7/83; F Elliott & Dr JR Young, Golborne for preservation 6/85.

1787 [2] (1): Chassis new to Auty's Tours Ltd, Bury (LA) registered CEN 535 (with a Duple (1051/179) C36F body); withdrawn 12/55; WE Pashley, Bradwell (DE) 6/56; Sheffield United Tours Ltd, Sheffield (WR) 7/58; numbered J1 and to service 6/59; F Cowley, Salford (dealer) 11/61; Tantivy Motors Ltd, St Helier (CI) 24 re-registered J 25784 4/62; Tally Ho! Coaches, Castel (CI) 2/73.

1787 [3]: New to J Watts {Line Motors}, Warrington (CH) registered LTB 817P; unidentified dealer 7/85.

1787 [4]: New to DC Venner {Scarlet Coaches}, Minehead (SO) registered ATT 151L; WP Le Marquand (senior) {Holiday Coach Tours}, St Peter (CI) 5 registered J 3256 [2] 11/74; WP Le Marquand (junior) {Holiday Coach Tours}, St Peter (CI) 5 9/85; Holiday Tours Ltd {Holiday Coach Tours}, St Peter (CI) 5 3/87; renumbered 19 6/91; Tantivy Holiday Coach Tours Ltd, St Helier (CI) 19 2/93.

1787 [5]: New to PWJ, JH & N Manning & E Stone, Challow (OX) registered G154 ELJ.

1931: Chassis new as a lorry registered D749 ULG.

2424: New to N Davis, Leigh (HA) registered TNG 184G.

2445 [1] (2): New to R Hearn, Harrow Weald (LN) registered ORO 966D; KS Jhimb, Southall (LN) 4/72.

2445 [2]: New to JG Wilson {Wilson's Coaches}, Carnwath (LK) registered NVA 75L, JD Campbell, Linlithgow (LO) at an unknown date; RD Garratt {Coalville Coaches}, Whitwick (LE) by6/82; Smith, Thorne (SY) at an unknown date; T Anelay {Black & White Coaches}, Scunthorpe (LI) by3/84.

3989 [1] (2): New to Fred Newton West End Garage Ltd, Dingwall (RY) registered MJS 808; Highland Omnibuses Ltd, Inverness (IV) A12 10/65; Milburn Motors Ltd, Glasgow (dealer) 4/68; Blair & Palmer Ltd, Carlisle (CU) 12/68; S & N Motors Ltd, Bishopbriggs (dealer) 10/72; James Gibson & Sons, Moffat (DF) 11/72; withdrawn by3/74; Maxwelltown High School, Dumfries (XDF) 1975; unidentified school, Southampton (XHA) by8/81.

3989 [2] (9): New to Court Garages (Torquay) Ltd (DN) registered 610 STT; AA Pitcher Ltd {Tantivy}, St Helier (CI) 6 re-registered J 22095 3/67; Tantivy Motors Ltd, St Helier (CI) 6 12/68.

3989 [3]: New to Greenslades Tours Ltd, Exeter (DN) 351 registered PFJ 351M; Western National Omnibus Co Ltd, Exeter (DN) 4/78; to service 5/78; withdrawn 1/80; JK & KN Wilby, Hibaldstow (LI) 8/80; Arlington Motor Co Ltd, Potters Bar (dealer) 7/83; Wacton Trading / Coach Sales, Bromyard (dealer) 8/83; Wiltshire County Council (Lackham College), Laycock (XWI) 8/83.

4510 [1] (44): New to Guernsey Motors Ltd, St Peter Port (CI) 44; fitted with a Perkins P6 oil engine 3/57; Guernsey Airport, Forest (XCI) for internal transport 6/70; withdrawn 11/73 (registration re-allocated elsewhere); Guernsey Old Car Club for preservation 1/80; re-registered 2725 4/80; fitted with a petrol engine 5/82.

5260 (12): New to Wharf Trading, Portsmouth (GHA) as a Bedford / Hawson van registered MRV 60G; R Help, St Peter Port (GCI) re-registered 5261 8/73; D Ferbrache, St Sampson (GCI) 6/74; withdrawn 6/79.

5779 [1] (7): New to Salopia Saloon Coaches Ltd, Whitchurch (SH) registered FNT 231D; J Birbeck {Blue Eagle Tours}, St Helier (CI) 27 re-registered J 9143 1/68; Blue Eagle Ltd, St Helier (CI) 27 5/68; renumbered 11 1972; Tantivy Holidays Ltd, St Helier (CI) 41 5/75.

6289: New to Guernsey Motors Ltd, St Peter Port (CI) 54; fitted with a Perkins P6 oil engine 2/55; reseated to B33F at an unknown date; withdrawn 4/60; living accommodation at Frie au Four, St Saviour at an unknown date.

6430 [1] (8): New to Jersey Coach Transport Ltd {Rover Tours}, St Helier (CI) *Rover Fourteen* registered J 35662; Tantivy Motors Ltd, St Helier (CI) 25 11/75; withdrawn 4/80.

6430 [3]: New to Blue Coach Tours Ltd, St Helier (CI) 12 registered J 60118; renumbered 32 4/84; fitted with an oil engine 1990.

6430 [4]: New as a demonstrator with Optare Ltd, Crossgates registered D939 KNW; South Midland Ltd, Witney (OX) 29 6/87; Thames Transit Ltd, Cowley (OX) 29 12/88; Lancaster City Transport (LA) 239 9/89; renumbered M9 2/90; Reading Transport Ltd (BE) 214 10/92; Optare Ltd (dealer), Crossgates 2/99.

6430 [5] (58): New to Luton & District Transport Ltd (BD) 302 registered F302 MNK (as B35F); LDT Ltd, Luton (BD) 302 5/95; Crosville Wales Ltd, Llandudno Junction (GD) SSC302 11/97; Arriva Cymru Ltd, Llandudno Junction (GD) SSC302 4/98; Wacton Trading / Coach Sales, Bromyard (dealer) 1/02.

6430 [6]: New to Durham County Council, Pity Me (XDM) registered T292 FRB (as C22FL); Durham County Council, Meadowfield (DM) 2/08.

6768 [2] (6): New to Greenslades Tours Ltd, Exeter (DN) registered AFJ 79B; numbered 444 6/71; renumbered 285 1/75; RK & RE Webber, Blisland (CO) 1/76; LJ Hubber {Streamline Coaches}, Newquay (CO) 2/78; RK & RE Webber, Blisland (CO) 6/79.

6768 [3] (11): New to MJ & L Pressley {Angela Coaches}, Bursledon (HA) registered MPX 945R.

6768 [4]: New to Nebard's Ltd, Wakefield (WY) registered WUA 655X.

6769 [2] (7): New to Devon General Omnibus & Touring Co Ltd, Exeter (DN) 5 registered 5 RDV; Western National Omnibus Co Ltd, Exeter (DN) 5 1/71; Greenslades Tours Ltd, Exeter (DN) 5/71; renumbered 435 6/71; numbered 293 1/75; withdrawn 1975; RK & RE Webber {Webber Bros}, Blisland (CO) 4/75.

7091 [1]: New to CA Smith {Silver Badge Motors}, Windermere (WT) registered GJM 6; J Birbeck {Blue Eagle Tours}, St Helier (CI) 22 re-registered J 1852 3/62; Blue Eagle Ltd, St Helier (CI) 22 5/68; renumbered 17 1972; Tantivy Motors Ltd, St Helier (CI) (not operated) 5/75; LD Miles {Tally Ho! Coaches}, Castel (CI) 11/76.

7091 [2] (6): New to G Hill {Jersey Tours}, St Helier (CI) 9 registered J 6901; Tantivy Motors Ltd, St Helier (CI) 31 12/70.

7269 (3): New to CA Smith {Silver Badge Motors}, Windermere (WT) registered GJM 5; J Birbeck {Blue Eagle Tours}, St Helier (CI) 23 re-registered J 1858 3/62; Blue Eagle Ltd, St Helier (CI) 23 5/68; renumbered 16 1972; Tantivy Motors Ltd, St Helier (CI) (not operated) 5/75; LD Miles {Tally Ho! Coaches}, Castel (CI) 10/76.

8225 [4]: New to Premium Tours Ltd, London WC1 (LN) registered AM03 BCK (as M16).

8226 [2] (3): New to Salopia Saloon Coaches Ltd, Whitchurch (SH) registered 5184 AW; J Birbeck {Blue Eagle Tours}, St Helier (CI) 25 re-registered J 2688 11/65; Blue Eagle Ltd, St Helier (CI) 25 5/68; renumbered 15 1972; Tantivy Motors Ltd, St Helier (CI) 43 5/75; withdrawn 4/80.

8226 [3] (3): New to WN & SM Warrington, Ilam (ST) registered CRF 699N; R Cooper, Upper Elkstone (ST) 3/81; JA Evans, Tregaron (DD) 3/83; Wacton Trading / Coach Sales, Bromyard (dealer) 9/84.

8227 [2] (4): New to Salopia Saloon Coaches Ltd, Whitchurch (SH) registered 5183 AW; J Birbeck {Blue Eagle Tours}, St Helier (CI) re-registered J 2687; 24 11/65; Blue Eagle Ltd, St Helier (CI) 24 5/68; renumbered 15 1972; Tantivy Motors Ltd, St Helier (CI) 52 5/75; withdrawn 4/80.

8227 [3]: New to Ford Motor Co Ltd, Warley as a demonstration vehicle.

8227 [4] (4): New to Corvedale Motor Co Ltd, Ludlow (SH) registered BUX 208L; Alpha Coaches {Brighton} Ltd (ES) 2/75; A & AR Turner, Chulmleigh (DN) 2/76.

8227 [5]: New to Taff-Ely Transport Ltd, Pontypridd (MG) registered E961 PME (as B37F); Arlington Motor Co Ltd, Enfield (dealer) 10/88; JMT (1987) Ltd, St Helier (CI) re-registered J 45700 [3] 11/88 (as C37F); numbered 19 by2/89; Arlington Motor Co Ltd, Enfield (dealer) 5/89; WMA Howarth {Silverline}, Merthyr Tydfil (MG) re-registered E961 PME 9/89; withdrawn 1/97; GD Handy {Sixty-sixty Coaches}, Merthyr Tyfil (MG) (not operated) 2/97; Wacton Trading / Coach Sales, Bromyard (dealer) 4/97.

8228 [2] (8): New to Greenslades Tours Ltd, Exeter (DN) registered AFJ 82B; numbered 447 6/71; renumbered 288 1/75; Midland Red Omnibus Co Ltd, Birmingham (dealer) 12/75; Paul Sykes Organisation Ltd, Blackerhill (dealer) 1/76; Seymours Ltd {Mascot Motors}, St Clement (CI) 2 re-registered J 16590 1/76; to service 6/76; moved to St Helier (CI) 3/78; withdrawn 12/80; intended for WP Simon {Riduna Buses}, Alderney (CI), but diverted en-route to Guernsey.

8228 [3] (2): New to Ben Stanley Ltd, Hersham (SR) registered JPC 547N; H Luckett & Co Ltd, Wallington (HA) 2/78.

8228 [4]: New to Olsen Bros Ltd, Strood (KT) registered KBH 450N; K O'Sullivan, Huyton (MY) 12/78; KJ Wills {Mid Devon Coaches}, Bow (DN) 2/81.

8229 [2] (9): New to Greenslades Tours Ltd, Exeter (DN) registered AFJ 77B (as C36F); reseated to C40F 4/66; reseated to C41F 4/72; numbered 442 6/71; renumbered 283 1/75; Midland Red Omnibus Co Ltd, Birmingham (dealer) 12/75; Paul Sykes Organisation Ltd, Blackerhill (dealer) 1/76; Seymours Ltd {Mascot Motors}, St Clement (CI) 6 re-registered J 16654 2/76; to service 4/76; moved to St Helier (CI) 3/78; withdrawn 12/80; intended for WP Simon {Riduna Buses}, Alderney (CI), but diverted en-route to Guernsey.

8230 [2] (10): New to Greenslades Tours Ltd, Exeter (DN) registered AFJ 86B; numbered 451 6/71; renumbered 251 1/75; Midland Red Omnibus Co Ltd, Birmingham (dealer) 12/75; Paul Sykes Organisation Ltd, Blackerhill (dealer) 1/76; Seymours Ltd {Mascot Motors}, St Clement (CI) 7 re-registered J 16706 2/76; to service 4/76; moved to St Helier (CI) 3/78; withdrawn 12/80; intended for WP Simon {Riduna Buses}, Alderney (CI), but diverted en-route to Guernsey.

8231 [2] (11): First recorded with GH Gough, Morestead (XHA) registration unknown.

9438 [2] (5): Jersey Coach Transport Ltd {Rover Tours}, St Helier (CI) Rover Nine registered J 1465 [2]; Tantivy Motors Ltd, St Helier (CI) 5 11/75; withdrawn 3/83.

9438 [3]: New to McClure, Renfrew (SC) registered LDS 997Y; Salvador Caetano (UK) Ltd, Northampton (dealer) 4/88.

9969 [1] (1): New to PJ, J & D Bryan {Reliable Cars}, Didcot (BE) registered ARX 705B; Jackson's of Altrincham Ltd (CH) at an unknown date; LF Garrard & RC Hollis {Holgar}, Hillingdon (MX) 5/68; HJ Fox, Hayes (MX) 5/72.

9969 [2] (10): New to Jersey Coach Transport Ltd {Rover Tours}, St Helier (CI) Rover Eleven registered J 2465; Tantivy Holidays Ltd, St Helier (CI) 18 11/75; withdrawn 4/80.

9969 [3]: New to HG Boon, Boreham (EX) registered BNO 134L; DJ Lively {Western Coaches}, Hereford (HW) 1/78; DD Buchanan {Western Coaches}, Stretton Sugwas (HW) 21 7/80; WD Davies {Stretton Coaches}, Hereford (HW) 21 3/83.

10152: New to R Davison {Northgate Motors}, Gloucester (GL) registered 8009 FH; WHM Terraneau, South Molton (DN) 2/67; GA Morse, Veryan (CO) 9/69; withdrawn 8/77.

10739 [1]: New to D James, Llangeitho (CG) registered KEJ 687H; Seymours Ltd {Mascot Motors}, St Helier (CI) 17 re-registered J 20361 4/75; withdrawn 6/87.

10797: New to Embankment Motor Co (Plymouth) Ltd (DN) registered MDR 525H; Wallace Arnold Tours Ltd, Leeds (WY) 5/74; Seymours Ltd {Mascot Motors}, St Helier (CI) 17 re-registered J 16898 6/76; withdrawn 6/87.

11033: New to Devon Mental Hospital, Exeter (XDN) registered VOD 313; RAE, Farnborough (XHA) at an unknown date.

11840: New to CW Sworder & Sons Ltd, Walkern (HT) registered UJH 346; AA Pitcher Ltd, St Helier (CI) 17 re-registered J 30366 4/64; Tantivy Motors Ltd, St Helier (CI) 17 12/68; Tally Ho! Coaches, Castel (CI) 2/74.

12359: New to Humberside Social Services (XHE) registered SAT 201R (as B10FL); Hardwick, Shafton (status / use unknown) 10/85; J Sykes, Carlton (dealer) 11/85.

12723 [4] (71): New to South East London & Kent Bus Co Ltd {Selkent}, Ilford (LN) MRL151 registered H151 UUA 9/94; moved to London SE26 (LN) 1/94; Metrobus Ltd, Orpington (not operated) 1/98; Guernseybus Ltd, St Peter Port (CI) 71 3/98.

12727 [4] (72): New to South East London & Kent Bus Co Ltd {Selkent}, Ilford (LN) MRL142 registered H142 UUA 9/94; moved to London SE26 (LN) 1/94; Guernseybus Ltd, St Peter Port (CI) 72 4/98.

12859 (14): New to La Motte Garages Ltd, Grouville (XCI) registered J 48139; Swan Rent-a-Car, St Peter Port (XCI) re-registered J 60691 6/79; Swan Rent-a-Car, St Peter Port (XCI) 1/80.

13456: New to Reliance Car Hire & Taxi Service (Gravesend) Ltd (KT) registered XWF 69T; Reliance Coaches of Gravesend Ltd (KT) 1/80; C Thomas {Victoria Auto Services}, Chichester (WS) 3/80; unidentified owner, Wakefield at an unknown date; JR Holyhead, Tettanhall (WM) 6/87.

17314 (67): New to London Buses Ltd, London SW1 (LN) MRL216 registered J216 BWU (as B26F); London Northern Bus Co Ltd, Harrow (LN) 10/94; MTL London Northern Ltd, Harrow (LN) MRL216 10/95; Guernseybus Ltd, St Peter Port (CI) 67 9/98.

18109 (104): New to Flights Hallmark Ltd, Hounslow (LN) 10013 registered SF10 EBN; renumbered 14013 9/11; Flights Hallmark Ltd, Birmingham (WM) 14013 c4/13; Plaxton, Anston (dealer) 10/13.

18221 [1] (52E): New to B McGowan {Whitestar}, Neilston (SC) registered PO17 EKD.

18264 [3] (70): New to South East London & Kent Bus Co Ltd {Selkent}, Ilford (LN) MRL147 registered H147 UUA 9/94; East London Bus & Coach Co Ltd, Ilford (LN) 12/97; Metrobus Ltd, Orpington (LN) (not operated) 1/98; Guernseybus Ltd, St Peter Port (CI) 70 4/98.

18267 [4] (73): New to South East London & Kent Bus Co Ltd {Selkent} MRL164 registered H564 WWR 9/94; moved to London SE26 (LN) 1/94; Guernseybus Ltd, St Peter Port (CI) 73 2/98.

19660 [3] (79): New to South East London & Kent Bus Co Ltd {Selkent}, Ilford (LN) MRL168 registered H168 WWT; moved to London SE26 (LN) 1/94; withdrawn 9/97; Metrobus Ltd, Orpington (LN) (not operated) 11/97; Guernseybus Ltd, St Peter Port (CI) 79 1/98.

19662 [3] (80): New to South East London & Kent Bus Co Ltd {Selkent}, Ilford (LN) MRL167 registered H167 WWT; moved to London SE26 (LN) 1/94; withdrawn 9/97; Metrobus Ltd, Orpington (LN) (not operated) 11/97; Guernseybus Ltd, St Peter Port (CI) 80 1/98.

19675 [4] (78): New to Kentish Bus & Coach Co Ltd, Northfleet (KT) 968 registered J968 JNL; Metrobus Ltd, Orpington (LN) 12/95; Guernseybus Ltd 5/97.

19676 [3] (75): New to Kentish Bus & Coach Co Ltd, Northfleet (KT) 967 registered J967 JNL; Metrobus Ltd, Orpington (LN) 12/95; Guernseybus Ltd 10/96.

19677 [4] (76): New to Kentish Bus & Coach Co Ltd, Northfleet (KT) 971 registered J971 JNL; Metrobus Ltd, Orpington (LN) 12/95; Guernseybus Ltd 9/96.

19678 [4] (77): New to Kentish Bus & Coach Co Ltd, Northfleet (KT) 972 registered J972 JNL; Metrobus Ltd, Orpington (LN) 12/95; Guernseybus Ltd 9/96.

20716 (69): New to London Buses Ltd, London SW1 (LN) MRL220 registered J220 BWU (as B26F); London Northern Bus Co Ltd, Harrow (LN) 10/94; MTL London Northern Ltd, Harrow (LN) MRL220 10/95; Guernseybus Ltd, St Peter Port (CI) 69 9/98.

24493: New to West Midlands Travel Ltd, Birmingham (WM) 671 registered F671 YOG; Wacton Trading / Coach Sales, Bromyard (dealer) by5/98.

24603 (88): New to South East London & Kent Bus Co Ltd {Selkent}, Ilford (LN) MRL165 registered H165 WWT; moved to London SE26 (LN) 1/94; Metrobus Ltd, Orpington (LN) 68 11/97; renumbered 915 8/98; Guernseybus Ltd, St Peter Port (CI) 88 3/00; entered service 4/00.

24775 [2] (90): New to South East London & Kent Bus Co Ltd {Selkent}, Ilford (LN) MRL161 registered H161 WWT; moved to London SE26 (LN) 1/94; Metrobus Ltd, Orpington (LN) 67 11/97; renumbered 913 8/98; Guernseybus Ltd, St Peter Port (CI) 90 3/00; entered service 6/00.

29728 [3] (74): New to Kentish Bus & Coach Co Ltd, Northfleet (KT) 963 registered J963 JNL; Metrobus Ltd, Orpington (LN) 12/95; Guernseybus Ltd, St Peter Port (CI) 74 2/97.

31921 [2] (171): New to Western National Ltd, Truro (CO) 3313 registered AFJ 736T; Guernseybus Ltd, St Peter Port (CI) 171 1/93; shortened to 32ft (in order to comply with maximum legal length on Guernsey) prior to entry into service; to service 5/96; transferred to the States of Guernsey, St Peter Port 11/00.

33541 (84): New to Cambus Ltd, Cambridge (CM) 962 registered J962 DWX; Guernseybus Ltd, St Peter Port (CI) 84 3/00; to service 4/00.

34518 (85): New to Cambus Ltd, Cambridge (CM) 960 registered J960 DWX; Guernseybus Ltd, St Peter Port (CI) 85 3/00; to service 4/00.

38243: New to Leicester Citybus Ltd (LE) 851 registered D851 CRY; Loughborough Coach & Bus Co Ltd (LE) M851 7/88; Derby City Transport Ltd (DE) 074 9/89.

38290: New to Leicester Citybus Ltd (LE) 854 registered D854 CRY; Loughborough Coach & Bus Co Ltd (LE) M854 7/88; Derby City Transport Ltd (DE) 075 8/89.

38293 [1]: New to Leicester Citybus Ltd (LE) 845 registered D845 CRY; Loughborough Coach & Bus Co Ltd (LE) M845 7/88; Derby City Transport Ltd (DE) 066 8/89.

38296: New to Leicester Citybus Ltd (LE) 853 registered D853 CRY; Loughborough Coach & Bus Co Ltd (LE) M853 7/88; Derby City Transport Ltd (DE) 072 9/89.

38327: New to A Jones, Pontypridd (MG) registered G917 GTG; N Collinson {Stonehouse Minibus}, Stonehouse (SC) 4/91; Gardiner Bros Ltd, Spennymoor (DM) 9/92.

38328: New to London Buses Ltd, London SW1 (LN) OV14 registered D346 JUM; Memory Lane Bus Co Ltd, Caerleon (GT) by3/95; Globe Luxury Coaches Ltd, Barnsley (SY) 3/95.

38393: New to as a demonstrator with Optare Ltd, Crossgates registered E456 VUM; CJ Springham {Crystal Cars}, Dartford (LN) 12/88; MJ & C Ryan, Langridge (AV) at an unknown date.

38406 [1]: New to Reading Transport Ltd (BE) registered F607 SDP (as B28F); reseated to B27F 3/90; Optare Ltd, Crossgates (dealer) 10/91; R & I Tours Ltd, London NW10 (LN) 230 11/91; re-registered RIB 7017 3/93; reseated to B26F by 6/94; re-registered F721 TLW 3/95; M Lawrenson, Earlestown (MY) 3/95.

38406 [2] (52): New to Educational Holidays GuernseyLtd {Island Coachways}, St Peter Port (CI) registered 8228 [5]; re-registered 38406 [2] 8/99; Guernseybus Ltd, St Peter Port (CI) 172 8/99 (as C45F); returned to Island Coachways Ltd, St Peter Port (CI) 11/00 52.

38509: New to Country Lion (Northampton) Ltd (NO) registered YN06 OPX; re-registered L 7 JSF 11/06; re-registered YN06 OPX 12/12.

39138 [2] (53): New to Educational Holidays GuernseyLtd {Island Coachways}, St Peter Port (CI) registered 8225 [2]; re-registered 39138 [2] 8/99; numbered 62 11/00; Guernseybus Ltd, St Peter Port (CI) 160 8/99 (as C45F); returned to Island Coachways Ltd, St Peter Port (CI) 11/00 53.

40527 (65): New to London Buses Ltd, London SW1 (LN) MRL210 registered J210 BWU (as B26F); London Northern Bus Co Ltd, Harrow (LN) 10/94; MTL London Northern Ltd, Harrow (LN) MRL210 10/95; Guernseybus Ltd, St Peter Port (CI) 65 9/98.

44525: New to BB Hire Cars Ltd, St Peter Port (XCI); hired to Guernseybus Ltd (CI) 9 5/88-10/88 (qv); Central Taxis Ltd, St Peter Port (CI) 12/88.

47979 (89): New South East London & Kent Bus Co Ltd {Selkent}, Ilford (LN) MRL163 registered H163 WWT; moved to London SE26 (LN) 1/94; withdrawn 9/97; Wealden PSV Sales Ltd, Five Oak Green (dealer) 11/97; Metrobus Ltd, Orpington (LN) 11/97; numbered 914 8/98; Guernseybus Ltd, St Peter Port (CI) 89 3/00; to service 5/00.

48161 (66): New to London Buses Ltd, London SW1 (LN) MRL214 registered J214 BWU (as B26F); London Northern Bus Co Ltd, Harrow (LN) 10/94; MTL London Northern Ltd, Harrow (LN) MRL214 10/95; Guernseybus Ltd, St Peter Port (CI) 66 9/98.

49377: New to Central Taxis Ltd, St Peter Port (CI).

51735 [1]: New to an unidentified owner as a van registered DSO 89T; Sealink, St Peter Port (GCI) as a luggage van at an unknown date.

52097: New to SA Bebb Ltd, Llantwit Fardre (MG) registered E 66 SUH; WS Yeates Ltd, Loughborough (dealer) 4/90; DA Bond, Willington (DM) 10/90.

52141 (16B): New to an unidentified UK owner registered YK59 YEE (as M16); Bontour, St Peter, Jersey (registration unknown) c10/15.

56206 (68): New to London Buses Ltd, London SW1 (LN) MRL218 registered J218 BWU (as B26F); London Northern Bus Co Ltd, Harrow (LN) 10/94; MTL London Northern Ltd, Harrow (LN) MRL218 10/95; Guernseybus Ltd, St Peter Port (CI) 67 9/98.

56624: Acquired from Nationaal Reumafonds, den Haag (O-NL) registered JS-35-JJ.

58677: New to AJ & MD Lovering, Combe Martin (DN) registered RTT 7N; Chepstow Minibus Co (GT) 4/78; M Smith, Llanmartin (GT) 3/79; Kerricabs Ltd, Newport (GT) 6/84; DD Jones, Meidrim (DD) by5/86; JA Evans, Tregaron (DD) 4/90.

59610 (17P): New to an unidentified UK owner registered CX14 RXZ (as M16).

61973 (86): New to East Surrey Bus Services Ltd, South Godstone (SR) 26 registered J326 PPD; Metrobus Ltd, Orpington (LN) 917 6/97; Guernseybus Ltd, St Peter Port (CI) 86 3/00; to service 5/00.

62067 (87): New East Surrey Bus Services Ltd, South Godstone (SR) 34 registered G972 WPA; Metrobus Ltd, Orpington (LN) 911 6/97; Guernseybus Ltd, St Peter Port (CI) 87 3/00; to service 4/00.

64991: New to West Midlands Police (XWM) registered F 56 BJW.

66867 (46): New to Avon County Council, Bristol (XAV) 483/15 registered F396 RHT (as B16FL); City & Council of Bristol (XAV) 4/96; WJ Amies {Courtesy Cars}, Shrewsbury (SH) 1/99.

66868 (44): New to London Borough of Redbridge (LN) registered H557 JEV.

69101 (59): New to Luton & District Transport Ltd (BD) 303 registered F303 MNK (as B35F); LDT Ltd, Luton (BD) 303 5/95; Crosville Wales Ltd, Llandudno Junction (GD) SSC303 11/97; Arriva Cymru Ltd, Llandudno Junction (GD) SSC303 4/98; Wacton Trading / Coach Sales, Bromyard (dealer) 1/02.

70011 (11): New to National Car Parks, Paisley (SC) registered AE54 MWF (as B23F).

70055 (55): New to National Car Parks, Paisley (SC) registered AE54 NUB (as B23F).

70066 (66): New to EMA Carparks, Nottingham East Midlands Airport (LE) 3 registered MV 54 EEM; Nottingham East Midlands Airport, Castle Donington (LE) 3 1/06; Manchester Airport (GM) 12/06; National Car Parks, Luton Airport (BD) 2/08.

70077 (77): New to EMA Carparks, Nottingham East Midlands Airport (LE) 2 registered FJ 05 HYM; Nottingham East Midlands Airport, Castle Donington (LE) 2 1/06; Manchester Airport (GM) 12/06; National Car Parks, Luton Airport (BD) 7/07.

70088 (88): New to EMA Carparks, Nottingham East Midlands Airport (LE) 6 registered FJ 05 HYK; Nottingham East Midlands Airport, Castle Donington (LE) 6 1/06; Manchester Airport (GM) 12/06; National Car Parks, Luton Airport (BD) 7/07.

70099 (99): New to EMA Carparks, Nottingham East Midlands Airport (LE) 1 registered FJ 05 HYL; Nottingham East Midlands Airport, Castle Donington (LE) 1 1/06; Manchester Airport (GM) 12/06; National Car Parks, Luton Airport (BD) 6/07.

77056 (56): New to National Car Parks, Paisley (SC) registered AE54 MWC (as B23F); Hansar Finance Ltd, Cheadle Hulme (dealer) by10/07; O'Hara {Row Travel}, Clifton (GM) 12/07; M Travel, Old Trafford (GM) 9/08; Hansar Finance Ltd, Cheadle Hulme (dealer) 11/08.

77091 (91): New to National Car Parks, Paisley (SC) registered AE54 MWD (as B23F); Hansar Finance Ltd, Cheadle Hulme (dealer) by10/07; O'Hara {Row Travel}, Clifton (GM) 12/07; Hansar Finance Ltd, Cheadle Hulme (dealer) 9/08.

J 26019: New to Nash's Luxury Coaches Ltd, Ventnor (IW) registered HDL 304; Southern Vectis Omnibus Co Ltd, Newport (IW) 104 6/56; Barnard & Barnard Ltd, London SE26 (dealer) 9/60; Mascot Motors Ltd, St Helier (CI) 17 4/61; Mrs P Skinner {Kultex Exchanges Familiaux}, St John (XCI) 6/79; Dr JR Young, Nottingham (dealer / preservationist) 9/85; Herefordshire Transport Collection for preservation 2/87.

MXX 481: New to London Transport Executive, London SW1 (LN) RF504 (LTE body number 7934, as B41F); reseated to B39F 3/59; Sterrett, Gosport (XHA) 5/79.

TUN 627: New to A Mates, Chirk (DH); JH Williams {Hadyn's Coaches}, Chirk (DH) 4/70; withdrawn 4/72; Direct Coal & Haulage {Mosswood Coaches}, Wetley Rocks (ST) 7/72; withdrawn 1/73; Canyon Travel Ltd, Hereford (HR) 25 3/73; TJ O'Brien, Farnworth (LA) 8/73; K Rimmer, St Helens (LA) 3/74; G Ashton {Regina}, St Helens (MY) 11/74; M Shaw, St Helens (MY) 10/75; Ashall & Sharp {Status Travel}, Haydock (MY) 10/75; D Ashall, (Haydock?) for preservation (at North West Transport Museum) by4/79.

510 PYB: New to Darch & Willcox Ltd {Comfy-Lux Coaches}, Martock (SO) (as C43F); E & TW Jones {Joseph Jones & Sons}, Ystradgynlais (BC) 2/65; Edwards Coaches Ltd, Joys Green (GL) 6/68; withdrawn 12/81.

D898 NUA: New as a demonstrator with Optare Ltd, Crossgates (as B25F); Blackpool Transport Services Ltd (LA) 8/87; reseated DP19F 1988; reseated DP21F by6/90; Optare Ltd, Crossgates (dealer) 9/96; Reading Transport Ltd (BE) 218 10/96; Optare Ltd, Crossgates (dealer) c12/98.

Notes:

In the 1986 season, a joint service with Dean Forest Coaches Ltd, Joy's Green (GL) was operated in the UK to and from Weymouth. 2445 [2] (ex NVA 75L) was operated by Educational Holidays Guernsey Ltd together with two vehicles below from Dean Forest Coaches Ltd.

CAR 162K	AEC Reliance	6U3ZR7881	Plaxton	728840	C51F	3/72
CXD 301M	Bedford YRT	DW454625	Plaxton	7411TX537	C53F	6/74

70011 (ex AE54 MWF) (11): Owned by States of Guernsey and leased to Island Coachways Ltd.

70012-70044 (12-44): Owned by States of Guernsey and leased to Island Coachways Ltd following the demise of Guernseybus Ltd.

70012-70034 (12-34): Reseated to B34F before or shortly afterward entering service.

70055 (ex AE54 NUB) (55), 70066 (ex MV54 EEM) (66), 70077 (ex FJ05 HYM) (77), 70088 (ex FJ05 HYK) (88), 70099 (ex FJ05 HYL) (99), 77056 (ex AE54 MWD) (56), 77091 (ex AE54 MWD) (91): Owned by States of Guernsey and leased to Island Coachways Ltd.

1787 [1] (ex 898 FUF, 1787 [1]): Was on hire 5/86-9/86; named 'Earl Grey'; acquired 4/88 and to service 5/88.

1787 [2] (ex J 25784, CEN 535) (1): Fitted with the 1972 Plaxton (728442) C45F body from Ford R192 WLJ 578K – ex Fairtax Foxhound Ltd, Melton Mowbray (LE), altered to 7ft 4in wide and to service 7/80; re-registered 8230 [3] 4/86.

1787 [3] (ex LTB 817P): Altered to 7ft 4in wide, named 'Portinfer', re-registered 8230 [4] and to service 5/88.

1787 [4] (ex J 3256 [2], ATT 151L): Named 'Ladies Bay' and to service 6/93.

1787 [5] (ex G154 ELJ): To service 4/95; numbered 51 11/00.

1931 (ex D749 ULG): Fitted with a replica tram body built on a reconstructed lorry chassis by Educational Holidays Guernsey Ltd {Island Coachways} as O20/22D.

2424: Re-registered 20412 9/77.

2445 [1] (ex ORO 966D) (2): Altered to 7ft 4in wide and to service 5/79.

2445 [2] (ex NVA 75L): Named *'Portinfer'*; use on Guernsey was limited due to its 8ft 2½in width with its principle use on a jointly operated (with Dean Forest Coaches Ltd, Joy's Green (GL)) coach service within the UK to and from Weymouth.

2609 (51): Named *'Joan-Mary'*.

3989 [1] (ex MTS 808) (2): Altered to 7ft 4in wide and to service 8/78.

3989 [2] (ex 610 STT) (9): Altered to 7ft 4in wide.

3989 [3] (ex PFJ 351M): Named *'Havelet Bay'* and to service 3/90.

3989 [4]: Numbered 49 11/00.

4510 [1] (ex 2725, 4510 [1]) (44): To service 6/84; named *'Katie'*.

5260 (ex 5261, MRV 60G): Rebuilt as a minibus by Educational Holidays Guernsey Ltd {Island Coachways} as C17F; to service 12/81.

5779 [1] (ex J 9143, FNT 231D) (7): Altered to 7ft 4in wide.

5779 [2]: Named 'Portelet Bay'; numbered 48 11/00.

6289: Acquired for spares.

6430 [1] (ex J 35662) (8): Altered to 7ft 4in wide.

6430 [2]: Named 'Pembroke Bay'; reseated to C43F 8/91.

6430 [4] (ex D939 KNW): Numbered 61 11/00.

6430 [6] (48): Re-registered 23374 5/18.

6430 [7] (54): Named *'Kit'*.

6768 [2] (ex AFJ 79B) (6): To service 10/81.

6768 [4] (ex WUA 655X): Named *'Petit Bot'*; received Public Service Omnibus plate ph90 5/93.

6768 [5]: Named *'Moulin Huet'*; numbered 50 11/00; re-registered 53849 by5/14.

6769 [2] (ex 5 RDV) (7): To service 5/82.

8225 [2]: Named *'Perelle Bay'*.

8226 [2] (ex J 2688, 5184 AW) (3): Altered to 7ft 4in wide.

8226 [3] (ex CRF 699N) (3): Altered to 7ft 4in wide; named *'Cobo Bay'*; to service 12/84.

8226 [4]: Numbered 45 11/00.

8227 [2] (ex J 2687, 5183 AW) (4): Altered to 7ft 4in wide and to service 7/81.

8227 [4] (ex BUX 208L) (4): Altered to 7ft 4in wide; named *'Fermain'*; to service 4/85.

8227 [3]: Was of limited use as it was too wide for use on the island (7ft 6in).

8227 [5] (ex E961 PME): Numbered 56 11/00.

8228 [2] (ex J 16590, AFJ 82B) (8): To service 5/81.

8228 [4] (ex KBH 450N): Altered to 7ft 4in wide; named *'Rocquaine'*; to service 5/85.

8228 [5]: Named *'Roquaine Bay'*.

8229 [2] (ex J 16654, AFJ 77B) (9): To service 1/81.

8230 [2] (ex J 16706, AFJ 86B) (10): To service 1/81.

8230 [5]: Numbered 47 11/00; being used for spares 9/17.

8230 [6] (53): Named *'Lily'*.

9438 [2] (ex J 1465 [2] (5): Altered to 7ft 4in wide.

9438 [3] (ex LDS 977Y): Named *'Petit Port'*.

9438 [4]: Numbered 64 11/00.

9969 [1] (ex ARX 705B) (1): Altered to 7ft 4in wide and to service 2/79.

9969 [2] (ex J 2465) (10): Altered to 7ft 4in wide and to service 5/84.

9969 [3] (ex BNO 134L): Altered to 7ft 4in wide, named *'Vazon Bay'* and to service 10/88.

9969 [4]: Was built as B—D, but the rear doorway was filled in before entering service; numbered 57 11/00; reseated C43F and received Public Service Omnibus plate 105 6/05; re-registered 52728 by2/13; received Public Service Omnibus plate 58 by3/19.

10739 [1] (ex J 20361, KEJ 687H): Altered to 7ft 4in wide and named 'Perelle'.

10797 (ex J 16898, MDR 525H): Altered to 7ft 4in wide, named 'Saints' and to service 10/87.

11840 (ex J 30366, UJH 346): Acquired for spares.

18221 [1] (52E): Named *'Dora'*; Re-registered 8227 [7] 1/19.

23196: Reseated to B18F and 108 5/96; numbered 63 11/00.

24539: Named *'Saint-Pierre du Bois'*.

24603 (ex H165 WWT) (88): Was set aside to be transferred to the NatWest Island Games Committee fleet 6/03, but in the event was not used.

34518 (ex J960 DWX) (85): Was set aside to be transferred to the NatWest Island Games Committee fleet 6/03, but in the event was not used.

38243 (ex D851 CRY): Named *'Roadrunner 5'* and to service 12/95; numbered 58 11/00.

38290 (ex D854 CRY): Named *'Roadrunner 1'*; to service 2/94; numbered 59 11/00.

38293 [1] (ex D845 CRY): Named *'Roadrunner 2'*; to service 2/94.

38296 (ex D853 CRY): Named '*Roadrunner 4*' and to service 9/95.

38327 (ex G917 GTG): Named '*Roadrunner 5*' and to service 7/95.

38328 (ex D346 JUM): Named '*Roadrunner 3*' and to service 9/95; numbered 60 11/00.

38393 (ex E456 VUM): Named '*Roadrunner 9*' and to service 9/95.

38406 [1] (ex F721 JLW, RIB 7017, F607 SDP): Named '*Roadrunner 8*' and to service 9/95; re-registered 8228 [6] 8/99; numbered 73 3/01; received Public Service Omnibus plate 58 1/03.

39138 [1]: Re-registered 8225 [3] 8/99.

47979 (ex H163 WWT) (89): Was set aside to be transferred to the NatWest Island Games Committee fleet 6/03, but in the event was not used.

51735 [1]: Its registration is also recorded as 51537; rebuilt as a minibus by Educational Holidays Guernsey Ltd {Island Coachways}, as M--; re-registered 8225 [1] 9/90; re-registered 10739 [2] 8/91.

52141 (ex J ?????, YK59 YEE): Named '*Bonnie*'.

56624 (ex JS-35-JJ): Converted to right-hand drive by Educational Holidays Guernsey Ltd {Island Coachways} and to accommodate wheelchairs.

58677 (ex RTT 7N): Named '*Saints Bay*' and to service 7/90.

59610 (ex CX14 RXZ): Named '*Mia*'.

62417 (2): Re-registered 3989 [5] by1/14.

64991 (ex F 56 BJW): Numbered 54 11/00.

65119 (1): Re-registered 8227 [6] by4/08; re-registered 18221 [2] 1/19.

65802 (43): Named '*Ohlin-Naomi*'; renumbered 3 by8/05.

66867 (ex F396 RHT): Reseated B37F and to service 9/01.

66868 (ex H557 JEV) (44): Reseated B37F and to service 9/01; renumbered 4 by8/05.

77819 (10): Named '*La buse de chentenaire*'.

J 26019 (ex HDL 304): Acquired for preservation but found to be in poor condition and uneconomic to restore.

MXX 481: Did not operate for Educational Holidays Guernsey Ltd.

TUN 627: Acquired for spares.

510 PYB: Did not operate for Educational Holidays Guernsey Ltd.

D898 NUA: Did not operate for Educational Holidays Guernsey Ltd.

Disposals:

1787 [1] (ex 898 FUF, 1787 [1]): Lakeland Motor Museum, Holker Hall for preservation re-registered 898 FUF 6/93; Greet, Broadhempson for preservation 3/94; Intransit Ltd, St Sampson (CI) 11 re-registered 1787 [1] 2/13; moved to St Sampson (CI) by9/13; fitted with a Cummins engine by3/18.

1787 [4] (ex J 3256 [2], ATT 151L): Wacton Trading / Coach Sales, Bromyard (dealer) 12/94; body scrapped 1/95; chassis exported to Pakistan.

1787 [5] (ex G154 ELJ) (51): Unidentified owner by6/09.

1787 [6]: Intransit Ltd, St Peter Port (CI) re-registered 55184 2/13; moved to St Sampson (CI) by9/13.

1931 (ex D749 ULG): W Whittaker, West Bromwich (WM) re-registered D749 ULG 2/97; R Tonk, Edgbaston by1/02; American Adventure {Gullivers Kingdom}, Shipley (XDE) 1/04; unidentified owner 5/12; noted Cardiff 9/12; last licence expired 4/13.

2445 [1] (ex ORO 966D) (2): Wacton Trading / Coach Sales, Bromyard (dealer) 1983.

2445 [2] (ex NVA 75L): Lonsdale Coaches (Sales) Ltd, Heysham (dealer) 2/85; Dean Forest Coaches Ltd, Joy's Green (GL) re-registered NVA 75L (not operated) 2/85; Barker, Hest Bank (LA) 2/85; SM Emerton Ltd, Cranfield (BD) 10/86; MJ Key, Worcester (HW) 5/89; Rover Coaches (Bromsgrove) Ltd (HW) 4/90; last licence expired 5/90.

3989 [1] (ex MTS 808) (2): No known disposal.

3989 [2] (ex 610 STT) (9): Traject Ltd {Abbeyways}, Halifax (WY) (not operated) 11/89; J Sykes, Carlton (dealer) 8/94; WH Fowler & Sons (Coaches) Ltd, Holbeach Drove for preservation 8/94; CL Harmer {Renown European}, Bexhill-on-Sea for preservation 3/98; Renown Coaches Ltd, Bexhill-on-Sea (ES) for preservation 10/98; advertised for sale 10/99; unidentified owner by4/02.

3989 [3] (ex PFJ 351M): G Blacker {Needabus}, Pitsea (EX) re-registered PFJ 351M 11/92; named "*Carol Anne*" by5/93; GH Brailey, Canvey Island (EX) 12/94; last licence expired 2/96; unidentified dealer for scrap c2/96.

3989 [4] (49): Unidentified dealer for scrap 11/14.

3989 [5] (ex 62417) (2): No known disposal.

4510 [1] (ex 2725, 4510 [1]) (44): Wacton Trading / Coach Sales, Bromyard (dealer) 9/92; Maple. Jacksons Hill (IS) re-registered VVS 913 4/93; moved to Porthcressa (IS) by10/95; withdrawn 3/97; Twynham, Hugh Town (IS) 7/98; to service 3/99; reseated B28F by5/02; Lucas, Hugh Town (IS) 10/06; S Hendra, Truro for preservation 12/14 (collected 4/15); P Whear, Redruth for preservation 11/17; Prof JF Kennedy, Tenbury Wells for preservation 7/18.

5260 (ex 5261, MRV 60G) (12): Wacton Trading / Coach Sales, Bromyard (dealer) by1987.

5779 [1] (ex J 9143, FNT 231D) (7): Traject Ltd {Abbeyways}, Halifax (WY) (not operated) 11/89; J Sykes, Carlton (dealer) 8/94; WH Fowler & Sons (Coaches) Ltd, Holbeach Drove for preservation 1/95; CL Harmer {Renown European}, Bexhill-on-Sea for preservation 3/98; Renown Coaches Ltd, Bexhill-on-Sea for preservation 10/98; unidentified dealer / owner by4/02; travellers, Upper Beeding as a caravan by11/04.
5779 [2] (48): Unidentified dealer for scrap by5/07.
6289: Broken up for spares 1987.
6430 [1] (ex J 35662) (8): Traject Ltd {Abbeyways}, Halifax (WY) (not operated) 11/89; J Sykes, Carlton (dealer) for scrap 8/94.
6430 [2]: Blue Coach Tours Ltd, St Helier (CI) 32 re-registered J 80977 5/95; Tantivy Blue Coach Tours Ltd, St Helier (CI) 11 11/96; scrapped 5/08.
6430 [3] (ex J 60118): Wacton Trading / Coach Sales, Bromyard (dealer) 3/98.
6430 [4] (ex D939 KNW) (61): Wacton Trading / Coach Sales, Bromyard (dealer) by12/01;   re-registered D939 KNW by8/02; IR Phillips {I & S Coaches}, Hereford (HR) (not used) 8/02; unidentified dealer for scrap by8/05; last licence expired 9/06.
6430 [5] (ex F302 MNK) (58): Unidentified dealer for scrap by6/06.
6768 [2] (ex AFJ 79B) (6): WP Simon {Riduna Buses}, Alderney (CI) re-registered AY   58 [2] 1/84; re-registered AY   586 [1] 1985; withdrawn c1988; noted un-registered and accident damaged at Torquay docks 1989; unidentified dealer (probably Peterborough Passenger Vehicle Spares) 1990, but not collected and stored in the yard of Torbay Seaways, Torre Station; P Platt, Exeter for preservation spares 1991; being dismantled at Winkleigh 10/91.
6768 [3] (ex MPX 945R) (11): A Charlesworth {Melksham Coaches}, Melksham (WI) re-registered MPX 945R by9/88; Taw & Torridge Coaches Ltd, Merton (DN) 7/90; N Squires {Norman's Garage}, Torquay (DN) 8/95; last licence expired 4/96; Dennis, Lympstone (XDN) by1997; C Shears, Winkleigh for preservation 3/98.
6768 [4] (ex WUA 655X): R Spandler {Alderney Taxi & Hire Cars}, Alderney (CI) re-registered AY   1773; unidentified owner 9/01.
6769 [2] (ex 5 RDV) (7): Wacton Trading / Coach Sales, Bromyard (dealer) 12/84; Truscott, Roche for preservation 12/84; D Rundell, Falmouth for preservation 1/99; Falmouth Coaches Ltd {King Harry Coaches} (CO) 7/02; converted to a recovery vehicle by12/03; re-registered YCV 365B 10/05; derelict in a field by5/19.
7091 [1] (ex J 1852, GJM 6): No known disposal.
7091 [2] (ex J 6901): R Gaudion (Methodist Boys Club}, Vale (XCI) 1987.
7269 (ex J 1858, GJM 5) (3): No known disposal.
8225 [3] (ex 39138 [1]): Unidentified owner by6/09.
8225 [4] (ex AM03 BCK): Converted to a luggage van by5/17.
8226 [2] (ex J 2688, 5184 AW) (3): Wacton Trading / Coach Sales, Bromyard (dealer) 10/84.
8226 [3] (ex CRF 699N) (3): Broken up by Guernseybus Ltd; remains to Wacton Trading / Coach Sales, Bromyard (dealer) 4/96.
8226 [4] (45): No known disposal
8227 [2] (ex J 2687, 5183 AW) (4): Wacton Trading / Coach Sales, Bromyard (dealer) 10/84.
8227 [3]: JMT (1978) Ltd, St Helier (CI) 24 re-registered J 34191 3/85; JMT (1987) Ltd, St Helier (CI) 24 11/87; scrapped 2/03.
8227 [4] (ex BUX 208L) (4): Broken up on the premises by12/97.
8227 [5] (ex E961 PME) (56): Unidentified owner by6/09.
8228 [2] (ex J 16590, AFJ 82B) (8): WP Simon {Riduna Buses}, Alderney (CI) re-registered AY   91 [3] 1/84; J Main {Riduna Buses}, Alderney (CI) 5/85; withdrawn 1986; C Shears & P Platt, Exeter (as dealer) 7/90; Wacton Trading / Coach Sales, Bromyard (dealer) for scrap 3/93.
8228 [3] (ex JPC 547N) (2): W Errington {Victoria Hotel}, Alderney (CI) re-registered AY 1858; 10/84; J Main {Riduna Buses}, Alderney (CI) 3/86; unidentified dealer / operator, Torquay c1988.
8228 [4] (ex KBH 450N): Holiday Tours Ltd, St Peter (dealer) 2/92; Clarendon Coaches Ltd, St Helier (CI) (not operated) by1/93; Tantivy Holiday Coach Tours Ltd, St Helier (CI) (not operated) 1/93; not traced further.
8228 [6] (ex 38406 [1], F721 JLW, RIB 7017, F607 SDP) (73): MJ Perry {Bromyard Omnibus Co}, Bromyard (HR) 177 re-registered F721 TLW 5/03 (as B33F); to service 8/03; named 'Lionel' by 6/04; Evans Coaches (Tregaron) Ltd (DD) 7/04 (as B26F); GR Lewis, Llangeitho (DD) 10/05 (as B29F); withdrawn 4/07; last licence expired 4/08; unidentified dealer for scrap by9/09.
8229 [2] (ex J 16654, AFJ 77B) (9): Wacton Trading / Coach Sales, Bromyard (dealer) 12/84; Truscott, Roche for preservation 12/84; D Rundell, Falmouth for preservation 1/99; re-registered AFJ 77B 4/99; Falmouth Coaches Ltd {King Harry} for preservation 7/02.

8230 [2] (ex J 16706, AFJ 86B) (10): Wacton Trading / Coach Sales, Bromyard (dealer) 12/84; R Wilson, Bovey Tracey for preservation 12/84; re-registered AFJ 86B by5/88; D Sayer et al, Halifax for preservation 10/91; A & J Purvis, Seaburn for preservation 10/94; J Purvis, Seaburn for preservation 8/97; D Waymann, Oldham for preservation by6/99; B Botley, Lee-on-Solent for preservation by12/01; D Joseph, Ilford for preservation 6/11.

8230 [3] (ex 1787 [2], J 25784, CEN 535) (1): Northern Lights, Landes du Marche (XCI) re-registered 10155 [2] 1986; Offshore Radio, St Martin (GCI) as a mobile studio 1990.

8230 [4] (ex 1787 [3], LTB 817P): Wacton Trading / Coach Sales, Bromyard (dealer) 2/98.

8230 [5] (47): Unidentified dealer for scrap 4/18.

8231 [2] (ex -?-) (11): No known disposal.

9438 [2] (ex J 1465 [2] (5): Wacton Trading / Coach Sales, Bromyard (dealer) 7/88; A Webster, Barrow-on-Soar for preservation 9/88; Wacton Trading / Coach Sales, Bromyard (dealer) 2/92; I Wareing (& Sullivan?), Gyffylliog, Ruthin as a mobile caravan 6/92; re-registered JNP 631C 10/92; last licence expired 7/03.

9438 [3] (ex LDS 997Y): Unidentified owner 12/96.

9438 [4] (64): No known disposal.

9969 [1] (ex ARX 705B) (1): No known disposal.

9969 [2] (ex J 2465) (10): Wacton Trading / Coach Sales, Bromyard (dealer) 7/88; Richards, Cheltenham as a caravan 9/88.

9969 [3] (ex BNO 134L): No known disposal.

10152 (ex 8009 FH): North Social Club (Northerners Football team} (XCI) 2/81.

10739 [1] (ex J 20361, KEJ 687H): Wacton Trading / Coach Sales, Bromyard (dealer) 12/89; Traject Ltd {Abbeyways}, Halifax (WY) (not operated) 1/90; probably to J Sykes, Carlton (dealer) for scrap 8/94.

10739 [2] (ex 8225 [1], 51735 [1] or 51537), DSO 89T): No known disposal.

10797 (ex J 16898, MDR 525H): Wacton Trading / Coach Sales, Bromyard (dealer) 12/89; Traject Ltd {Abbeyways}, Halifax (WY) (not operated) 12/89; J Sykes, Carlton (dealer) for scrap 8/94.

11033 (ex VOD 313): ME Ruggiada, St Sampson (XCI) (for overland journey overseas) 9/78.

11840 (ex J 30366, UJH 346): Broken up at an unknown date.

12359 (ex SAT 201R): Presstoon Travel Ltd, Bilton (WK) by2/89; re-registered SAT 201R 1990; R Garratt, Ashby (LE) 8/92; private owner 1/93; last licence expired 9/94.

12723 [4] (ex H151 UUA) (71): NatWest Island Games Committee (CI) 71 6-7/03; unidentified UK dealer 7/03.

12727 [4] (ex H142 UUA) (72): No known disposal.

12859 (ex J 60691, 18939, J 48139) (14): No known disposal.

13456 (ex XWF 69T): Kerricabs Ltd, Newport (GT) 3/90; withdrawn 12/90; Wacton Trading / Coach Sales, Bromyard (dealer) 9/92.

17314 (ex J216 BWU) (67): NatWest Island Games Committee (CI) 67 6-7/03; unidentified UK dealer 7/03; R Wilson, Gourock (SC) re-registered J216 BWU (not operated) 12/03; Caledonian Coach Co Ltd {Caledonia Buses / Linn Park Buses}, Glasgow (SC) 10/04; last licence expired 3/07; unidentified dealer for scrap by12/08.

18047: States Airport, Forest (XCI) 4/06.

18221 [2] (ex 8227 [6], 65119)) (1): Island Taxis Ltd, St Peter Port (CI) 1/19.

18264 [3] (ex H147 UUA) (70): NatWest Island Games Committee (CI) 70 6-7/03; unidentified UK dealer 7/03.

18267 [4] (ex H564 WWR) (73): Scrapped 3/01.

19660 [3] (ex H168 WWT) (79): NatWest Island Games Committee (CI) 79 6-7/03; unidentified UK dealer 7/03; RJ, S & CJ Goulden {Master Travel}, Welwyn Garden City (HT) (not operated) by5/04; unidentified dealer for scrap by7/15.

19662 [3] (ex H167 WWT) (80): NatWest Island Games Committee (CI) 80 6-7/03; unidentified UK dealer 7/03; R Wilson, Gourock (SC) (not operated) 12/03.

19675 [4] (ex J968 JNL) (78): NatWest Island Games Committee (CI) 78 6-7/03; unidentified UK dealer 7/03; R Wilson, Gourock (SC) (not operated) 12/03.

19676 [3] (ex J967 JNL) (75): NatWest Island Games Committee (CI) 75 6-7/03; unidentified UK dealer 7/03; R Wilson, Gourock (SC) re-registered J967 JNL (not operated) 12/03; Caledonian Coach Co Ltd {Caledonia Buses / Linn Park Buses}, Glasgow (SC) 3/05; last licence expired 2/07; unidentified dealer for scrap by12/08.

19677 [4] (ex J971 JNL) (76): NatWest Island Games Committee (CI) 76 6-7/03; unidentified UK dealer 7/03; R Wilson, Gourock (SC) (not operated) 12/03; unidentified dealer for scrap by12/06.

19678 [4] (ex J972 JNL) (77): NatWest Island Games Committee (CI) 77 6-7/03; unidentified UK dealer 7/03; R Wilson, Gourock (SC) (not operated) 12/03; unidentified dealer for scrap by12/06.

20412 (ex 2424, TNG 184G): No known disposal.

20716 (ex J220 BWU) (69): NatWest Island Games Committee (CI) 69 6-7/03; unidentified UK dealer 7/03; noted disused on the premises of CR Craske, Sutton (NK) 1/05 (owner unknown).

23196 (63): Private owner, Guernsey by4/09.

23374 (ex 6430 [6]) (48): Tantivy Blue Coach Tours Ltd, St Helier (CI) 7/18 (see below).

24493 (ex F671 YOG): Scrapped by12/01.

24539: Wacton Trading / Coach Sales, Bromyard (dealer) by6/09.

24603 (ex H165 WWT) (88): Unidentified UK dealer 7/03; RJ, S & CJ Goulden {Master Travel}, Welwyn Garden City (HT) (not operated) by1/05; unidentified dealer for scrap 6/05.

24775 [2] (ex H161 WWT) (90): NatWest Island Games Committee (CI) 90 6-7/03; unidentified UK dealer 7/03; R Wilson, Gourock (SC) (not operated) 12/03; unidentified dealer for scrap by12/06.

29728 [3] (ex J963 JNL) (74): NatWest Island Games Committee (CI) 74 6-7/03; unidentified UK dealer 7/03; R Wilson, Gourock (SC) (not operated) 12/03; unidentified dealer for scrap by12/06.

31921 [2] (ex AFJ 736T) (171): Rexquote Ltd, Bishops Lydeard (SO) (not operated) 11/01; A Goddard, West Ewell for preservation 3/03; re-registered AFJ 736T by6/18; P Emery, Chase Terrace for preservation 6/18.

33541 (ex J962 DWX) (84): NatWest Island Games Committee (CI) 84 6-7/03; unidentified UK dealer 7/03; RJ, S & CJ Goulden {Master Travel}, Welwyn Garden City (HT) 13 re-registered J962 DWX 2/06; last licence expired 2/13; unidentified dealer for scrap by5/15.

34518 (ex J960 DWX) (85): Unidentified UK dealer by7/03; R Wilson, Gourock (SC) (not operated) 12/03; unidentified dealer for scrap by12/06.

38243 (ex D851 CRY) (58): Scrapped by6/02.

38290 (ex D854 CRY): Scrapped by6/02.

38293 [1] (ex D845 CRY): No known disposal.

38296 (ex D853 CRY): No known disposal.

38327 (ex G917 GTG): No known disposal.

38328 (ex D346 JUM) (60): Wacton Trading / Coach Sales, Bromyard (dealer) by12/01.

38393 (ex E456 VUM): Blythswood Motors Ltd, Glasgow (dealer) 1/98; Dickson, Erskine (SC) 2/98; Beattie {Direct}, Renfrew (SC) 5/03; last licence expired 10/03; unidentified dealer by1/06.

38406 [2] (ex 8228 [5]: Sarnia Autos, St Peter Port (dealer) 11/09; Mr Pink, Portsmouth (as a caravan?) by9/12.

39138 [2] (ex 8225 [2]: Unidentified dealer for scrap by5/07.

40527 [2] (ex J210 BWU) (65): NatWest Island Games Committee (CI) 65 6-7/03; unidentified UK dealer 7/03; RA Giles {KG Motors}, Caerphilly (MG) by10/03; re-registered J210 BWU 11/03; IA Tomlinson, Winsford (CH) by5/06; MJ Perry {Bromyard Omnibus Co}, Bromyard (HW) 5/06; re-registered J555 BUS 5/06; to service 6/06; DT Brundrit {RML Travel}, Burslem (ST) MRL210 10/06; re-registered J555 RML and named 'Gladys' 11/06; re-registered J210 BWU 7/08; withdrawn 11/08; last licence expired 11/10; unidentified dealer for scrap c11/10.

44525: Central Transfers, St Peter Port (CI) 3/90; Guernseybus Ltd, St Peter Port (CI) 3 1/91; Central Transfers Ltd, St Peter Port (CI) 3 1/95; Intransit Ltd, St Peter Port (CI) 3 12/96; withdrawn 9/03.

47979 (ex H163 WWT) (89): No known disposal.

48161 (ex J214 BWU) (66): No known disposal.

49377: Central Transfers, St Peter Port (CI) 3/90; Guernseybus Ltd, St Peter Port (CI) 2 1/91; Central Transfers Ltd, St Peter Port (CI) 2 1/95; withdrawn at an unknown date.

52097 (ex E 66 SUH): Brouard, Guernsey (XCI) 2/98.

52728 (ex 9969 [4]) (57): No known disposal.

53849 (ex 6768 [5]) (50): Unidentified dealer for scrap 11/16.

56206 (ex J218 BWU) (68): NatWest Island Games Committee (CI) 68 6-7/03; unidentified UK dealer 7/03; unidentified owner as a mobile caravan re-registered J218 BWU 8/05.

56624 (ex JS-35-JJ): Unidentified owner, Lincolnshire 9/92.

58677 (ex RTT   7N): Holiday Tours Ltd, St Peter (dealer) 2/92; Clarendon Coaches Ltd, St Helier (CI) re-registered J 46545 5/92; withdrawn 10/92; Holiday Tours Ltd, St Peter (dealer) for scrap c10/92.

61973 (ex J326 PPD) (86): NatWest Island Games Committee (CI) 86 6-7/03; unidentified UK dealer 7/03; R Wilson, Gourock (SC) (not operated) 12/03; unidentified dealer for scrap by12/06.

62067 (ex G972 WPA) (87): Unidentified dealer c7/03; exported to France by7/10; dumped in a field off the D62 road near Linieres-Bouton and being used for spares.

64991 (ex F 56 BJW) (54): Unidentified dealer for scrap by4/05.

65802 (3, ex 43): Tantivy Blue Coach Tours Ltd, St Helier (CI) 11/18 (see below).

66867 (ex F396 RHT) (46): Unidentified UK dealer 11/09.

66868 (ex H557 JEV) (4, ex 44): Unidentified UK dealer 11/09.

69101 (ex F303 MNK) (58): Unidentified dealer for scrap by6/06.

70011 (ex AE54 MWF) (11): CT Plus Guernsey Ltd, St Peter Port (CI) DCS10 4/12; renumbered 214 4/17; renumbered 1114 10/18.

70012 (12): CT Plus Guernsey Ltd, St Peter Port (CI) DM1 4/12; renumbered 419 4/17; withdrawn 7/17; unidentified dealer by10/18.

70013 (13): CT Plus Guernsey Ltd, St Peter Port (CI) DM2 4/12; renumbered 420 4/17; withdrawn 7/17; unidentified UK dealer 9/17.

70014 (14): CT Plus Guernsey Ltd, St Peter Port (CI) DM3 4/12; renumbered 421 4/17; withdrawn 9/18; unidentified dealer by10/18.

70015 (15): CT Plus Guernsey Ltd, St Peter Port (CI) DM4 4/12; renumbered 422 4/17; withdrawn 7/17; unidentified dealer by10/18.

70016 (16): CT Plus Guernsey Ltd, St Peter Port (CI) DM5 4/12; renumbered 423 4/17; withdrawn 10/18; unidentified dealer 10/18.

70017 (17): CT Plus Guernsey Ltd, St Peter Port (CI) DM6 4/12; renumbered 424 4/17; withdrawn 10/18; unidentified dealer 10/18.

70018 (18): CT Plus Guernsey Ltd, St Peter Port (CI) DM7 4/12; renumbered 425 4/17; withdrawn 10/18; unidentified dealer by11/18.

70019 (19): CT Plus Guernsey Ltd, St Peter Port (CI) DM8 4/12; renumbered 426 4/17; withdrawn 9/18; unidentified dealer by10/18.

70020 (20): CT Plus Guernsey Ltd, St Peter Port (CI) DM9 4/12; renumbered 427 4/17; withdrawn 10/18; unidentified dealer 10/18.

70021 (21): CT Plus Guernsey Ltd, St Peter Port (CI) DM10 4/12; being used for spares by4/17; renumbered 428 (on paper) 4/17; unidentified dealer for scrap 7/17.

70022 (22): CT Plus Guernsey Ltd, St Peter Port (CI) DM11 4/12; renumbered 429 4/17; withdrawn 9/18; unidentified dealer by10/18.

70023 (23): CT Plus Guernsey Ltd, St Peter Port (CI) DM12 4/12; renumbered 430 4/17; withdrawn 9/18; unidentified dealer by10/18.

70024 (24): CT Plus Guernsey Ltd, St Peter Port (CI) DM13 4/12; renumbered 431 4/17; withdrawn 9/18; unidentified dealer by10/18.

70025 (25): CT Plus Guernsey Ltd, St Peter Port (CI) DM14 4/12; renumbered 432 4/17; withdrawn 9/18; unidentified dealer by10/18.

70026 (26): CT Plus Guernsey Ltd, St Peter Port (CI) DM15 4/12; renumbered 433 4/17; retained for use as a driver training vehicle 2019.

70027 (27): CT Plus Guernsey Ltd, St Peter Port (CI) DM16 4/12; renumbered 434 4/17; withdrawn 10/18; unidentified dealer 10/18.

70028 (28): CT Plus Guernsey Ltd, St Peter Port (CI) DM17 4/12; renumbered 435 4/17; withdrawn 7/17; unidentified UK dealer 9/17.

70029 (29): CT Plus Guernsey Ltd, St Peter Port (CI) DM18 4/12; renumbered 436 4/17; withdrawn 10/18; unidentified dealer 10/18.

70030 (30): CT Plus Guernsey Ltd, St Peter Port (CI) DM19 4/12; renumbered 437 4/17; withdrawn 7/17; unidentified dealer by10/18.

70031 (31): CT Plus Guernsey Ltd, St Peter Port (CI) DM20 4/12; renumbered 438 4/17; withdrawn 7/17; unidentified dealer by10/18.

70032 (32): CT Plus Guernsey Ltd, St Peter Port (CI) DM21 4/12; renumbered 439 4/17; withdrawn 10/18; unidentified dealer 10/18.

70033 (33): CT Plus Guernsey Ltd, St Peter Port (CI) DM22 4/12; renumbered 440 4/17; withdrawn 7/17; unidentified dealer by10/18.

70034 (34): CT Plus Guernsey Ltd, St Peter Port (CI) DM23 4/12; renumbered 441 4/17; withdrawn 7/17; unidentified dealer by11/18.

70035 (35): CT Plus Guernsey Ltd, St Peter Port (CI) DM24 4/12; renumbered 442 4/17; withdrawn 2/19; retained for use as a driver training vehicle 2/19.

70036 (36): CT Plus Guernsey Ltd, St Peter Port (CI) DM25 4/12; renumbered 443 4/17; withdrawn 11/18; unidentified dealer 11/18.

70037 (37): CT Plus Guernsey Ltd, St Peter Port (CI) DM26 4/12; renumbered 444 4/17; withdrawn 7/17; unidentified dealer 9/17.

70038 (38): CT Plus Guernsey Ltd, St Peter Port (CI) DM27 4/12; being used for spares by4/17; renumbered 445 (on paper) 4/17; unidentified dealer for scrap 7/17.

70039 (39): CT Plus Guernsey Ltd, St Peter Port (CI) DM28 4/12; renumbered 446 4/17; withdrawn 9/18; States Airport, Forest (XCI) 9/18.

70040 (40): CT Plus Guernsey Ltd, St Peter Port (CI) DM29 4/12; renumbered 447 4/17; withdrawn 9/18; unidentified dealer by10/18.

70041 (41): CT Plus Guernsey Ltd, St Peter Port (CI) DM30 4/12; renumbered 448 4/17; withdrawn 9/18; unidentified dealer by10/18.

70042 (42): CT Plus Guernsey Ltd, St Peter Port (CI) DM31 4/12; renumbered 449 4/17; withdrawn 9/18; unidentified dealer by1/19.

70043 (43): CT Plus Guernsey Ltd, St Peter Port (CI) DM32 4/12; renumbered 450 4/17; withdrawn 10/18; unidentified dealer 10/18.

70044 (44): CT Plus Guernsey Ltd, St Peter Port (CI) DM33 4/12; renumbered 451 4/17; withdrawn 7/17; unidentified UK dealer 9/17.

70055 (ex AE54 NUB) (55): CT Plus Guernsey Ltd, St Peter Port (CI) DCS11 4/12, renumbered 215 4/17; renumbered 1115 10/18.

70066 (ex MV54 EEM) (66): CT Plus Guernsey Ltd, St Peter Port (CI) DCS13 4/12; renumbered 216 4/17; renumbered 1116 10/18.
70077 (ex FJ05 HYM) (77): CT Plus Guernsey Ltd, St Peter Port (CI) DCS14 4/12; renumbered 217 4/17; renumbered 1117 10/18.
70088 (ex FJ05 HYK) (88): CT Plus Guernsey Ltd, St Peter Port (CI) DCS15 4/12; renumbered 218 4/17; renumbered 1118 10/18.
70099 (ex FJ05 HYL) (99): CT Plus Guernsey Ltd, St Peter Port (CI) DCS17 4/12; renumbered 219 4/17; renumbered 1119 10/18.
77056 (ex AE54 MWD) (56): CT Plus Guernsey Ltd, St Peter Port (CI) DCS12 4/12; renumbered 220 4/17; renumbered 1120 10/18.
77091 (ex AE54 MWD) (91): CT Plus Guernsey Ltd, St Peter Port (CI) DCS16 4/12; renumbered 221 4/17; renumbered 1121 10/18.
J 26019 (ex HDL 304): Broken up at an unknown date.
MXX 481: Wacton Trading / Coach Sales, Bromyard (dealer) 12/84; R Brown, Motcombe for preservation 1/85; R Brown, Motcombe (DT) 9/85-11/85; on loan to Classis Buses, Winchester (HA) 5/89-1/91; R Brown, Motcombe (DT) 1/91-10/91; P Weal, Leicester for preservation 5/92; R Brown, Shaftsbury (DT) 1/93; re-registered KSJ 622 12/97; M Nash, Weybridge for preservation 3/98; re-registered MXX 481 3/98; B Crowther {Classic Coaches}, Booker (BK) c3/99; M Nash, Weybridge for preservation 11/00; M & S Betterton, Tivetshall for preservation 9/04; Alpha Bus Co Ltd, Soulbury for preservation by9/11.
TUN 627: Partially dismantled by9/80.
510 PYB: Wacton Trading / Coach Sales, Bromyard (dealer) at an unknown date.
D898 NUA: Wildcards, Guernsey (GCI) as a van re-registered 41951 4/00; unidentified dealer for scrap 6/00, for scrap.

One of 23374 (ex 6430 [6]) (48) and 65802 (3, ex 43) was re-registered J142754 in 5/19 by Tantivy Blue Coach Tours Ltd, St Helier (CI).

ISLAND TAXIS LTD

Guelles Road, ST PETER PORT
PO Box 381, ST PETER PORT (by5/17)

Island Taxis Ltd was a taxi-bus operator from 2003. Following the collapse of Delta Taxis Ltd, some school contracts were gained.

14031	Renault Master	Atlas		M16	12/04	4/10	#
	VF1FDCUM631836424						
27803	Renault Master ?	?		M16	by7/06	4/10	#
36113	Renault Master	Red Kite Conversions		M16	10/05	4/10	#
	VF1PDMUL633467236						
56660	Renault Master	Cymric	RM97/2246	M14	5/97	4/10	by5/11
	VF1FB30AK15537481						
56690	Renault Master	Cymric	RM95/1537	M14	5/95	4/10	by5/11
	VF1FB30AH12482772						
62812	Toyota HDB30R	Caetano	351007	C18F	6/93	4/10	by12/15
	HBB3000002152						
67463	Toyota BB50R	Caetano	051214	C27F	6/01	4/10	by12/18
	TW043BB5000001644						
66959	Toyota BB50R	Caetano	951204	C27F	6/01	by5/11	#
	TW043BB5000001549						
13195	Toyota Hiace ?	GM		M7	by7/10	by7/10	by12/18
68875	Toyota Hiace ?	GM		M7	by7/10	by7/10	by12/18
11612	Toyota BB50R 0001426	Caetano	951106	C29F	1/00	6/14	by3/18
37141	Mercedes Benz 811D	Plaxton 928.5MEY0271		C33F	8/92	4/15	by12/18
	WDB6703032P167781						
42992	Mercedes Benz O814D	Plaxton 978.5MZE7667		C32F	6/98	6/15	#
	WDB6703742N066569						
X645 AKW	Mercedes Benz O814D	Plaxton 998.5MZE0456		C33F	10/00	c8/15	----
	WDB6703742N084956						
15216 [2]	Mercedes Benz O814D	Plaxton 008.5MZE3169		C33F	10/00	8/15	#
	WDB6703742N066569						
37424	Toyota BB50R	Caetano	951118	C26F	3/00	11/16	#
	TW043BB5000001448						
52478	Renault Master ?	?		M16	-/--	-/--	#

| 18221 [2] | Mercedes Benz O814D WDB6703742N117428 | Plaxton 058.5MAE5977 | C33F | 5/05 | 1/19 | # |

Vehicles marked # were still in service at the date of this Fleet History.

Public Service Omnibus plates:

13195: t59	37141: 137	66959: ph24
14031: ph8	42992: 138	67463: ph22
15216 [2]: 139	52478: 130	68875: t147
27803: ph31	56660: ph24	
36113: ph30	62812: ph23	

Previous histories:

11612: New to Translinc Ltd, Lincoln (LI) registered V749 EJF; Translinc Ltd, Derby (DE) 065.090 6/05; CJ Reynolds, Caister (NK) 2/10; named '*Lady Jackalyn*'; re-registered BIG 7558 6/10; AJ Charter, Litlington (CM) 2/13.

14031: New to Delta Taxis Ltd, Vale (CI) 9.

15216 [2]: New to Moffat & Williamson Ltd, Gauldry (FE) registered X937 MSP; Plaxton, South Anston (dealer) 10/05; RL Fraser {Black Isle Coaches}, Duncanston (HI) 10/05; re-registered GNT 184 by5/06; re-registered X937 MSP 10/08; J Davies & S Jenkins, Loanhead (LO) 10/08; moved to Newtongrange (LO) and re-registered J 6 EGT 6/09; withdrawn 6/13; D MacMillan {MacMillan's Coaches}, Bearsden (SC) 9/13; re-registered X937 MSP 3/14; Drew Wilson Coach Sales Ltd, Carluke (dealer) 7/15.

18221 [2]: New to Island Coachways Ltd, St Peter Port (CI) 1 registered 65119; re-registered 8227 [6] by4/08; re-registered 18221 [2] 1/19.

27803: New to Island Taxis Ltd, St Peter Port (XCI).

36113: New to Island Taxis Ltd, St Peter Port (XCI) (having been first registered CN 55 EXG in the UK) 10/05.

37141: New to DRR & AR James, Sherston (WI) registered K 30 ARJ; AR James {Andybus}, Tetbury (GL) 9/94; re-registered K691 RMW by9/95; E Brown {ERB Services}, Newcastle upon Tyne (TW) 9/95; ERB Services Ltd, Byker (TW) C5 10/99; G Johnson {Nightingale Coaches}, Greencroft (DM) 9/02; re-registered PJI 800 10/02; A Cunningham {A & A Coach Travel}, Boroughbridge (NY) 6/09; Hodsons Coaches (Clitheroe) Ltd (LA) 11/12; named '*Pendle Broomstick*'.

37424: New to Horseman Coaches Ltd, Reading (BE) registered W 58 SJH; D Jackson {Leisure Travel}, Baguley (GM) 9/00; moved to Timperley (GM) by10/08; White House Farm, Grantham (LI) 7/12; GJ Bishop, Barroway Drove (NK) 3/13; South Devon Transgender Association, Paignton (XDN) 4/16.

42992: New to MH Elcock & Son Ltd, Madeley (SH) registered R496 XAW (as C31F); NG Baynes, Allendale (ND) 2/02; re-registered K 5 NGB 6/04; reseated C32F by7/04; re-registered R496 XAW 3/06; B Breen {B-Line Coaches}, Motherwell (SC) 3/06; Hunter's Coaches Ltd, Moortown (WY) 3/15.

52478: Its origins are unknown.

56660: New to Delta Taxis Ltd, Vale (CI); numbered 2 6/01.

56690: New to Delta Taxis Ltd, Vale (CI); numbered 3 6/01.

62812: New to Capital Coaches Ltd, West Drayton (LN) 26 registered K 26 VRY; Hertz Rent a Car Ltd, London SW10 (LN) 26 8/93; Blue Bird Taxis Ltd, Vale (CI) 9/98; Delta Taxis Ltd, Vale (CI) 7 1/04; withdrawn 3/10.

66959: New to Delta Taxis Ltd, Vale (CI) 1.

67463: New to Blue Bird Taxis Ltd, Vale (CI); Delta Taxis Ltd, Vale 6 (CI) 1/04; withdrawn 3/10.

X645 AKW: New to Bibby's of Ingleton Ltd (NY); named '*Dales Cheetah*'; re-registered BIB 1106 by8/02; re-registered X645 AKW 1/04; Ridings Coaches Ltd, Swarcliffe (WY) 3/04; M Crook & M Savery {Ridings Coaches}, Swarcliffe (WY) 5/05; Glenesk Travel Ltd, Edzell (TE) 6/10; Drew Wilson Coach Sales Ltd, Carluke (dealer) by8/15.

Notes:

14031: Re-registered 11188 and received Public Service Omnibus plate ph25 by5/10; re-registered 38225 10/15; received Public Service Omnibus plate 132 by5/17; numbered 3 2018.

15216 [2] (ex X937 MSP, J 6 EGT, X937 MSP, GNT 184, X937 MSP): Numbered 9 2018.

27803: Received Public Service Omnibus plate ph26 by5/11; received Public Service Omnibus plate 134 by5/17; numbered 1 2018.

36113 (ex CN 55 EXG): Received Public Service Omnibus plate 136 and numbered 2 2018.

37141 (ex PJI 800, K691 RMW, K 30 ARJ): Numbered 10 2018.

37424 (ex W 58 SJH): Has yet to enter service.

42992 (ex R496 XAW, K 5 NGB, R496 XAW): Numbered 8 2018; re-registered 18992 by2019.

52478: Numbered 4 2018.

66959: Received Public Service Omnibus plate 135 and numbered 2 2018.
67463: Received Public Service Omnibus plate 131 and numbered 7 2018; being cannibalised for spares by12/18.
X645 AKW: Was intended to be re-registered 15216 [1] but proved to be unsuitable.

Disposals:
11612 (ex BIG 7558, V749 EJF): Unidentified non-PSV owner, Guernsey (XCI) by3/18.
13195: No known disposal.
56660: Unidentified owner by5/11.
56690: Unidentified owner by5/11.
62812 (ex K 26 VRY): Unidentified owner by12/15.
68875: No known disposal.
X645 AKW (ex BIB 1106, X645 AKW): Drew Wilson Coach Sales Ltd, Carluke (dealer) c8/15.

LAMBOURNE TAXIS LTD {Luxibus}   Willow Grange, Baliffs Cross Rpad, ST ANDREW

12912	Renault Master	?	?	M16	by7/12	by7/12	#
36862	Ford Transit	?	Ford	M16	-/--	by5/17	#
60178	Mercedes Benz	?	?	M16	-/--	by11/18	#
66328	Toyota	?	Caetano	C26F	-/--	11/18	#

Vehicles marked # were still in service at the date of this Fleet History.

Public Service Omnibus plates:
12912: ph31   60178: ph2
36862: ph47   66328: ph44

Previous histories:
36862: Probably new to an unidentified UK operator.
60178: Probably new to an unidentified UK operator.
66328: New to an unidentified UK operator.

AE LANGMEAD {The Robin}   St Jacques, ST PETER PORT
Langmead operated his 'Robin' service from St Peter Port to Grandes Rocques from 1925 to September 1928 when he sold the business to Guernsey Motors Ltd.

	Ford TT	?	F Mallett	Ch--	-/--	-/23?	-/--
	Wallace 25 hp	B510	?	Ch20	by7/21	-/25?	9/28
	Renault PB	?	Underhill	OB20F	-/--	-/26	9/28

Previous histories:
Ford: Its origins are unknown.
Renault: Its origins are unknown.
Wallace: Probably new to Sansum's Central Garage, Paignton (DN) registered TA 1738 (as C20-); last licensed 3/25.

Notes:
Ford: Named 'Ste Jacqueline'.

Disposals:
Ford: No known disposal.
Renault: Guernsey Motors Ltd, St Peter Port (CI) 20 9/28; withdrawn c1936.
Wallace (ex TA 1738): Guernsey Motors Ltd, St Peter Port (CI) 35 9/28; withdrawn c1928.

Frederick LE CHEMINANT {Saints Bus Service}   Rue Maze, ST MARTIN
Frederick Le Cheminant was a builder and a carter from the horse-bus days. He operated services from St Peter Port to Saints Bay (which he was running in January 1922) and Pleinmont before selling out to Guernsey Motors Ltd. Le Cheminant became an Inspector with that company until after World War II.

	Ford TT	?	Le Cheminant	OB14R	-/--	by9/22	8/25
2251	International	?	?	Ch24	-/--	by9/22	8/25
	Oldsmobile	?	?	Ch10	-/--	-/--	8/25

Previous histories:
>The previous histories of these vehicles are not known, all being first recorded with F Le Cheminant on the dates shown.

Notes:
>In addition, one (possibly both) of the Panhards listed below were acquired:

Panhard 1 ton		? ?		OB18R	-/--	-/--	-/--
Panhard 30 cwt		? ?		OB24R	-/--	-/--	-/--

>These were first recorded with AJ Dingle, St Peter Port (CI) at an unknown date; TW Sarre, St Peter-in-the-Wood (CI) by3/21; for sale by auction 3/21.

Disposals:
>Ford: Guernsey Motors Ltd, St Peter Port (CI) 48 8/25; withdrawn c1935.
>Oldsmobile: Guernsey Motors Ltd, St Peter Port (CI) 47 8/25; withdrawn c1935.
>2251: Guernsey Motors Ltd, St Peter Port (CI) 46 8/25; withdrawn 9/37; scrapped 3/39; remains impressed by German Military Authorities (Military Truck Compound) (GOV) for scrap metal 12/42.

J LE HURAY {New Windsor Private Hotel}   **Kings Road, ST PETER PORT**
Le Huray operated a courtesy coach for the for the New Windsor Private Hotel.

5407	Toyota Hiace	RH320021752	Toyota	M8	12/83	12/83	-/86

Disposal:
>5407: DW Clunn, Alderney (CI) re-registered AY   38 1986; withdrawn at an unknown date.

Nic A LENFESTEY {Lorina}   **La Villetole, PLEINMONT**
Nic Lenfestey opened the Pleinmont Picnic House and a motor garage before starting the Lorina bus service in 1925 (Lorina was a popular mailboat of the day). All his vehicles were Heaver bodied Reos painted blue and cream. The service ran from St Peter Port to Pleinmont (operated jointly with the Watson Greys company) before being taken over by Guernsey Motors Ltd on 4 February 1939.

1		Reo Speed Wagon	?	Heaver	C23D	1/25	1/25	8/29
2	1419	Reo Speed Wagon F	110536	Heaver	C24D	3/26	3/26	2/39
3	2719	Reo Sprinter	FAX1430	Heaver	B25F	10/29	10/29	2/39
4	3901 [1]	Reo (Speed Wagon?)	TDX20285	Heaver	B29F	6/34	6/34	2/39
5	2714	Reo Sprinter	FAA11138	Heaver	B25F	10/29	5/37	2/39

Previous history:
>2714 (5): New to HN & HK Falla {Blue Bird}, Vale (CI) 7 (as B22F); reseated to B25F at an unknown date.

Notes:
>1419 (2): Rebuilt to OB20D at an unknown date.
>2714: Fitted with a Silver Crown engine.
>3901 [1]: Fitted with a Silver Crown engine.

Disposals:
>1: Destroyed by fire 8/29.
>1419 (2): Guernsey Motors Ltd, St Peter Port (CI) 2/39; impressed by German Military Authorities (Military Truck Compound) (GOV) 10/42; scrapped locally at an unknown date (or sent to France for scrapping).
>2714 (5): Guernsey Motors Ltd, St Peter Port (CI) 48 2/39; impressed by States of Guernsey Military Transport Service, St Peter Port (GOV) 11/41; German Military Authorities (Fortress Engineer Staff) (GOV) 7/42; returned to Guernsey Motors Ltd 48 at an unknown date; withdrawn 9/49.
>2719 (3): Guernsey Motors Ltd, St Peter Port (CI) 44 2/39; impressed by States of Guernsey Military Transport Service, St Peter Port (GOV) 11/41; AP Delaney, Castel (GOV) 10/42; returned to Guernsey Motors Ltd 44 by8/44; renumbered 11 1945; withdrawn 9/48; Watson's Garage Ltd {The Greys}, St Martin (CI) 11/48; broken up for spares 1949.
>3901 [1] (4): Guernsey Motors Ltd, St Peter Port (CI) 46 2/39; impressed by AP Delaney, Castel (GOV) 10/42; returned to Guernsey Motors Ltd 46 by8/44; fitted with an Austin engine 1947; withdrawn 9/49; living accommodation, La Ramee, St Peter Port (later as a shed) 1/50.

LES BLANC BOIS LTD   **Rue Cohu, CASTEL**
Operated a courtesy coach for residential homes.

39281	Bedford Midi	GV606299	Bedford	M11	1/86	1/86	9/89

Public Service Omnibus plate:
39281: ph43

Disposal:
39281: Private owner, Guernsey 9/89.

Joe LE VALLIANT & Jack E ROBERT {Britannia}   **Chelsea House, 27 Glategny Esplanade, ST PETER PORT**
Joe Le Valliant was a driver with Guernsey Motors up to 1921 before teaming up with Jack Robert. They operated a service from St Peter Port to St Saviour from 1921 to August 1925, before being taken over by Guernsey Motors Ltd. The Britannia name came from the stables of that name in Trinity Square where they rented garage space.

	Oldsmobile 1 ton	?	?	Ch15	-/--	-/--	8/25
434	Reo Speed Wagon	?	?	OB25F	-/--	-/--	8/25

Previous histories:
The previous histories of these vehicles are not known.

Disposals:
Oldsmobile: Guernsey Motors Ltd, St Peter Port (CI) 50 8/25; withdrawn c1940.
434: Guernsey Motors Ltd, St Peter Port (CI) 49 8/25; withdrawn c1935; impressed by German Military Authorities (Military Truck Compound) (GOV) 10/42; scrapped locally at an unknown date (or sent to France for scrapping).

A spare body was also acquired by Guernsey Motors Ltd.

D A LOCKE
A motor wagonette was acquired in February 1905 and a service from St Peter Port to Cobo and Pleinmont was operated from April to around July 1905. No other details are known.

AH MARQUAND {Shorncliffe Hotel}   **Rohais, ST PETER PORT**
Marquand provided a courtesy coach for the Shorncliffe Hotel.

2877 [2]	Volkswagen Microbus	296387	Volkswagen	M10	12/57	6/60	c-/70

Previous history:
2877 [2]: New to Jackson's Garage, St Peter Port (XCI); S Vaudin, St Peter Port (XCI) 1/58; withdrawn 6/58; Le Chalet Hotel, St Martin (XCI) 5/58; withdrawn 5/60.

Disposal:
2877 [2]: Private owner, Guernsey c1970.

John Henry MILLER   **Britannia Livery Stables, Trinity Square, ST PETER PORT**
John Miller was a operator who operated horse buses in July 1913 before converting to motor buses in early 1920. Services were operated out of St Peter Port, to St Martin, Forest, Cobo, St Saviour, Grandes Rocques and Pleinmont. He was a fierce competitor of Guernsey Motors for a time but was bought out by them in October 1921 after they took over the tenancy of the Britannia Livery Stables where he garaged his vehicles.

1		Maxwell 25 cwt	?	T Davies	B18R	-/--	2/20	10/21
2	1151	Maxwell 25 cwt	?	T Davies	OB18R	-/--	4/20	10/21
3		Maxwell 25 cwt	?	T Davies	Ch20	-/--	6/20	10/21
	313	Maxwell 25 cwt	?	T Davies	OB18R	-/--	7/21	10/21
		Maxwell 25 cwt	?	T Davies	?	-/--	by-/21	10/21
		De Dion Bouton	?	T Davies	?	-/--	-/21	10/21
	658	Maxwell 25 cwt	?	(chassis only)		-/--	10/21	10/21
	659 [1]	Guy	?	Guy	B--F	-/--	10/21	10/21

Previous histories:
The previous histories of these vehicles are not known, all being first recorded with JH Miller on the dates shown.

Notes:
A number of Pierce-Arrow lorries were operated, some of which were convertible to charabancs and used to carry passengers. Those still in use when the buses were sold in 10/21 remained in the haulage fleet.

Disposals:
De Dion-Bouton: Guernsey Motors Ltd, St Peter Port (CI) 29 10/21; withdrawn by1935.
Maxwell (new by1921): (one of 27, 28, 30 – two of these rebodied Baico OB19F 1926); withdrawn by1939.
1: Guernsey Motors Ltd, St Peter Port (CI) (one of 27, 28, 30 – two of these rebodied Baico OB19F 1926); withdrawn by1939.
3: Guernsey Motors Ltd, St Peter Port (CI) (one of 27, 28, 30 – two of these rebodied Baico OB19F 1926); withdrawn by1939.
313: Guernsey Motors Ltd, St Peter Port (CI) 32 10/21; rebuilt as a small-wheeled 'Toast Rack Tourabout' and bodied by Guernsey Motors T14 1933; impressed by German Military Authorities (Military Truck Compound) (GOV) 10/42; scrapped locally at an unknown date (or sent to France for scrapping).
1151 (2): Guernsey Motors Ltd, St Peter Port (CI) 31; probably reseated / rebuilt as B16F c1930; withdrawn by1939; impressed by German Military Authorities (Military Truck Compound) (GOV) 10/42; scrapped locally at an unknown date (or sent to France for scrapping).
658: Guernsey Motors Ltd, St Peter Port (CI) 33 10/21; fitted with a B—R body at an unknown date; overturned and its roof demolished 1/27; rebodied B18F at an unknown date; impressed by German Military Authorities (Military Truck Compound) (GOV) 10/42; scrapped locally at an unknown date (or sent to France for scrapping).
659 [1]: Guernsey Motors Ltd, St Peter Port (CI) 34 10/21 (as B—F); chassis returned to Guy Motors 3/23; body to Packard 3641 (2) 7/29.

MOORE'S HOTEL
JB PARKER LTD   Le Pollet, ST PETER PORT
RUNNYMEADE LTD (-/--)
Courtesy coaches were operated for the Moore's Hotel. Later OGH Hotel and Le Chalet Hotel were also served as was (from the 1980s), the Old Government House Hotel.

2203	Volkswagen Microbus	456003	Volkswagen	M10	7/59	7/59	7/65
16646	Commer 1500LB	343260	Rootes	M11	7/65	7/65	3/72
6898	Ford Transit	BC05LM51955	Ford	M14	2/72	2/72	-/83
35836	Ford Transit	BDVZDY11437	Ford	M14	12/83	12/83	8/90

Public Service Omnibus plate:
35836: ph68

Notes:
35836: Re-registered 24453.

Disposals:
2203: Private owner, Guernsey 7/65; scrapped 1969.
6898: Private owner, Guernsey re-registered 25369 1983.
16646: Tally Ho! Coaches, Castell (CI) 3/72; re-registered 16779 2/77; A Nash, Castell (XCI) 9/77; re-registered 19414 at an unknown date; G Archenoul, St Sampson (XCI) 8/79; scrapped 9/79.
24453 (ex 35836): Moore's Hotel, St Peter Port (XCI) 8/90.

NATWEST ISLAND GAMES COMMITTEE
This operator was formed to run vehicles to ferry competitors, organisers and others connected with the Island Games between various venues, hotels etc during the week of 28 June to 4 July 2003. In addition, a series of routes were operated at frequent intervals. The fleet comprised mainly of 16 Optare vehicles owned by States of Guernsey and which were former Guernseybus Ltd vehicles that had later been leased to Island Coachways Ltd. Six former JMT Fords augmented the fleet. The operation was not formally licensed but was authorised and approved by the States Traffic Committee.

71	12723 [4]	Optare MR03	VN1033	Optare	1033	B26F	12/90	6/03	7/03
67	17314	Optare MR03	VN1161	Optare	1161	B31F	1/92	6/03	7/03
70	18264 [3]	Optare MR03	VN1029	Optare	1029	B26F	12/90	6/03	7/03
79	19660 [3]	Optare MR03	VN1071	Optare	1071	B26F	5/91	6/03	7/03
80	19662 [3]	Optare MR03	VN1070	Optare	1070	B26F	5/91	6/03	7/03
78	19675 [4]	Optare MR03	VN1148	Optare	1148	B25F	11/91	6/03	7/03
75	19676 [3]	Optare MR03	VN1147	Optare	1147	B25F	11/91	6/03	7/03
76	19677 [4]	Optare MR03	VN1151	Optare	1151	B25F	11/91	6/03	7/03
77	19678 [4]	Optare MR03	VN1134	Optare	1134	B25F	11/91	6/03	7/03
69	20716	Optare MR03	VN1165	Optare	1165	B31F	2/92	6/03	7/03
90	24775 [2]	Optare MR03	VN1053	Optare	1053	B26F	5/91	6/03	7/03
Jsy06	29346	Ford R1015	BCRSEA40558	Wadham Stringer 9099/85		B45F	10/85	6/03	7/03
74	29728 [3]	Optare MR03	VN1143	Optare	1143	B25F	11/91	6/03	7/03
84	33541	Optare MR03	VN1206	Optare	1206	B29F	5/92	6/03	7/03
Jsy01	35766	Ford R1015	BCRSEA40554	Wadham Stringer 1131/86		B45F	12/86	6/03	7/03
Jsy03	39823	Ford R1015	BCRSEA40555	Wadham Stringer 1129/86		B45F	11/86	6/03	7/03
65	40527	Optare MR03	VN1155	Optare	1155	B31F	11/91	6/03	7/03
Jsy05	46710	Ford R1015	BCRSEA40556	Wadham Stringer 1130/86		B45F	1/87	6/03	7/03
Jsy04	47638	Ford R1015	BCRSEA40557	Wadham Stringer 8537/84		B45F	10/84	6/03	7/03
Jsy02	50129	Ford R1015	BCRSEA40551	Wadham Stringer 8536/84		B45F	12/84	6/03	7/03
68	56206	Optare MR03	VN1163	Optare	1163	B31F	1/92	6/03	7/03
86	61973	Optare MR01	VN1058	Optare	1058	B33F	8/91	6/03	7/03

Previous histories:

12723 [4] (71): New to South East London & Kent Bus Co Ltd {Selkent}, Ilford (LN) MRL151 registered H151 UUA 9/94; moved to London SE26 (LN) 1/94; Metrobus Ltd, Orpington (not operated) 1/98; Guernseybus Ltd, St Peter Port (CI) 71 3/98; transferred to the States of Guernsey, St Peter Port and leased to Island Coachways Ltd, St Peter Port (CI) 71 11/00.

17314 (67): New to London Buses Ltd, London SW1 (LN) MRL216 registered J216 BWU (as B26F); London Northern Bus Co Ltd, Harrow (LN) 10/94; MTL London Northern Ltd, Harrow (LN) MRL216 10/95; Guernseybus Ltd, St Peter Port (CI) 67 9/98; transferred to the States of Guernsey, St Peter Port and leased to Island Coachways Ltd, St Peter Port (CI) 67 11/00.

18264 [3] (70): New to South East London & Kent Bus Co Ltd {Selkent}, Ilford (LN) MRL147 registered H147 UUA 9/94; East London Bus & Coach Co Ltd, Ilford (LN) 12/97; Metrobus Ltd, Orpington (LN) (not operated) 1/98; Guernscybus Ltd, St Peter Port (CI) 70 4/98; transferred to the States of Guernsey, St Peter Port and leased to Island Coachways Ltd, St Peter Port (CI) 70 11/00.

19660 [3] (79): New to South East London & Kent Bus Co Ltd {Selkent}, Ilford (LN) MRL168 registered H168 WWT; moved to London SE26 (LN) 1/94; withdrawn 9/97; Metrobus Ltd, Orpington (LN) (not operated) 11/97; Guernseybus Ltd, St Peter Port (CI) 79 1/98; transferred to the States of Guernsey, St Peter Port and leased to Island Coachways Ltd, St Peter Port (CI) 79 11/00.

19662 [3] (80): New to South East London & Kent Bus Co Ltd {Selkent}, Ilford (LN) MRL167 registered H167 WWT; moved to London SE26 (LN) 1/94; withdrawn 9/97; Metrobus Ltd (LN) (not operated) 11/97; Guernseybus Ltd, St Peter Port (CI) 80 1/98; transferred to the States of Guernsey, St Peter Port and leased to Island Coachways Ltd, St Peter Port (CI) 80 11/00.

19675 [4] (78): New to Kentish Bus & Coach Co Ltd, Northfleet (KT) 968 registered J968 JNL; Metrobus Ltd, Orpington (LN) 12/95; Guernseybus Ltd 5/97; transferred to the States of Guernsey, St Peter Port and leased to Island Coachways Ltd, St Peter Port (CI) 78 11/00.

19676 [3] (75): New to Kentish Bus & Coach Co Ltd, Northfleet (KT) 967 registered J967 JNL; Metrobus Ltd, Orpington (LN) 12/95; Guernseybus Ltd 10/96; transferred to the States of Guernsey, St Peter Port and leased to Island Coachways Ltd, St Peter Port (CI) 75 11/00.

19677 [4] (76): New to Kentish Bus & Coach Co Ltd, Northfleet (KT) 971 registered J971 JNL; Metrobus Ltd, Orpington (LN) 12/95; Guernseybus Ltd 9/96; transferred to the States of Guernsey, St Peter Port and leased to Island Coachways Ltd, St Peter Port (CI) 76 11/00.

19678 [4] (77): New to Kentish Bus & Coach Co Ltd, Northfleet (KT) 972 registered J972 JNL; Metrobus Ltd, Orpington (LN) 12/95; Guernseybus Ltd 9/96; transferred to the States of Guernsey, St Peter Port and leased to Island Coachways Ltd, St Peter Port (CI) 77 11/00.

20716 (69): New to London Buses Ltd, London SW1 (LN) MRL220 registered J220 BWU (as B26F); London Northern Bus Co Ltd, Harrow (LN) 10/94; MTL London Northern Ltd, Harrow (LN) MRL220 10/95; Guernseybus Ltd, St Peter Port (CI) 69 9/98; transferred to the States of Guernsey, St Peter Port and leased to Island Coachways Ltd, St Peter Port (CI) 69 11/00.

24775 [2] (90): New to South East London & Kent Bus Co Ltd {Selkent}, Ilford (LN) MRL161 registered H161 WWT; moved to London SE26 (LN) 1/94; Metrobus Ltd, Orpington (LN) 5/00; renumbered 913 8/98; Guernseybus Ltd, St Peter Port (CI) 90 3/00; entered service 6/00; transferred to the States of Guernsey, St Peter Port and leased to Island Coachways Ltd, St Peter Port (CI) 90 11/00.

29346 (Jsy06): New to JMT (1978) Ltd, St Helier (CI) 42 registered J 42259; JMT (1987) Ltd, St Helier (CI) 42 12/87; withdrawn 9/02.

29728 [3] (74): New to Kentish Bus & Coach Co Ltd, Northfleet (KT) 963 registered J963 JNL; Metrobus Ltd, Orpington (LN) 12/95; Guernseybus Ltd, St Peter Port (CI) 74 2/97; transferred to the States of Guernsey, St Peter Port and leased to Island Coachways Ltd, St Peter Port (CI) 74 11/00.

33541 (84): New to Cambus Ltd, Cambridge (CM) 962 registered J962 DWX; Guernseybus Ltd, St Peter Port (CI) 84 3/00; to service 4/00; transferred to the States of Guernsey, St Peter Port and leased to Island Coachways Ltd, St Peter Port (CI) 84 11/00.

35766 (Jsy01): New to JMT (1978) Ltd, St Helier (CI) 17 registered J 40820; JMT (1987) Ltd, St Helier (CI) 17 12/87; withdrawn 9/02.

39823 (Jsy03): New to JMT (1978) Ltd, St Helier (CI) 18 registered J 40853; JMT (1987) Ltd, St Helier (CI) 18 12/87; withdrawn 9/02.

40527 (65): New to London Buses Ltd, London SW1 (LN) MRL210 registered J210 BWU (as B26F); London Northern Bus Co Ltd, Harrow (LN) 10/94; MTL London Northern Ltd, Harrow (LN) MRL210 10/95; Guernseybus Ltd, St Peter Port (CI) 65 9/98; transferred to the States of Guernsey, St Peter Port and leased to Island Coachways Ltd, St Peter Port (CI) 65 11/00.

46710 (Jsy05): New to JMT (1978) Ltd, St Helier (CI) 25 registered J 40865; JMT (1987) Ltd, St Helier (CI) 23 12/87; withdrawn 9/02.

47638 (Jsy04): New to JMT (1978) Ltd, St Helier (CI) 23 registered J 43063; JMT (1987) Ltd, St Helier (CI) 25 12/87; withdrawn 9/02.

50129 (Jsy02): New to JMT (1978) Ltd, St Helier (CI) 20 registered J 43037; JMT (1987) Ltd, St Helier (CI) 20 12/87; withdrawn 9/02.

56206 (68): New to London Buses Ltd, London SW1 (LN) MRL218 registered J218 BWU (as B26F); London Northern Bus Co Ltd, Harrow (LN) 10/94; MTL London Northern Ltd, Harrow (LN) MRL218 10/95; Guernseybus Ltd, St Peter Port (CI) 67 9/98; transferred to the States of Guernsey, St Peter Port and leased to Island Coachways Ltd, St Peter Port (CI) 68 11/00.

61973 (86): New to East Surrey Bus Services Ltd, South Godstone (SR) 26 registered J326 PPD; Metrobus Ltd, Orpington (LN) 917 6/97; Guernseybus Ltd, St Peter Port (CI) 86 3/00; to service 5/00; transferred to the States of Guernsey, St Peter Port and leased to Island Coachways Ltd, St Peter Port (CI) 86 11/00.

Disposals:

12723 [4] (ex H151 UUA) (71): Unidentified UK dealer 7/03.

17314 (ex J216 BWU) (67): Unidentified UK dealer 7/03; R Wilson, Gourock (SC) re-registered J216 BWU (not operated) 12/03; Caledonian Coach Co Ltd {Caledonia Buses / Linn Park Buses}, Glasgow (SC) 10/04; last licence expired 3/07; unidentified dealer for scrap by12/08.

18264 [3] (ex H147 UUA) (70): Unidentified UK dealer 7/03.

19660 [3] (ex H168 WWT) (79): Unidentified UK dealer 7/03; RJ, S & CJ Goulden {Master Travel}, Welwyn Garden City (HT) (not operated) by5/04; unidentified dealer for scrap by7/15.

19662 [3] (ex H167 WWT) (80): Unidentified UK dealer 7/03; R Wilson, Gourock (SC) (not operated) 12/03.

19675 [4] (ex J968 JNL) (78): Unidentified UK dealer 7/03; R Wilson, Gourock (SC) (not operated) 12/03.

19676 [3] (ex J967 JNL) (75): Unidentified UK dealer 7/03; R Wilson, Gourock (SC) re-registered J967 JNL (not operated) 12/03; Caledonian Coach Co Ltd {Caledonia Buses / Linn Park Buses}, Glasgow (SC) 3/05; last licence expired 2/07; unidentified dealer for scrap by12/08.

19677 [4] (ex J971 JNL) (76): Unidentified UK dealer 7/03; R Wilson, Gourock (SC) (not operated) 12/03; unidentified dealer for scrap by12/06.

19678 [4] (ex J972 JNL) (77): Unidentified UK dealer 7/03; R Wilson, Gourock (SC) (not operated) 12/03; unidentified dealer for scrap by12/06.

20716 (ex J220 BWU) (69): Unidentified UK dealer 7/03; noted disused on the premises of CR Craske, Sutton (NK) 1/05 (owner unknown).

24775 [2] (ex H161 WWT) (90): Unidentified UK dealer 7/03; R Wilson, Gourock (SC) (not operated) 12/03; unidentified dealer for scrap by12/06.

29346 (ex J 42259) (Jsy06): Unidentified owner by12/03.

29728 [3] (ex J963 JNL) (74): Unidentified UK dealer 7/03; R Wilson, Gourock (SC) (not operated) 12/03; unidentified dealer for scrap by12/06.

33541 (ex J962 DWX) (84): Unidentified UK dealer 7/03; RJ, S & CJ Goulden {Master Travel}, Welwyn Garden City (HT) 13 re-registered J962 DWX 2/06; last licence expired 2/13; unidentified dealer for scrap by5/15.
35766 (ex J 40820) (Jsy01): States Airport, Forest (XCI) 7/03.
39823 (ex J 40853) (Jsy03): Exported to France 8/03.
40527 (ex J210 BWU) (65): Unidentified UK dealer 7/03; RA Giles {KG Motors}, Caerphilly (MG) by10/03; re-registered J210 BWU 11/03; IA Tomlinson, Winsford (CH) by5/06; MJ Perry {Bromyard Omnibus Co}, Bromyard (HW) 5/06; re-registered J555 BUS 5/06; to service 6/06; DT Brundrit {RML Travel}, Burslem (ST) MRL210 10/06; re-registered J555 RML and named 'Gladys' 11/06; re-registered J210 BWU 7/08; withdrawn 11/08; last licence expired 11/10; unidentified dealer for scrap c11/10.
46710 (ex J 40865) (Jsy05): Unidentified owner 8/03.
47638 (ex J 43063) (Jsy04): C Miller, Edinburgh for preservation 8/03; current 11/07.
50129 (ex J 43037) (Jsy02): States Airport, Forest (XCI) 7/03; Universal Limos (Guernsey) Ltd, St Peter Port (CI) re-registered 73140 12/06; withdrawn 7/08.
56206 (ex J218 BWU) (68): Unidentified UK dealer 7/03; unidentified owner as a mobile caravan re-registered J218 BWU 8/05.
61973 (ex J326 PPD) (86): Unidentified UK dealer 7/03; R Wilson, Gourock (SC) (not operated) 12/03; unidentified dealer for scrap by12/06.

AV NEWTON {Channel Islands Hotel}   **Glategny Esplanade, ST PETER PORT**
The Channel Islands Hotel held three licences for island tours from May 1934 up to December 1939.

3777	Dennis GL	70631	Willmott		C13F	-/--	1/35	11/45

Previous history:
3777: Its origins are unknown.

Disposal:
3777: Guernsey Railway Co Ltd, St Peter Port (CI) 3 12/45; body rebuilt to B26F; WP Simon {Riduna Buses}, Alderney (CI) re-registered AY 59 [1] 9/47; withdrawn 1951.

OATLANDS VILLAGE   **Les Gigands, ST SAMPSON**

72103	Bedford OB	132303	Duple	46694	C29F	3/50	7/12	10/13

Public Service Omnibus plate:
72103: ph31

Previous history:
72103: New to RS Webb, Armscote (WK) registered JUE 860; Harvey, Chedworth 4/64; Handover, Chedworth 6/71 (or 11/72); J Williams, Minster Lovell for preservation 3/77; J Dodsworth (Coaches) Ltd, Boroughbridge for preservation 4/84; Kenzie, Shepreth for preservation 11/08.

Disposal:
72103 (ex JUE 860): Kenzie, Shepreth for preservation re-registered JUE 860 4/15; R Webb, Armscote for preservation 5/15.

JS Le C OGIER {La Girouette Hotel}   **ST SAVIOUR**
Le C Ogier operated a courtesy coach for La Girouette Hotel.

10801	Ford Transit	BDVZDU24130	Ford		M11	12/83	12/83	12/88

Public Service Omnibus plate:
10801: ph84

Disposal:
10801: Private owner, Guernsey 12/88.

OLD GOVERNMENT HOUSE HOTEL

Ann's Place, ST PETER PORT

Courtesy coaches for the hotel guests were provided by the Old Government House Hotel. After 1962, cars and minibuses performed this service.

3410	Bedford WHB	? ?		C14F	-/35	-/35	10/42
5201	Austin K8/CVC	1077 ?		C14F	7/48	7/48	7/62

Disposal:
3410: Impressed by German Military Authorities (Military Truck Compound) (GOV) 10/42.
5201: Unidentified owner as a mobile snack bar 7/62; scrapped 2/72.

PARAGON

Henry C COLLENETTE

Nocq Road and Lowlands, ST SAMPSON

Harold K FALLA {Paragon} (7/48)   Durrington, Les Banques, ST SAMPSON

Henry Collenette lost a leg in World War I but spent five years in the UK learning the motor trade and then spending time with his Uncles' (the Collenette Bros) Shamrock operation. He started on his own in October 1923 and ran a bus service from St Peter Port to L'Ancresse. A route to Bordeaux was taken over from Guernsey Railway Co in 1925. On 28 July 1948 he sold out to Harold Falla who had previously operated Blue Bird and who had shared the service to L'Ancresse with him. Falla retired and sold out to Guernsey Railway Co on 17 January 1963.

1		Dodge LB	A134200	Underhill		OB18F	8/24	8/24	-/30
2	1415	Dodge A	A302112	FT Bennett		OB22F	6/25	6/25	-/30
3		Dodge LB	A586023	Strachan & Brown		B22F	-/26	-/26	-/30
3	511	Dodge LER	D217761	Strachan		B22D	10/29	10/29	7/48
4	1845	Dodge LER	D225913	Strachan		B27F	-/30	-/30	12/35
5	3013	Dodge LER	D226722	Strachan		B27F	6/31	6/31	7/41
1	3216	Commer 6TK/1	28322	Strachan		B29F	7/32	7/32	7/48
6	3810	Leyland KP3	2775	Strachan		B29F	6/34	6/34	1/63
2	864	Leyland KP3	4143	Strachan		B29F	6/35	6/35	1/63
4	1596	Dodge RBF	505	Strachan		FB32F	8/36	8/36	6/40
7	99	Dodge LER	D217768	?		FB30F	-/30	7/39	9/40
4	1532	Leyland KP2	1302	Brush		B20F	-/32	5/46	7/48
5	3923	Commer Commando	17A0822	Strachan	51015	B33F	1/48	1/48	1/63
4	3924	Commer Commando	17A0793	Strachan	51166	B33F	7/48	7/48	1/63
3	3925	Albion SpFT3L	70693J	Strachan	50934	B31F	9/48	9/48	1/63
1	2981	Reo FAX	1691	Heaver		FB32F	5/31	1/49	12/52
7	4818	Albion FT39AB	70792B	Heaver		B33F	11/49	11/49	1/63

Police plates:

864 (2): 149	3923 (5): 151	4818 (7): 194
2981 (1): 138	3924 (4): 173	
3810 (6): 147	3925 (3): 182	

511 (3), 1532 (4) and 3216 (1) probably had plates 146, 148 and 150 (order unknown)

Previous histories:
99 (7): New to an unidentified UK operator (as B—F).
1532 (4): New to North Western Road Car Stockport (CH) 616 registered JA 2216; withdrawn 1940; F Cowley, Salford (dealer) 1945; JC Broadhead, Bollington (dealer) at an unknown date.
2981 (1): New to HN & HK Falla {Blue Bird}, Vale (CI) 8 (with a Heaver B27F body); converted to forward control, rebodied Heaver FB32F and renumbered 1 12/36; impressed by States of Guernsey Civil Transport Service, St Peter Port (GOV) 2/41; returned 5/45.

Notes:
99 (7) (ex -?-): Rebuilt to forward control with a full front body by HC Collenette.
511 (3): Reseated to B23D 6/31; impressed by States of Guernsey Civil Transport Service, St Peter Port (GOV) by7/44; returned 5/45.
864 (2): Impressed by States of Guernsey Military Transport Service, St Peter Port (GOV) 9/42; German Military Authorities (Fortress Engineer Staff) (GOV) 12/42; returned at an unknown date; converted to forward control and re-bodied Heaver (9731) FB35F 1951; fitted with a Perkins P6 oil engine 1953.

1532 (ex JA 2216) (4): Width reduced to 7ft in order to comply with Guernsey's maximum width regulations, before entering service.

2981 (1): S Le Poidevin, St Peter Port 4/53; unidentified owner as a mobile shop (GCI) at an unknown date.

3216 (1): Impressed by States of Guernsey Civil Transport Service, St Peter Port (GOV) 9/42; German Military Authorities (Fortress Engineer Staff) (GOV) 12/42; returned at an unknown date; reseated to B26F at an unknown date.

3810 (6): Impressed by States of Guernsey Civil Transport Service, St Peter Port (GOV) 2/41; States of Guernsey Military Transport Service, St Peter Port (GOV) 9/42; German Military Authorities (Fortress Engineer Staff) (GOV) 12/42; returned at an unknown date; converted to forward control and re-bodied Heaver (9521) FB35F 6/50; fitted with a Perkins P6 oil engine 1953.

3923 (5): Fitted with a Perkins P6 oil engine 1953.

3924 (4): Fitted with a Perkins P6 oil engine 1953.

3925 (3): Fitted with a Perkins P6 oil engine 1953.

4818 (7): Fitted with an Albion oil engine at an unknown date.

Disposals:

1: Le Tocq, Guernsey (dealer) for scrap 1930.

3: Renouf, Guernsey (GCI) as a mobile shop 1930.

99 (7) (ex -?-): Impressed by German Military Authorities (Military Truck Compound) (GOV) 5/41; scrapped locally at an unknown date (or sent to France for scrapping).

511 (3): W Hobbs, St Peter Port 3/49; VW Kesterton, St Peter Port 11/50; Simon, Vale 9/52 and scrapped.

864 (2): Guernsey Railway Co Ltd, St Peter Port (CI) 42 1/63; renumbered 25 8/63; withdrawn 9/66; unidentified owner (minus engine) 3/68.

1415 (2): Guernsey Railway Co Ltd, St Peter Port (CI) 22 1931; withdrawn 12/37.

1532 (ex JA 2216) (4): Chassis broken up for spares 1948; body to WJ Rugg, St Sampson as a summer house 1948.

1596 (4): Impressed by German Military Authorities (Military Truck Compound) (GOV) 5/41; scrapped locally at an unknown date (or sent to France for scrapping).

1845 (4): Guernsey Railway Co Ltd, St Peter Port (CI) 3 12/35 (as B22F); States of Guernsey Military Transport Services, St Peter Port (GOV) 7/41; German Military Authorities (Military Truck Compound) (GOV) 12/42; scrapped locally at an unknown date (or sent to France for scrapping).

3013 (5): Impressed by States of Guernsey Military Transport Services, St Peter Port (GOV) 7/41; German Military Authorities (LPA Paris) (GOV) 9/42; German Military Authorities (Military Truck Compound) (GOV) 12/42; scrapped locally at an unknown date (or sent to France for scrapping).

3216 (1): Chassis scrapped 7/48; body to C Bougourd, Alderney 1949.

3810 (6): Guernsey Railway Co Ltd, St Peter Port (CI) 41 1/63; renumbered 24 8/63; withdrawn 9/67; dumped at Priaulx's Quarry, St Sampson 3/68.

3923 (5): Guernsey Railway Co Ltd, St Peter Port (CI) 43 1/63; renumbered 26 8/63; K Rive, St Sampson as living accommodation 9/65.

3924 (4): Guernsey Railway Co Ltd, St Peter Port (CI) 44 1/63; renumbered 27 8/63; withdrawn 9/64.

3925 (3): Guernsey Railway Co Ltd, St Peter Port (CI) 45 1/63; renumbered 28 8/63; withdrawn 9/65.

4818 (7): Guernsey Railway Co Ltd, St Peter Port (CI) 46 1/63; rebuilt with a standard destination box 6/63; renumbered 29 8/63; withdrawn 9/72; F Mallett & Son Ltd, St Peter Port (GCI) as a flatbed lorry 1/73; withdrawn 1975.

PETIT BOT MINIBUS SERVICE

David MASON {Petit Bot Minibus Service} — Clovelly, Le Varclin, ST MARTIN

JA DE GARIS {Petit Bot Minibus Service} (3/72) — Candie Road, CASTEL

David Mason operated a seasonal minibus service from Le Bourg to Petit Bot from 1963 until 1972 when the business was taken over by JA De Garis until he retired at the end of the 1981 season. The service was awarded to Guernseybus from the 1982 season and several operators have run it since.

13786	Bedford CALV	4239152	Martin Walter	M12	6/63	6/63	12/69
9118	Volkswagen Microbus	406856	Volkswagen	M10	4/59	5/65	6/68
6083	Volkswagen Microbus	2228080908	Volkswagen	M8	6/68	6/68	6/70
23201	Ford Transit	BC05JK50010	Ford	M12	5/70	5/70	11/81

Police plate:

23201: 245

Public Service Omnibus plates:

9118: 241   13786: 245   23201: 245

Previous history:
9118: New to H Pitchler, Vale (XCI); H Field, St Peter Port (XCI) at an unknown date.

Disposals:
6083: Eight private owners from 6/70; re-registered 13172 6/88; last licensed 11/88; scrapped 3/92.
9118: E Wells, St Peter Port (XCI) 6/68; various private owners; scrapped 1/76.
13786: Private owner, Guernsey 12/69.
23201: IG Scott, Kings Mills (XCI) re-registered 28989 11/81; G Scott & Co, St Peter Port (XCI) re-registered 10155 [1] 2/84; various private owners at unknown dates; scrapped 3/86.

WN PRIAULX / OZANNE BROS {Primrose}   Avondale, FOREST
Wn Priaulx together with his son-in-law and brother (Ozanne Bros) established the Avondale Motor Garage in 1922 and started a bus and taxi service from St Peter Port to Pleinmont. The services were actually run by the Ozannes with Priaulx financing the business. It was sold to UU Ash and subsequently (in stages) to Guernsey Motors Ltd.

348	Maxwell	?	?	Ch20	-/--	10/22?	5/24
	Napier	?	Ridley	Ch16	-/--	-/--	5/24
885	Vulcan 30 cwt	?	?	Ch20	-/24	-/24	5/24
987:	Vulcan 3 ton	?	?	Ch28	-/24	-/24	5/24

Previous histories:
Napier: Its origins are unknown.
348: Its origins are unknown.

Notes:
885: Named 'Queen of the Isles'.
987: Named 'Princess Ena'.

Disposals:
Napier: UU Ash, St Peter Port (dealer) c5/24; Guernsey Motors Ltd, St Peter Port (CI) 44 5/24; withdrawn at an unknown date (1930s).
348: UU Ash, St Peter Port (dealer) c5/24; Guernsey Motors Ltd, St Peter Port (CI) 45 5/24 (as Ch14); Impressed by German Military Authorities (Military Truck Compound) (GOV) 11/42.
885: UU Ash, St Peter Port (CI) 5/24; Guernsey Motors Ltd, St Peter Port (CI) 60 10/31; impressed by German Military Authorities (Military Truck Compound) (GOV) 1/41; scrapped locally at an unknown date (or sent to France for scrapping).
987: UU Ash, St Peter Port (CI) 5/24; Guernsey Motors Ltd, St Peter Port (CI) 61 10/31; impressed by German Military Authorities (Military Truck Compound) (GOV) 1/41; scrapped locally at an unknown date (or sent to France for scrapping).

FJK REYNOLDS {Cliffways Hotel}   Calais, ST MARTIN
The Cliffways Hotel was unusual in that it ran a full-sized coach in the postwar period without incurring displeasure from the major operators or indeed, the authorities. He actually purchased vehicles from both the Motors and Railway companies with their full knowledge of their intended use, probably because the hotel was some distance from the nearest bus route.

3041	Renault	SX488467	?	C15-	7/31	5/52	9/55
3460	Bedford OB	31380	Mulliner	B32F	9/46	9/55	10/61
4414	Bedford OB	105646	Mulliner	T383 B28F	5/49	11/61	9/69

Police plate:
4414: ph54

Previous histories:
3041: New to Commercial Company of the Channel Islands, St Peter Port (CI) 7/31; withdrawn 3/40; G Vidamour, Forest at an unknown date; AJ Snell, Forest (CI) 4/49.
3460: New to Sarre Transport Ltd, St Peter-in-the-Wood (CI) 4; moved to St Peter Port (CI) at an unknown date; Guernsey Railway Co Ltd, St Peter Port (CI) 41 11/51; fitted with a Perkins P6 oil engine from 1/52 to 2/53.
4414: New to Sarre Transport Ltd, St Peter-in-the-Wood (CI) 20; moved to St Peter Port (CI) at an unknown date; Guernsey Motors Ltd, St Peter Port (CI) 60 11/51; withdrawn 9/61.

Disposals:
3041: Scrapped 9/55.
3460: W Laine, Vale as living accommodation 10/61.
4414: LF Le Noury, St Sampson 3/72; scrapped by5/73.

WT ROBILLIARD {Reindeer} 48 Victoria Road, ST PETER PORT
Beldene, Belmont Road, ST PETER PORT (-/--)

The Reindeer operation was named after a well-known mailboat of the day. Robilliard operated a service from St Peter Port to L'Eree from September 1927 to November 1928, together with private hire work.

48 [2]	Maxwell 30 cwt	?	?		Ch20	-/--	6/23	-/--
1601	GMC	?	FT Bennett		OB22F	-/--	-/--	11/28

Previous histories:
The previous histories of these vehicles is unknown.

Notes:
48 [2]: Its body was said to have been built in Southampton; it was supplied by K Millard, Guernsey (dealer).

Disposals:
48 [2]: UU Ash, St Peter Port (CI) at an unknown date (as Ch22); Guernsey Motors Ltd, St Peter Port (CI) 63 10/31 (as Ch18); impressed by German Military Authorities (Military Truck Compound) (GOV) 1/41; scrapped locally at an unknown date (or sent to France for scrapping).
1601: Guernsey Motors Ltd, St Peter Port (CI) 7 11/28 (as OB23F); impressed by German Military Authorities (Military Truck Compound) (GOV) 10/42; scrapped locally at an unknown date (or sent to France for scrapping).

ROYAL HOTEL
JG WAY Le Pollet, ST PETER PORT
COMMERCIAL COMPANY OF THE CHANNEL ISLANDS Royal Hotel, Glategny Esplanade, ST PETER PORT

JG Way operated a hotel bus for Gardner's Royal Hotel, used to convey golfers between St Peter Port and the course at L'Ancresse. From March 1920, a Guernsey Motors bus was painted in a special livery for use of the guests and this was used, probably for most of that decade. In 1931, the Commercial Company of the Channel Islands took over the contract.

Prior to World War I, the Commercial Company held three island tour licences although no vehicles are known to have been operated. Postwar operations were restricted however to providing a courtesy vehicle for the Royal Hotel. After June 1960, an estate car and later a minibus were used to convey guests.

	MMC 15 hp	?	?		B10-	-/--	3/07	-/--
3041	Renault	SX488457	?		C15-	7/31	7/31	3/40
5895	Morris CVF.13/5	73322	Wadham		C19F	8/48	8/48	6/60

Previous history:
MMC: Its origins are unknown.

Notes:
MMC: Was a small motor bus, probably the first motor bus on Guernsey.
5895: Was fitted with 2+1 seating.

Disposals:
MMC 15 hp: No known disposal.
3041: G Vidamour, Forest at an unknown date; AJ Snell, Forest (CI) 4/49; FJK Reynolds {Cliffways Hotel}, St Martin (CI) 5/52; scrapped 9/55.
5895: AJ Snell, Forest (CI) 6/60; WS Le Poidevin, Castel (XCI) 11/64; Guernsey Motors Ltd, St Peter Port (CI) (not operated) 1/66; broken up by11/68.

ST MARGARET'S LODGE HOTEL Forest Road, ST MARTIN

St Margaret's Lodge Hotel ran courtesy minibus for the hotel patrons in the late 1980s and early 1990s.

49628	Renault Master	00957674R	Holdsworth		M14	2/88	2/88	-/--
30021	DAF 400	?	DAF		M16	3/94	3/94	-/--

Public Service Omnibus plate:
49628: ph14

Disposals:
30021: No known disposal.
49628: No known disposal.

SARNIA CABS
22 Havilland Street, ST MARTIN

The vehicle was owned by Comfi Cabs Ltd, St Peter Port, but the licence was in the name of Sarnia Cabs. After 1988, the name was used by Vaudin's United Taxis, St Sampson.

50797	Ford A510	BCLWWS31590	Wadham Stringer	B14F	12/79	5/87	-/88

Public Service Omnibus plate:
50797: ph1

Previous history:
50797: New to Bedfordshire Ambulance Service (XBD) registered KPP 123V.

Disposal:
50797: No known disposal.

Thomas W SARRE
Le Crocq, ST PETER-IN-THE-WOOD

Thomas Sarre had been a horse-bus operator from the 1890s but started a motor bus service between St Peter Port and Pleinmont. He ran horse-buses again during the Occupation and later founded Sarre Transport Ltd in 1946.

	Panhard 1 ton	?	?		OB18R	-/--	by3/21	by3/21
	Panhard 30 cwt	?	?		OB24R	-/--	by3/21	by3/21
2224	International 25 hp	5520	T Le Huray		Ch19	-/--	-/21	-/--
	International 25 cwt	?	?		OB19F	-/--	by8/22	8/22

Previous histories:
Both Panhards: First recorded with AJ Dingle, St Peter Port (CI).
Second International: Probably new to TW Sarre.

Notes:
2224: Ordered by TW Sarre, St Peter-in-the Wood (CI) but not operated (or possibly even delivered); its registration may not have been its original, but a later re-registration.

Disposals:
Both Panhards: For sale by auction 3/21 –one, possibly both of these to F Le Cheminant {Saints Bus Service}, St Martin (CI) at an unknown date.
Second International: Guernsey Motors Ltd, St Peter Port (CI) 42 8/22 (as OB22C); withdrawn c1929.
2224: HJ Ozanne, Guernsey (dealer) by8/22; Guernsey Motors Ltd, St Peter Port (CI) 41 8/22; scrapped 3/39.

SARRE TRANSPORT LTD {Wayfarer}
Le Crocq, Pitronnerie Road, ST PETER-IN-THE-WOOD
Trinity Square, ST PETER PORT (-/--)

Sarre Transport Ltd was started by Thomas Sarre in March 1946. Sarre had operated horse-buses from the 1890s and again during the Occupation and ran early motor buses in 1920/21. With these credentials, he gained the financial backing of some wealthy individuals who provided most of the capital.

On 30 April 1946, he acquired WJ Rugg's Wayfarer business – Sarre continuing with the Wayfarer fleet name – and started to run services from St Peter Port to Pleinmont, L'Eree and Grandes Rocques as well as island tours.

An impressive fleet of Mulliner bodied Bedford OBs was quickly established. The 1946 deliveries were to utility specification, but later ones more luxuriously appointed. The livery was crimson with broken white and brown wings.

After the initial investment, the company did not perform well financially and when an offer was tabled by Red & White, it was accepted on 1 November 1951. The assets were divided equally between Guernsey Motors and Guernsey Railway Co, both by then Red & White subsidiaries.

6	1633	Dodge	HLW628	WJ Rugg		B25F	3/34	4/46	5/49
7	2711	Dodge	PLW29	WJ Rugg		B25F	-/--	4/46	11/51
4	3060	Dodge UG30	8343213	WJ Rugg		OB21F	10/31	4/46	11/51
3	4085	Dodge	KB228	WJ Rugg		B25F	3/35	4/46	11/51
2	1557	Bedford OB	24340	Mulliner		B32F	5/46	5/46	11/51
1	1558	Bedford OB	23960	Mulliner		B32F	5/46	5/46	11/51
5	1560	Bedford OB	23382	Mulliner		B32F	5/46	5/46	11/51
6	1951	Bedford OB	29502	Mulliner		B32F	9/46	9/46	11/51
9	3458	Bedford OB	33376	Mulliner		B32F	9/46	9/46	11/51
4	3460	Bedford OB	31380	Mulliner		B32F	9/46	9/46	11/51
3	4101	Bedford OB	30485	Mulliner		B32F	9/46	9/46	11/51
12	2818	Bedford OB	43166	Mulliner		B32F	3/47	3/47	11/51
11	2819	Bedford OB	43097	Mulliner		B32F	3/47	3/47	11/51
13	2851	Bedford OB	43367	Mulliner		B32F	3/47	3/47	11/51
10	2877 [1]	Bedford OB	43412	Mulliner		B32F	4/47	4/47	11/51
14	5181	Bedford OB	70827	Mulliner	SP209	B31F	3/48	3/48	11/51
15	5182	Bedford OB	72578	Mulliner	SP205	B28F	4/48	4/48	11/51
16	5183	Bedford OB	72585	Mulliner	SP210	B31F	5/48	5/48	11/51
17	5184	Bedford OB	76076	Mulliner	SP207	B28F	6/48	6/48	11/51
18	5185	Bedford OB	75989	Mulliner	SP206	B31F	6/48	6/48	11/51
19	5186	Bedford OB	77409	Mulliner	SP208	B28F	6/48	6/48	11/51
20	4414	Bedford OB	105646	Mulliner	T383	B28F	5/49	5/49	11/51
21	4426	Bedford OB	108594	Mulliner	T384	B28F	7/49	7/49	11/51

Police plates:

1557 (2): 124	2851 (13): 59	4426 (21): 148
1558 (1): 120	2877 [1] (10): 60	5181 (14): 157
1560 (5): 125	3060 (4): 124	5182 (15): 179
1633 (6): 122	3458 (9): 122	5183 (16): 163
1951 (6): 127	3460 (4): 126	5184 (17): 167
2711 (7): 123	4085 (3): 121	5185 (18): 166
2818 (12): 128	4101 (3): 123	5186 (19): 170
2819 (11): 119?	4414 (20): 191	

Previous histories:

1633 (6): New to WJ Rugg {Wayfarer}, St Sampson (CI) 6; impressed by States of Guernsey Civil Transport Service, St Peter Port (GOV) 2/41; converted to gazogene propulsion at an unknown date; returned to WJ Rugg 5/45.

2711 (7): Chassis purchased second hand in Jersey and fitted with a WJ Rugg body; WJ Rugg {Wayfarer}, St Sampson (CI) 7 1938.

3060 (4): New to WJ Rugg {Wayfarer}, St Sampson (CI) (as OB22F); WJ Rugg {Wayfarer}, St Sampson (CI) 4/32; reseated to OB21F at an unknown date; transferred to States of Guernsey Civil Transport Service, St Peter Port (GOV) at some point during the period 11/40 to 6/44.

4085 (3): New to WJ Rugg {Wayfarer}, St Sampson (CI) 3.

Notes:

Two of the Dodges were probably renumbered 7 and 8 at an unknown date.

2711 (7): Renumbered 22 and received Police plate 118 at an unknown date.

Disposals:

1557 (2): Guernsey Motors Ltd, St Peter Port (CI) 9 11/51; dismantled 12/55.

1558 (1): Guernsey Motors Ltd, St Peter Port (CI) 1 11/51; withdrawn 1956; Vazon, Castel as a shed 2/57.

1560 (5): Guernsey Motors Ltd, St Peter Port (CI) 42; withdrawn 7/58; WP Simon, Alderney (CI) re-registered AY 59 [4] 10/58 (as B33F); withdrawn 1960.

1633 (6): SA Noel, St Peter Port (dealer) 5/49; WP Simon, Alderney (CI) re-registered AY 101 [1] 1949; withdrawn 1951.

1951 (6): Guernsey Railway Co Ltd, St Peter Port (CI) 43 11/51; fitted with a Perkins P6 oil engine from 3/52 to 3/54; withdrawn 9/55; A Martel, Delancey, St Sampson (GCI) as a mobile shop 4/56; unidentified owner, St Sampson as living accommodation 3/63.

2711 (22, ex 7): Guernsey Motors Ltd, St Peter Port (CI) 61 (not operated) 11/51; Vandertang's Nurseries, Vale as an office 9/55; broken up when the site was sold at an unknown date.

2818 (12): Guernsey Motors Ltd, St Peter Port (CI) 20 11/51; withdrawn 9/56; unidentified owner 2/57.

2819 (11): Guernsey Railway Co Ltd, St Peter Port (CI) 46 11/51; fitted with a Perkins P6 oil engine from 2/52 to 11/54; withdrawn 9/54; unidentified owner as a non-PSV 4/56.

2851 (13): Guernsey Motors Ltd, St Peter Port (CI) 56 11/51; withdrawn 9/57; Normandy Laundry, St Peter Port as a store 3/59.

2877 [1] (10): Guernsey Railway Co Ltd, St Peter Port (CI) 45 11/51; fitted with a Perkins P6 oil engine from 1/52 to 1/54; reseated to B29F at an unknown date; withdrawn 9/57; unidentified owner (minus engine) 10/57.

3060 (4): Guernsey Railway Co Ltd, St Peter Port (CI) (not operated) 11/51; scrapped 9/53.

3458 (9): Guernsey Railway Co Ltd, St Peter Port (CI) 44; fitted with a Perkins P6 oil engine from 1/52 to 10/53; reseated to B33F at an unknown date; withdrawn 9/56; Victoria Hotel, St Sampson as living accommodation 3/57; exported to Bombay (O-IND) at an unknown date.

3460 (4): Guernsey Railway Co Ltd, St Peter Port (CI) 41 11/51; fitted with a Perkins P6 oil engine from 1/52 to 2/53; FJK Reynolds {Cliffways Hotel}, St Martin (XCI) 9/55; W Laine, Vale as living accommodation 1961.

4085 (3): Guernsey Railway Co Ltd, St Peter Port (CI) (not operated) 11/51; Le Poidevin, St Peter Port 10/53.

4101 (3): Guernsey Motors Ltd, St Peter Port (CI) 10 11/51; dismantled 12/55.

4414 (20): Guernsey Motors Ltd, St Peter Port (CI) 60 11/51; withdrawn 9/61; FJK Reynolds {Cliffways Hotel}, St Martin (CI) 11/61; withdrawn 9/69; LF Le Noury, St Sampson 3/72; scrapped by5/73.

4426 (21): Guernsey Railway Co Ltd, St Peter Port (CI) 50 11/51; withdrawn 9/63; WP Simon, Alderney (CI) re-registered AY   59 [8] 2/64; withdrawn 1965.

5181 (14): Guernsey Railway Co Ltd, St Peter Port (CI) 47 11/51; withdrawn 9/60; unidentified owner, Les Vardes, St Sampson as living accommodation 1/61; at Camp du Roi 4/63; scrapped at an unknown date.

5182 (15): Guernsey Railway Co Ltd, St Peter Port (CI) 48 11/51; withdrawn 9/62; JT Carre, Guernsey 10/63.

5183 (16): Guernsey Railway Co Ltd, St Peter Port (CI) 49 11/51; withdrawn 9/61; WP Simon, Alderney (CI) re-registered AY   59 [6] 3/62 (as B33F); withdrawn 1963.

5184 (17): Guernsey Motors Ltd, St Peter Port (CI) 57 11/51; withdrawn 9/62; St Anthony's Hotel, Vale as living accommodation 3/63.

5185 (18): Guernsey Motors Ltd, St Peter Port (CI) 58 11/51; withdrawn 9/62; JT Carre, Guernsey 10/63.

5186 (19): Guernsey Motors Ltd, St Peter Port (CI) 59 11/51; unidentified owner 3/61.

AJ SNELL   Le Bourg, FOREST

Snell was a private hire and taxi operator.

| 3041 | Renault | SX488457 | ? | | C15- | 7/31 | 4/49 | 5/52 |
| 5895 | Morris CVF.13/5 | 73322 | Wadham | | C19F | 8/48 | 6/60 | 11/64 |

Previous histories:
3041: New to Commercial Company of the Channel Islands, St Peter Port (CI) 7/31; withdrawn 3/40; G Vidamour, Forest at an unknown date.
5895: New to Commercial Company of the Channel Islands, St Peter Port (CI); withdrawn 5/40; G Vidamour, Forest at an unknown date.

Disposals:
3041: FJK Reynolds {Cliffways Hotel}, St Martin (CI) 5/52; scrapped 9/55.
5895: WS Le Poidevin, Castel (XCI) 11/64; Guernsey Motors Ltd, St Peter Port (CI) (not operated) 1/66; broken up by11/68.

JW STACEY   Ivy Garage, Colborne Road, ST PETER PORT

Stacey was a private hire operator.

1963	Reo	?	?		B20F	-/--	-/30	11/42
651	Chevrolet	?	?		B18F	-/--	-/33	11/42
882	Reo Speed Wagon F	84066	?		Ch19	-/23	3/33	3/36
2047	Reo Sprinter LWB	FAX579	Bence		B24F	3/28	-/35	11/42

Previous histories:
651: Its origins are unknown.
882: New to CR Watson {The Greys}, St Martin (CI) (as Ch20); Mrs SE Watson {The Greys}, St Martin (CI) 9/31.
1963: Its origins are unknown.
2047: New to HN & HK Falla {Falla Bros / Blue Bird}, Vale (CI) 5.

Disposals:
651: Impressed by German Military Authorities (Military Truck Compound) (GOV) 11/42; scrapped locally at an unknown date (or sent to France for scrapping).
882: Converted to a lorry by JW Stacey 3/36; scrapped 8/39.
1963: Impressed by German Military Authorities (Military Truck Compound) (GOV) 11/42; scrapped locally at an unknown date (or sent to France for scrapping).
2047: Impressed by German Military Authorities (Military Truck Compound) (GOV) 11/42; scrapped locally at an unknown date (or sent to France for scrapping).

Ernest STEAD {La Rapide}   **East View, L'Islet, ST SAMPSON**
Ayton, Ville au Roi Estate, ST PETER PORT (-/--)
After spells as a driver for Blue Bird and Guernsey Railway Co, Ernest Stead started his own operation which was in direct competition to Guernsey Motors on a service from St Peter Port to Cobo. It was not until January 1930 that they came to an agreement to run the service jointly. In 1938, he became manager of Guernsey Railway Co Ltd whilst still running his own La Rapide business until 1944.

1		Ford TT	?	Underhill	OB21F	5/25	5/25	12/28
2	1073	Dodge LB	?	FT Bennett	OB23F	8/25	8/25	-/31
3	1295	Dodge A	A577835	FT Bennett	OB21F	4/26	4/26	-/32
4?	2501	Dodge LER	?	FT Bennett	OB20F	6/29	6/29	9/42
1?	3135	Vulcan Duchess	?	Strachan	B27F	1/32	1/32	9/41
2	3625	Vulcan Duchess	D135?	Strachan	B29F	12/33	12/33	9/41
3?	2787	Vulcan Duchess	D190	Strachan	B29F	1/38	1/38	1/44

Notes:
2787: Its chassis number is also recorded as D170; impressed by States of Germany Military Transport Service, St Peter Port (GOV) 2/41; returned at an unknown date.
3135: Its chassis number is recorded as 20205, but this may be an engine number.
3625: Its chassis number is also recorded as D85.

Disposals:
1: Guernsey Railway Co Ltd, St Peter Port (CI) 4 11/28; chassis scrapped 7/30; body to 1931 Ford AA 1389 (4) of Guernsey Railway Co Ltd.
2: No known disposal.
1073 (2): Guernsey Motors Ltd, St Peter Port (CI) 3/34 (as OB18F); Impressed by German Military Authorities (Military Truck Compound) (GOV) 10/42; scrapped locally at an unknown date (or sent to France for scrapping).
1295 (3): Guernsey Motors Ltd, St Peter Port (CI) 3/34; Guernsey Railway Co Ltd (CI) 15 9/34; withdrawn 12/36; scrapped 12/39.
2501: Impressed by German Military Authorities (Military Truck Compound) (GOV) 9/42; scrapped locally at an unknown date (or sent to France for scrapping).
2787: Guernsey Railway Co Ltd, St Peter Port (CI) 1 1/44; withdrawn 9/50; unidentified owner (minus engine) 6/51.
3135: Impressed by States of Germany Military Transport Service, St Peter Port (GOV) 9/41; German Military Authorities (Fortress Engineer Staff) (GOV) 3/43; scrapped locally at an unknown date (or sent to France for scrapping).
3625 (2): Impressed by States of Germany Military Transport Service, St Peter Port (GOV) 9/41; German Military Authorities (Garrison Commander) (GOV) 10/42; scrapped locally at an unknown date (or sent to France for scrapping).

TALLY HO! COACHES
AW CARRE {Tally Ho! Cabs}   **16 Mount Row, ST PETER PORT**
AW CARRE & J BLUNDELL {Tally Ho! Coaches} (-/74)
Lionel D MILES {Tally Ho! Coaches} (by10/76)   **Le Menage Hotel, CASTEL**
Tally Ho! Cabs (later Coaches) started in a small way with a small minibus operation in 1966, but soon added a succession of Bedford SB coaches. Lionel Miles took over the business in 1976 but in the following year, he formed Educational Holidays, Guernsey Ltd and transferred the last two coaches to that company.

2500	Commer 1500LB	013124	Rootes		M11	4/61	11/66	6/70
7482	Commer Q4	18B1156	Pearson		C30F	-/--	3/68	1/70
5482	Commer Q4	18A6589	Plaxton	43	C31F	-/--	4/69	3/71
8370	Ford 400E	?	Ford		M11	4/58	12/70	6/72
13110	Bedford SB	3708	Duple	1006/296	C35F	5/52	3/71	9/74
16646	Commer 1500LB	343260	Rootes		M11	7/65	3/72	9/77
16412	Bedford SBG	28463	Duple	1051/179	C36F	5/54	5/73	10/74
11840	Bedford SBG	37194	Duple	1055/320	C38F	4/55	2/74	9/77
7269	Bedford SB3	77291	Plaxton	602914	C41F	3/60	10/76	7/77
7091 [1]	Bedford SB3	77295	Plaxton	602921	C41F	3/60	11/76	12/77
8555	Commer 1500LB	342914	Rootes		M14	6/65	2/77	8/78

Police plates:

2500: ph62	7482: ph12	16412: ph12
5482: ph12	11840: ph62	16646: ph77
7091 [1]: ph62	13110: ph62	

Previous histories:

2500: New to CG Baxter {Exclusive Drive Hire}, St Peter Port (XCI).

5482: Chassis new to War Department (GOV) 1943-46; Beales & Swinhoe, Dormanstown (NR) bodied Plaxton (43) C31F registered HYN 728 10/48; FW Parker, Spalding (HD as C30F) at an unknown date; AA Pitcher Ltd {Tantivy Coaches}, St Helier (CI) 7 re-registered J 14064 2/53; Tantivy Motors Ltd, St Helier (CI) 5 12/68; withdrawn 4/69.

7091 [1]: New to CA Smith {Silver Badge Motors}, Windermere (WT) registered GJM 6; J Birbeck {Blue Eagle Tours}, St Helier (CI) 22 re-registered J 1852 3/63; Blue Eagle Ltd, St Helier (CI) 22 5/68; renumbered 17 1972; Tantivy Motors Ltd, St Helier (CI) (not operated) 5/75.

7269: New to CA Smith {Silver Badge Motors}, Windermere (WT) registered GJM 5; J Birbeck {Blue Eagle Tours}, St Helier (CI) 23 re-registered J 1858 3/62; Blue Eagle Ltd, St Helier (CI) 23 5/68; renumbered 16 1972; Tantivy Motors Ltd, St Helier (CI) (not operated) 5/75.

7482: Chassis new to War Department (GOV) 1943-46; unidentified owner and fitted with a Pearson C30F body (registration unknown) at an unknown date; AA Pitcher Ltd {Tantivy Coaches}, St Helier (CI), re-registered J 14065 and numbered 9 2/53; withdrawn 1/68.

8370: New to FNG Ross {Cleveland Hotel}, St Peter Port (XCI); Bougourd Bros, St Peter Port (dealer) 3/68; Fossey, Vale 4/68.

8555: New to EA Burbridge {La Favorita Hotel}, St Peter Port (XCI); La Favorita Hotel Ltd, St Peter Port (XCI) 7/69; two private owners from 3/71.

11840: New to CW Sworder & Sons Ltd, Walkern (HT) registered UJH 346; AA Pitcher Ltd, St Helier (CI) 17 re-registered J 30366 4/64; Tantivy Motors Ltd, St Helier (CI) 17 12/68.

13110: New to Essex County Coaches Ltd, London E15 (LN) registered EJD 508 (as C33F); J Birbeck {Blue Eagle Tours}, St Helier (CI) 11 re-registered J 7992 4/57; Blue Eagle Ltd, St Helier (CI) 11 5/68; withdrawn 1970.

16412: New to Auty's Tours Ltd, Bury (LA) registered CEN 535; withdrawn 12/55; WE Pashley, Bradwell (DE) 6/56; Sheffield United Tours Ltd, Sheffield (WR) 7/58; numbered J1 and to service 6/59; F Cowley, Salford (dealer) 11/61; AA Pitcher Ltd {Tantivy Coaches}, St Helier (CI) 24 re-registered J 25784 4/62; Tantivy Motors Ltd, St Helier (CI) 24 12/68; withdrawn 2/73.

16646: New to JB Parker Ltd {Moore's Hotel}, St Peter Port (CI).

Notes:

16646: Re-registered 16779 2/77.

Disposals:

2500: Scrapped 7/72.

5482 (ex J 14064, HYN 728): H Dessau, St Peter-in-the-Wood 9/72 and scrapped.

7091 [1] (ex J 1852, GJM 6): Educational Holidays Guernsey Ltd {Island Coachways}, Castel (CI) 7/77; withdrawn 1981.

7269 (ex J 1858, GJM 5): Educational Holidays Guernsey Ltd {Island Coachways}, Castel (CI) 12/77; withdrawn 9/81.

7482 (ex J 14065):. D Le Noury, D Le Gallez & R Bougourd, Vale 1/70; scrapped by6/72.

8370: For private owners, Guernsey from 6/72; last licensed 1979.

8555: Three private owners, Guernsey as a van from 8/78; scrapped by8/86.

11840 (ex J 30366, UJH 346): LD & B Miles {Le Menage Hotel}, Castel (XCI) 9/77; Educational Holidays Guernsey Ltd, St Peter Port (CI) for spares 10/78; broken up at an unknown date.

13110 (ex J 7992, EJD 508): Scrapped 7/75.

16412 (ex J 25784, CEN 535): Airport Fire Service, Forest, Guernsey as a training unit at an unknown date; chassis to Educational Holidays Guernsey Ltd {Island Coachways}, St Peter Port (CI) for the rebuild of 1787 [2]; modified and fitted with a the 1972 Plaxton (728442) C45F body from Ford R192 WLJ 578K 5/79; Altered to 7ft 4in wide and to service 7/80; re-registered 8230 [3] 4/86; Northern Lights, Landes du Marche (XCI) re-registered 10155 [2] 1986; Offshore Radio, St Martin (GCI) as a mobile studio 1990.

16779 (ex 16646): A Nash, Castell (XCI) 9/77; re-registered 19414 at an unknown date; G Archenoul, St Sampson (XCI) 8/79; scrapped by9/79.

TAXICO LTD　　　　　　　　　　　　　　　　　　**Westbourne House, Stanley Road, ST PETER PORT**

48830	Renault Master	G500687	?		M10L	10/85	5/95	9/96

Previous history:
48830: New to St John's Ambulance (XCI) 12 registered 5616; unidentified dealer re-registered 48830 by5/95.

Disposal:
48830 (ex 5616): Private owner, Guernsey 9/96.

R TORODE {Windmill Hotel}　　　　　　　　　　　　　　**Rue Poudreuse, ST MARTIN**
Torode operated a courtesy coach for the Windmill Hotel.

2730	Toyota Hiace	RH20E029183	Toyota	M11	12/78	12/78	12/90

Police plate (Public Service Omnibus plates after 1981):
2730: ph5

Disposal:
2730: No known disposal.

TRIDENT TRAVEL　　　　　　　　　　　　　　　　　**Weighbridge, ST PETER PORT**
Trident Travel operated harbour transfers for visitors.

27503	Leyland Sherpa	002198N	Leyland	M11	3/75	-/75	-/80

Police plate:
27503: ph78

Previous history:
27503: New to Ruette Braye & La Lacheurs Motors Ltd, St Martin (XCI).

Disposal:
27503: No known disposal.

UNIVERSAL LIMOS GUERNSEY LTD　　　　　　**St Pierre Park Hotel, Rohais, ST PETER PORT**
Universal Limos had a history stretching back to the mid-1990s when the company was originally named Guernsey Chauffeur Drive Ltd. It changed its name to Universal Limos (Guernsey) Ltd in around 2002, but to 2004, just supplied limousines for weddings and other special occasions. In August of that year, a licence was granted to operate an excursion from St Peter Port to the north of the island and west to Pleinmont. It also provided party buses on occasions. A night-bus service was started in March 2005.

Other plans did not come to fruition including a proposal to buy amphibious vehicles from Puddleducks on Jersey an application was also refused to run a road train – a vehicle had been acquired from a wildlife park in Germany.

Licences were suspended on more than one occasion and the authorities finally revoked them on 27 June 2008.

53948	AEC Routemaster	RML2566	Park Royal	L5852	H40/32R	8/66	8/04	2/07
CUV 274C	AEC Routemaster	RML2274	Park Royal	L5809	H40/32R	7/65	8/04	----
65346	AEC Routemaster	3P2RH2173	Park Royal	B49994	H40/31F	4/64	5/05	3/08
50129	Ford R1015	BCRSEA40551	Wadham Stringer 8536/84		B45F	12/84	12/06	6/08
68523	Bristol VRT/SL3/6LXB	3/267	ECW	20949	O43/27D	7/76	6/07	6/08
69788	Bristol VRT/SL3/6LXB	3/1060	ECW	22760	H43/31F	1/78	10/07	6/08

Public Service Omnibus plates:

    53948: ph12   65346: ph21   50129 (as 73140): ph123

Previous histories:

    50129: New to JMT (1978) Ltd, St Helier (CI) 20 registered J 43037; JMT (1987) Ltd, St Helier (CI) 20 12/87; withdrawn 9/02; NatWest Island Games Committee (CI) Jsy02 6/03; States Airport, Forest (XCI) as a shuttle bus 7/03.

    53948: New to London Transport Executive, London SW1 (LN) RML2566 registered JJD 566D; London Central Bus Co Ltd, London SE13 (LN) RML2566 4/89; Metroline Travel Ltd, Harrow (LN) RML2566 7/93; International Coachlines Ltd, Thornton Heath (LN) 3/04.

    65346: New to Northern General Transport Ltd, Gateshead (DM) 2101 registered RCN 701; renumbered 3085 1975; London Transport Executive, London SW1 (LN) RMF2771 8/80; T Aston Buses, Epsom (XSR) 7/81; converted to a mobile restaurant 1982; Time Transport Ltd, Thornton Heath (SR) 10/92; International Coachlines Ltd, Thornton Heath (LN) 5/96; re-registered EYY 776B 5/05.

    68523: New to Bristol Omnibus Co Ltd (AV) C5055 registered LEU 263P (as H43/27D); renumbered 5055 c8/78; rebuilt to O43/27D 8/86; Badgerline Ltd, Weston-super-Mare (AV) 8622 2/93; to service 3/93; Bristol Omnibus Co Ltd (AV) 8622 1/96; S Munden {Bristol Bus & Coach Sales}, Bristol (dealer) 4/00; AJ Curtis {Riduna Buses}, Alderney (CI) re-registered AY 586 [3] 5/02.

    CUV 274C: New to London Transport Executive, London SW1 (LN) RML2274; Metroline Travel Ltd, Harrow (LN) RML2274 4/89; International Coachlines Ltd, Thornton Heath (LN) 3/04.

    69788: New to Western National Omnibus Co Ltd, Exeter (DN) 1117 registered VDV 117S; Western National Ltd, Truro (CO) 1117 1/83; First Western National Buses Ltd, Truro (CO) 3/99; withdrawn 4/03; A Hardwick, Carlton (dealer) 7/03; I Peacock, Stockton (CD) 8/03; Stephenson's of Easingwold Ltd, Tholthorpe (NY) 9/03; Tees Valley Luxury Coaches Ltd, Eaglescliffe (CD) 9/05.

Notes:

    50129 (ex J 43037): Re-registered 73140 12/06.

    53948 (ex JJD 566D): Received Public Service Omnibus plate 120 5/05.

    65346 (ex EYY 776B, RCN 701): Operated as a 'party bus'.

    CUV 274C: Did not operate for Universal Limos (Guernsey) Ltd.

Disposals:

    53948 (ex JJD 566D): Penn, Bagshot for preservation 2/07; re-registered JJD 566D 9/07; Ghost Bus Tours Ltd, Bloomsbury (LN) 4/08; burnt out and scrapped 11/12.

    65346 (ex EYY 776B, RCN 701): Unidentified UK owner re-registered EYY 776B 3/08.

    68523 (ex AY 586 [3], LEU 263P): S Munden {Bristol Bus & Coach Sales}, Bristol (dealer) 8/10; re-registered LEU 263P 10/10; R Smith, Glastonbury for preservation 10/10; J Pratt, Weston-super-Mare for preservation 2/11; J Pratt, Weston-super-Mare (SO) 5/11; Crosville Motor Services Ltd, Weston-super-Mare (SO) 2/12; withdrawn 4/18.

    69788 (ex VDV 117S): S Munden {Bristol Bus & Coach Sales}, Bristol (dealer) re-registered VDV 117S 6/09.

    73140 (ex 50129, J 43037): Party & Funbus, St Peter Port (XCI) 7/08; unidentified owner, Jersey by9/11; Signature Coaches ARL, Trinity (CI) for spares over the winter of 2014/15; EMR Jersey Ltd, Bellozane (dealer) for scrap by12/15.

    CUV 274C: No known disposal.

VAUDIN'S UNITED TAXIS   **Belgreve Lane, ST SAMPSON**

Vaudin's United Taxis operated airport and harbour transfers, taking over from Sarnia Cabs. Operations ceased in May 1991 with the vehicles passing to Central Transfers Ltd.

34932	Toyota Hiace	60V00009946	Toyota	M14	6/84	4/88	6/91
43361	Ford Transit	BDVZJE65999	Ford	M11	9/88	6/90	11/90
44993	Mazda E2200	143200708730	Mazda	M8	5/91	5/91	6/91

Public Service Omnibus plates:

    34932: ph34   43361: ph34   44993: t132

Previous histories:

    34932: New to RL Gaudion {L'Islet Cabs}, St Sampson (CI).

    43361: New to BB Hire Cars Ltd, St Peter Port (XCI).

Notes:
>   34932: Was withdrawn between 6/90 and 4/91.
>   43361: Was withdrawn following an accident.

Disposals:
>   34932: Central Transfers Ltd, St Peter Port (CI) 6/91; withdrawn 7/94.
>   43361: No known disposal.
>   44993: Central Transfers Ltd, St Peter Port (CI) 6/91; DIta Taxis Ltd, St Peter Port (CI) 7/94; withdrawn at an
>   unknown date.

WAGGA-WAGGA

GH LUXON {Wagga-Wagga}   **New Road, ST SAMPSON**
WJ RUGG {Wagga-Wagga} (8/25)   **Brock Road, ST SAMPSON**
                                             Nocq Road, ST SAMPSON (4/27)

GH Luxon ran a service from St Peter Port to St Sampson three days a week before being taken over by WJ Rugg in August 1925.

	Ford TT	?	?		Ch15	-/--	c-/22	-/--

Previous history:
>   Ford: Its origins are unknown.

Disposal:
>   Ford: No known disposal.

Charles R WATSON {The Greys}   **Les Cornus, ST MARTIN**
Mrs SE WATSON {The Greys} (9/31)
WATSON BROS {The Greys) (-/43)
WATSON'S GARAGE LTD {The Greys} (7/70)

Charles Watson had been a carter in the early years of the century and later ran the service from St Peter Port to Pleinmont jointly with Lenfestey's Lorina operation. Watson died in 1931 and the operation was taken over by his widow until 1943, after which his sons took over. On 1 February 1978, the business was sold to Guernsey Railway Co, the last of the old independent still in existence.

1112	Berliet 16 hp	14249	?		B20-	-/--	c-/22	4/36
	Oldsmobile	?	?		Ch20	-/--	-/--	-/23
882	Reo Speed Wagon F	84066	?		Ch20	-/23	-/23	3/33
732 [1]	Reo Speed Wagon F	128113	Heaver		Ch22	-/24	-/24	1/39
2317	Reo Sprinter	FAX5789	?		B22F	-/28	-/28	12/42
1737	Reo Sprinter	FAX1754	Heaver		B27F	5/31	5/31	3/59
3409	Vulcan Countess	D40	Vulcan		B31F	4/33	4/33	9/77
3944	Leyland KP3	2992	Heaver		B29F	9/34	9/34	12/60
1559	Albion PH115	25006L	Heaver		B29F	7/36	7/36	2/78
3120	Reo C	?	FT Bennett		B26F	-/32	-/37	2/43
653	Albion PH115	25026I	Heaver		B29F	8/39	8/39	2/78
2719	Reo Sprinter	FAX1430	Heaver		B25F	10/29	11/48	-/49
732 [2]	Albion FT3AB	70739A	Reading	5840	B36F	2/50	2/50	2/78
3992	Albion FT39N	73234E	Reading	8898	B36F	5/52	5/52	2/78
1787 [1]	Albion FT39AN	73737B	Reading	5176	B36F	6/54	6/54	2/78
1309	Albion NS3N	82052F	Reading	7116	B36F	6/60	6/60	2/78

Police plates:
>   653: 133   1737: 130   3944: 134
>   732 [2]: 153   1787 [1]: 84   3992: 130
>   1309: 134   2719: 153
>   1559: 131   3409: 132

Previous histories:

Berliet: Its origins are unknown.

Oldsmobile: Its origins are unknown.

2719: New to NA Lenfestey {Lorina}, Pleinmont (CI); Guernsey Motors Ltd, St Peter Port (CI) 44 2/39; impressed by States of Guernsey Military Transport Service, St Peter Port (GOV) 11/41; AP Delaney, Castel (GOV) 10/42; returned to Guernsey Motors Ltd 44 by8/44; renumbered 11 1945.

3120: New to HN & HK Falla {Falla Bros / Blue Bird}, Vale (CI) 4.

Notes:

653: Impressed by States of Guernsey Civil Transport Service, St Peter Port (GOV) 2/41; returned 5/45; rebodied Reading (2908) FB32F 1953; fitted with a Perkins P6 oil engine 2/64.

732 [2]: Was fitted with an Albion oil engine before entering service (the first oil-engine bus on Guernsey); its front-end was rebuilt 5/61.

882: Was fitted with the body from the Oldsmobile.

1559: Impressed by States of Guernsey Civil Transport Service, St Peter Port (GOV) 2/41; converted to gazogene at an unknown date; returned 5/45; rebodied Reading (5185) FB32F 2/55; fitted with a Leyland Cub engine 6/58; fitted with a Morris engine and radiator 1/63; fitted with a BMC engine 5/75.

1737: Impressed by States of Guernsey Military Transport Service, St Peter Port (GOV) 8/41; returned 1942.

3409: Impressed by States of Guernsey Military Transport Service, St Peter Port (GOV) 11/41; returned by3/44; fitted with a Albion petrol engine 1948/49; rebodied Reading FB32F 6/53; fitted with a Perkins P6 oil engine 5/67.

3944: Impressed by States of Guernsey Civil Transport Service, St Peter Port (GOV) 2/41; converted to gazogene at an unknown date; returned 5/45.

Disposals:

Berliet: Converted to a van by Mrs SE Watson 4/36; scrapped 12/39.

Oldsmobile: Body to 1923 Reo; chassis presumed scrapped.

653: Guernsey Railway Co Ltd, St Peter Port (CI) 24 2/78; withdrawn 2/78; K Rowland, St Asaph for preservation 3/80; N Hirst, M Ponder & T Quinn, Coventry for preservation c4/82; re-registered DFP 496 by8/83; LT Shaw, Tamworth for preservation by9/88; M Bowring, Lydney for preservation 8/93.

732 [1]: Converted to a lorry with Mrs SE Watson / Watson Bros 1/39; used until the late 1940s.

732 [2]: Guernsey Railway Co Ltd, St Peter Port (CI) 22 2/78; A Wood, St Martin for preservation re-registered 1982 3/80; North West Transport Museum, Warrington for preservation 10/82; F Elliott & Dr JR Young, Golborne for preservation 3/85; unidentified owner, Tamworth possibly for preservation 4/92; 'Adam & Lee', location unknown as a caravan by5/93; re-registered OFF 605 by11/93; last licence expired 9/94; Fyffe, Carnoustie (dealer) for scrap c10/01.

882: JW Stacey, Vale (CI) 3/33; converted to a lorry by JW Stacey 3/36; scrapped 8/39.

1309: Guernsey Railway Co Ltd, St Peter Port (CI) 23 2/78; fitted with a Bedford engine 1980; withdrawn 11/80; Guernseybus Ltd, St Peter Port (CI) 23 2/81; re-registered 31235 [1] 8/82; withdrawn 12/83; Dr JR Young, Nottingham (dealer / preservationist) 1/85.

1559: Guernsey Railway Co Ltd, St Peter Port (CI) 5 (not operated) 2/78; J Foley, Guernsey Motor Museum for preservation 3/80; F Help, Guernsey as a caravan 1982; D & A Ridley, Orpington for preservation by12/84; unidentified preservationist (M Verrechia?), Felbridge by12/00.

1737: Le Prevost, St Saviour as living accommodation 3/59; broken up mid-1960s.

1787 [1]: Guernsey Railway Co Ltd, St Peter Port (CI) 20 2/78; withdrawn 9/79; ; hired to Educational Holidays Guernsey Ltd {Island Coachways}, St Peter Port (CI) 5/86-9/86 and acquired 4/88; to service 5/88; Lakeland Motor Museum, Holker Hall for preservion re-registered 898 FUF 6/93; R Greet, Broadhempson for preservation 3/94; Intransit Ltd, St Peter Port (CI) 11 re-registered 1787 [1] 2/13; moved to St Sampson (CI) by9/13; fitted with a Cummins engine by3/18.

2317: Impressed by German Military Authorities (Military Truck Compound) (GOV) 12/42; scrapped at an unknown date (or exported to France).

2719: Broken up for spares 1949.

3120: Impressed by German Military Authorities (Military Truck Compound) (GOV) 2/43; scrapped at an unknown date (or exported to France).

3409: Guernsey Railway Co Ltd, St Peter Port (CI) 25 (not operated) 2/78; G Hatton, Woolston for preservation 3/80; Dr JR Young, Nottingham (dealer / preservationist) 7/84; H Glover, Nuneaton for preservation 5/96; re-registered MSJ 702 6/98; moved to Shirebrook by10/04; P Harris, Mansfield Woodhouse for preservation 9/13; D Maskell, Wilstead for preservation 4/14; T Smith, Sandbach for preservation; current 8/17.

3944: Simon, St Sampson as living accommodation 10/62; scrapped mid-1960s.

3992: Guernsey Railway Co Ltd, St Peter Port (CI) 21 2/78; withdrawn 9/79; B Jolly, Guernsey Old Car Club for preservation 3/80; A Tracey, London E7 for preservation 2/84; moved to Merthyr Tydfil by9/89; moved to Evesham by6/90; C White, Harston for preservation 1992; D Roizer, Leicester for preservation spares c6/93; broken up for spares 1993.

JW WAY   Way's Garage, Bosq Lane, ST PETER PORT

JW Way ran wedding and funeral cars, but also had licences for three island tours up to the outbreak of War.

1613		Bedford WLB		108403	Duple		2854	C22F	-/32	-/32	9/39

Disposal:
1613: Impressed by German Military Authorities (Military Truck Compound) (GOV) 10/42; scrapped locally at an unknown date (or sent to France for scrapping).

WAYFARER

C LE GALLEZ {Wayfarer}   Jesmond Dene, Victoria Avenue, ST SAMPSON

Ernest RUGG {Wayfarer} (11/27)   Grande Maison Road, ST SAMPSON

William J RUGG {Wayfarer} (4/32)   Nocq Road, ST SAMPSON

Le Gallez started a service between St Peter Port and Grandes Rocques before being taken over by the Rugg family (who also built bodies) in November 1927. William Rugg lost an arm in an accident during the War years and when peacetime arrived, he offered to sell the business to Sarre Transport Ltd which took place pm 23 April 1946.

		Overland 1 ton	?	?			OB18F	12/24	12/24	7/29
2		Overland 1 ton	?	?			OB18F	11/27	11/27	-/29
1	597	Bean Model 11	2069/11W	Willowbrook	2215	B20F	9/29	9/29	11/41
2	2799	Bean Model 11	1223/11W	Willowbrook	2408	B20F	1/30	1/30	11/41
3	1940	Ford A	3735545	WJ Rugg		OB18F	10/30	10/30	6/35
	3060	Dodge UG30	8343213	WJ Rugg		B21F	10/31	10/31	4/46
5	1765	Reo Sprinter	FAX10234	Heaver		B24F	4/29	7/33	7/41
6	1633	Dodge	HLW628	WJ Rugg		B25F	3/34	3/34	4/46
3	4085	Dodge	KB228	WJ Rugg		B25F	3/35	3/35	4/46
7	2711	Dodge	PLW29	WJ Rugg		B25F	-/--	-/38	4/46

Police plates:
1633 (6): 122   3060: 124
2711 (7): 123   4085 (3): 121

Previous histories:
1765 (5): New to HN & HK Falla {Falla Bros / Blue Bird}, Vale (CI) 6.
2711 (7): Its chassis purchased second hand in Jersey and fitted with a WJ Rugg body.

Notes:
First Overland: Numbered 1 11/27.
597 (1): Reseated to B22F 4/32; rebuilt by WJ Rugg mid-1930s.
1633 (6): Impressed by States of Guernsey Civil Transport Service, St Peter Port (GOV) 2/41; converted to gazogene propulsion at an unknown date; returned to WJ Rugg 5/45.
1765 (5): Body rebuilt by WJ Rugg before entering service.
2799 (2): Reseated to B22F 4/32; rebuilt by WJ Rugg mid-1930s.
3060: Was initially operated by WJ Rugg in a separate venture called 'The Kingsway' which operated under a private hire licence; transferred to 'The Wayfarer' fleet and numbered 4 4/32; rebuilt to OB21F at an unknown date; transferred to States of Guernsey Civil Transport Service, St Peter Port (GOV) at some or all of the period 2/41 to 5/45.

Disposals:
1 (First Overland): No known disposal.
2 (Second Overland): Damaged in an accident 1929.
597 (1): Impressed by States of Guernsey Military Transport Service, St Peter Port (GOV) 11/41; German Military Authorities (Military Truck Compound) (GOV) 12/42; scrapped locally at an unknown date (or sent to France for scrapping).
1633 (6): Sarre Transport Ltd, St Peter-in-the-Wood (CI) 6 4/46; moved to St Peter Port (CI) at an unknown date; SA Noel, St Peter Port (dealer) 5/49; WP Simon, Alderney (CI) re-registered AY 101 [1] 1949; withdrawn 1951.

1765 (5): Impressed by States of Guernsey Military Transport Service, St Peter Port (GOV) t/41; German Military Authorities (Fortress Engineer Staff) (GOV) 7/42; scrapped locally at an unknown date (or sent to France for scrapping).

1940 (3): Guernsey Railway Co Ltd, St Peter Port (CI) 1 6/35; rebuilt by Guernsey Railway Co Ltd to B18F at an unknown date; impressed by German Military Authorities (Military Truck Compound) (GOV) 8/41; scrapped locally at an unknown date (or sent to France for scrapping).

2711 (7): Sarre Transport Ltd, St Peter-in-the-Wood (CI) 7 4/46; moved to St Peter Port (CI) at an unknown date; renumbered 22 at an unknown date; Guernsey Railway Co Ltd, St Peter Port (CI) 61 (not operated) 11/51; Vandertang's Nurseries, Vale as an office 9/55; broken up when the site was sold at an unknown date.

2799 (2): Impressed by States of Guernsey Military Transport Service, St Peter Port (GOV) 2/42; German Military Authorities (Military Truck Compound) (GOV) 12/42; scrapped locally at an unknown date (or sent to France for scrapping).

3060 (4): Sarre Transport Ltd, St Peter-in-the-Wood (CI) 4 4/46; moved to St Peter Port (CI) at an unknown date; Guernsey Railway Co Ltd, St Peter Port (CI) (not operated) 11/51; scrapped 9/53.

4085 (3): Sarre Transport Ltd, St Peter-in-the-Wood (CI) 3 4/46; moved to St Peter Port (CI) at an unknown date; Guernsey Railway Co Ltd, St Peter Port (CI) (not operated) 11/51; Le Poidevin, St Peter Port 10/53.

A WINDSOR   Charroterie, ST PETER PORT

Windsor ran a small garage and car hire firm.

2070	Chevrolet 18 hp	? ?	C12F	-/26	-/--	2/43

Previous history:
2070: Its origins are unknown.

Disposal:
2070: Impressed by German Military Authorities (Military Truck Compound) (GOV) 2/43.

WARTIME

Following the occupation of Guernsey by the German Military Forces on 30 June 1940, bus and coach services for the general public ceased with vehicles initially impressed by the authorities. A ban on the supply of petrol and the civilian use of motor vehicles led to a few individuals seeking authority to run horse bus services and several licences were issued:

	Dates operated bus services
WJ Belbem, Vale	7/40 to ?
J De Carteret, St Peter-in-the-Wood	7/40 – 8/42
Mrs HT McKane, Vale	7/40 to ?
T Sarre, St Peter-in-the-Wood	7/41 to ?
P Le Feuvre, St Sampson	?

Thomas Sarre was of course a former bus operator who operated in the early 1920s before running into financial difficulties and would start up Sarre Transport Ltd immediately after the War.

In November 1940 the German Authorities incorporated the States of Guernsey Civil Transport Service with an aim to provide a pool of transport for all needs, bar emergency and other essential services. Initially this comprised of commercial vehicles whose main function was to provide general haulage and delivery services to local depots. Prior to this, in August 1940 a morning and evening bus service to the airport was commissioned for local workers with it providing other services in and around St Peter Port between times. The Civil Transport Service later widened its scope to provide a skeleton bus service to most parts of the island with vehicles converted to Brandt Gazogene power – a charcoal burning plant that produced gas.

In February 1941, the States of Guernsey Military Transport Service was established involving all types of vehicles impressed from the civilian population. In some instances, the vehicle's owner would drive with the vehicle. From 1942, this state of affairs gave way to direct control by various individual military establishments (or 'feldposts').

One significant deviation from the above occurred in October 1942 when seven former Military Transport Service buses passed to AP Delaney of Castel. He fulfilled a contract to provide transport for staff at Organization Todt, which was responsible for engineering projects, specifically on Guernsey building a series of coastal defences around the island using forced labour. Delaney also acted as a civilian translator.

Only the immediate previous and subsequent operators are listed in this section – full details of vehicle histories are included elsewhere.

STATES OF GUERNSEY CIVIL TRANSPORT SERVICE La Pollet, ST PETER PORT

567 [1]	Packard E	?	Guernsey Motors	B29F	-/--	2/41	5/45
653	Albion PH115	25026I	Heaver	B29F	8/39	2/41	5/45
1559	Albion PH115	25006L	Heaver	B29F	7/36	2/41	5/45
1633	Dodge	HLW628	WJ Rugg	B25F	3/34	2/41	5/45
1814	Vulcan Duchess	D177	Vulcan	B29F	7/37	2/41	5/45
2981	Reo FAX	1691	Heaver	FB32F	5/31	2/41	5/45
3774	Dennis Falcon	280007	Dennis	B34C	4/39	2/41	11/41
3810	Leyland KP3	2775	Strachan	B29F	6/34	2/41	9/42
5499	Reo (Speed Wagon?)	909	Heaver	FB35F	4/39	2/41	5/45
27	Dennis Falcon	280011	Dennis	B31F	10/39	7/41	5/45
3944	Leyland KP3	2992	Heaver	B29F	9/34	2/41	5/45
4869	Albion PK115	25011G	Heaver	FB35F	10/36	5/41	5/45
4879	Reo Gold Crown	5372	Heaver	FB35F	7/37	5/41	5/45
1127	Dennis Arrow Minor	255045	Dennis	B29F	10/38	2/43	5/45
511	Dodge LER	D217761	Strachan	B23D	10/29	by7/44	5/45
3450	Vulcan Duke (Duchess)	3XS63	Metcalfe	B19F	2/30	-/--	5/45
3060	Dodge UG30	8343213	WJ Rugg	B21F	10/31	-/--	by5/45

Previous operators:
27: States of Guernsey Military Transport Service, St Peter Port (GOV).
511: HC Collenette, St Sampson (CI) 3.
567 [1]: Guernsey Motors Ltd, St Peter Port (CI) 23.
653: Mrs SE Watson {The Greys}, St Martin (CI).
1127: States of Guernsey Military Transport Service, St Peter Port (GOV).
1559: Mrs SE Watson {The Greys}, St Martin (CI).
1633: WJ Rugg {Wayfarer}, St Sampson (CI) 6.

1814: Guernsey Motors Ltd, St Peter Port (CI) 20.
2981: HN & HK Falla {Blue Bird}, Vale (CI) 1.
3060: WJ Rugg {The Kingsway}, St Sampson (CI) 4.
3450: States of Guernsey Military Transport Service, St Peter Port (GOV).
3774: Guernsey Railway Co Ltd, St Peter Port (CI) 9.
3810: HC Collenette {Paragon}, St Sampson (CI) 6.
3944: Mrs SE Watson {The Greys}, St Martin (CI).
4869: HN & HK Falla {Blue Bird}, Vale (CI) 5.
4879: HN & HK Falla {Blue Bird}, Vale (CI) 4.
5499: HN & HK Falla {Blue Bird}, Vale (CI) 7.

Notes:
27: Converted to Gazogene propulsion 9/42 and received licence no. 257.
1127: Converted to gazogene propulsion 3/43 and received licence no. 258.
1559: Converted to gazogene propulsion at an unknown date and received licence no. 259.
1633: Converted to gazogene propulsion at an unknown date and received licence no. 265.
1814: Converted to gazogene propulsion 9/42 and received licence no. 261.
3450: Was originally registered 2791.
3944: Converted to gazogene propulsion at an unknown date and received licence no. 260.
4869: Converted to gazogene propulsion 8/42 and received licence no. 262.
4879: Converted to gazogene propulsion 11/42 and received licence no. 263.
5499: Fitted with a Gold Crown engine; converted to gazogene propulsion 1/43 and received licence no. 264.

Initial disposals:
27: Returned to Guernsey Motors Ltd 5/45.
511: Returned to HC Collenette {Paragon}, St Sampson (CI) 3 5/45.
567 [1]: Returned to Guernsey Motors Ltd, St Peter Port (CI) 23 5/45.
653: Returned to Watson Bros {The Greys}, St Martin (CI) 5/45.
1127: Returned to Guernsey Motors Ltd, St Peter Port (CI) 28 5/45.
1559: Returned to Watson Bros {The Greys}, St Martin (CI) 5/45.
1633: Returned to WJ Rugg {Wayfarer}, St Sampson (CI) 6.
1814: Returned to Guernsey Motors Ltd, St Peter Port (CI) 20 5/45.
2981: Returned to HN & HK Falla {Blue Bird}, Vale (CI) 1 5/45.
3060: Returned to WJ Rugg {Wayfarer}, St Sampton (CI) 4 by5/45.
3450 (ex 2791): Returned to Guernsey Motors Ltd, St Peter Port (CI) 29 5/45.
3774: States of Guernsey Military Transport Service, St Peter Port (GOV) 11/41.
3810: States of Guernsey Military Transport Service, St Peter Port (GOV) 9/42.
3944: Returned to Watson Bros {The Greys}, St Martin (CI) 5/45.
4869: Returned to HN & HK Falla {Blue Bird} 5/45.
4879: Returned to HN & HK Falla {Blue Bird} 5/45.
5499: Returned to HN & HK Falla {Blue Bird} 5/45.

STATES OF GUERNSEY MILITARY TRANSPORT SERVICE   Ash's Garage, Grange, ST PETER PORT

448	Packard E	?	?	B29F	-/--	7/40	12/42
465	Packard E	?	Guernsey Motors	B29F	-/--	7/40	4/41
558	Vulcan Duchess	D125	Vulcan	B29F	8/35	7/40	8/42
612	Packard E	?	Guernsey Motors	B29F	-/--	7/40	by10/42
624	Vulcan Duchess	D150	Vulcan	B29F	6/36	7/40	10/42
630	Vulcan Duchess	D151	Vulcan	B29F	7/36	7/40	7/42
737	Packard E	?	Guernsey Motors	B29F	-/--	7/40	12/42
784	Packard E	?	Guernsey Motors	B29F	-/--	7/40	12/42
1088	Packard E	?	Baico	COB25F	-/--	7/40	9/42
1846	Vulcan Duchess	D152	Vulcan	B29F	6/36	7/40	8/42
2982	Vulcan Duchess	D51	Vulcan	B26F	5/31	7/40	7/42
2985	Vulcan Duchess	D52	Vulcan	B26F	4/31	7/40	11/42
2987	Vulcan Duchess	D53	Vulcan	B26F	4/31	7/40	12/42
3641	Packard E	?	Guernsey Motors	B29F	-/--	7/40	12/42
4222	Vulcan Duchess	D41	?	B24R	3/30	7/40	12/42
4444	Vulcan Duchess	D55	Guernsey Motors	B29F	12/30	7/40	12/42
4684	Vulcan Duchess	D48	Vulcan	B27F	10/30	7/40	10/42
27	Dennis Falcon	280011	Dennis	B31F	10/39	2/41	7/41
759	Vulcan RF	RF319	Guernsey Motors	B35F	-/35	2/41	11/42
848	Dennis Falcon	200032	Dennis	B34C	3/40	2/41	9/42

879	Dennis Falcon	280033	Dennis		B34C	3/40	2/41	8/42
937	Packard E	?	Guernsey Motors		B29F	-/--	2/41	12/42
1127	Dennis Arrow Minor	255045	Dennis		B29F	10/38	2/41	2/43
1322	Morris CS.2.13/80	1009C30753	Guernsey Railway		B33F	7/37	2/41	7/42
2783	Vulcan Duke	3XS68	Metcalfe		B19F	1/30	2/41	12/42
2787	Vulcan Duchess	D190	Strachan		B29F	1/38	2/41	-/--
2793	Vulcan Duke	3XS64	Metcalfe		B19F	3/30	2/41	12/42
3450	Vulcan Duke (Duchess)	3XS63	Metcalfe		B19F	2/30	2/41	-/--
2972 [1]	Vulcan Duke	(3XS)44	Vulcan		B26F	5/29?	3/41	9/42
118	Vulcan Duchess	D87	Guernsey Railway		B29F	5/34	4/41	11/42
931	Vulcan Duchess	D59	Guernsey Railway		B29F	4/33	4/41	11/42
2792	Vulcan Duke	3XS62	Metcalfe		B19F	2/30	4/41	7/42
3405	Vulcan Duchess	D62	Guernsey Railway		B29F	5/33	4/41	11/42
1398	Dodge PLB	1038	Guernsey Railway		B25F	8/35	7/41	by3/44
1473	Morris Director	048RP	Guernsey Railway		B25F	5/32	7/41	by3/44
1765	Reo Sprinter	FAX10234	Heaver		B24F	4/29	7/41	7/42
1845	Dodge LER	D225913	Strachan		B22F	-/30	7/41	12/42
3013	Dodge LER	D226722	Strachan		B27F	6/31	7/41	9/42
3193	Dodge	8343439	Guernsey Railway		B26F	2/32	7/41	11/42
1737	Reo Sprinter	FAX1754	Heaver		B27F	5/31	8/41	-/42
1940	Ford A	3735545			B18F	4/32	8/41	3/43
			Rugg / Guernsey Railway					
3688	Vulcan Duchess	D86	Guernsey Railway		B29F	12/33	8/41	11/42
3135	Vulcan Duchess	?	Strachan		B27F	1/32	9/41	3/43
3625	Vulcan Duchess	D135?	Strachan		B29F	12/33	9/41	10/42
597	Bean Model 11	2069/11W	Willowbrook	2215	B20F	9/29	11/41	12/42
2714	Reo Sprinter	FAA11138	Heaver		B25F	10/29	11/41	7/42
2719	Reo Sprinter	FAX1430	Heaver		B25F	11/29	11/41	10/42
3409	Vulcan Countess	D40	Vulcan		B31F	4/33	11/41	by3/44
3774	Dennis Falcon	280007	Dennis		B34C	4/39	11/41	11/42
2377	Bean Model 11	1573/11W	Willowbrook	2214	B20F	8/28	1/42	11/42
2799	Bean Model 11	1223/11W	Willowbrook	2408	B20F	1/30	2/42	12/42
722	Bedford WTB	18200	Thurgood	724	C20F	6/39	4/42	12/42
864	Leyland KP3	4143	Heaver	9731	FB35F	6/35	9/42	12/42
3216	Commer 6TK/1	28322	Strachan		B29F	7/32	9/42	12/42
3810	Leyland KP3	2775	Strachan		B29F	6/34	9/42	12/42

Previous operators:
27: Guernsey Motors Ltd, St Peter Port (CI) 50.
118: Guernsey Railway Co Ltd, St Peter Port (CI) 16.
448: Guernsey Motors Ltd, St Peter Port (CI) 42.
465: Guernsey Motors Ltd, St Peter Port (CI) 5.
558: Guernsey Motors Ltd, St Peter Port (CI) 12.
597: E Rugg {Wayfarer}, St Sampson (CI) 1 4/32.
612: Guernsey Motors Ltd, St Peter Port (CI) 24.
624: Guernsey Motors Ltd, St Peter Port (CI) 9.
630: Guernsey Motors Ltd, St Peter Port (CI) 55.
722: Guernsey Motors Ltd, St Peter Port (CI) 41.
737: Guernsey Motors Ltd, St Peter Port (CI) 38.
759: Guernsey Railway Co Ltd, St Peter Port (CI) 8.
784: Guernsey Motors Ltd, St Peter Port (CI) 38.
848: Guernsey Railway Co Ltd, St Peter Port (CI) 10.
864: HC Collenette {Paragon}, St Sampson (CI) 2.
879: Guernsey Motors Ltd, St Peter Port (CI) 11.
931: Guernsey Motors Ltd, St Peter Port (CI) 12.
937: Guernsey Motors Ltd, St Peter Port (CI) 1.
1088: Guernsey Motors Ltd, St Peter Port (CI) 4.
1127: Guernsey Motors Ltd, St Peter Port (CI) 28.
1322: Guernsey Railway Co Ltd, St Peter Port (CI) 7.
1398: Guernsey Railway Co Ltd, St Peter Port (CI) 2.
1473: Guernsey Railway Co Ltd, St Peter Port (CI) 24.
1737: Mrs SE Watson {The Greys}, St Martin (CI).
1765: WJ Rugg {Wayfarer}, St Sampson (CI) 5.
1845: Guernsey Railway Co Ltd, St Peter Port (CI) 3.

1846: Guernsey Motors Ltd, St Peter Port (CI) 10.
1940: Guernsey Railway Co Ltd, St Peter Port (CI) 1.
2377: Guernsey Railway Co Ltd, St Peter Port (CI) 19.
2714: Guernsey Motors Ltd, St Peter Port (CI) 48.
2719: Guernsey Motors Ltd, St Peter Port (CI) 44.
2783: Guernsey Motors Ltd, St Peter Port (CI) 17.
2787: EA Stead {La Rapide}, St Peter Port (CI) (3?).
2792: Guernsey Motors Ltd, St Peter Port (CI) 56.
2793: Guernsey Motors Ltd, St Peter Port (CI) 57.
2799: E Rugg {Wayfarer}, St Sampson (CI) 2 4/32.
2972 [1]: Guernsey Motors Ltd, St Peter Port (CI) 30.
2982: Guernsey Motors Ltd, St Peter Port (CI) 19.
2985: Guernsey Motors Ltd, St Peter Port (CI) 47.
2987: Guernsey Motors Ltd, St Peter Port (CI) 15.
3013: HC Collenette {Paragon}, St Sampson (CI) 5.
3135: EA Stead {La Rapide}, St Peter Port (CI) (1?).
3193: Guernsey Railway Co Ltd, St Peter Port (CI) 23.
3216: HC Collenette {Paragon}, St Sampson (CI) 1.
3405: Guernsey Railway Co Ltd, St Peter Port (CI) 14.
3409: Mrs SE Watson {The Greys}, St Martin (CI).
3450: Guernsey Motors Ltd, St Peter Port (CI) 55.
3625: EA Stead {La Rapide}, St Peter Port (CI) 2.
3641: Guernsey Motors Ltd, St Peter Port (CI) 2.
3688: Guernsey Railway Co Ltd, St Peter Port (CI) 15.
3774: States of Guernsey Civil Transport Services, St Peter Port (GOV).
3810: States of Guernsey Civil Transport Services, St Peter Port (GOV).
4222: Guernsey Motors Ltd, St Peter Port (CI) 11.
4444: Guernsey Motors Ltd, St Peter Port (CI) 16.
4684: Guernsey Motors Ltd, St Peter Port (CI) 13.

Notes:
879: Used as a military band coach.
2714: Fitted with a Silver Crown engine.
2787: Its chassis number is also recorded as D170.
2972 [1]: Was possibly originally registered EY 3586.
3450: Was originally registered 2791.
3625: Its chassis number is also recorded as D85.
4222: Was originally registered ED 4838.
4444: Was originally registered VO 4935.
4684: Was originally registered IB 4689.

Initial disposals:
27: States of Guernsey Civil Transport Service, St Peter Port (GOV) 7/41.
118: German Military Authorities (Fortress Engineer Staff) (GOV) 11/42.
448: German Military Authorities (Military Truck Compound) (GOV) 12/42.
465: German Military Authorities (Military Truck Compound) (GOV) 4/41.
558: German Military Authorities (Air Force Local Command) (GOV) 8/42.
597: German Military Authorities (Military Truck Compound) (GOV) 12/42.
612: German Military Authorities (Military Truck Compound) (GOV) by10/42.
624: AP Delaney, Castel (GOV) 10/42.
630: German Military Authorities (Fortress Engineer Staff) (GOV) 7/42.
722: German Military Authorities (Garrison Commander) (GOV) 12/42.
737: German Military Authorities (Military Truck Compound) (GOV) 12/42.
759: German Military Authorities (Fortress Engineer Staff) (GOV) 11/42.
784: German Military Authorities (Military Truck Compound) (GOV) 12/42.
848: German Military Authorities (Garrison Commander) (GOV) 9/42.
864: German Military Authorities (Fortress Engineer Staff) (GOV) 12/42.
879: German Military Authorities (Garrison Commander) (GOV) 8/42.
931: German Military Authorities (Fortress Engineer Staff) (GOV) 11/42.
937: German Military Authorities (Military Truck Compound) (GOV) 12/42.
1088: German Military Authorities (LPA Paris) (GOV) 9/42.
1127: States of Guernsey Civil Transport Service, St Peter Port (GOV) 2/43.
1322: German Military Authorities (Organization Todt) (GOV) 7/42.
1398: Returned to Guernsey Railway Co Ltd 2 by3/44.

1473: Guernsey Railway Co Ltd, St Peter Port (CI/) 24 by3/44.
1737: Returned to Watson Bros {The Greys}, St Martin (CI) 1942.
1765: German Military Authorities (Fortress Engineer Staff) (GOV) 7/42.
1845: German Military Authorities (Military Truck Compound) (GOV) 12/42.
1846: German Military Authorities (Air Force Construction Staff) (GOV) 8/42.
1940: German Military Authorities (Military Truck Compound) (GOV) 3/43.
2377: German Military Authorities (Fortress Engineer Staff) (GOV) 11/42.
2714: German Military Authorities (Fortress Engineer Staff) (GOV) 7/42.
2719: AP Delaney, Castel (GOV) 10/42.
2783: German Military Authorities (Military Truck Compound) (GOV) 12/42.
2787: Returned to EA Stead {La Rapide}, St Peter Port (CI) at an unknown date.
2792: German Military Authoritied (Fortress Engineer Staff) (GOV) 7/42.
2793: German Military Authorities (Military Truck Compound) (GOV) 12/42.
2799: German Military Authorities (Military Truck Compound) (GOV) 12/42.
2972 [1] (ex EY 3586?): German Military Authorities (Air Force Local Command) (GOV) 9/42.
2982: German Military Authorities (Fortress Engineer Staff) (GOV) 7/42.
2985: German Military Authorities (Military Truck Compound) (GOV) 11/42.
2987: German Military Authorities (Military Truck Compound) (GOV) 12/42.
3013: German Military Authorities (LPA Paris) (GOV) 9/42.
3135: German Military Authorities (Fortress Engineer Staff) (GOV) 3/43.
3193: German Military Authorities (Military Truck Compound) (GOV) 12/42.
3216: German Military Authorities (Fortress Engineer Staff) (GOV) 12/42.
3405: German Military Authorities (Fortress Engineer Staff) (GOV) 11/42.
3409: Returned to Watson Bros {The Greys}, St Martin (CI) by3/44.
3450 (ex 2791): States of Guernsey Civil Transport Service, St Peter Port (GOV).
3625: German Military Authorities (Garrison Commander) (GOV) 10/42.
3641: German Military Authorities (Military Truck Compound) (GOV) 12/42.
3688: German Military Authorities (Fortress Engineer Staff) (GOV) 11/42.
3774: German Military Authorities (Garrison Commander) (GOV) 11/42.
3810: German Military Authorities (Fortress Engineer Staff) (GOV) 12/42.
4222 (ex ED 5838): German Military Authorities (Military Truck Compound) (GOV) 12/42.
4444 (ex VO 4935): German Military Authorities (Fortress Engineer Staff) (GOV) 12/42.
4684 (ex IB 4689): AP Delaney, Castel (GOV) 10/42.

AP DELANEY   Cobo Stores, CASTEL

465	Packard E	?	Guernsey Motors	B29F	-/--	10/42	by8/44
612	Packard E	?	Guernsey Motors	B29F	-/--	10/42	by8/44
624	Vulcan Duchess	D150	Vulcan	B29F	6/36	10/42	by8/44
2719	Reo Sprinter	FAX1430	Heaver	B25F	10/29	10/42	by8/44
3901 [1]	Reo (Speed Wagon?)	TDX20285	Heaver	B29F	6/34	10/42	by8/44
4684	Vulcan Duchess	D48	Vulcan	B27F	10/30	10/42	by8/44
2793	Vulcan Duke	3XS64	Metcalfe	B19F	3/30	-/--	by8/44

Previous operators:
465: German Military Authorities (Military Truck Compound) (GOV).
612: German Military Authorities (Military Truck Compound) (GOV).
624: States of Guernsey Military Transport Service, St Peter Port (GOV).
2719: States of Guernsey Military Transport Service, St Peter Port (GOV).
2793: German Military Authorities (Military Truck Compound) (GOV).
3901 [1]: Guernsey Motors Ltd, St Peter Port (CI) 46.
4684: States of Guernsey Military Transport Service, St Peter Port (GOV).

Notes:
465: Re-registered 295 [1] 10/42.
612: Re-registered 372 [1] 10/42.
2793: Re-registered 266 at an unknown date.
3901 [1]: Fitted with a Silver Crown engine.
4784: Was originally registered IB 4689.

Initial disposals:
266 (ex 2793): Returned to Guernsey Motors Ltd 57 by8/44.
295 [1] (ex 465): Returned to Guernsey Motors Ltd 5 by8/44.
372 [1] (ex 612): Returned to Guernsey Motors Ltd 24 by8/44.
624: Returned to Guernsey Motors Ltd 9 by8/44.

2719: Returned to Guernsey Motors Ltd 44 by8/44.
3901 [1]: Returned to Guernsey Motors Ltd 46 by8/44.
4684 (ex IB 4689): Returned to Guernsey Motors Ltd 1 by8/44.

FORTRESS ENGINEER STAFF   FELDPOST 07691

630	Vulcan Duchess	D151	Vulcan		B29F	7/36	7/42	-/--
1765	Reo Sprinter	FAX10234	Heaver		B24F	4/29	7/42	-/--
2714	Reo Sprinter	FAA11138	Heaver		B25F	10/29	7/42	-/--
2982	Vulcan Duchess	D51	Vulcan		B26F	5/31	7/42	-/--
118	Vulcan Duchess	D87	Guernsey Railway		B29F	5/34	11/42	-/--
759	Vulcan RF	RF319	Guernsey Railway		B35F	-/35	11/42	-/--
931	Vulcan Duchess	D59	Guernsey Railway		B29F	4/33	11/42	-/--
3193	Dodge	8343439	Guernsey Railway		B26F	2/32	11/42	-/--
3405	Vulcan Duchess	D62	Guernsey Railway		B29F	5/33	11/42	-/--
3688	Vulcan Duchess	D86	Guernsey Railway		B29F	12/33	11/42	-/--
864	Leyland KP3	4143	Heaver	9731	FB35F	6/35	12/42	-/--
2792	Vulcan Duke	3XS62	Metcalfe		B19F	2/30	12/42	-/--
3216	Commer 6TK/1	28322	Strachan		B29F	7/32	12/42	-/--
3810	Leyland KP3	2775	Strachan		B29F	6/34	12/42	-/--
4444	Vulcan Duchess	D55	Guernsey Motors		B29F	12/30	12/42	-/--
3135	Vulcan Duchess	?	Strachan		B27F	1/32	3/43	-/--

Previous operators:
118: States of Guernsey Military Transport Service, St Peter Port (GOV).
630: States of Guernsey Military Transport Service, St Peter Port (GOV).
759: States of Guernsey Military Transport Services, St Peter Port (GOV).
864: States of Guernsey Military Transport Service, St Peter Port (GOV)
931: States of Guernsey Military Transport Service, St Peter Port (GOV).
1765: States of Guernsey Military Transport Service, St Peter Port (GOV).
2714: States of Guernsey Military Transport Service, St Peter Port (GOV).
2792: States of Guernsey Military Transport Service, St Peter Port (GOV).
2982: States of Guernsey Military Transport Service, St Peter Port (GOV).
3135: States of Germany Military Transport Service, St Peter Port (GOV).
3193: States of Guernsey Military Transport Service, St Peter Port (GOV).
3216: States of Guernsey Civil Transport Service, St Peter Port (GOV).
3405: States of Guernsey Military Transport Service, St Peter Port (GOV).
3688: States of Guernsey Military Transport Service, St Peter Port (GOV).
3810: States of Guernsey Military Transport Services, St Peter Port (GOV).
4444: States of Guernsey Military Transport Service, St Peter Port (GOV).

Notes:
2714: Fitted with a Silver Crown engine.
4444: Was previously registered VO 4935.

Initial disposals:
Unless otherwise stated, vehicles were scrapped locally or in France at unknown dates.

118: Returned to Guernsey Railway Co Ltd at an unknown date.
864: Returned HC Collenette {Paragon}, St Sampson (CI) 2 at an unknown date.
931: Returned to Guernsey Railway Co Ltd at an unknown date.
2714: Returned to Guernsey Motors Ltd 48 at an unknown date.
2982: Returned to Guernsey Motors Ltd 19 at an unknown date.
3216: Returned HC Collenette {Paragon}, St Sampson (CI) 1 at an unknown date.
3688: Returned to Guernsey Railway Co Ltd at an unknown date.
3810: Returned to HC Collenette {Paragon}, St Sampson (CI) 6 at an unknown date.
4444 (ex VO 4935): Returned to Guernsey Motors Ltd 16 at an unknown date.

AIR FORCE CONSTRUCTION STAFF   FELDPOST L36047

1846	Vulcan Duchess	D152	Vulcan	B29F	6/36	8/42	-/--

Previous operator:
1846: States of Guernsey Military Transport Service, St Peter Port (GOV).

Initial disposal:
1846: Returned to Guernsey Motors Ltd 10 at an unknown date.

AIR FORCE LOCAL COMMAND   FELDPOST L43025

558	Vulcan Duchess	D125	Vulcan	B29F	8/35	8/42	-/--
2972 [1]	Vulcan Duke	(3XS)44	Vulcan	B26F	5/29?	9/42	11/42

Previous operators:
558: States of Guernsey Military Transport Service, St Peter Port (GOV).
2972 [1]: States of Guernsey Military Transport Service, St Peter Port (GOV).

Notes:
2972 [1]: Was possibly originally registered EY 3586.

Initial disposals:
Unless otherwise stated, vehicles were scrapped locally or in France at unknown dates.

2972 [1] (ex EY 3586?): German Military Authorities (Military Truck Compound) (GOV) 11/42.

LPA PARIS   FELDPOST L08901

1088	Packard E	?	Baico	COB25F	-/--	9/42	12/42
3013	Dodge LER	D226722	Strachan	B27F	6/31	9/42	12/42

Previous operators:
1088: States of Guernsey Military Transport Service, St Peter Port (GOV).
3013: States of Guernsey Military Transport Service, St Peter Port (GOV).

Initial disposals:
1088: German Military Authorities (Military Truck Compound) (GOV) 12/42.
3013: German Military Authorities (Military Truck Compound) (GOV) 12/42.

GARRISON COMMANDER   FELDPOST 47098

722	Bedford WTB	18200	Thurgood	724	C20F	6/39	8/42	-/--
879	Dennis Falcon	280033	Dennis		B34C	3/40	8/42	6/45
848	Dennis Falcon	280032	Dennis		B34C	3/40	9/42	-/--
3625	Vulcan Duchess	D135?	Strachan		B29F	12/33	10/42	-/--
3774	Dennis Falcon	280007	Dennis		B34C	4/39	11/42	-/--

Previous operators:
722: States of Guernsey Military Transport Service, St Peter Port (GOV).
848: States of Guernsey Military Transport Services, St Peter Port (GOV).
879: States of Guernsey Military Transport Services, St Peter Port (GOV).
3625: States of Germany Military Transport Service, St Peter Port (GOV).
3774: States of Guernsey Military Transport Services, St Peter Port (GOV).

Notes:
879: Was used as a military band coach
3625: Its chassis number is also recorded as D85.

Disposals:
Unless otherwise stated, vehicles were scrapped locally or in France at unknown dates.

722: Returned to Guernsey Motors Ltd 41 at an unknown date.
879: Returned to Guernsey Railway Co Ltd 11 6/45.

ORGANIZATION TODT   FELDPOST 41639

1322	Morris CS.2.13/80	1009C30753	Guernsey Railway	B33F	7/37	7/42	-/--

Previous operator:
1322: States of Guernsey Military Transport Service, St Peter Port (GOV).

Disposal:
1322: Scrapped locally at an unknown date (or sent to France for scrapping).

MILITARY TRUCK COMPOUND   FELDPOST 35346

No.	Make	Chassis	Body builder		Body			
465	Packard E	?	Guernsey Motors		B29F	-/--	4/41	10/42
99	Dodge LER	D217768	?		FB30F	-/30	5/41	-/--
1596	Dodge RBF	505	Strachan		FB32F	8/36	5/41	-/--
2501	Dodge LER	?	FT Bennett		OB20F	6/29	9/42	-/--
48 [2]	Maxwell 30 cwt	?	?		Ch18	6/23	10/42	-/--
313	Maxwell 25 cwt	?	Guernsey Motors		T14	-/--	10/42	-/--
400	Packard E	?	Baico		COB23F	-/--	10/42	-/--
413	Packard E	?	Guernsey Motors		Ch27	-/--	10/42	-/--
441	Berliet	?	(chassis only)			-/28	10/42	-/--
507	Reo 25 hp	?	?		OB25F	-/--	10/42	-/--
612	Packard E	?	Guernsey Motors		B29F	-/--	by10/42	10/42
658	Maxwell 25 cwt	?	?		B18F	-/--	10/42	-/--
659 [2]	Guy 25 hp	?	Baico		OB25F	7/23	10/42	-/--
742	Packard E	?	Baico		COB23F	-/--	10/42	-/--
745	Packard E	?	Baico		COB23F	-/--	10/42	-/--
753	Packard E	?	Guernsey Motors		Ch23	-/--	10/42	-/--
885	Vulcan 30 cwt	?	?		Ch19	-/24	10/42	-/--
987	Vulcan 3 ton	?	?		Ch28	-/24	10/42	-/--
1016	Vulcan Duchess	D12-	Vulcan		B29F	8/35	10/42	-/--
1073	Dodge LB	?	FT Bennett		OB18F	8/25	10/42	-/--
1151	Maxwell 25 cwt	?	?		B16F	-/--	10/42	-/--
1389	Ford AA	4488900			B21F	7/31	10/42	-/--
			Underhill / Guernsey Railway					
1419	Reo Speed Wagon F	110536	Heaver		OB20D	3/26	10/42	-/--
1601	GMC	?	FT Bennett		OB23F	-/--	10/42	-/--
1613	Bedford WLB	108403	Duple	2854	C22F	-/32	10/42	-/--
2220	Vulcan Duke	3XS06	Spicer		Ch19	11/27	10/42	-/--
2341	Commer 6TK/1	?	Heaver		B28F	-/33	10/42	-/--
2536	Packard E	?	Baico		COB25F	-/--	10/42	-/--
3410	Bedford WHB	?	?		C14F	-/35	10/42	-/--
176	Overland	?	Guernsey Motors		B14F	-/--	11/42	-/--
348	Maxwell	?	?		Ch14	-/--	11/42	-/--
434	Reo Speed Wagon	?	?		OB25F	-/--	11/42	-/--
651	Chevrolet	?	?		B18F	-/--	11/42	-/--
744	Maxwell 30 cwt	?	Guernsey Motors		T14	-/22	11/42	-/--
1027	Packard E	?	Baico		COB25F	-/--	11/42	-/--
1963	Reo	?	?		B20F	-/--	11/42	-/--
2047	Reo Sprinter LWB	FAX579	Bence		B24F	3/28	11/42	-/--
2377	Bean Model 11	1573/11W	Willowbrook	2214	B20F	8/28	11/42	-/--
2972 [1]	Vulcan Duke	(3XS)44	Vulcan		B26F	5/29?	11/42	-/--
2985	Vulcan Duchess	D52	Vulcan		B26F	4/31	11/42	-/--
448	Packard E	?	?		B29F	-/--	12/42	-/--
597	Bean Model 11	2069/11W	Willowbrook	2215	B20F	9/29	12/42	-/--
737	Packard E	?	Guernsey Motors		B29F	-/--	12/42	-/--
784	Packard E	?	Guernsey Motors		B29F	-/--	12/42	-/--
937	Packard E	?	Guernsey Motors		B29F	-/--	12/42	-/--
1088	Packard E	?	Baico		COB25F	-/--	12/42	-/--
1845	Dodge LER	D225913	Strachan		B22F	-/30	12/42	-/--
1957	Packard E	?	Baico		COB25F	-/--	12/42	-/--
2317	Reo Sprinter	FAX5789	?		B22F	-/28	12/42	-/--
2783	Vulcan Duke	3XS68	Metcalfe		B19F	1/30	12/42	-/--
2793	Vulcan Duke	3XS64	Metcalfe		B19F	3/30	12/42	-/--
2799	Bean Model 11	1223/11W	Willowbrook	2408	B20F	1/30	12/42	-/--
2987	Vulcan Duchess	D53	Vulcan		B26F	4/31	12/42	-/--
3013	Dodge LER	D226722	Strachan		B27F	6/31	12/42	-/--
3641	Packard E	?	Guernsey Motors		B29F	-/--	12/42	-/--
4222	Vulcan Duchess	D41	?		B24R	3/30	12/42	-/--
2070	Chevrolet 18 hp	?	?		C12F	-/26	2/43	-/--
3120	Reo C	?	FT Bennett		B26F	-/32	2/43	-/--
1940	Ford A	3735545	?		B18F	4/32	3/43	-/--

Previous operators:
   48: Guernsey Motors Ltd, St Peter Port (CI) 63.
   99: HC Collenette {Paragon}, St Sampson (CI) 7.
   176: Guernsey Motors Ltd, St Peter Port (CI) 65.
   313: Guernsey Motors Ltd, St Peter Port (CI) 32.
   348: Guernsey Motors Ltd, St Peter Port (CI) 45.
   400: Guernsey Motors Ltd, St Peter Port (CI) 40.
   413: Guernsey Motors Ltd, St Peter Port (CI) 21.
   434: Guernsey Motors Ltd, St Peter Port (CI) 49.
   441: Guernsey Railway Co Ltd, St Peter Port (CI) 21.
   448: States of Guernsey Military Transport Service, St Peter Port (GOV).
   465: States of Guernsey Military Transport Service, St Peter Port (GOV).
   507: Guernsey Motors Ltd, St Peter Port (CI) 49.
   597: States of Guernsey Military Transport Service, St Peter Port (GOV).
   612: States of Guernsey Military Transport Service, St Peter Port (GOV).
   651: JW Stacey, St Peter Port (CI).
   658: Guernsey Motors Ltd, St Peter Port (CI) 33.
   659 [2]: Guernsey Motors Ltd, St Peter Port (CI) 34.
   737: States of Guernsey Military Transport Service, St Peter Port (GOV).
   742: Guernsey Motors Ltd, St Peter Port (CI) 39.
   744: Guernsey Motors Ltd, St Peter Port (CI) 43.
   745: Guernsey Motors Ltd, St Peter Port (CI) 36.
   753: Guernsey Motors Ltd, St Peter Port (CI) 8.
   784: States of Guernsey Military Transport Service, St Peter Port (GOV).
   885: Guernsey Motors Ltd, St Peter Port (CI) 60.
   937: States of Guernsey Military Transport Service, St Peter Port (GOV).
   987: Guernsey Motors Ltd, St Peter Port (CI) 61.
   1016: Guernsey Motors Ltd, St Peter Port (CI) 14.
   1027: Guernsey Motors Ltd, St Peter Port (CI) 22.
   1073: Guernsey Motors Ltd, St Peter Port (CI) 62.
   1088: German Military Authorities (LPA Paris) (GOV).
   1151: Guernsey Motors Ltd, St Peter Port (CI) 31.
   1389: Guernsey Railway Co Ltd, St Peter Port (CI) 4.
   1419: Guernsey Motors Ltd, St Peter Port (CI).
   1596: HC Collenette {Paragon}, St Sampson (CI) 4.
   1601: Guernsey Motors Ltd, St Peter Port (CI) 7.
   1613: JW Way, St Peter Port (CI).
   1845: States of Guernsey Military Transport Services, St Peter Port (GOV).
   1940: States of Guernsey Military Transport Service, St Peter Port (GOV).
   1957: Guernsey Motors Ltd, St Peter Port (CI) 52.
   1963: JW Stacey, St Peter Port (CI).
   2047: JW Stacey, St Peter Port (CI).
   2070: A Windsor, St Peter Port (CI).
   2220: UU Ash, St Peter Port (CI).
   2317: Mrs SE Watson {The Greys}, St Martin (CI).
   2341: HN & HK Falla {Blue Bird}, Vale (CI) 3.
   2377: States of Guernsey Military Transport Service, St Peter Port (GOV).
   2501: E Stead {La Rapide}, St Peter Port (CI (4?).
   2536: Guernsey Motors Ltd, St Peter Port (CI) 3.
   2783: States of Guernsey Military Transport Service, St Peter Port (GOV).
   2793: States of Guernsey Military Transport Service, St Peter Port (GOV).
   2799: States of Guernsey Military Transport Service, St Peter Port (GOV).
   2972 [1]: German Military Authorities (Air Force Local Command) (GOV).
   2985: States of Guernsey Military Transport Service, St Peter Port (GOV).
   2987: States of Guernsey Military Transport Service, St Peter Port (GOV).
   3013: German Military Authorities (LPA Paris) (GOV).
   3120: Mrs SE Watson {The Greys}, St Martin (CI).
   3410: Old Government House Hotel, St Peter Port (CI).
   3641: States of Guernsey Military Transport Service, St Peter Port (GOV).
   4222: States of Guernsey Military Transport Service, St Peter Port (GOV).

Notes:

The 1921 Baico OB25F bodies from Guernsey Motors Ltd 25-26 were probably impressed 12/42 (the Packard E chassis (registrations unknown) that these were fitted to were scrapped 1940. The remains of Guernsey Motors Ltd 2251 (46) (International) which was scrapped 3/39 were acquired (for scrap metal) 12/42.

99: Was originally registered in the UK.
2220: Was originally registered WM 1405.
2972 [1]: Was possibly originally registered EY 3586.
4222: Was originally registered ED 5838.

Initial disposals:

Unless otherwise stated, vehicles were scrapped locally or in France at unknown dates.

465: AP Delaney, Castel (CI) 10/42.
612: AP Delaney, Castel (CI) 10/42.
2793: AP Delaney, Castel (GOV) at an unknown date.

ALDERNEY

Alderney is the smallest of the Channel Islands with conventional motor transport covering an area of about 3 square miles and with a population of about 2,000. It has one parish – St Anne – which covers the whole of the island. It was unique amongst the islands in that it was entirely evacuated on 23 June 1940 at the time of the German invasion, who remained there until 16 May 1945. By then, everything had been damaged or destroyed on the island which had been turned into a fortress. With the assistance of the UK, the island was restored and the inhabitants started to return in December 1945.

The States of Alderney headed by a President, is the legislature of the island although some matters since the War have been devolved to the States of Guernsey.

Alderney also operates the only surviving railway in the Channel Islands, opened in 1847 and operated by the Admiralty. It runs from Braye Harbour to the quarry at Mannez. In the mid-1970s, discussions were held to investigate the potential for carrying passengers and these came to fruition in 1980. Since 1987, the carriages have been former London Underground tube cars, hauled by steam locomotives. Alderney also has an airport (with flights to Guernsey and Southampton).

The major bus operator has been Riduna Buses (Riduna being the island's Latin name). It was opened in 1947 and operated for 70 years under a succession of owners, only ceasing in 2017 following the ill-health of its last owner. Other than that, there are only two operators of minibus surviving at present:

> A1 Taxis
> Alderney Taxis

Alderney's vehicle registrations are prefixed 'AY' and numbers constantly reused (indeed Riduna Buses AY 59 has been recorded on 17 different PSVs).

A1 TAXIS   **Westways, Allee es Fees, ALDERNEY**

AY	97 [1]	Ford Transit	Devcoplan	?	B16FL	2/98	by12/12	by6/14
		WF0AXXBDVATE02317						
AY	2139	Citroen Relay	AVB		M11	11/05	3/14	#
		VF7ZAAMFA17689914						
AY	97 [2]	Ford Transit	Devcoplan	2100.2	B14FL	2/98	by6/14	#
		WF0AXXBDVATE02316						
AY	1658	FIAT Ducato	FIAT		M16	10/10	1/15	#
		ZFA25000001780047						

Vehicles marked # were still in service at the date of this Fleet History.

Previous histories:
> AY   97 [1]: New to Wakefield Metropolian District Council (XWY) 3045 registered R 45 JUB (as B12FL); Somerset Transport Services Ltd, Paulton (SO) 9/04 (as (DP16FL); SK & DH Young {CT Coaches}, Radstock (SO) 6/08; Somerset Transport Services Ltd, Paulton (SO) 9/08; withdrawn by7/11.
> AY   97 [2]: New to Wakefield Metropolian District Council (XWY) 3043 registered R 43 JUB (as B12FL); Heaton's Motor Co, Abram (dealer) 3/05; SK & DH Young {CT Coaches}, Radstock (SO) by4/04 (as B11FL); reseated to B8FL by7/05; withdrawn by10/13.
> AY   1658: New to 1st Call Auto Rentals, Gloucester (XGL) registered VX 60 CPE.
> AY   2139: New to Beverley Community Lift (XEY) registered YY 55 KNV and named 'Bluebell'.

Notes:
> A Citroen Relay registered AY 1919 may also be operated, by no other details are known.

ABC TAXIS   **Les Jumelles, Longis Road, ALDERNEY**

ALDERNEY TOURS (by5/12)

AY	59 [15]	Peugeot Boxer	Crystals		1156	M15	3/95	9/07	1/08
		VF3233J5215063495							
AY	1495	Peugeot Boxer	?	Excel		M15	-/--	by5/12	#

Vehicles marked # were still in service at the date of this Fleet History.

Previous histories:

AY   59 [15]: New to CJ Springham, Dartford (KT) as a non-PSV registered M388 SPY (as M11L); Crystals Coaches Ltd, London SW10 (LN) 3/98; re-registered CSU 906 by1/04; re-registered M388 SPY 4/04; AJ Curtis {Riduna Buses}, Alderney (CI) 10/04.

AY 1495: Its origins are unknown.

Disposal:

AY   59 [15] (ex M388 SPY, CSU 906, M388 SPY): Unidentified UK dealer 1/08; unidentified owners 6/09 and 3/13.

JA BLIGH   Bligh's Hotel, Les Butes, ALDERNEY

AY 446	Commer 1500LB	?	?	M11	-/--	-/--	-/--

Notes:

AY 446: No further information is known about this vehicle other than it was operated during the 1960s.

'BLUE BIRD'

A charabanc known as the 'Blue Bird' was operated during the 1920s. No other details are known of either operator or vehicle.

BRITISH EUROPEAN AIRWAYS CORPORATION   ALDERNEY Airport

BEA provided a bus service to the airport from April 1947 to March 1956.

	?	Ford	?	?		?	-/--	4/47	4/49
2008	AY 169	Bedford KZ	94785	Spurling		B11D	1/49	4/49	3/56

Previous histories:

Unidentified Ford: Its origins are unknown.

AY   169: New to British European Airways Corporation, Heathrow (LN) 2020 as a non-PSV crew-car registered TMY 42.

Disposals:

Unidentified Ford: No known disposal.

AY 169 (ex TMY 42) (2008): Unidentified (local) dealer / operator 6/56.

CHANNEL ISLANDS AIRWAYS   ALDERNEY Airport

A 6-wheel Steyr was operated from June 1945 to March 1947 prior to BEA taking over the service. No other details are known.

CG CHARLIER

AY 2246 [1]	Ford Transit	BDVZMD60750	Ford	M12	-/--	11/91	by4/94
AY 2246 [2]	Renault Master	10284137	Walsall Motor Bodies	M16	4/94	4/94	by12/95

Previous history:

AY 2246 [1]: Its origins are unknown.

Disposal:

AY 2246 [1]: No known disposal.

AY 2246 [2]: Blue Coach Tours Ltd, St Helier (CI) 16 re-registered J 12633 3/96; Tantivy Blue Coach Tours Ltd, St Helier (CI) 108 11/96; scrapped 1/04.

DW CLUNN   Melford House, Le Banquage, ALDERNEY

AY 38	Toyota Hiace	RH320021752	Toyota	M8	12/83	-/86	-/--

Previous history:

AY 38: New to J Le Huray {New Windsor Private Hotel}, St Peter Port (CI) registered 5407.

Disposal:

AY 38: No known disposal.

W ERRINGTON {Victoria Hotel / Taxi & Leisure}   Victoria Street, ALDERNEY

AY	414	Austin J2BA	6786	BMC		M12	-/--	c-/65	-/--
AY	1878	Ford Transit	BDVZ??544952	Ford		M14	-/--	-/84	-/85
AY	1858	Bedford J2SZ10	DW112856	Caetano	75/24	C20F	6/75	10/84	10/85

Previous histories:
AY   414: Its origins are unknown.
AY 1858: New to Ben Stanley Ltd, Hersham (SR) registered JPC 547N; H Luckett & Co Ltd, Wallington (HA)
2/78; Educational Holidays Guernsey Ltd {Island Coachways}, St Peter Port (CI) 2 re-registered
8228 [3] 6/83.
AY 1878: Its origins are unknown.

Disposals:
AY   414: No known disposal.
AY 1858: J Main {Riduna Buses}, Alderney (CI) 3/86; unidentified dealer / operator, Torquay c1988.
AY 1878: No known disposal.

S GAUDION   Victoria Street, St Anne, ALDERNEY
Gaudion was a charabanc operator from 1923 to 1935, but no details of vehicles operated are known.

GRAND HOTEL   Les Butes, ALDERNEY

AY	218	Volkswagen	? ?	?	-/--	-/--	-/--

Notes:
AY   218: No further information is known about this vehicle.

AJ LANGLOIS {Riduna Bus Service}   Newtown, ALDERNEY

AY	14	Chevrolet 30 cwt	? ?	C18F	5/31	5/31	12/34
AY	34	Chevrolet 30 cwt	? ?	B18F	5/31	5/31	12/34

Disposals:
AY   14: WJ Simon, Alderney (CI) 12/34.
AY   34: WJ Simon, Alderney (CI) 12/34.

MIKE'S TAXI   Victoria Street, ALDERNEY

AY	1772 [1]	Freight Rover	SAZZKPST7BN513102	Freight Rover	M11	2/86	2/86	2/89
AY	1041	Ford Transit	BDVZCG54852	Ford	M11	-/82	-/88	-/90
AY	1772 [2]	Peugeot-Talbot	SDB280A1100523760	Peugeot-Talbot	M11	2/89	2/89	3/91
AY	1774	Renault Trafic	00741945	Holdsworth	M11	-/--	3/90	3/91

Previous histories:
AY 1041: New to an unidentified Jersey non-PSV operator; unidentified Guernsey non-PSV operator
registered 16638 at an unknown date.
AY 1774: New to an unidentified Jersey non-PSV operator registered J 61552; unidentified Guernsey non-
PSV operator registered 44492 at an unknown date.

Disposals:
AY 1041 (ex 16638, -?-): No known disposal.
AY 1772 [1]: Talbot, Guernsey (XCI) 1989.
AY 1772 [2]: Unidentified Guernsey non-PSV operator 3/91.
AY 1774 (ex 44492, J 61552): Unidentified Guernsey non-PSV operator registered 60310 3/91.

J NEWTON {The Bonnie}   Victoria Street, ALDERNEY

Ford TT		?	Underhill?	?	-/--	8/23	-/--
Ford TT		?	F Mallett	OB22F	4/25	-/31	-/--
Reo Speed Wagon		?	FT Bennett	OB22F	5/26	-/31	-/--

Previous histories:
First Ford: The identity of this vehicle is unknown. It was supplied by Bougourd Bros, St Peter Port (dealer), but J Newton was probably its first operator.
Second Ford: Possibly new to VA Mallett {Blue Bird}, St Sampson (CI) 2 registered 1480; HN & HK Falla {Blue Bird}, Vale (CI) 2 11/25.
Reo: Possibly new to HN & HK Falla {Blue Bird}, Vale (CI) 4 registered 1319.

Disposals:
First Ford (ex -?-): No known disposal.
Second Ford (ex 1480): No known disposal.
Reo (ex 1319): No known disposal.

RIDUNA BUSES

WP SIMON {Riduna Buses}   5 High Street & Mare Jean Bott, ALDERNEY
                                           Newtown, ALDERNEY (-/--)
J MAIN {Riduna Buses} (5/85)   Braye Street, Braye, ALDERNEY
ND MACDONALD {Riduna Buses} (6/93)   6a Clos des Mouriaux, ALDERNEY
AJ CURTIS {Riduna Buses} (1/96)   Victoria Street, ALDERNEY
                                           High Street, ALDERNEY (by-/98)
                                           Westways, Allee es Fees, ALDERNEY (-/--)

Reg		Chassis	Chassis no	Body	Body no	Type	Date	In	Out
AY	59 [1]	Dennis GL	70631	Willmott		B26F	1/35	9/47	-/51
AY	129 [1]	Bean Model 14	1051/14W	Willowbrook		B26F	1/30	4/48	-/49
AY	101 [1]	Dodge	HLW628	WJ Rugg		B25F	3/34	-/49	-/51
AY	129 [2]	Dodge PLB	1038	Guernsey Railway		B29F	8/35	1/50	-/54
AY	101 [2]	Bedford WTB	18200	Thurgood	724	C20F	6/39	4/54	by2/60
AY	59 [2]	Bedford OB	40851	Mulliner		B33F	1/47	2/55	12/56
AY	59 [3]	Bedford OB	40830	Mulliner		B33F	1/47	1/56	12/57
AY	59 [4]	Bedford OB	23382	Mulliner		B33F	5/46	10/58	-/60
AY	59 [5]	Bedford OB	73174	Mulliner	SP214	B33F	6/48	2/60	-/61
AY	101 [3]	Bedford OB	76145	Mulliner	SP213	B33F	6/48	2/60	-/62
AY	59 [6]	Bedford OB	72585	Mulliner	SP210	B33F	5/48	3/62	-/63
AY	59 [7]	Bedford OB	73023	Mulliner	SP212	B33F	4/48	-/63	by2/64
AY	101 [4]	AEC Regal III	9621A328	Duple	45345	C32F	5/49	-/62	-/67
AY	59 [8]	Bedford OB	108594	Mulliner	T384	B28F	7/49	2/64	-/65
J	20096	Austin K4/CXB	133328	Mann Egerton		FC31F	5/49	6/65	-/66
AY	81 [1]	AEC Regal IV	9822S1558	Weymann	M5592	B44F	11/52	7/66	9/80
AY	59 [9]	AEC Reliance	MU3RV1158	Weymann	M7474	C41F	4/56	4/67	12/73
AY	666	Ford 400E	BC58EMG37417	Ford		M12	-/--	6/68	by-/79
AY	750 [1]	Leyland PSUC1/1	524411	Saunders-Roe	1452	B44F	1/53	4/69	c-/80
AY	91 [1]	AEC Reliance	MU3RV1226	Weymann	M7681	DP44F	3/57	6/71	c-/82
AY	59 [10]	Leyland PSUC1/1	596365	MCCW		B45F	7/60	2/74	c-/82
XAE	329	Leyland PSUC1/2	565252	Duple	1070/8	C41C	7/56	by5/74	----
AY	305 [1]	AEC Reliance	2MU4RA4906	Harrington	2830	C41F	3/64	4/80	-/86
AY	750 [2]	AEC Reliance	2MU4RA5075	Harrington	2962	C41F	5/64	4/80	11/87
AY	59 [11]	AEC Reliance	6MU4R7455	Willowbrook	69426	DP49F	5/71	-/82	-/84
AY	91 [2]	AEC Reliance	6MU4R7453	Willowbrook	69424	DP49F	5/71	-/82	-/84
AY	58 [2]	AEC Reliance	2MU4RA4905	Harrington	2829	C41F	3/64	1/84	c-/88
AY	91 [3]	AEC Reliance	2MU4RA4908	Harrington	2832	C41F	3/64	1/84	-/86
AY	1858	Bedford J2SZ10	DW112856	Caetano	75/24	C20F	6/75	3/86	-/88
AY	2153	Ford Transit	BDVZCJ29015	Ford		M14	-/--	1/88	c6/93
AY	91 [4]	Bedford SB3	CW451648	Duple	264/1854	C41F	4/73	4/88	by9/01
AY	305 [2]	Bedford VAS2	0T481354	Duple	215/31	C29F	-/70	4/88	by10/01
AY	586 [2]	Bedford SB3	1T485646	Duple	232/49	C41F	5/71	4/88	1/96
AY	750 [3]	Bedford SB3	CW451719	Duple	264/1856	C41F	5/73	4/88	by11/01
AY	59 [12]	Freight Rover Sherpa	AN276293	Wadham Stringer	1824	M15	6/87	6/93	by12/94
AY	593 [1]	Freight Rover Sherpa	AN276338	Wadham Stringer	1823	M15	6/87	6/93	by12/94
AY	81 [2]	Bedford YLQ	KW450567	Plaxton	8010QC006	C45F	2/80	by1/94	4/96
AY	593 [2]	Bedford J6L	CW119879	Pennine	1242	B35F	5/74	6/94	3/97
AY	59 [13]	Freight Rover Sherpa	238771	Freight Rover		M17	3/85	4/95	by9/01
AY	81 [3]	Albion FT39AN	73821D	Heaver		B35F	1/57	1/96	by8/12

AY									
AY	593 [3]	Leyland CU435	566466	Duple	137/5557	B31F	11/81	3/98	6/03
AY	1114 [1]	Dodge S56	209269	Mellor	022876	B20FL	5/92	5/99	12/03
AY	91 [6]	Bedford SB3	ET102376	Duple	8301/0098	C41F	3/84	11/01	3/06
AY	586 [3]	Bristol VRT/SL3/6LXB	3/267	ECW	20949	O43/27D	7/76	5/02	6/07
AY	59 [14]	Volkswagen LT31	?	Devon Conversions		M15	by12/89	by4/04	10/04
AY	593 [4]	Renault	?	Wadham Stringer		B29F	by2/89	by10/04	12/07
AY	1114 [2]	Renault S56 SDGB56A0GKD221320		Robin Hood	20371	B23FL	6/89	by10/04	10/07
AY	59 [15]	Peugeot Boxer VF3233J5215063495		Crystals	1156	M15	3/95	10/04	9/07
AY	91 [7]	Renault PP160.09 VF6JN1E2400015288		Wadham Stringer 4098/93		C37C	6/93	3/06	4/12
AY	59 [16]	Dennis Dart	9.8SDL3002/124	Carlyle	C25-020	B39F	5/90	1/08	by6/14
AY	586 [4]	Ford Transit SFAVXXBDVVME61503		Dormobile		C16F	7/93	by12/08	by9/14
AY	328	Optare MR17	VN2330	Optare		B31F	3/00	by12/09	by6/14
AY	593 [5]	Mercedes-Benz 609D WDB6680622N044508		Pilcher-Greene		C16FL	8/96	7/10	by9/17
AY	59 [17]	Dennis Dart	9SDL3034/1803	NCME	4693	B35F	4/94	by6/14	by9/17

Previous histories:

AY 58 [2]: New to Greenslades Tours Ltd, Exeter (DN) registered AFJ 79B; numbered 444 6/71; renumbered 285 1/75; RK & RE Webber, Blisland (CO) 1/76; LJ Hubber {Streamline Coaches}, Newquay (CO) 2/78; RK & RE Webber, Blisland (CO) 6/79; Educational Holidays Guernsey Ltd {Island Coachways}, St Peter Port (CI) 6 registered 6768 [2] 8/81; to service 10/81.

AY 59 [1]: New to AV Newton {Channel Island Hotel}, St Peter Port (CI) 3 registered 3777 (as C13F); withdrawn 11/45; Guernsey Railway Co Ltd, St Peter Port (CI) 12/45; body rebuilt to B26F by Guernsey Railway Co Ltd.

AY 59 [2]: New to Guernsey Railway Co Ltd, St Peter Port (CI) 23 registered 3087; withdrawn 9/54.

AY 59 [3]: New to Guernsey Railway Co Ltd, St Peter Port (CI) 25 registered 3088; withdrawn 9/55.

AY 59 [4]: New to Sarre Transport Ltd, St Peter-in-the-Wood (CI) 5 registered 1560 (as B32F); moved to St Peter Port (CI) at an unknown date; Guernsey Railway Co Ltd, St Peter Port (CI) 42 11/51; withdrawn 7/58.

AY 59 [5]: New to Guernsey Railway Co Ltd, St Peter Port (CI) 29 registered 5190 (as B31F); withdrawn 9/59.

AY 59 [6]: New to Sarre Transport Ltd, St Peter-in-the-Wood (CI) 16 registered 5183 (as B31F); moved to St Peter Port (CI) at an unknown date; Guernsey Railway Co Ltd, St Peter Port (CI) 49 11/51; reseated to B32F at an unknown date; withdrawn 9/61.

AY 59 [7]: New to Guernsey Railway Co Ltd, St Peter Port (CI) 20 registered 5188 (as B31F); withdrawn 9/61.

AY 59 [8]: New to Sarre Transport Ltd, St Peter-in-the-Wood (CI) 21 registered 4426; moved to St Peter Port (CI) at an unknown date; Guernsey Railway Co Ltd, St Peter Port (CI) 50 11/51; withdrawn 9/63.

AY 59 [9]: New to Birch Bros (Transport) Ltd, London NW5 (LN) K34 registered RYT 34; F Cowley, Salford (dealer) 5/66.

AY 59 [10]: New to East Midland Motor Services Ltd, Mansfield (NG) R381 registered 381 ENN; withdrawn 1972; F Cowley, Salford (dealer) 7/72.

AY 59 [11]: New to City of Oxford Motor Services Ltd (OX) 52 registered SWL 52J.

AY 59 [12]: New to Board of Health, Guernsey (XCI) registered 50562.

AY 59 [13]: New to Meon Cross School, Buckfastleigh (XDN) registered B 97 WOR.

AY 59 [14]: Its origins are unknown.

AY 59 [15]: New to Springham, Dartford (KT) as a non-PSV registered M388 SPY (as M11L); Crystals Coaches Ltd, London SW10 (LN) 3/98; re-registered CSU 906 by1/04; re-registered M388 SPY 4/04.

AY 59 [16]: New as a demonstration vehicle with Carlyle Group Ltd, Edgbaston registered G141 GOL (as B36F); loaned to Shearings Ltd, Wigan (GM) 127 5/90-6/91; loaned to Arrowline (Travel) Ltd, Knutsford (CH) 6/91-c8/91; Stevensons of Uttoxeter Ltd, Spath (ST) 41 2/92; reseated to B39F 3/92; reseated to B36F by9/94; Midland Red (North) Ltd, Cannock (ST) S307 5/96; renumbered 541 by8/97; renumbered 2061 6/03; withdrawn 1/06; DJ Wardle, Norton (ST) 11 2/06; re-registered RLZ 3218 3/06; loaned to D & G Coach & Bus Ltd, Adderley Green (ST) 4/07; unidentified dealer / operator 10/07; last licence expired 1/08.

AY   59 [17]: New to Kentish Bus & Coach Co Ltd, Dartford (KT) 156 registered L156 YVK; Maidstone &
District Motor Services Ltd, Maidstone (KT) 3156 8/97; Arriva Kent Thameside Ltd, Maidstone
(KT) 3156 1/99; Arriva Kent & Sussex Ltd, Maidstone (KT) 3156 7/07; Wealden PSV Sales Ltd,
Five Oak Green (dealer) 1/09; JD Judge, Corby (NO) 3/09; Wealden PSV Sales Ltd, Five Oak
Green (dealer) 3/09; last licence expired 4/10.

AY   81 [1]: New to Western Welsh Omnibus Co Ltd, Cardiff (GG) 540 registered GUH 540; withdrawn 9/65.

AY   81 [2]: New to Capital Coaches Ltd, Hayes (LN) registered GPA 623V; withdrawn 9/85; Parfitt's Motor
Services Ltd, Rhymney Bridge (MG) 3/86; Owen's Motors Ltd, Knighton (PS) 10/89; Spa
Coaches Ltd, Droitwich (HW) 6/92; P Anslow, Garndiffaith (GT) 9/92.

AY   81 [3]: New to Guernsey Railway Co Ltd, St Peter Port (CI) 60 registered 3338 [1]; renumbered 160
8/73; G Bailey, Castel for preservation 4/80; Dr JR Young, Nottingham (dealer / preservationist)
1/88; AJ Curtis, Midsomer Norton (AV) for preservation by7/90; re-registered YFF 660 4/95.

AY   91 [1]: New to Aldershot & District Traction Co Ltd (HA) 294 registered RCG 612 (as DP43F); withdrawn
12/68; F Cowley, Salford (dealer) 1/69.

AY   91 [2]: New to City of Oxford Motor Services Ltd (OX) 52 registered SWL 50J.

AY   91 [3]: New to Greenslades Tours Ltd, Exeter (DN) registered AFJ 82B; numbered 447 6/71;
renumbered 288 1/75; Midland Red Omnibus Co Ltd, Birmingham (dealer) 12/75; Paul Sykes
Organisation Ltd, Blackerhill (dealer) 1/76; Seymours Ltd {Mascot Motors}, St Helier (CI) 2 re-
registered J 16590 1/76; to service 6/76; moved to St Clement (CI) 3/78; W Simon {Riduna
Buses}, Alderney (CI), but diverted en-route to Educational Holidays Guernsey Ltd {Island
Coachways}, St Peter Port (CI) 8 12/80; re-registered 8228 [2] and to service 7/81.

AY   91 [4]: New to Tantivy Motors Ltd, St Helier (CI) 24 registered J 43803.

AY   91 [6]: New to Guiton Group Ltd {Blue Coach Tours}, St Helier (CI) 23 registered J 26626; Blue Coach
Tours Ltd, St Helier (CI) 23 7/84; Tantivy Blue Coach Tours Ltd, St Helier (CI) 44.

AY   91 [7]: New to London Borough of Greenwich (XLN) registered K903 PBP (as DP36C); unidentified
dealer / operator 4/05.

AY   101 [1]: New to WJ Rugg {Wayfarer}, St Sampson (CI) 6 registered 1633; impressed by States of
Guernsey Civil Transport Service, St Peter Port (GOV) 2/41; converted to gazogene propulsion
at an unknown date; returned to WJ Rugg 5/45; Sarre Transport Ltd, St Peter-in-the-Wood (CI)
6 4/46; SA Noel, St Peter Port (dealer) 5/49.

AY   101 [2]: New to Guernsey Motors Ltd, St Peter Port (CI) 41 registered 722; impressed by States of
Guernsey Military Transport Service, St Peter Port (GOV) 2/41; German Military Authorities
(Garrison Commander) (GOV) 8/42; returned to Guernsey Motors Ltd 41 at an unknown date.

AY   101 [3]: New to Guernsey Railway Co Ltd, St Peter Port (CI) 28 registered 5189 (as B31F); fitted with a
Perkins P6 oil engine 8/51-2/53; withdrawn 9/59.

AY   101 [4]: New to Devon General Omnibus & Touring Co Ltd, Exeter (DN) TCR621 registered JOD 621;
Western Welsh Omnibus Co Ltd, Cardiff (GG) 534 1/52; to service 3/53; Passenger Vehicle
Disposals Ltd, Dunchurch (dealer) 5/61.

AY   129 [1]: New to Guernsey Railway Co Ltd, St Peter Port (CI) 20 registered 2751; withdrawn 9/47.

AY   129 [2]: New to Guernsey Railway Co Ltd, St Peter Port (CI) 2 registered 1398 (as B25F); chassis
lengthened and reseated to B29F 2/38; impressed by States of Guernsey Military Transport
Services, St Peter Port (GOV) 7/41; returned to Guernsey Railway Co Ltd by3/44; withdrawn
9/49.

AY   305 [1]: New to Greenslades Tours Ltd, Exeter (DN) registered AFJ 80B; numbered 445 6/71;
renumbered 286 1/75; Midland Red Omnibus Co Ltd, Birmingham (dealer) 12/75; Paul Sykes
Organisation Ltd, Blackerhill (dealer) 1/76; Seymours Ltd {Mascot Motors}, St Helier (CI) 8
registered J 16841 2/76; to service 3/76; moved to St Clement (CI) 3/78.

AY   305 [2]: New G Hill {Jersey Tours}, St Helier (CI) 11 as an un-registered vehicle (it was diverted from
Hills Tours Ltd, West Bromwich (ST) – registration BEA 480J allocated but not taken up); Tantivy
Motors Ltd, St Helier (CI) (un-registered) 12/70; numbered 29 and registered J 26408 4/71.

AY   328: New to Mrs A Jones {Shamrock}, Pontypridd (MG) registered W674 DDN; Bebb Travel plc, Llantwit
Fardre (MG) 10/06; Lewis Travel UK plc, Greenwich (LN) 2/08; IA Tomlinson, Winsford (CH)
12/08; Wrexham Electrical Systems (XCL) as a mobile catering van 4/09; unidentified dealer
11/09; last licence expired 11/09.

AY   586 [2]: New to Blue Eagle Ltd, St Helier (CI) 29 registered J 38084; renumbered 9 1972; Tantivy Motors
Ltd, St Helier (CI) 37 5/75.

AY   586 [3]: New to Bristol Omnibus Co Ltd (AV) C5055 registered LEU 263P (as H43/27D); renumbered
5055 c8/78; rebuilt to O43/27D 8/86; Badgerline Ltd, Weston-super-Mare (AV) 8622 2/93; to
service 3/93; Bristol Omnibus Co Ltd (AV) 8622 1/96; S Munden {Bristol Bus & Coach Sales},
Bristol (dealer) 4/00.

AY   586 [4]: New to East Sussex County Council, Lewes (ES) WM.370 registered K572 SKP (as C12F);
unidentified dealer 10/06.

AY   593 [1]: New to Board of Health, Guernsey (XCI) registered 50563.

AY   593 [2]: New to Guernsey Railway Co Ltd, St Peter Port (CI) 117 registered 25704; Guernseybus Ltd, St Peter Port (CI) 117 2/81; re-registered 3338 [2] 8/92.

AY   593 [3]: New to Lothian Regional Transport, Edinburgh (LO) 166 registered HSC 166X; withdrawn 5/88; R Irvine {Tiger Coaches}, Salsburgh (dealer) 10/90; R Irvine {Tiger Coaches}, Salsburgh (SC) 5/91; CW Christie {M Line Coaches}, Alloa (CE) 1/93; HJ & CE Heaton, Leigh (GM) 9/93; FG Lovett {Toftwood Travel}, Rainhill (MY) 2/94; Houston Ramm Bus & Coach Sales, Sudden (dealer) 1/96; C Bentley {CB Travel}, Birmingham (WM) 2/96; re-registered CIB 9623 c3/96; re-registered HSC 166X 9/96.

AY   593 [4]: New to Ministry of Defence (GOV); said to have been re-registered F481 BUH 2/89 (although this is doubtful as this registration was allocated to an ERF lorry).

AY   593 [5]: New to East Sussex County Council {Selsey Community Bus}, Lewes (ES) AZ31 registered P826 OGT.

AY   666: New to an unidentified Guernsey operator registered 10735; Bougourd Bros, St Peter Port (dealer) by6/68.

AY   750 [1]: New to Ribble Motor Services Ltd, Preston (LA) 408 registered ERN 776; withdrawn 1968; F Cowley, Salford (dealer) 1/69.

AY   750 [2]: New to Greenslades Tours Ltd, Exeter (DN) registered AFJ   85B; numbered 450 6/71; renumbered 250 1/75; Midland Red Omnibus Co Ltd, Birmingham (dealer) 12/75; Paul Sykes Organisation Ltd, Blackerhill (dealer) 1/76; Seymours Ltd {Mascot Motors}, St Helier (CI) 15 registered J 16868 2/76; to service 4/76; moved to St Clement (CI) 3/78.

AY   750 [3]: New to Tantivy Motors Ltd, St Helier (CI) 33 registered J 43805.

AY   1114 [1]: New to Board of Health, Guernsey (XCI) registered 41898.

AY   1114 [2]: New to Gwent County Council Social Services (XGT) 557592 registered F270 DBO; last licence expired 5/04.

AY   1858:   New to Ben Stanley Ltd, Hersham (SR) registered JPC 547N; H Luckett & Co Ltd, Wallington (HA) 2/78; last licence expired 2/84; Educational Holidays Guernsey Ltd {Island Coachways}, St Peter Port (CI) 2 registered 8228 [3] 2/84; W Errington {Victoria Hotel / Taxi & Leisure}, Alderney (CI) 10/84.

AY   2153: New to BB Hire Cars Ltd, St Peter Port (XCI) registered 45260; hired to Guernseybus Ltd, St Peter Port (CI) 10 5/86-11/86.

J 20096: New to DA Battwell & LS Garner {Uxbridge Coaches}, London W5 (LN) registered UMP 77; J Byrne {Shamrock Tours}, St Helier (CI) 7/58.

XAE 329: New to Mrs A Wild {A Ball & Sons / Eagle Coaches}, Bristol (GL); Kirkby & Sons (Sales) Ltd, South Anston (dealer) 12/73.

Notes:

AY   58 [2] (ex 6768 [2], AFJ   79B): Re-registered AY   586 [1] 1985.

AY   59 [12] (ex 50562): Re-registered AY   184 by12/94.

AY   91 [4] (ex J 43803): Was out of use from c6/93 to c12/97; registered AY   750 [4] by12/97.

AY   305 [2] (ex J 26408): Was out of use from 5/94 to c3/98.

AY   593 [1] (ex 50563): Re-registered AY   89 7/94.

AY   593 [2] (ex 3338 [2], 25704): The Bedford model type J6L is incomplete, possibly J6LZ; to service 7/94.

AY   750 [3] (ex J 43805): Re-registered AY   91 [5] by1/96.

J 20096 (ex UMP   77): Believed to have not been registered locally on Alderney.

XAE 329: Acquired for spares.

Disposals:

AY   59 [1] (ex 3777): No known disposal.

AY   59 [2] (ex 3087): No known disposal.

AY   59 [3] (ex 3088): No known disposal.

AY   59 [4] (ex 1560): No known disposal.

AY   59 [5] (ex 5190): No known disposal.

AY   59 [6] (ex 5183): No known disposal.

AY   59 [7] (ex 5188): No known disposal.

AY   59 [8] (ex 4426): No known disposal.

AY   59 [9] (ex RYT   34): No known disposal.

AY   59 [10] (ex 381 ENN): Chassis sold for use as a boat trailer; body dumped in the sea.

AY   59 [11] (ex SWL   52J): Reduced to a frame on the premises 1988.

AY   59 [13] (ex B 87 WOR): No known disposal.

AY   59 [14]: Unidentified dealer, presumably for scrap by6/14.

AY   59 [15] (ex M388 SPY, CSU 906, M388 SPY): ABC Taxis, Alderney (CI) 9/07; unidentified UK dealer 1/08; unidentified owners 6/09 and 3/13.

AY   59 [16] (ex RLZ 3218, G141 GOL): Unidentified dealer, presumably for scrap by6/14.

AY 59 [17] (L156 YVK): S Boxall, M Welch & C Thorn, Bromley for preservation re-registered L156 YVK 8/18.
AY 81 [1] (ex GUH 540): Believed still on Alderney, derelict 9/97.
AY 81 [2] (ex GPA 623V): Unidentified UK dealer / operator 4/96.
AY 81 [3] (ex YFF 660, 3338 [1]): SK & DH Young {CT Coaches}, Radstock (SO) for preservation re-registered YFF 660 by8/12.
AY 89 (ex AY 593 [1], 50563): Unidentified owner as a builder's van by12/94.
AY 91 [1] (ex RCG 612): No known disposal.
AY 91 [2] (ex SWL 50J): Converted to a fire tender at Alderney Airport; scrapped 1990.
AY 91 [3] (ex 8228 [2], J 16590, AFJ 82B): C Shears & P Platt, Exeter (as dealer) 7/90; Wacton Trading / Coach Sales, Bromyard (dealer) for scrap 3/93.
AY 91 [5] (ex AY 750 [3] J 43805): Believed to be still on the premises, derelict 2017.
AY 91 [6] (ex J 26626): Wacton Trading / Coach Sales, Bromyard (dealer) 4/06; Pointmost Ltd {Girlings of Plymouth}, Ivybridge (DN) (not operated) by10/06; AC Myall {CG Myall & Son}, Bassingbourn (CM) for preservation 10/10.
AY 91 [7] (ex K903 PBP): Unidentified dealer, Guernsey for scrap 4/12.
AY 101 [1] (ex 1633): No known disposal.
AY 101 [2] (ex 722): No known disposal.
AY 101 [3] (ex 5189): No known disposal.
AY 101 [4] (ex JOD 621): No known disposal.
AY 129 [1] (ex 2751): No known disposal.
AY 129 [2] (ex 1398): No known disposal.
AY 184 (ex AY 59 [12], 50562): Unidentified owner as a builder's van by12/94.
AY 305 [1] (ex J 16841, AFJ 80B): Peterborough Passenger Vehicle Spares (dealer) 1990; unidentified dealer, Barnsley for scrap at an unknown date.
AY 305 [2] (ex J 26408): Unidentified owner by10/01.
AY 328 (ex W674 DDN): Unidentified dealer, presumably for scrap by6/14.
AY 586 [1] (ex AY 58 [2], 6768 [2], AFJ 79B): Noted un-registered and accident damaged at Torquay docks 1989; unidentified dealer (probably Peterborough Passenger Vehicle Spares) 1990, but not collected and stored in the yard of Torbay Seaways, Torre Station; P Platt, Exeter for preservation spares and being dismantled at Winkleigh 10/91.
AY 586 [2] (ex J 38084): Unidentified dealer 1/96.
AY 586 [3] (ex LEU 263P): Universal Limos (Guernsey) Ltd, St Peter Port (CI) registered 68523 6/07; withdrawn 7/08; S Munden {Bristol Bus & Coach Sales}, Bristol (dealer) 8/10; re-registered LEU 263P 10/10; R Smith, Glastonbury for preservation 10/10; J Pratt, Weston-super-Mare for preservation 2/11; J Pratt, Weston-super-Mare (SO) 5/11; Crosville Motor Services Ltd, Weston-super-Mare (SO) 2/12; withdrawn 4/18.
AY 586 [4] (ex K572 SKP): Unidentified dealer for scrap by9/17.
AY 593 [2] (ex 3338 [2], 25704): Wacton Trading / Coach Sales, Bromyard (dealer) 3/97.
AY 593 [3] (ex HSC 166X, CIB 9623, HSC 166X): Unidentified dealer / operator 6/03; noted Norfolk possibly as a caravan by5/04.
AY 593 [4] (ex F481 BUH, -?-): Derelict at Alderney Airport by6/14.
AY 593 [5] (ex P826 OGT): Not yet disposed.
AY 666 (ex 10735): Converted to a truck for WP Simon's associated garage business by1979.
AY 750 [1] (ex ERN 776): No known disposal.
AY 750 [2] (ex J 16868, AFJ 85B): Unidentified owner, Torbay c6/89; Peterborough Passenger Vehicle Spares (dealer) 1990; unidentified dealer, Barnsley for scrap at an unknown date.
AY 750 [4] (ex AY 91 [4], J 43803): Unidentified dealer by9/01.
AY 1114 [1] (ex 41898): Unidentified dealer / operator 12/03.
AY 1114 [2] (ex F270 DBO): Exported to West Africa 10/07.
AY 1858 (ex 8228 [3], JPC 547N): Unidentified dealer / operator, Torquay c1988.
AY 2153 (ex 45260): Unidentified dealer / operator c6/93.
J 20096 (ex UMP 77): No known disposal.
XAE 329: No known disposal.

Many of the vehicles with no known disposals remained derelict on Alderney for years after withdrawal.

WJ SIMON   5 High Street & Huret, ALDERNEY

AY	5	Bedford WHB	100081	Duple	2959	B14F	4/33	4/33	6/40
AY	14	Chevrolet 30 cwt	?	?		C18F	5/31	12/34	-/--
AY	34	Chevrolet 30 cwt	?	?		B18F	5/31	12/34	by-/38
AY	32	Morris	?	?		B18F	-/--	-/--	6/40
AY	58 [1]	Dodge	?	?		B22F	-/--	-/39	6/40
2227		Bean Model 11	1044/11W	Willowbrook	2157	B20F	5/28	3/40	----

Previous histories:
2227: New to Guernsey Railway Co Ltd, St Peter Port (CI) 18; withdrawn 12/38.
AY   14: New to AJ Langlois {Riduna Bus Service}, Alderney (CI).
AY   32: Its origins are unknown.
AY   34: New to AJ Langlois {Riduna Bus Service}, Alderney (CI).
AY   58 [1]: Its origins are unknown.

Notes:
2227: Probably never shipped to Alderney following the outbreak of WW2.

Disposals:
AY   5: Abandoned at the evacuation of Alderney 6/40.
AY   14: Converted to a lorry at an unknown date; abandoned at the evacuation of Alderney 6/40.
AY   32: Abandoned at the evacuation of Alderney 6/40.
AY   34: No known disposal.
AY   58 [1]: Abandoned at the evacuation of Alderney 6/40.

R SPANDLER {Alderney Taxi & Hire Cars}					8 Braye Street, ALDERNEY		
AY 1741 [1]	Freight Rover	8N213432	Freight Rover		M11	2/85	2/85	1/89
AY 1741 [2]	Freight Rover	7N839778	Freight Rover		M11	2/89	2/89	4/96
AY 1950	Bedford VAS5	DT102073	Marshall	280880	B30F	3/83	10/92	by10/04
AY 1773	FIAT 60-10	300127	Caetano	181156	C18F	9/81	4/95	9/01
AY 2475	LDV 200	CN969294	LDV		M8	4/96	4/96	9/01

Previous histories:
AY 1773: New to Nebard's Ltd, Wakefield (WY) registered WUA 655X; Educational Holidays Guernsey Ltd {Island Coachways}, St Peter Port (CI) re-registered 6768 [4] named 'Petit Bot' 8/88.
AY 1950: New to Ministry of Defence (GOV) registered 26 KA 49.

Disposals:
AY 1741 [1]: Unidentified UK dealer / operator 1/89.
AY 1741 [2]: Unidentified dealer / operator 4/96.
AY 1773 (ex WUA 655X): Unidentified dealer / operator 9/01.
AY 1950 (ex 26 KA 49): Unidentified dealer / operator by10/04.
AY 2475: Unidentified dealer / operator 9/01.

DP WHITE {Marina's Cars}					1 Whitegates, ALDERNEY		
AY 1671	Ford Transit	Ford		M14	3/91	3/91	4/99
	SFAZXXBDVZLB25664						

Disposal:
AY   1671: Unidentified UK dealer / operator registered H686 CDM 4/99; JM Woods & RJ Willmitt {Regal Travel}, West Derby (MY) by11/00; unidentified dealer / operator 3/02; scrapped 1/06.

GA WOOLFE   **Belle Vue Hotel, The Butes, ALDERNEY**
A charabanc was operated in the summer of 1922 but no other details are known.

SARK

Sark has a population of about 500 and an area of just over 2 square miles. It has always prohibited motor vehicles from its roads, a rule that was relaxed after World War II to permit tractors to use the roads for the purpose of hauling trailers loaded with freight and luggage up the steep hill leading from Creux Harbour, through a tunnel of rock to the hotels and houses high above. This is tolerated out of regard for the local horses who previously had to undertake this arduous task role. In more recent times, 'buses' have also been hauled on tours of the island.

The island like the rest of the Channel Islands was occupied by the German forces between 1940 and 1945, although unlike the other islands, it was completely evacuated before the forces landed.

A Sark tractor bus. (Mike Streete)

NON-PSVs

Many vehicles were relegated to non-PSV work on the Island and these are listed where known, in the main body of this Fleet History. A handful of vehicles (minibuses excepted) that arrived on the island and were solely put to non-PSV use are listed below, but records are scanty.

BRITISH SHOWJUMPING ASSOCIATION GUERNSEY   **ST MARTIN**

| PSC 310G | Leyland PDR1A/1 | 901246 | Alexander | J13/866/58 | H--/--D | 7/69 | by3/93 | -/-- |
| BPF 131Y | Leyland ONTL11/1R | ON787 | Roe | GO8715 | H43/29F | 7/83 | by7/07 | -/-- |

Previous histories:

PSC 310G: New to Edinburgh Corporation (LO) 310; Lothian Regional Transport (LO) 310 5/75; withdrawn 1983; J Whiting, Pontefract (dealer) 3/84.

BPF 131Y: New to London Country Bus Services Ltd, Reigate (SR) LR31; London Country North East Ltd, Hertford (HT) LR31 9/86; Sovereign Bus & Coach Co Ltd, Hertford (HT) LR31 1/89; moved to Welwyn Garden City (HT) 2/90; renumbered 31 1992; withdrawn 1/93; Keighley & District Travel Ltd, Keighley (WY) 972 1/93; Sovereign Bus & Coach Co Ltd, Stevenage (HT) 31 2/96; withdrawn with accident damage 1/98; Eastville Coaches Ltd, Bristol (GL) 4/98; also used as required by Turners Coachways (Bristol) Ltd, Bristol (GL) from c8/00; Ensign (Bus Sales) Ltd, Purfleet 12/03.

Notes:

These vehicles were used as static grandstands.

FLEWITT   **ALDERNEY**

| F266 YTJ | Ld ONCL10/1RZ | ON11034 | Northern Counties 3788 | H47/30F | 4/89 | by7/11 | -/-- |

Previous history:

F266 YTJ: Arriva Merseyside (MY) 3266 -/--; Arriva North West (MY) 3266 4/05; Travelspeed, Burnley (LA) 166 9/06; GP Ripley, Carlton (dealer) by10/07; PJ Leyland, Fulwood (LA) 10/07; moved to Weeton (LA) 7/09.

Notes:

F266 YTJ: Converted for use as a café / shop.

G PERCY TRENTHAM   **FOREST**

| GV 4123 | Dodge PLB | 1096 | Thurgood | 579 | B20F | 2/36 | -/59 | -/60 |

Previous history:

GV 4123: New to HS & WHS Theobold & Son, Long Melford (WF); G Percy Trentham, Pangbourne (contractor) c5/57.

Notes:

GV 4123:   Was used during the remaking of the Airport runway in 1959.

GUERNSEY RIDING & HUNT CLUB

| KAG 859 | Leyland PD2/30 | 571148 | Alexander | 5171 | L31/28RD7/57 | 6/77 | # |

Previous history:

KAG 859: New to Western SMT (SC) 1378; Ensign Bus Co Ltd, Hornchurch (dealer) 2/75; transferred to the contract fleet and hired to Lesney Products Ltd {Matchbox Toys}, London E9 (XLN) 8/75-4/77.

Notes:

KAG 859: Was acquired engineless for use as a grandstand.

ROCKHOPPER   Le Huret, ALDERNEY & Rock Aviation, States Airport, FOREST
BLUE ISLANDS LTD (4/06)   The Grange, ST PETER PORT

Rockhopper was a local airline based on Alderney although the vehicle operated airside on Guernsey and so was not registered locally. Blue Islands was the remodeled and renamed successor to Rockhopper and based a vehicle on both Guernsey and Jersey airports.

G883 WML	Renault S75	Reeve Burgess	17986	B25F	2/90	3/04	4/06
	SGDB75A0GLD222671						
M559 SRE	Mercedez Benz	Marshall	C19-277	B23F	8/94	4/06	-/--
	WDB6690032N021700						

Previous histories:

G883 WML: New to London Buses Ltd, London SW1 (LN) RB13; Yorkshire Traction Ltd, Barnsley (SY) (not operated) by8/94; Lincolnshire Road Car Co Ltd, Lincoln (LI) 383 8/94; renumbered 183 at an unknown date; London Bus Group, Beeston Regis for preservation 9/03.

M559 SRE: New to PMT Ltd, Stoke-on-Trent (ST) MMM559; First PMT Ltd, Stoke-on-Trent (ST) 559 8/01; Houston Ramm Bus & Coach Sales, Sudden (dealer) 6/02; White {Swift}, New Cumnock (SC) by3/03; unidentified dealer 8/05.

Notes:

A third vehicle operated but based at Jersey Airport was R196 LBC – details of this can be found included under the Delta Taxis Ltd heading.

G883 WML: Named 'Rocky 1'. It passed to Alderney Shipping, Guernsey (use unknown) 4/06.
M559 SRE: Named 'Blue 1'.

DC TRAISNEL METALWORKS   Les Buttes (later Bridge Avenue), ST SAMPSON

TVF 870	Bristol SC4LK	113.018	ECW	9196	C33F	7/56	by7/78	4/86

Previous history:

TVF 870: New to Eastern Counties Omnibus Co Ltd, Norwich (NK) LSC870; Ben Jordan, Coltishall (dealer) by5/68; VC Transport, Leigh-on-Sea (EX) B16 5/68; CG Goodger {Riverway}, Harlow (LN) 10/68; C Warburton, Harlow (EX) 3/69; withdrawn 2/70; W Norths (PV) Ltd, Sherburn in Elmet (dealer) by3/71; Mrs Coates, Holymoorside (XNY) 3/71.

Notes:

TVF 870: Used for living accommodation (also recorded as a storeshed); used for fire-fighting practice at Guernsey airport 8/87 and destroyed.

HORSE BUS OPERATORS

GUERNSEY OMNIBUS CO
GUERNSEY RAILWAY CO LTD

Guernsey Omnibus Co was founded early in 1888 in competition to the tramway and quickly became the largest horse bus operator on the island. The steam tramway found itself unable to compete with the frequent bus services and ceased operating in January 1889. The revived electric tramway operations under Guernsey Railway Co however thrived and eventually took over the horse buses on the St Peter Port to St Sampson Service on 24 April 1895. Other services lasted longer with the final horses disappearing in 1911.

Services run were:

St Peter Port to St Sampson's Bridge	3/1888
St Sampson's Bridge to Bordeaux (seasonal)	6/1889
St Peter Port to Rohais	2/1891
Half Way to L'Islet	3/1891
St Peter Port to Cobo (via Rohais) (seasonal)	5/1891
Half Way to L'Ancresse (seasonal)	6/1892

New buses:

(1)	WT Crane	2 horse double-deck	12/14	3/1888	7/1895
(2)	WT Crane	2 horse double-deck	12/14	3/1888	7/1895
(3)	WT Crane	2 horse double-deck	12/14	3/1888	1/1902
(4)	WT Crane	1 horse single-deck	12/2	11/1888	7/1911
(5)	WT Crane	1 horse single-deck	12/2	11/1888	3/1892
(6)	WT Crane	1 horse single-deck	12/2	11/1888	3/1892
(7)	WT Crane	1 horse single-deck	12/2	11/1888	5/1905
(8)	WT Crane	1 horse single-deck	12/2	11/1888	5/1905
(9)	WT Crane?	2 horse double-deck	32	6/1889	10/1904
(10)	WT Crane?	2 horse double-deck	32	6/1889	10/1904
(11)	WT Crane?	2 horse wagonette	16	6/1891	7/1911
(12)	WT Crane?	2 horse wagonette	16	6/1891	7/1911
(5)	WT Crane?	2 horse double-deck	32	3/1892	10/1904
(6)	WT Crane?	2 horse double-deck	32	3/1892	10/1904
	S Frampton	1 horse wagonette	12	4/1896	5/1905
	S Frampton	1 horse wagonette	12	4/1896	5/1905
	ex-Bartlet	?	?	4/1904	5/1907
	ex-W Stagg	2 horse single-deck	18	4/1905	2/1911
	ex-W Stagg	1 horse single-deck	12	4/1905	7/1911

Notes:

The fleet numbers are based on scraps of information gleaned from archived material.

WT Crane was a well-known London coachbuilder of the day. The later vehicles may however have been built by a different firm as there are detail differences between these and the earlier examples.

11-12 were known as 'American Waggonettes' and had transverse garden seating.

All the vehicles attributed to WT Crane (apart from the first 5 and 6) were transferred to Guernsey Railway Co Ltd in May 1895.

The last three were acquired on the dates shown (dates new are unknown). Nothing is known about Bartlet – he does not appear to have been a horse bus operator. William Stagg (of Vale) was a former Guernsey Railway Co Ltd contractor (since 1895) who set up in competition in 6/1903 before returning to the company as an employee (with his vehicles) in 4/1905.

Disposals:

Whilst it is recorded where (and when) most of the buses were disposed to, tying these to individual fleet numbers is a matter of some conjecture.

1-2: Andrews, London 7/1895.

3: WS Freeman, London 2/1902.

4, 11-12, ex-W Stagg 1 horse single-deck: Three of these sold by auction 7/1911; the fourth was retained for possible use after 7/1911.

5-6 (first): No known disposals.

5-6 (second), 9, 10: Broken up 10/1904.

7-8, two S Frampton wagonettes: T Miller Davis, St Peter Port (CI) 5/1905.

ex-Bartlet bus: Broken up 5/1907.

ex-W Stagg 2 horse single-deck: JJ Brice 2/1911.

OTHER OPERATORS

The following were known to have operated horse buses and were generally part of wider livery-stables businesses. Most of these ran services from St Peter Port (Town Church) to St Sampson's Bridge.

<u>Dates operated bus services</u>

J Roberts, St Peter Port	1837-1852
Buses: *Defiance* (1838-1849); *Defiance no 2* (1840); *Favourite* (1842-1849), *Jenny Lind* (1848-1852)	
J Thomas, St Peter Port	1838-1849
Buses: *Sarnian Granite* (1838-1840); *Victoria* (1840-1849), *Nelson* (1842-1849); *Albert* (1848-1849)	
GW Lewis, St Peter Port	1841
J Pike, St Sampson	1843-5/1845
Bus: *Albert*	
C Waterman, St Sampson	1845-5/1847
Bus: *Red Rover*	
R Collings	1851-1859
Buses: *Times* (1851-1859); *Fancy* (1853-1859); *Jenny Lind* (1854-1859); *Nelson* (1856-1859)	
W Miller, St Peter Port	1853-1869
Buses: *Favourite* (1853-1869); *Rover* (1855-1859); *Favourite no 2* (1860-1869)	
A Mallett, St Sampson	1858-1868
Buses: *Eclipse* (1858-1864); *Eclipse no 2* (1860-1863)	
J Norton, St Peter Port	1861-1863
Buses: *Queen no 1*, *Queen no 2* (1861-1863)	
GB Debenham, St Sampson	4/1868-1874

Cab operators began to appear in the 1860s although the quality of these services was variable:

J Norton, St Peter Port	1861-1863
J Thomas	1864
J Dibden	1864-1868
D Winterflood	1864-1868
J Palmer	1864-1867
N Denty	1865-1866
J Le Gallais	1865-1868
R Brice	1866-1868
T McLean	1866
J Webb	1868
A Gibbs	1868
J Brown	1868-1877
J Cleale	1868
J Phillips	1881-1886
G Brand	1872
R Brett	1872-1879
W Phillips	1876
J Palmer	1877
J Wiscombe	1877
W Brown	1877
D Chapman	1877
T Roberts	1877-1880
W de Beauchamp	1879
N Guilbert	1882
J Endicott	1885
W McDonald	1886

INDEX OF OPERATORS & FLEET NAME CROSS REFERENCE

Operators are generally listed in alphabetical order of the formal title. However, where business have changed hands (frequently in the case of some of the larger independents), they are listed under the fleet name.

This comprehensive listing of operator and fleetnames may therefore be useful:

ALDERNEY

MILITARY

REGISTRATION CROSS REFERENCE

Guernsey									
A48	38	501	46	784	16	1322	44	1787 [1]	156
A81	38	502	46	784	160	1322	161	1787 [2]	120
A82	38	503	46	784	167	1322	166	1787 [3]	120
A83	38	505	46	848	44	1337 [1]	44	1787 [4]	121
A83	63	506	46	848	160	1337 [2]	44	1787 [5]	121
		507	23	848	166	1379	27	1787 [6]	116
3	28	507	167	864	52	1389	43	1787 [6]	123
27	25	511	145	864	145	1389	167	1814	24
27	160	511	160	864	161	1398	43	1814	160
27	160	558	22	864	165	1398	161	1833	26
48 [1]	38	558	160	879	44	1398	175	1845	43
48 [2]	18	558	166	879	161	1410	106	1845	145
48 [2]	104	567 [1]	16	879	166	1415	42	1845	161
48 [2]	148	567 [1]	160	882	151	1415	145	1845	167
48 [2]	167	567 [2]	28	882	156	1419	25	1846	26
80	39	597	158	885	21	1419	139	1846	160
83	38	597	161	885	104	1419	167	1846	165
99	145	597	167	885	147	1463 [1]	31	1864	26
99	167	612	16	885	167	1463 [1]	55	1916	30
118	42	612	160	917	106	1463 [2]	62	1931	121
118	161	612	164	931	42	1463 [2]	64	1940	43
118	165	612	167	931	161	1473	42	1940	158
176	25	624	23	931	165	1473	161	1940	161
176	167	624	160	932	28	1480	106	1940	167
261	26	624	164	937	18	1480	173	1951	48
266	21	630	23	937	161	1506	27	1951	150
266	164	630	160	937	167	1529 [1]	31	1957	19
291	45	630	165	987	21	1529 [1]	55	1957	167
295 [1]	17	651	151	987	104	1529 [2]	62	1963	151
295 [1]	164	651	167	987	147	1529 [2]	64	1963	167
295 [2]	28	653	58	987	167	1532	145	1982	31
313	15	653	156	994	39	1557	30	1982	55
313	140	653	160	995	87	1557	150	2027	31
313	167	658	15	1016	22	1558	30	2027	55
348	18	658	140	1016	167	1558	150	2047	106
348	147	658	167	1027	19	1559	58	2047	151
348	167	659 [1]	15	1027	167	1559	150	2047	167
372 [1]	16	659 [1]	140	1035	105	1559	156	2070	159
372 [1]	164	659 [2]	18	1073	22	1559	160	2070	167
372 [2]	28	659 [2]	167	1073	152	1560	48	2125	46
374	29	671	104	1073	167	1560	150	2126	46
400	16	722	25	1088	19	1560	174	2203	141
400	167	722	161	1088	160	1596	145	2220	22
413	15	722	166	1088	166	1596	167	2220	104
413	167	722	175	1088	167	1601	20	2220	167
434	18	732 [1]	156	1112	156	1601	148	2224	17
434	140	732 [2]	58	1127	25	1601	167	2224	149
434	167	732 [2]	156	1127	160	1613	158	2227	41
437	105	737	16	1127	161	1613	167	2227	177
441	41	737	160	1151	15	1633	150	2239 [2]	60
441	167	737	167	1151	140	1633	158	2247	30
448	20	742	16	1151	167	1633	160	2251	18
448	165	742	167	1216	39	1633	175	2251	138
448	167	744	17	1292	26	1737	156	2251	169
465	16	744	167	1295	22	1737	161	2317	156
465	160	745	16	1295	43	1765	106	2317	167
465	164	745	167	1295	152	1765	158	2341	106
465	167	753	20	1309	58	1765	161	2341	167
478	14	753	167	1309	64	1765	165	2377	41
499	46	759	44	1309	156	1787 [1]	58	2377	161
500	46	759	160	1319	106	1787 [1]	116	2377	167
		759	165	1319	173	1787 [1]	120	2388 [1]	54

2388 [1]	64	2819	150	3193	165	3989 [3]	120	4879	160
2388 [2]	77	2840	22	3216	145	3989 [4]	121	5126	44
2411	26	2840	104	3216	161	3989 [5]	131	5181	48
2424	120	2851	30	3216	165	3990	33	5181	150
2441	26	2851	150	3324	50	3990	106	5182	48
2445 [1]	120	2877 [1]	48	3338 [1]	50	3992	59	5182	150
2445 [2]	120	2877 [1]	150	3338 [1]	175	3992	156	5183	48
2486	30	2877 [2]	140	3338 [2]	67	4021	26	5183	150
2493 [1]	35	2959	27	3338 [2]	176	4022 [1]	26	5183	174
2493 [1]	55	2960	33	3338 [3]	84	4022 [2]	31	5184	30
2493 [1]	64	2960	106	3338 [4]	71	4022 [2]	55	5184	150
2493 [2]	81	2961	33	3405	42	4023	27	5185	30
2500	153	2961	106	3405	161	4024	27	5185	150
2501	152	2965	22	3405	165	4029	31	5186	30
2501	167	2965	104	3409	58	4029	55	5186	150
2536	20	2972 [1]	24	3409	156	4038	31	5187	46
2536	167	2972 [1]	161	3409	161	4038	55	5188	46
2599	114	2972 [1]	166	3410	145	4052	42	5188	174
2609	123	2972 [1]	167	3410	167	4076	31	5189	46
2616	50	2972 [2]	35	3450	21	4076	55	5189	175
2634 [1]	54	2972 [2]	55	3450	160	4085	48	5190	46
2634 [1]	64	2972 [2]	64	3450	161	4085	150	5190	174
2634 [2]	79	2972 [3]	82	3458	48	4085	158	5191	46
2636	50	2972 [4]	84	3458	150	4101	30	5192	46
2659	14	2976	21	3460	48	4101	150	5201	145
2711	30	2981	106	3460	147	4151	28	5260	120
2711	150	2981	145	3460	150	4222	23	5261	125
2711	158	2981	160	3462	27	4222	160	5389	114
2714	25	2982	21	3625	152	4222	167	5407	139
2714	106	2982	160	3625	161	4252	106	5407	171
2714	139	2982	165	3625	166	4392	28	5482	153
2714	161	2985	21	3641	20	4400	27	5499	33
2714	165	2985	160	3641	160	4400	47	5499	106
2719	25	2985	167	3641	167	4414	30	5499	160
2719	139	2987	21	3688	42	4414	147	5502	29
2719	156	2987	161	3688	161	4414	150	5579 [1]	111
2719	161	2987	167	3688	165	4426	48	5579 [2]	71
2719	164	3013	145	3774	44	4426	150	5597 [2]	73
2725	29	3013	161	3774	160	4426	174	5616	154
2725	125	3013	166	3774	161	4444	23	5779 [1]	120
2730	154	3013	167	3774	166	4444	160	5779 [2]	120
2751	41	3041	147	3777	45	4444	165	5779 [3]	123
2751	175	3041	148	3777	144	4492	28	5895	34
2783	21	3041	151	3777	174	4493	29	5895	148
2783	161	3060	48	3787	114	4495	28	5895	151
2783	167	3060	150	3810	52	4496	28	5967	33
2787	45	3060	158	3810	145	4498	28	5967	106
2787	152	3060	160	3810	160	4499	38	6083	146
2787	161	3087	46	3810	161	4507	28	6148	31
2791	25	3087	174	3810	165	4508	28	6148	55
2791	175	3088	46	3901 [1]	25	4510 [1]	28	6173	31
2792	21	3088	174	3901 [1]	139	4510 [1]	120	6173	55
2792	161	3089	46	3901 [1]	164	4512	28	6188	31
2792	165	3090	46	3901 [2]	29	4548	29	6188	55
2793	21	3117	45	3923	52	4683	29	6286	29
2793	162	3118	45	3923	145	4684	24	6287	29
2793	164	3120	106	3924	52	4684	160	6288	29
2793	167	3120	156	3924	145	4684	164	6289	29
2799	158	3120	167	3925	52	4818	52	6289	120
2799	161	3135	152	3925	145	4818	145	6290	29
2799	167	3135	161	3944	156	4869	33	6351	70
2818	30	3135	165	3944	160	4869	106	6430 [1]	120
2818	150	3193	42	3989 [1]	120	4869	160	6430 [2]	120
2819	48	3193	161	3989 [2]	120	4879	106	6430 [3]	121

6430 [4]	121	8228 [2]	120	10485 [1]	55	12724	65	14867	53
6430 [5]	122	8228 [2]	175	10485 [1]	64	12725	32	14867	65
6430 [6]	123	8228 [3]	120	10486	32	12725	55	15206	116
6430 [7]	124	8228 [3]	172	10486	55	12725	65	15216 [1]	138
6432	47	8228 [3]	176	10487	32	12726	32	15216 [2]	136
6433	47	8228 [4]	120	10487	55	12726	55	15562	114
6434	47	8228 [5]	93	10487	64	12726	65	15872	83
6435	47	8228 [5]	121	10488 [1]	51	12727 [1]	51	15975	111
6436	47	8228 [6]	131	10488 [1]	64	12727 [1]	65	16213	33
6436	63	8229 [1]	32	10488 [2]	70	12727 [2]	72	16213	55
6437	47	8229 [1]	55	10489 [1]	51	12727 [3]	76	16213	65
6438	48	8229 [2]	120	10489 [1]	64	12727 [4]	92	16214	33
6439	48	8230 [1]	50	10489 [2]	71	12727 [4]	121	16214	55
6440	48	8230 [2]	120	10489 [2]	96	12728 [1]	51	16214	65
6441	49	8230 [3]	129	10532	108	12728 [1]	65	16215	53
6442	49	8230 [4]	129	10558	67	12728 [2]	73	16215	65
6443	49	8230 [5]	121	10633	75	12728 [3]	85	16216	53
6768 [1]	31	8230 [6]	123	10735	176	12833	115	16216	65
6768 [1]	55	8231 [1]	50	10739 [1]	120	12859	120	16412	153
6768 [2]	124	8231 [2]	120	10739 [2]	131	12912	138	16646	141
6768 [2]	174	8370	154	10797	120	12924	115	16646	153
6768 [3]	120	8555	153	10801	144	13110	153	16697	107
6768 [4]	120	9118	146	11033	120	13172	147	16779	141
6768 [4]	178	9434 [1]	35	11188	113	13195	136	16779	153
6768 [5]	121	9434 [1]	51	11188	137	13456	120	16938	67
6769 [1]	49	9434 [1]	55	11612	136	13704	116	17052	107
6769 [2]	120	9434 [1]	64	11671	51	13786	146	17314	92
6770	49	9434 [2]	82	11671	65	14031	112	17314	121
6771	31	9435	35	11672	51	14031	136	17314	142
6771	55	9435	51	11672	65	14223 [1]	34	17337	116
6772	49	9435	55	11673	51	14223 [1]	55	18047	121
6773	31	9435	64	11673	65	14223 [1]	65	18109	123
6773	55	9436 [1]	32	11674	32	14223 [2]	78	18221 [1]	123
6776	114	9436 [1]	55	11674	55	14223 [2]	85	18221 [2]	131
6898	141	9436 [1]	64	11674	64	14223 [2]	96	18221 [2]	137
7091 [1]	120	9436 [2]	73	11675 [1]	32	14223 [2]	109	18262	34
7091 [1]	153	9436 [2]	96	11675 [1]	55	14531 [1]	34	18262	55
7091 [2]	120	9437	32	11675 [1]	65	14531 [1]	55	18262	65
7269	120	9437	55	11675 [2]	72	14531 [1]	65	18262	96
7269	153	9437	64	11676	32	14531 [2]	80	18263	34
7482	153	9438 [1]	32	11676	55	14531 [3]	85	18263	55
7798	104	9438 [1]	55	11676	65	14626 [1]	52	18263	65
7799	104	9438 [1]	64	11840	120	14626 [1]	65	18264 [1]	34
8225 [1]	131	9438 [2]	120	11840	153	14626 [2]	72	18264 [1]	55
8225 [2]	93	9438 [3]	120	11926	116	14627	33	18264 [1]	65
8225 [2]	120	9438 [4]	121	12034	116	14627	55	18264 [2]	84
8225 [3]	131	9438 [5]	123	12045	116	14627	65	18264 [3]	91
8225 [4]	123	9439 [1]	32	12162	75	14627	96	18264 [3]	121
8226 [1]	32	9439 [1]	55	12359	120	14628	33	18264 [3]	142
8226 [1]	55	9439 [1]	64	12523	81	14628	55	18265 [1]	53
8226 [2]	120	9439 [2]	70	12614	58	14628	65	18265 [1]	65
8226 [3]	120	9969 [1]	120	12614	65	14651	52	18265 [2]	84
8226 [4]	121	9969 [2]	120	12614	111	14651	65	18266 [1]	53
8227 [1]	32	9969 [3]	120	12723 [1]	32	14838 [1]	34	18266 [1]	65
8227 [1]	55	9969 [4]	121	12723 [1]	55	14838 [1]	55	18266 [2]	84
8227 [2]	120	10026	86	12723 [1]	65	14838 [1]	65	18267 [1]	53
8227 [3]	120	10152	120	12723 [2]	72	14838 [2]	80	18267 [1]	65
8227 [4]	120	10155 [1]	147	12723 [2]	143	14838 [3]	85	18267 [2]	79
8227 [5]	121	10155 [2]	133	12723 [3]	76	14857 [1]	53	18267 [3]	84
8227 [6]	131	10155 [2]	154	12723 [4]	91	14857 [1]	65	18267 [4]	92
8227 [7]	130	10484 [1]	32	12723 [4]	121	14857 [2]	79	18267 [4]	121
8228 [1]	32	10484 [1]	55	12723 [4]	142	14859 [1]	53	18718	67
8228 [1]	55	10484 [1]	64	12724	32	14859 [1]	65	18939	127
8228 [1]	118	10485 [1]	32	12724	55	14859 [2]	78	19414	141

19414	154	21902	55	28403	65	31906 [3]	76	31923 [3]	87
19660 [1]	54	21902	65	28404	57	31906 [4]	71	31924 [1]	70
19660 [1]	65	21903	34	28404	65	31907 [1]	61	31924 [2]	87
19660 [2]	77	21903	55	28989	147	31907 [1]	66	31925 [1]	70
19660 [3]	91	21903	65	29090	100	31907 [2]	73	31925 [2]	71
19660 [3]	121	21904	54	29110	77	31907 [3]	76	31925 [3]	88
19660 [3]	142	21904	65	29131	101	31907 [4]	82	31925 [4]	91
19661	54	21905	54	29191	100	31908 [1]	60	31926	70
19661	65	21906 [1]	54	29333	100	31908 [1]	66	31927 [1]	70
19662 [1]	54	21906 [1]	65	29346	142	31908 [2]	85	31927 [2]	91
19662 [1]	65	21906 [2]	67	29694	86	31908 [3]	86	31928	70
19662 [2]	84	23069	116	29726	58	31909 [1]	60	31929	70
19662 [3]	65	23172	75	29726	65	31909 [1]	66	31930 [1]	70
19662 [3]	91	23196	121	29727	58	31909 [2]	81	31930 [2]	92
19662 [3]	121	23201	146	29727	65	31909 [3]	85	32057	103
19662 [3]	142	23337	114	29728 [1]	58	31910 [1]	62	32464	105
19663 [1]	54	23374	130	29728 [1]	65	31910 [1]	66	32751	89
19663 [1]	65	24018	71	29728 [2]	82	31910 [2]	69	32758	101
19663 [2]	77	24453	141	29728 [3]	90	31910 [3]	73	33040	100
19675 [1]	34	24493	121	29728 [3]	121	31911 [1]	62	33541	93
19675 [1]	55	24539	121	29728 [3]	142	31911 [1]	66	33541	121
19675 [1]	65	24603	94	29729 [1]	58	31911 [2]	73	33541	142
19675 [2]	78	24603	121	29729 [1]	65	31912 [1]	60	34516	100
19675 [3]	71	24775 [1]	76	29729 [2]	82	31912 [1]	66	34518	93
19675 [4]	90	24775 [2]	94	29730 [1]	58	31912 [2]	73	34518	121
19675 [4]	121	24775 [2]	121	29730 [1]	65	31913 [1]	62	34740	73
19675 [4]	142	24775 [2]	142	29730 [2]	82	31913 [1]	66	34796	116
19676 [1]	34	25278	67	29730 [2[	96	31913 [2]	73	34857	100
19676 [1]	55	25474	89	29731 [1]	58	31914 [1]	60	34932	108
19676 [1]	65	25701 [1]	57	29731 [1]	65	31914 [1]	66	34932	115
19676 [2]	78	25701 [1]	65	29731 [2]	80	31914 [2]	76	34932	155
19676 [3]	90	25701 [2]	76	29732 [1]	58	31914 [3]	72	35295	101
19676 [3]	121	25702 [1]	57	29732 [1]	66	31915 [1]	60	35428	101
19676 [3]	142	25702 [1]	65	29732 [2]	80	31915 [1]	66	35694	101
19677 [1]	34	25702 [2]	86	29733 [1]	58	31915 [2]	76	35698	84
19677 [1]	55	25703	57	29733 [1]	66	31915 [3]	72	35766	142
19677 [1]	65	25703	65	29733 [2]	82	31916 [1]	60	35836	141
19677 [2]	77	25703	96	29776	115	31916 [1]	66	35888	114
19677 [3]	79	25704	57	29904	115	31916 [2]	76	35888	117
19677 [4]	90	25704	65	30021	148	31916 [3]	75	35940	87
19677 [4]	121	25704	176	30455	107	31917 [1]	60	36113	136
19677 [4]	142	25845	89	30715	108	31917 [1]	66	36394	114
19678 [1]	34	25912	58	30715	115	31917 [2]	76	36676	107
19678 [1]	55	25912	65	30752	110	31917 [3]	75	36862	138
19678 [1]	65	25912	111	30752	116	31918 [1]	60	37141	136
19678 [2]	77	26209	107	30888	115	31918 [1]	66	37424	136
19678 [3]	82	26209	112	30938	87	31918 [2]	75	37487	112
19678 [4]	90	26248	116	31235 [1]	67	31918 [3]	74	37603	116
19678 [4]	121	26943	100	31235 [1]	156	31919 [1]	60	38225	113
19678 [4]	142	26960	106	31235 [2]	73	31919 [1]	66	38243	121
19797	110	26984	93	31235 [2]	96	31919 [2]	73	38273	111
19797	112	27237	89	31901	61	31919 [3]	74	38290	121
19797	116	27308	89	31901	66	31920 [1]	60	38293 [1]	121
20234	116	27503	154	31902	60	31920 [1]	66	38293 [2]	107
20412	130	27718	100	31902	66	31920 [2]	76	38293 [2]	112
20582	114	27803	136	31903	60	31920 [3]	87	38296	121
20716	92	28231	82	31903	66	31921 [1]	70	38327	121
20716	121	28274	111	31904	60	31921 [2]	86	38328	121
20716	142	28401	65	31904	66	31921 [2]	87	38393	121
21173	107	28401	57	31905	61	31921 [2]	122	38406 [1]	121
21901	34	28402 [1]	57	31905	66	31922 [1]	70	38406 [2]	93
21901	55	28402 [1]	65	31906 [1]	60	31922 [2]	87	38406 [2]	121
21901	65	28402 [2]	86	31906 [1]	66	31923 [1]	70	38509	123
21902	34	28403	57	31906 [2]	75	31923 [2]	71	39121	81

39138 [1]	121	49193	77	61973	121	70023	97	77091	123
39138 [2]	93	49195	77	61973	142	70023	122	77819	123
39138 [2]	121	49282	107	62067	94	70024	97		
39138 [3]	123	49282	112	62067	122	70024	122	**Alderney**	
39281	140	49377	85	62417	123	70025	97	AY 5	177
39823	142	49377	108	62812	107	70025	122	AY 14	172
40527	92	49377	109	62812	112	70026	97	AY 14	177
40527	121	49377	110	62812	136	70026	122	AY 32	177
40527	142	49377	120	63798	101	70027	97	AY 34	172
40631	101	49628	148	64098	102	70027	122	AY 34	177
40869	101	49641	101	64153	102	70028	97	AY 38	137
41158	107	49679	101	64189	102	70028	122	AY 38	171
41898	176	49768	116	64193	102	70029	97	AY 58 [1]	177
41951	136	50109	123	64195	102	70029	122	AY 58 [2]	132
42625	101	50129	142	64198	102	70030	97	AY 58 [2]	173
42838	116	50129	154	64198	107	70030	122	AY 59 [1]	45
42896	84	50188	77	64202	102	70031	97	AY 59 [1]	144
42992	136	50414	107	64203	102	70031	122	AY 59 [1]	173
43234	75	50524	116	64918	107	70032	97	AY 59 [2]	46
43361	155	50562	174	64918	112	70032	122	AY 59 [2]	173
44492	172	50563	174	64991	121	70033	97	AY 59 [3]	46
44525	81	50797	149	65075	117	70033	122	AY 59 [3]	173
44525	85	51537	131	65119	123	70034	98	AY 59 [4]	49
44525	108	51668	101	65119	123	70034	122	AY 59 [4]	150
44525	109	51735 [1]	120	65161	79	70035	98	AY 59 [4]	173
44525	110	51735 [2]	101	65346	154	70035	122	AY 59 [5]	47
44525	116	52097	121	65802	122	70036	98	AY 59 [5]	173
44525	120	52141	123	66328	138	70036	122	AY 59 [6]	49
44850	75	52408	116	66867	122	70037	98	AY 59 [6]	151
44925	101	52478	136	66868	122	70037	122	AY 59 [6]	173
44993	108	52728	130	66959	112	70038	98	AY 59 [7]	47
44993	112	53428	89	66959	136	70038	123	AY 59 [7]	173
44993	155	53467	89	67463	107	70039	98	AY 59 [8]	49
45038	75	53499	83	67463	112	70039	123	AY 59 [8]	151
45093	84	53515	83	67463	136	70040	98	AY 59 [8]	173
45144	81	53516	83	68523	154	70040	123	AY 59 [9]	173
45260	75	53849	130	68523	177	70041	98	AY 59 [10]	173
45260	176	53948	154	68875	136	70041	123	AY 59 [11]	173
45833	84	54361	116	69101	122	70042	98	AY 59 [12]	173
46088	81	54537	89	69788	154	70042	123	AY 59 [13]	173
46710	142	55159	89	70011	97	70043	98	AY 59 [14]	174
46893	101	55184	118	70011	123	70043	123	AY 59 [15]	170
46921	81	55184	131	70012	97	70044	98	AY 59 [15]	174
47312	88	56206	92	70012	122	70044	123	AY 59 [16]	174
47635	107	56206	121	70013	97	70055	98	AY 59 [17]	174
47638	142	56206	142	70013	122	70055	123	AY 81 [1]	173
47878	101	56302	101	70014	97	70066	98	AY 81 [2]	173
47979	94	56624	120	70014	122	70066	123	AY 81 [3]	50
47979	121	56650	112	70015	97	70077	98	AY 81 [3]	173
48032	101	56660	112	70015	122	70077	123	AY 89	176
48161	92	56660	136	70016	97	70088	98	AY 91 [1]	173
48161	121	56690	112	70016	122	70088	123	AY 91 [2]	173
48641	116	56690	136	70017	97	70099	98	AY 91 [3]	132
48701	75	58054	107	70017	122	70099	123	AY 91 [3]	173
48701	85	58054	112	70018	97	72103	144	AY 91 [4]	173
48701	109	58228	116	70018	122	73140	144	AY 91 [5]	176
48701	110	58651	79	70019	97	73140	155	AY 91 [6]	174
48702	75	58677	120	70019	122	73861	116	AY 91 [7]	174
48702	85	59610	123	70020	97	74271	116	AY 97 [1]	170
48702	109	60174	102	70020	122	76357	116	AY 97 [2]	170
48702	110	60178	138	70021	97	76385	116	AY 101 [1]	150
48702	116	60310	172	70021	122	77056	98	AY 101 [1]	158
48830	154	60317	101	70022	97	77056	123	AY 101 [1]	173
49192	77	61973	94	70022	122	77091	98	AY 101 [2]	25

AY 101 [2] 173	J 1852 153	F 2440 113	LLU 804 88	268 KTA 60
AY 101 [3] 47	J 1858 126	F 2442 113	LSV 201 67	268 KTA 66
AY 101 [3] 173	J 1858 153		LSV 748 56	271 KTA 61
AY 101 [4] 173	J 1942 81	BJ 415 113	LUC 196 84	271 KTA 66
AY 129 [1] 41	J 2465 126	BJ 416 113	MIB 650 114	272 KTA 60
AY 129 [1] 173	J 2687 126	CW 7706 23	MJS 808 125	272 KTA 66
AY 129 [2] 43	J 2688 126	DS 6468 56	MSJ 702 59	278 KTA 61
AY 129 [2] 173	J 3256 [2] 125	ED 5838 23	MSJ 702 157	278 KTA 66
AY 169 171	J 5567 81	ED 5838 163	MSV 412 56	280 KTA 61
AY 184 176	J 5660 82	ED 5838 169	MXX 481 120	280 KTA 66
AY 218 172	J 6901 126	EY 3586 24	OAS 624 82	286 KTA 61
AY 305 [1] 173	J 7992 153	EY 3586 163	OFF 605 59	286 KTA 66
AY 305 [2] 173	J 8392 45	EY 3586 166	OFF 605 156	510 PYB 120
AY 328 174	J 9143 125	EY 3586 169	PJI 800 137	5 RDV 125
AY 414 172	J 12633 171	GV 4123 180	RCG 612 175	610 STT 125
AY 446 171	J 14064 153	GD 9128 22	RCN 701 155	210 UXO 69
AY 586 [1] 132	J 14065 153	GD 9128 104	RFO 375 63	266 UYH 57
AY 586 [1] 176	J 16590 126	IB 4689 24	RFO 829 56	839 XUJ 83
AY 586 [2] 173	J 16590 175	IB 4689 163	RIB 7017 128	840 XUJ 81
AY 586 [3] 155	J 16654 126	IB 4689 164	RLZ 3218 174	
AY 586 [3] 174	J 16841 175	JA 2216 145	RSJ 747 56	ACH 845A 84
AY 586 [4] 174	J 16868 126	LE 9177 39	RYT 34 174	AFJ 77B 126
AY 593 [1] 173	J 16898 176	LE 9177 63	TFO 249 57	AFJ 79B 125
AY 593 [2] 67	J 16706 126	LE 9956 40	TFO 249 126	AFJ 79B 174
AY 593 [2] 173	J 20096 173	LF 8055 39	TMY 42 171	AFJ 80B 175
AY 593 [3] 174	J 20096 176	LF 8508 39	TUN 627 120	AFJ 82B 126
AY 593 [4] 174	J 20361 126	LF 8660 40	TVF 870 181	AFJ 82B 175
AY 593 [5] 174	J 22095 125	TA 1738 19	UJH 346 127	AFJ 85B 176
AY 666 173	J 25784 124	TA 1738 138	UJH 346 53	AFJ 86B 126
AY 750 [1] 173	J 25784 153	VO 4935 23	UMP 77 176	ARX 705B 126
AY 750 [2] 173	J 26019 12o	VO 4935 163	VHO 462 68	EBW 112B 68
AY 750 [3] 173	J 26408 175	VO 4935 165	VOD 313 127	EYY 776B 155
AY 750 [4] 176	J 26626 175	WM 1405 22	VVS 913 29	YCV 365B 132
AY 1041 172	J 26896 69	WM 1405 169	VVS 913 131	BDV 244C 69
AY 1114 [1] 174	J 29184 79		XAE 329 173	BDV 245C 62
AY 1114 [2] 174	J 30366 127	BIB 1106 137	YFF 660 50	BDV 245C 66
AY 1495 170	J 30366 153	BIG 7558 137	YFF 660 175	BDV 251C 66
AY 1658 170	J 34191 132	CEN 535 124	YFO 127 57	BDV 251C 66
AY 1671 178	J 35662 125	CEN 535 153	YSL 334 81	BDV 253C 60
AY 1741 [1] 178	J 38084 175	CIB 9623 176		BDV 253C 66
AY 1741 [2] 178	J 40820 143	CSU 906 171	5183 AW 126	CUV 274C 154
AY 1772 [1] 172	J 40853 143	CSU 906 174	5184 AW 126	JNP 590C 68
AY 1772 [2] 172	J 40865 143	DFP 496 59	8009 FH 126	JNP 631C 133
AY 1773 132	J 42259 143	EJD 508 153	4234 NT 117	EDV 537D 60
AY 1773 178	J 43037 143	ERN 776 176	8439 RU 114	EDV 537D 66
AY 1774 172	J 43037 155	ESV 215 150	8439 RU 117	EDV 538D 60
AY 1858 132	J 43063 143	GJM 5 126		EDV 538D 66
AY 1858 172	J 43803 175	GJM 5 153	670 COD 70	EDV 539D 61
AY 1858 173	J 43805 176	GJM 6 125	395 DEL 56	EDV 539D 66
AY 1878 172	J 46467 111	GJM 6 153	346 EDV 60	EDV 550D 60
AY 1919 170	J 45700 [3] 126	GNT 184 137	346 EDV 66	EDV 550D 66
AY 1950 178	J 46545 134	GTB 906 81	356 EDV 61	EDV 552D 60
AY 2139 170	J 48139 127	GUH 540 125	356 EDV 66	EDV 552D 66
AY 2153 75	J 57640 58	HDL 314 129	358 EDV 62	EDV 554D 62
AY 2153 173	J 57640 111	HFO 742 51	381 ENN 174	EDV 554D 66
AY 2246 [1] 171	J 60118 125	HYN 728 153	842 FUF 57	EDV 558D 62
AY 2246 [2] 171	J 60691 127	JOD 621 175	898 FUF 59	EDV 558D 66
AY 2475 178	J 61552 172	JUE 860 144	898 FUF 117	FNT 231D 125
	J 68770 75	KAG 859 180	898 FUF 124	HFW 391D 68
Jersey	J 68771 75	KLB 719 88	898 FUF 157	JFL 93D 68
J 257 113	J 80977 132	KSU 288 56	417 HDV 61	JJD 566D 155
J 515 113		KXW 123 77	417 HDV 66	ORO 966D 125
J 1465 [2] 126	UK	KXW 476 79	430 HDV 60	MRV 60G 125
J 1852 125	F 1874 113	KYY 647 88	430 HDV 66	PSC 310G 180

TNG 184G	125	LTB 817P	124	A167 OOT	109	H142 UUA	92	J555 RML	144
KEJ 687H	126	MPX 945R	125	B287 KCH	108	H142 UUA	127	K 30 ARJ	137
MDR 525H	126	MUA 42P	76	B 97 WOR	174	H147 UUA	91	K455 EDT	87
WNG 105H	77	MUA 43P	76	C649 JUH	75	H147 UUA	127	K 5 NGB	137
XXE 135H	77	OJD 12R	79	C998 VLD	111	H147 UUA	142	K903 PBP	175
BEA 480J	175	OJD 43R	70	D845 CRY	128	H151 UUA	91	K691 RMW	137
SWL 50J	175	OJD 46R	86	D848 CRY	89	H151 UUA	127	K572 SKP	175
SWL 52J	174	OJD 47R	80	D851 CRY	128	H151 UUA	142	K 26 VRY	102
CAR 162K	129	OJD 48R	83	D853 CRY	128	H564 WWR	92	K 26 VRY	108
VOD 88K	73	OJD 50R	71	D854 CRY	128	H564 WWR	127	K 26 VRY	137
VOD 89K	73	OJD 52R	70	D823 EBJ	77	H161 WWT	94	L 7 JSF	128
VOD 89K	96	OJD 64R	83	D449 FRF	77	H161 WWT	127	L156 YVK	175
VOD 90K	73	OJD 67R	70	D346 JUM	128	H161 WWT	143	M651 FWK	117
VOD 120K	73	OJD 70R	70	D939 KNW	125	H163 WWT	94	M652 FWK	117
VOD 120K	96	OJD 72R	78	D634 NOE	111	H163 WWT	128	M388 SPY	171
WLJ 578K	129	OJD 73R	80	D126 NON	86	H165 WWT	94	M388 SPY	174
WLJ 578K	154	OJD 74R	71	D898 NUA	121	H165 WWT	127	M559 SRE	181
ATT 151L	125	OJD 90R	71	D749 ULG	125	H167 WWT	91	M139 UWY	108
BDV 316L	80	OJD 94R	83	D 64 YRF	84	H167 WWT	127	M139 UWY	112
BNO 134L	126	SAT 201R	127	D 66 YRF	84	H167 WWT	142	N876 PPK	108
BUX 208L	126	TPJ 63S	72	D 67 YRF	84	H168 WWT	91	N876 PPK	112
NVA 75L	125	VDV 117S	155	D 72 YRF	84	H168 WWT	127	P856 GRC	108
RPH 103L	78	AFJ 720T	89	E401 BHK	89	H168 WWT	142	P856 GRC	112
CXD 301M	129	AFJ 722T	87	E402 BHK	89	J555 BUS	93	P826 OGT	176
NTT 322M	80	AFJ 725T	88	E531 NFA	81	J555 BUS	144	Q402 JDV	63
PFJ 351M	125	AFJ 733T	87	E533 NFA	81	J210 BWU	92	Q147 OST	56
SPK 118M	73	AFJ 736T	87	E538 NFA	81	J210 BWU	128	R334 EFG	118
CRF 699N	126	AFJ 736T	127	E961 PME	126	J210 BWU	143	R 43 JUB	170
GPD 304N	82	AFJ 741T	88	E205 PWY	89	J214 BWU	92	R 45 JUB	170
GPD 312N	79	AFJ 743T	87	E206 PWY	89	J214 BWU	128	R196 LBC	112
HDL 415N	84	DSO 89T	128	E207 PWY	89	J216 BWU	92	R196 LBC	181
JFH 473N	82	ESU 953T	62	E214 PWY	89	J216 BWU	127	R496 XAW	137
JFJ 497N	84	ESU 953T	66	E217 PWY	89	J216 BWU	142	T292 FRB	125
JFJ 498N	84	XWF 69T	127	E219 PWY	89	J218 BWU	92	V749 EJF	137
JFJ 499N	75	DES 229V	62	E 66 SUH	128	J218 BWU	128	W674 DDN	175
JFJ 500N	75	DES 229V	66	E456 VUM	128	J218 BWU	143	W244 GSE	117
JFJ 501N	74	FDV 790V	84	F 56 BJW	128	J220 BWU	92	W314 SBC	117
JFJ 502N	74	FDV 791V	84	F481 BUH	176	J220 BWU	127	W 58 SJH	137
JFJ 503N	74	GPA 623V	175	F270 DBO	176	J220 BWU	143	X645 AKW	136
JFJ 504N	74	JPA 81V	56	F302 MNK	125	J960 DWX	93	X937 MSP	137
JFJ 505N	74	JPA 82V	56	F303 MNK	128	J960 DWX	127	Y831 HHE	117
JFJ 506N	74	JPA 83V	57	F396 RHT	128	J962 DWX	93		
JFJ 507N	72	JPA 84V	57	F607 SDP	128	J962 DWX	127	FY02 OTG	118
JFJ 508N	72	JPA 84V	118	F133 TCR	91	J962 DWX	143	AM03 BCK	126
JPC 547N	126	JPA 85V	57	F134 TCR	92	J 6 EGT	137	BU03 BGF	117
JPC 547N	172	KBC 258V	72	F721 TLW	128	J963 JNL	90	GN53 UJU	103
JPC 547N	176	KPP 123V	149	F795 WBF	83	J963 JNL	127	SF04 RHY	118
JUG 355N	76	GTX 758W	77	F796 WBF	83	J963 JNL	143	AE54 MWC	99
JUG 356N	76	GTX 759W	77	F797 WBF	83	J967 JNL	90	AE54 MWC	129
JUG 357N	76	MCX 402W	56	F799 WBF	83	J967 JNL	127	AE54 MWD	99
KBH 450N	126	HSC 166X	176	F671 YOG	127	J967 JNL	142	AE54 MWD	129
RTT 7N	128	KWO 568X	77	F266 YTJ	180	J968 JNL	90	AE54 MWF	98
KJD 403P	70	KWO 569X	77	G700 APB	108	J968 JNL	127	AE54 MWF	129
KJD 407P	80	NJB 356X	109	G700 APB	112	J968 JNL	142	AE54 NUB	98
KJD 417P	71	WUA 655X	125	G154 ELJ	125	J971 JNL	90	AE54 NUB	129
KJD 418P	82	WUA 655X	178	G124 FRE	84	J971 JNL	127	MV54 EEM	99
KJD 424P	70	BPF 131Y	180	G141 GOL	174	J971 JNL	142	MV54 EEM	129
KJD 425P	71	JGH 431Y	71	G917 GTG	128	J972 JNL	90	FJ05 HXZ	117
KJD 430P	71	JGH 431Y	96	G883 WML	181	J972 JNL	127	FJ05 HYK	99
KJD 432P	71	LDS 997Y	126	G137 WOW	91	J972 JNL	142	FJ05 HYK	129
KJD 437P	71	VPL 819Y	108	G972 WPA	94	J326 PPD	94	FJ05 HYL	99
KJD 438P	86			G972 WPA	128	J326 PPD	128	FJ05 HYL	129
LEU 263P	155	A167 OOT	78	H686 CDM	178	J326 PPD	143	FJ05 HYM	99
LEU 263P	175	A167 OOT	86	H557 JEV	128	J555 RML	93	FJ05 HYM	129

CN55 EXG	137	LK56 GYJ	117	LJ59 NFA	103	YN10 ACO	117	BL64 HJD	100
YN55 UJX	117	MX07 VUN	118	LX59 DGO	114	VX60 CPE	170	BL64 HJE	100
YY55 KNV	170	CB08 YPB	114	YK59 YEE	128	YJ60 CVO	114	PO17 EKD	127
YN06 OPX	128	YJ08 EFB	118	SF10 EBN	127	BU14 SZC	100		
EO56 NTJ	114	YN08 DLZ	114	SF10 EBV	117	CX14 RXZ	128		

HISTORICAL COUNTY CODES

GOV   Government Department

AD	Aberdeenshire	KK	Kirkcudbrightshire
AH	Armagh	KN	Kesteven division of Lincolnshire
AL	Argyllshire	KS	Kinross-shire
AM	Antrim	KT	Kent
AR	Ayrshire	LA	Lancashire
AS	Angus	LC	Lincoln (City)
AY	Isle of Anglesey	LE	Leicestershire
BC	Brecknockshire	LI	Lindsey division of Lincolnshire
BD	Bedfordshire	LK	Lanarkshire
BE	Berkshire	LN	London Postal area
BF	Banffshire	LY	Londonderry
BK	Buckinghamshire	ME	Merionethshire
BU	Buteshire	MH	Monmouthshire
BW	Berwickshire	MN	Midlothian
CG	Cardiganshire	MO	Montgomeryshire
CH	Cheshire	MR	Morayshire
CI	Channel Islands	MX	Middlesex
CK	Clackmannanshire	ND	Northumberland
CM	Cambridgeshire	NG	Nottinghamshire
CN	Caernarfonshire	NK	Norfolk
CO	Cornwall	NN	Nairnshire
CR	Carmarthenshire	NO	Northamptonshire
CS	Caithness	NR	North Riding of Yorkshire
CU	Cumberland	OK	Orkney Islands
DB	Dunbartonshire	OX	Oxfordshire
DE	Derbyshire	PB	Peebles-shire
DF	Dumfries-shire	PE	Pembrokeshire
DH	Denbighshire	PH	Perthshire
DM	County Durham	RD	Rutland
DN	Devon	RH	Roxburghshire
DO	Down	RR	Radnorshire
DT	Dorset	RW	Renfrewshire
EI	Eire	RY	Ross-shire & Cromarty
EK	East Suffolk	SD	Shetland Islands
EL	East Lothian	SH	Shropshire
ER	East Riding of Yorkshire	SI	Selkirkshire
ES	East Sussex	SN	Stirlingshire
EX	Essex	SO	Somerset
EY	Isle of Ely	SP	Soke of Peterborough
FE	Fife	SR	Surrey
FH	Fermanagh	ST	Staffordshire
FT	Flintshire	SU	Sutherland
GG	Glamorgan	TY	Tyrone
GL	Gloucestershire	WF	West Suffolk
HA	Hampshire	WI	Wiltshire
HD	Holland division of Lincolnshire	WK	Warwickshire
HN	Huntingdonshire	WL	West Lothian
HR	Herefordshire	WN	Wigtownshire
HT	Hertfordshire	WO	Worcestershire
IM	Isle of Man	WR	West Riding of Yorkshire
IS	Isles of Scilly	WS	West Sussex
IV	Inverness	WT	Westmorland
IW	Isle of Wight	YK	York (City)
KE	Kincardineshire		

Note: A 'G' prefix (eg GCI) indicates the vehicle had been converted to goods (eg lorry or van) and the operator was a goods operator (in this case, in the Channel Islands).

OVERSEAS COUNTRY CODES

O-B	Belgium
O-DK	Denmark
O-F	France
O-IND	India
O-M	Malta
O-NL	Netherlands
O-UAE	United Arab Emirates

ABBREVIATIONS USED FOR MANUFACTURERS

CIMGE	Channel Island Motor & General Engineering Co Ltd
ECW	Eastern Coach Works Ltd
LCB	Leicester Carriage Builders Ltd
MCCW	Metro-Cammell Carriage & Wagon Co Ltd
MCW	Metropolitan-Cammell Weymann Ltd
SCC	SC Coachbuilders
SCWC	Starbuck Car & Wagon Co Ltd

Guerseybus operated several ex-London RTs including 2634 [2] which it acquired in 1988. It was converted to open-top by the operator and was later re-registered 58651. In 2001 it passed to Island FM where it worked as a publicity vehicle for the radio station, re-registered again to 65161. Today it is in Malta. (The Bus Archive, Roy Marshall)

1931 was a 1987 FIAT 7.14 lorry chassis that was fitted with a tram body by Educational Holidays in 1992 - based on original 1897 tram no.3 which is in preservation. It operated on the sea front in St Peter Port for three years before being repatriated to the UK. (The Bus Archive, Roy Marshall)

AY 91 was used seven times on buses by Riduna. This was the first, being an 1957 AEC Reliance with Weymann bodywork new as Aldershot & District (HA) registered RCG 612. It served for 11 years from 1971-1982. (Geoffrey Morant, courtesy Richard Morant)

Watson Greys was an old established operator from the 1920s that was taken over by Guernsey Railway Co in 1978. Their grey liveried vehicles were a familiar sight on the island, exemplified by 3992, a 1952 Albion FT39N with Reading bodywork. (Geoffrey Morant, courtesy Richard Morant)

Front Cover Photograph: 16213 (97) was new to Guernsey Motors in 1965, passing to the Railway Co in 1973 and Guernseybus in 1981. It was withdrawn and sold for scrap in 1985. It is seen here in Railway Co malachite green livery and was an Albion NS3AN, one of the last deliveries of that make, with Reading B35F bodywork. (Geoffrey Morant).

ISBN: 978-1-910767-38-2

£16.00